Walt Disney World®, Universal Studios and Orlando

> "When it comes to information on regional history, what to see and do, and shopping, these guides are exhaustive."
>
> —*USAir Magazine*

> "Usable, sophisticated restaurant coverage, with an emphasis on good value."
>
> —Andy Birsh, *Gourmet Magazine* columnist

> "Valuable because of their comprehensiveness."
>
> —*Minneapolis Star-Tribune*

> "Fodor's always delivers high quality...thoughtfully presented...thorough."
>
> —*Houston Post*

> "An excellent choice for those who want everything under one cover."
>
> —*Washington Post*

Fodor's Travel Publications, Inc.
New York • Toronto • London • Sydney • Auckland

Fodor's Walt Disney World, Universal Studios and Orlando

Editorial Director: Karen Cure

Editor: Robert I. C. Fisher

Contributors: Robert Andrews, Robert Blake, Jennifer Burgess, Marianne Camas, Catherine Fredman, Barbara Freitag, Andrew Holleran, Anto Howard, Dawn Lawson, Bevin McLaughlin, Mary Meehan, Dee Rivers, Mary Ellen Schultz, Marshall Schwartzman, Lindy Shepherd, Dinah Spritzer, Rowland Stiteler, Nancy van Itallie

Creative Director: Fabrizio La Rocca

Cartographer: David Lindroth

Cover Photograph: Comstock, Inc.

Text Design: Between the Covers

Copyright

Special Sales

Fodor's Travel Publications are available at special discounts for bulk purchases for sales promotions or premiums. Special editions, including personalized covers, excerpts of existing guides, and corporate imprints, can be created in large quantities for special needs. For more information, contact your local bookseller or write to Special Markets, Fodor's Travel Publications, 201 East 50th Street, New York, NY 10022. Inquiries from Canada should be directed to your local Canadian bookseller or sent to Random House of Canada Ltd., Marketing Dept., 1265 Aerowood Drive, Mississaugua, Ontario L4W 1B9. Inquiries from the United Kingdom should be sent to Fodor's Travel Publications, 20 Vauxhall Bridge Road, London, England SW1 2SA.

MANUFACTURED IN THE UNITED STATES OF AMERICA

10 9 8 7 6 5 4 3 2 1

CONTENTS

ON THE ROAD WITH FODOR'S

By Karen Cure

MANY YEARS AGO, I wrote the *Official Guide to Walt Disney World*. After that, I was for many years the book's executive editor, and I followed the field of WDW books as it grew. And grew. And grew. But not until we at Fodor's produced the volume you now hold in your hands have I ever felt that there was a perfect guidebook to the most unusual of vacation kingdoms.

It's the best book for visiting with kids, for instance. If a ride routinely scares toddlers, we say so. I have two of my own, so I know how important that can be. But it's also a great guide for grown-ups on their own—that's how I traveled when I first visited Orlando. And it's also the book for people who can't stand waiting in line; I hate queuing up as much as you do, so we made sure to tell you how to avoid the crowds. I love what Disney does, and I've seen it at very close range and from behind the scenes. Yet we're not in Disney's pocket: The information in this guide originated with the authors and revisers and has not been authorized or endorsed by The Walt Disney Company or any of its affiliates. That way we can always say what we really think. We can also cover all of Orlando's many attractions with equal care, to help you decide how you want to spend your time.

Because this is a Fodor's guide, you'll find great writing. Our descriptions of the various theme-park rides don't merely recite historical facts or repeat what you read in a brochure. We also capture the magic of each attraction or ride, and we tell you enough about it so you can easily plan in advance what you want to see—and what you could miss.

About Our Writers

Our Orlando guidebook is a collaboration of a number of extraordinary writers.

Catherine Fredman's very first visit to Walt Disney World coincided with her 34th birthday, so, of course, she really got into the swing of the fireworks and laser shows. As part of that bang-up trip, she became a human projectile on Splash Mountain, memorized the lyrics of "It's a Small World," and outsmarted the hoardes in getting ol' big ears's autograph. She deftly manages to tickle every sentence's funny bone, a talent so irresistible it keeps her on the move across America for a variety of magazines. She picks up her mail and does her laundry in New York City.

A blizzard can keep some folks from their appointed rounds, but not Orlando-based **Marianne Camas,** especially when the action takes place at Blizzard Beach, Disney's newest water-park attraction. Marianne, now a pro at attaining flotation on the Summit Plummet ride, has been a fervent Disney fan since childhood—a proud possession is her Mickey ear gear in the orginal felt. Long before Disney came to Florida, grade-schooler Marianne pilgrimaged to Disneyland, where she stood in line for the Matterhorn so many times she can still recite the ride's P.A. announcement by heart. When not exploring Mouseville with her five-year-old niece (who's convinced her aunt owns the place), Marianne works as senior editor of AAA's *Car & Travel* magazine.

As one of Fodor's veteran Orlando writers, **Mary Meehan** has fearlessly traveled from the top of the Twilight Zone Tower of Terror to the foot of the Great Wall at Splendid China. Along the way, she has covered our After Dark beat. It's obviously difficult for someone who managed to snub Sylvester Stallone at the opening of Planet Hollywood to reach excitement saturation. After eight years in the newspaper/publishing trenches, she is now spokesperson for Hospice of Central Florida.

Good meals stick to your ribs; great meals stick in your mind. That's the belief of **Rowland Stiteler,** who has served as editor and dining critic of *Orlando* and *Central Florida* magazines. Always trying to beat the buffet blahs, he keeps an eye out for the hottest news in Floridian cuisine, from the newest northern Italian bistro to the coolest recipe for kumquat sorbet. As a rule, he feels many Central Florida restaurants put more emphasis on the sizzle than on the steak, but if you are willing to search it out, good dining—from haute to homey—can be found throughout the Orlando area. Stiteler, a journalist for 25 years, won top honors for best feature story in the 1994 Florida Magazine Association awards competition.

Anto Howard, Jennifer Burgess, Dee Rivers, and Lindy Shepard round out Fodor's roster of writers all of whom, with humor and meticulous detail, continue to bring you the lowdown on the amazing panorama that is Orlando. Robert I. C. Fisher, this edition's editor, is a confirmed Disneyaholic and travel buff. From his vantage as an art-history specialist, Fisher ranks the early pioneering Disney animators alongside Leonardo, Michelangelo, and other aesthetic groundbreakers of the past. His patron saint is Jiminy Cricket.

What's New

Big things are happening at Fodor's—and to this edition of *Walt Disney World, Universal Studios, and Orlando*.

Introducing Disney at-a-Glance

When it comes to vacations, it's true that getting started is half the fun, but visiting Walt Disney World for the first time can be a lot like trying to solve a gigantic jigsaw puzzle. The countless attractions inspire a thousand questions. Our new Disney at-a-glance guide, **Ready, Set, Disney!: Everything You Need to Know About Getting Started at Walt Disney World,** up front in Chapter 1, provides the answers. Now, 11 easy-to-digest topics turn WDW inside out, break down the major and minor parks, outline the main attractions, provide an overview of hotels and restaurants, and otherwise give you the lay of the land. It's part reference guide, part motivator, and after reading it, you'll be set to engineer a totally memorable vacation to the most fun place on earth.

A New Design

If this is not the first Fodor's guide you've purchased, you'll immediately notice our new look. More readable and easier to use than ever? We think so—and we hope you do, too.

Let Us Do Your Booking

Our writers have scoured the Orlando area to come up with an extensive and well-balanced list of the best B&Bs, inns, resorts, and hotels, both small and large, new and old. But you don't have to beat the bushes to come up with a reservation. Now we've teamed up with an established hotel-booking service to make it easy for you to secure a room at the property of your choice. It's fast, it's free, and confirmation is guaranteed. If your first choice is booked, the operators can line up your second right away. Just call 800/FODORS-1 or 800/363–6771; (0800/89–1030 when in Great Britain; 0014/800–12–8271 when in Australia; 1800/55–9101 when in Ireland).

Travel Updates

In addition, just before your trip, you may want to order a Fodor's Worldview Travel Update. From local publications all over Orlando and central Florida, the lively, cosmopolitan editors at Worldview gather information on concerts, plays, opera, dance performances, gallery and museum shows, sports competitions, and other special events that coincide with your visit. See the order blank at the back of this book, call 800/799–9609, or fax 800/799–9619.

How to Use This Book

Organization

Up front is the **Gold Guide,** comprised of two sections on gold paper that are chock-full of information about traveling within your destination as well as traveling in general. Both are in alphabetical order by topic. **Important Contacts A to Z** gives addresses and telephone numbers of organizations that offer destination-related services and detailed information. Here's where you'll find information about how to get to the Orlando area from wherever you are. **Smart Travel Tips A to Z,** the Gold Guide's second section, gives specific tips on how to get the most out of your travels, as well as information on how to accomplish what you need to in the Orlando area.

Following the Gold Guide, you'll find our introduction, **Destination: Walt Disney World, Universal Studios and Orlando.** After looking at Walt Disney World in our brand-new overview, **Ready, Set, Disney!: Everything You Need to Know About**

Getting Started at Walt Disney World, we explore all the other theme-park attractions of the Orlando area. For a quick look at the best of the best, our **Fodor's Choice** samples magical moments in store for you during your Orlando vacation.

At the end of the book you'll find our **Portrait** section, which includes "The Mouse and the Dynamo" by Andrew Holleran, a fascinating essay on the history of Walt Disney and his theme parks, and suggestions for other texts on the wonderful worlds of Disney.

Stars

Stars in the margin are used to denote highly recommended sights, attractions, hotels, and restaurants.

Restaurant and Hotel Criteria and Price Categories

Restaurants and lodging places are chosen with a view to giving you the cream of the crop in each location and in each price range. Price categories are as follows:

For restaurants:

CATEGORY	COST*
$$$$	over $40
$$$	$30–$40
$$	$20–$30
$	under $20

All prices are per person, excluding drinks, service, and 6% sales tax.

For hotels:

CATEGORY	COST*
$$$$	over $180
$$$	$120–$180
$$	$65–$120
$	under $65

All rates are for two adults traveling with up to two children during high season, plus 10% tax.

Hotel Facilities

Note that in general you incur charges when you use many hotel facilities. We wanted to let you know what facilities a hotel has to offer, but we don't always specify whether or not there's a charge, so when planning a vacation that entails a stay of several days, it's wise to ask what's included in the rate.

Dress Code in Restaurants

Orlando, Walt Disney World, and other Central Florida destinations are extremely casual, day and night. Men need a jacket or jacket and tie for only a handful of restaurants (which we note). Elsewhere, casual-smart resort wear is the norm except in fast-food eateries, where shorts, sneakers, and T-shirts are fine. Because restaurant air-conditioning can border on the glacial, always bring a sweater or jacket when you eat out.

Credit Cards

The following abbreviations are used: **AE,** American Express; **D,** Discover; **DC,** Diners Club; **MC,** MasterCard; and **V,** Visa.

Please Write to Us

Everyone who has contributed to *Walt Disney World, Universal Studios, and Orlando '96* has worked hard to make the text accurate. All prices and opening times are based on information supplied to us at press time, and the publisher cannot accept responsibility for any errors that may have occurred. The passage of time will bring changes, so it's always a good idea to call ahead and confirm information when it matters—particularly if you're making a detour to visit specific sights or attractions. When making reservations at a hotel or inn, be sure to mention if you have a disability or are traveling with children, if you prefer a private bath or a certain type of bed, or if you have specific dietary needs or any other concerns.

Were the restaurants we recommended as described? Did our hotel picks exceed your expectations? Have you discovered a new way to make your Walt Disney World trip more enjoyable? We would love your feedback, positive and negative. If you have complaints, we'll look into them and revise our entries when the facts warrant it. If you've happened upon a special place that we haven't included, we'll pass the information along to the writers so they can check it out. So please send a letter or postcard to us at Fodor's (we're at 201 East 50th Street, New York, New York 10022). We look forward to hearing from you. And in the meantime, have a wonderful trip!

Karen Cure
Editorial Director

World Time Zones

Numbers below vertical bands relate each zone to Greenwich Mean Time (0 hrs.).
Local times frequently differ from these general indications,
as indicated by light-face numbers on map.

Algiers, **29**

Anchorage, **3**

Athens, **41**

Auckland, **1**

Baghdad, **46**

Bangkok, **50**

Beijing, **54**

Berlin, **34**

Bogotá, **19**

Budapest, **37**

Buenos Aires, **24**

Caracas, **22**

Chicago, **9**

Copenhagen, **33**

Dallas, **10**

Delhi, **48**

Denver, **8**

Djakarta, **53**

Dublin, **26**

Edmonton, **7**

Hong Kong, **56**

Honolulu, **2**

Istanbul, **40**

Jerusalem, **42**

Johannesburg, **44**

Lima, **20**

Lisbon, **28**

London
(Greenwich), **27**

Los Angeles, **6**

Madrid, **38**

Manila, **57**

The Florida Peninsula

GEORGIA

Amelia Island

Jacksonville

Marys R.

ATLANTIC OCEAN

Osceola National Forest

St. Augustine

Suwannee River

Santa Fe R.

St. Johns River

Gainesville

Ocala National Forest

Ocala

Cedar Keys

Daytona Beach

Titusville

John F. Kennedy Space Center

Merritt Island

Cape Canaveral
Cocoa Beach

Tarpon Springs

Walt Disney World

Orlando

Busch Gardens

Winter Haven

Melbourne

Tampa

Clearwater

Cypress Gardens

Florida's Turnpike

Sebastian Inlet Recreation Area

Tampa Bay

St. Petersburg

Vero Beach

Bradenton

Manatee R.

Fort Pierce

Sarasota

Peace R.

Kissimmee R.

Hutchinson Island

Venice

Lake Okeechobee

Cape Coral

Caloosahatchee R.

West Palm Beach

Singer Island

Fort Myers

Captiva Island

Loxahatchee National Wildlife Refuge

Palm Beach

Sanibel Island

Boca Raton

Naples

Big Cypress National Preserve

Fort Lauderdale

Miami Beach

Gulf of Mexico

Miami

Biscayne Bay

Everglades National Park

Cape Sable

Florida Bay

0   100 miles

0   150 km

Key West

Florida Keys

IMPORTANT CONTACTS A TO Z

An Alphabetical Listing of Publications, Organizations, and Companies That Will Help You Before, During, and After Your Trip

Half the fun of traveling is looking forward to your trip—but when you look forward, don't just daydream. There are plans to be made, things to learn about, serious work to be done. The following organizations, books, and brochures will supplement the information in Fodor's *Walt Disney World, Universal Studios, and Orlando '96*. For related information, including both basic tips on visiting Walt Disney World and background information on many of the topics below, study Smart Travel Tips A to Z, the section that follows Important Contacts A to Z. The main information numbers for major attractions are listed under Visitor Information.

A

AIR TRAVEL

The major gateway to Walt Disney World is Orlando International Airport. Flying time is 2½ hours from New York, 3½ hours from Chicago, and 5 hours from Los Angeles.

The Orlando airport has Universal Studios and Walt Disney World gift shops, where tickets, maps, and information are available. Buying tickets here while waiting for your bags to be unloaded will save time later.

CARRIERS

Carriers serving Orlando International include **America West** (☎ 800/235–9292); **American Airlines** (☎ 800/433–7300); **Bahamasair** (☎ 800/222–4262); **British Airways** (☎ 800/247–9297); **Continental** (☎ 800/525–0280); **Delta** (☎ 800/221–1212), the official airline of Walt Disney World; **Icelandair** (☎ 800/223–5500); **Northwest** (☎ 800/225–2525); **Trans-Brasil** (☎ 800/872–3153); **TWA** (☎ 800/221–2000); **United Airlines** (☎ 800/241–6522); **USAir** (☎ 800/428–4322); and **Virgin Atlantic** (☎ 800/862–8621).

LOW-COST CARRIERS

For inexpensive, no-frills flights, contact **Kiwi International** (☎ 800/538–5494) and **Private Jet** (☎ 404/231–7571, 800/546–7571, or 800/949–9400).

COMPLAINTS

To register complaints about charter and scheduled airlines, contact the U.S. Department of Transportation's **Office of Consumer Affairs** (400 7th St. NW, Washington, DC 20590, ☎ 202/366–2220 or 800/322–7873).

CONSOLIDATORS

Established consolidators selling to the public include **Euram Tours** (1522 K St. NW, Suite 430, Washington DC, 20005, ☎ 800/848–6789) and **TFI Tours International** (34 W. 32nd St., New York, NY 10001, ☎ 212/736–1140 or 800/745–8000).

PUBLICATIONS

For general information about charter carriers, ask for the Office of Consumer Affairs' brochure **"Plane Talk: Public Charter Flights."** The Department of Transportation also publishes a 58-page booklet, **"Fly Rights"** ($1.75; Consumer Information Center, Dept. 133-B, Pueblo, CO 81009).

For other tips and hints, consult the Consumers Union's monthly **"Consumer Reports Travel Letter"** ($39 a year; Box 53629, Boulder CO 80322, ☎ 800/234–1970) and the newsletter **"Travel Smart"** ($37 a year; 40 Beechdale Rd., Dobbs Ferry, NY 10522, ☎ 800/327–3633); *The Official Frequent Flyer Guidebook,* by Randy Petersen ($14.99 plus $3 shipping; 4715-C Town Center Dr., Colorado Springs, CO 80916, ☎

719/597–8899 or 800/487–8893); *Air-fare Secrets Exposed,* by Sharon Tyler and Matthew Wonder (Universal Information Publishing; $16.95 plus $3.75 shipping from Sandcastle Publishing, Box 3070-A, South Pasadena, CA 91031, ☎ 800/655–0053); and *202 Tips Even the Best Business Travelers May Not Know,* by Christopher McGinnis ($10 plus $3.00 shipping; Irwin Professional Publishing, 1333 Burr Ridge Pkwy., Burr Ridge, IL 60521, ☎ 708/789–4000 or 800/634–3966).

ORLANDO AIRPORT TRANSFERS

BY BUS➤ Public buses operate between the airport and the main terminal of the **Tri-County Transit Authority** (1200 W. South St., Orlando, ☎ 407/841–8240), downtown.

BY LIMOUSINE➤ **Mears Transportation Group** (☎ 407/423–5566) will meet you at the gate, help you with your luggage, and whisk you away, in either an 11-passenger van, a town car, or a limo. Vans run to Walt Disney World and along U.S. 192 every 30 minutes; prices range from $12.50 one-way for adults ($8.50 for children 4–11) to $22 round-trip for adults ($16 children 4–11). Limo rates run around $50–$60 for a town car that will accommodate three or four and $90 for a stretch limo that will seat six. **Town & Country Limo** (☎ 407/828–3035) charges $30–$40

one-way for up to seven, depending on the hotel, and **First Class Transportation** (☎ 407/578–0022) charges $45 one-way for up to four people.

B

BETTER BUSINESS BUREAU

For local contacts, consult the **Council of Better Business Bureaus** (4200 Wilson Blvd., Arlington, VA 22203, ☎ 703/276–0100).

BUS TRAVEL

Greyhound Lines (555 N. Magruder Ave., Orlando, ☎ 407/292–3422 or 800/231–2222) serves Orlando from most American cities.

FROM THE HOTELS TO THE ATTRACTIONS

Scheduled service and charters linking just about every hotel and major attraction in the area are available from **Gray Line of Orlando** (☎ 407/422–0744), **Mears Transportation Group** (☎ 407/423–5566), **Phoenix Tours** (☎ 407/859–4211), and **Rabbit Bus Lines** (☎ 407/291–2424).

WITHIN ORLANDO

For information on local bus service, contact the **Tri-County Transit Authority Information Office** (1200 W. South St., Orlando, ☎ 407/841–8240).

C

CAR RENTAL

Major car-rental companies represented in Orlando include **Alamo** (☎ 800/327–9633,

0800/272–2000 in the U.K.), **Avis** (☎ 800/331–1212, 800/879–2847 in Canada), **Budget** (☎ 800/527–0700, 0800/181–181 in the U.K.), **Dollar** (☎ 800/800–4000, 800/800–6000 in Canada and U.K.), **Hertz** (☎ 800/654–3131, 800/263–0600 in Canada, 0181/679–1799 in the U.K.), and **National** (☎ 800/227–7368, 0181/950–5050 in the U.K., where it is known as Europcar). Rates in Orlando begin at $28 a day and $154 a week for an economy car with unlimited mileage.

CHILDREN AND TRAVEL

BABY-SITTING

Baby-sitting is widely available; ask at your hotel desk. **Fairy God-mothers** (☎ 407/277–3724) will care for infants and children in your hotel room or will take your youngsters to the theme parks. Walt Disney World's preschool and drop-off day-care facilities in the Lake Buena Vista area, **KinderCare,** will also send baby-sitters to your hotel room (☎ 407/827–5444). The KinderCare center proper accepts children who are potty trained and walking (☎ 407/827–5437; available daily 6 AM–8 PM); you don't have to stay at Disney to use the program. These programs charge between $5 and $10 an hour, depending on the ages and number of children and the type of service provided.

EDUCATIONAL PROGRAMS

Contact **Walt Disney World**'s Wonders Program (☎ 407/354–1855) and Kidventure Program (☎ 407/824–3784), **Sea World** (☎ 407/363–2380), and **Busch Gardens** (☎ 813/987–5555).

FLYING

Look into **"Flying with Baby"** ($5.95 plus $1 shipping; Third Street Press, Box 261250, Littleton, CO 80126, ☎ 303/595–5959), cowritten by a flight attendant. **"Kids and Teens in Flight,"** free from the U.S. Department of Transportation's Office of Consumer Affairs, offers tips for children flying alone. Every two years the February issue of **Family Travel Times** (*see* Know-How, *below*) details children's services on three dozen airlines.

KNOW-HOW

Family Travel Times, published 10 times a year by Travel with Your Children (TWYCH, 45 W. 18th St., New York, NY 10011, ☎ 212/206–0688; annual subscription $55), covers destinations, types of vacations, and modes of travel.

The **Family Travel Guides** catalogue ($1 postage; ☎ 510/527–5849) lists about 200 books and articles on family travel. Also check **Take Your Baby and Go! A Guide for Traveling with Babies, Toddlers and Young Children,** by Sheri Andrews, Judy Bor-

deaux, and Vivian Vasquez ($5.95 plus $1.50 shipping; Bear Creek Publications, 2507 Minor Ave., Seattle, WA 98102, ☎ 206/322–7604 or 800/326–6566). **The 100 Best Family Resorts in North America,** by Jane Wilford with Janet Tice ($12.95), and the two-volume **50 Great Family Vacations** ($18.95 per volume), both from Globe Pequot Press (plus $3 for shipping; Box 833, 6 Business Park Rd., Old Saybrook, CT 06475, ☎ 203/395–0440, 800/243–0495, or 800/962–0973 in CT), will help you plan your trip with children, from toddlers to teens.

TOUR OPERATORS

Contact **Rascals in Paradise** (650 5th St., Suite 505, San Francisco, CA 94107, ☎ 415/978–9800 or 800/872–7225).

Joint Walt Disney World–cruise packages have become increasingly popular since they debuted a few years ago. Two of the most popular include three- and four-day land packages to Walt Disney World plus cruises to the Bahamas on **Carnival Cruise Lines**' *Fantasy* (Box 526170, Miami, FL 33152-6170, ☎ 305/599–2600 or 800/327–9501); or aboard the Big Red Boats of **Premier Cruise Lines** (400 Challenger Rd., Cape Canaveral, FL 32920, ☎ 407/783–5061 or 800/473–3262).

CANADIANS

Contact **Revenue Canada** (2265 St. Laurent Blvd. S, Ottawa, Ontario K1G 4K3, ☎ 613/993–0534) for a copy of the free brochure **"I Declare/Je Déclare"** and for details on duties that exceed the standard duty-free limit.

U.K. CITIZENS

HM Customs and Excise (Dorset House, Stamford St., London SE1 9NG, ☎ 0171/202–4227) can answer questions about U.K. customs regulations and publishes **"A Guide for Travellers,"** detailing standard procedures and import rules.

COMPLAINTS

To register complaints under the provisions of the Americans with Disabilities Act, contact the U.S. Department of Justice's **Public Access Section** (Box 66738, Washington, DC 20035, ☎ 202/514–0301, TTY 202/514–0383, FAX 202/307–1198).

LODGING

For questions about or reservations at Disney-owned properties, call **WDW Special Request Reservations** (☎ 407/354–1853).

Disney properties that have wheelchair-accessible facilities include the **Yacht and Beach Club** and **Dixie Landings** (Walt Disney World Central Reservations,

☎ 407/934–7639, TTY 407/939–7670), the **All-Star Sports Resort** (☎ 407/939—5000), and the **All-Star Music Resort** (☎ 407/939—6000).

Other wheelchair-accessible hotels are the **Embassy Suites Resorts** at Lake Buena Vista (☎ 407/239–1144 or 800/362–2779, TTY 800/451–4833), which provides free transportation to the Disney parks, and the one on International Drive South (☎ or TTY 407/352–1400 or 800/433–7275); the **Hilton Gateway** on U.S. 192 in Kissimmee (☎ 407/396–4400 or 800/327–9170); the **Hampton Inn** (☎ 407/351–6716 or 800/231–8395); and the two **Motel Six** properties (5731 W. Irlo Bronson Memorial Hwy., Kissimmee 34746, ☎ 407/396–6333; 7455 W. Irlo Bronson Memorial Hwy., Kissimmee 34747, ☎ 407/396–6422).

Hotels with facilities for guests with vision impairments include the **Buena Vista Palace** in Walt Disney World Village (☎ 407/827–2727 or 800/327–2990) and the **Embassy Suites Resorts** at Lake Buena Vista and International Drive (*see above*).

See also Chapter 8 for details.

ORGANIZATIONS

The **Disabled Traveler's Helpline of Central Florida** (☎ 407/352–5209 or 800/945–2045, FAX 407/351–1901 or 800/677–

5224) can answer questions about the accessibility of many area attractions, hotels, and restaurants. Both Walt Disney World (☎ 407/824–4321) and Universal Studios (☎ 407/363–8000) publish guidebooks for guests with disabilities; allow six weeks for delivery. If you need the information in a hurry, send a large, self-addressed envelope with at least $1 in postage to the **Disabled Travelers Friendship Network** (Box 690801, Orlando, FL 32869–0801), which operates under the wing of the Disabled Traveler's Helpline and is affiliated with **Friends of the Family** (Box 690801, Orlando, FL 32869–0801, ☎ 407/856–7676 or 800/945–2045), which will customize your itinerary, supply tour guides who push wheelchairs, and meet you at the airport.

FOR TRAVELERS WITH HEARING IMPAIRMENTS➤ Contact the **American Academy of Otolaryngology** (1 Prince St., Alexandria, VA 22314, ☎ 703/836–4444, FAX 703/683–5100, TTY 703/519–1585).

FOR TRAVELERS WITH MOBILITY PROBLEMS➤ Contact the **Information Center for Individuals with Disabilities** (Fort Point Pl., 27–43 Wormwood St., Boston, MA 02210, ☎ 617/727–5540, 800/462–5015 in MA, TTY 617/345–9743); **Mobility International USA** (Box 10767, Eugene, OR 97440, ☎ and TTY 503/343–

1284, FAX 503/343–6812), the U.S. branch of an international organization based in Belgium (*see below*) that has affiliates in 30 countries; the **Travel Industry and Disabled Exchange** (TIDE, 5435 Donna Ave., Tarzana, CA 91356, ☎ 818/344–3640, FAX 818/344–0078); and **Travelin' Talk** (Box 3534, Clarksville, TN 37043, ☎ 615/552–6670, FAX 615/552–1182).

FOR TRAVELERS WITH VISION IMPAIRMENTS➤ Contact the **American Council of the Blind** (1155 15th St. NW, Suite 720, Washington, DC 20005, ☎ 202/467–5081, FAX 202/467–5085); or the **American Foundation for the Blind** (15 W. 16th St., New York, NY 10011, ☎ 212/620–2000, TTY 212/620–2158).

In the U.K.: Contact the **Royal Association for Disability and Rehabilitation** (RADAR, 12 City Forum, 250 City Rd., London EC1V 8AF, ☎ 0171/250–3222) or Mobility International (rue de Manchester 25, B1070 Brussels, Belgium, ☎ 00–322–410–6297), an international clearinghouse of travel information for people with disabilities.

PUBLICATIONS

Several free publications are available from the U.S. Information Center (Box 100, Pueblo, CO 81009, ☎ 719/948–3334): **"New Horizons for the Air Traveler with a Disability"** (address to Dept. 355A), describing legally mandated changes; the pocket-size **"Fly Smart"** (Dept. 575B), good on flight safety; and the Airport Operators Council's worldwide **"Access Travel: Airports"** (Dept. 575A).

Fodor's *Great American Vacations for Travelers with Disabilities* ($18; available in bookstores, or call 800/533–6478) details accessible attractions, restaurants, and hotels in U.S. destinations. The 500-page *Travelin' Talk Directory* ($35; Box 3534, Clarksville, TN 37043, ☎ 615/552–6670) lists people and organizations who help travelers with disabilities. For specialist travel agents worldwide, consult the *Directory of Travel Agencies for the Disabled* ($19.95 plus $2 shipping; Twin Peaks Press, Box 129, Vancouver, WA 98666, ☎ 206/694–2462 or 800/637–2256).

THEME PARKS
Walt Disney World (☎ 407/560–6233; TTY 407/827–5141), **Universal Studios** (☎ 407/354–6356; TTY 407/363–8265), and **Sea World** (☎ 407/351–3600; TTY 407/363–2395) make arrangements for guides who know sign language. Advance reservations are necessary; provide two weeks' notice if possible.

TRAVEL AGENCIES AND TOUR OPERATORS
The Americans with Disabilities Act requires that travel firms serve the needs of all travelers. However, some agencies and operators specialize in making group and individual arrangements for travelers with disabilities, among them **Access Adventures** (206 Chestnut Ridge Rd., Rochester, NY 14624, ☎ 716/889–9096), run by a former physical-rehab counselor; **Tailored Tours** (Box 797687, Dallas, TX 75379, ☎ 214/612–1168 or 800/628–8542); and **Travel Trends** (2 Allan Plaza, 4922–51 Ave., Box 3581, Leduc, Alberta T9E 6X2, ☎ 403/986–9000 or 800/661–2109 in Canada), which has group tours and is especially good for cruises. In addition, many general-interest operators and agencies (*see* Tour Operators, *below*) can also arrange vacations for travelers with disabilities.

FOR TRAVELERS WITH HEARING IMPAIRMENTS➤ One agency is **International Express** (7319-B Baltimore Ave., College Park, MD 20740, ☎ TDD 301/699–8836, FAX 301/699–8836), which arranges group and independent trips.

FOR TRAVELERS WITH MOBILITY PROBLEMS➤ A number of operators specialize in working with travelers who have mobility problems: **Access Tours** (Box 2985, Jackson, WY 83001, ☎ 307/733–6664 in summer; 2440 S. Forest, Tucson, AZ 85713, ☎ 602/791–7977 winter–mid-May), which organizes national park tours; **Hinsdale Travel Service** (201 E. Ogden Ave., Suite 100, Hinsdale, IL 60521, ☎ 708/325–1335 or 800/303–5521), a travel agency that will give you access to the services of wheelchair-user Janice Perkins; and **Wheelchair Journeys** (16979 Redmond Way, Redmond, WA 98052, ☎ 206/885–2210), which can handle arrangements worldwide.

FOR TRAVELERS WITH DEVELOPMENTAL DISABILITIES➤ Contact the nonprofit **New Directions** (5276 Hollister Ave., Suite 207, Santa Barbara, CA 93111, ☎ 805/967–2841).

MEDICAL SUPPLIES
Undoubtedly the best in town, **Care Medical Equipment** (☎ 407/856–2273 in Orlando, 407/933—1412 in Kissimmee, or 800/741–2282) does everything from renting wheelchairs and scooters to supplying oxygen. The organization is particularly effective at coordinating with hometown medical personnel to ensure the appropriate equipment. Prices are reasonable, and reliability is superior.

NURSING SERVICES
Rescare (1801 Lee Rd., Suite 175, Winter Park 32789, ☎ 407/740–5650, FAX 407/740–7178) reliably provides LPNs, home health aides, therapists, and RNs on call around the clock. Prices are reasonable, although professional services are never cheap. **Careteam** (1085 W. Morse Blvd., Suite

THE GOLD GUIDE / IMPORTANT CONTACTS

A, Winter Park 32789, ☎ 407/628–8845) has a similar setup, with similar prices and reliability.

DISCOUNTS

Options include **Entertainment Travel Editions** (fee $28–$53, depending on destination; Box 1068, Trumbull, CT 06611, ☎ 800/445–4137); **Great American Traveler** ($49.95 annually; Box 27965, Salt Lake City, UT 84127, ☎ 800/548–2812); **Moment's Notice Discount Travel Club** ($25 annually, single or family; 163 Amsterdam Ave., Suite 137, New York, NY 10023, ☎ 212/486–0500); **Privilege Card** ($74.95 annually; 3391 Peachtree Rd. NE, Suite 110, Atlanta GA 30326, ☎ 404/262–0222 or 800/236—9732); **Travelers Advantage** ($49 annually, single or family; CUC Travel Service, 49 Music Sq. W, Nashville, TN 37203, ☎ 800/548–1116 or 800/648–4037); and **Worldwide Discount Travel Club** ($50 annually for family, $40 single; 1674 Meridian Ave., Miami Beach, FL 33139, ☎ 305/534–2082).

DRIVING

If you want to have your car in Florida without driving it there, board the **Auto-Train** in Lorton, Virginia (☎ 703/690–3355), near Washington, DC. Its southern terminus is Sanford, Florida (☎ 407/323–4800), some 23 miles north of Orlando.

ROAD SERVICE

AAA Emergency Road Service (☎ 407/877–2266 or 800/222–4357). In Walt Disney World, there is a **Car Care Center** (*see* Essential Information *in* Chapter 2).

E

EMERGENCIES

Police or **ambulance** (☎ 911). All of the area's major theme parks have first-aid centers.

DOCTORS

Hospital emergency rooms are open 24 hours a day. The most accessible hospital is the **Orlando Regional Medical Center/Sand Lake Hospital,** in the International Drive area (9400 Turkey Lake Rd., ☎ 407/351–8500).

For minor medical problems, contact **Housemed** (2901 Parkway Blvd., Kissimmee, ☎ 407/396–1195, 407/648–9234 or 407/846–2093), which runs a clinic that's open 9–9 daily and a minor-emergency mobile service that offers hotel-room visits by physicians for minor medical care and dispenses nonnarcotic medication. Closer to Orlando, a block west of Kirkman Road, is **Centra Care** (6001 Vineland Rd., Orlando, ☎ 407/351–6682; open daily 8 AM–midnight). Near WDW, in Lake Buena Vista, the most convenient facility is the **Buena Vista Walk-in Medical Center,** next to the Walt Disney World Village entrance (Rte. 535, ☎ 407/828–3434), open daily 8–8;

it also provides free shuttle service from any of the Disney theme park's first-aid stations.

24-HOUR PHARMACIES

Eckerd Drugs (908 Lee Rd., Orlando, ☎ 407/644–6908) is just off I–4 at the Lee Road exit, and **Walgreen's** (6201 International Dr., ☎ 407/345–8311 or 407/345–8402) is opposite Wet 'n' Wild; **Walgreen's** (4578 S. Kirkman Rd., ☎ 407/293–8458) is just north of Universal Studios.

DENTISTS

Emergency dental referral (☎ 407/847–7474).

G

GAY AND LESBIAN TRAVEL

ORGANIZATIONS

The Genesis Foundation (Box 560213, Orlando, FL 32856, ☎ 407/857–5444, FAX 407/438–3695) has organized an annual Gay Day at Walt Disney World for the past five years. The **International Gay Travel Association** (Box 4974, Key West, FL 33041, ☎ 800/448–8550), a consortium of 800 businesses, can supply names of travel agents and tour operators.

PUBLICATIONS

The premier international travel magazine for gays and lesbians is **Our World** ($35 for 10 issues; 1104 N. Nova Rd., Suite 251, Daytona Beach, FL 32117, ☎ 904/441–5367). The 16-page monthly "Out & About" ($49 for 10 issues; ☎ 212/645–

6922 or 800/929–2268) covers gay-friendly resorts, hotels, cruise lines, and airlines.

TOUR OPERATORS

Cruises and resort vacations are handled by **Toto Tours** (1326 W. Albion Suite 3W, Chicago, IL 60626, ☎ 312/274–8686 or 800/565–1241).

TRAVEL AGENCIES

The largest agencies serving gay travelers are **Advance Travel** (10700 Northwest Freeway, Suite 160, Houston, TX 77092, ☎ 713/682–2002 or 800/695–0880), **Islanders/Kennedy Travel** (183 W. 10th St., New York, NY 10014, ☎ 212/242–3222 or 800/988–1181), **Now Voyager** (4406 18th St., San Francisco, CA 94114, ☎ 415/626–1169 or 800/255–6951), and **Yellowbrick Road** (1500 W. Balmoral Ave., Chicago, IL 60640, ☎ 312/561–1800 or 800/642–2488). **Skylink Women's Travel** (746 Ashland Ave., Santa Monica, CA 90405, ☎ 310/452–0506 or 800/225—5759) works with lesbians.

I

INSURANCE

Travel insurance covering baggage, health, and trip cancellation or interruptions is available from **Access America** (Box 90315, Richmond, VA 23286, ☎ 804/285–3300 or 800/284–8300), **Carefree Travel Insurance** (Box 9366, 100 Garden City Plaza, Garden City,

NY 11530, ☎ 516/294–0220 or 800/323–3149), **Near** (Box 1339, Calumet City, IL 60409, ☎ 708/868–6700 or 800/654–6700), **Travel Guard International** (1145 Clark St., Stevens Point, WI 54481, ☎ 715/345–0505 or 800/826–1300), and **Wallach & Company** (107 W. Federal St., Box 480, Middleburg, VA 22117, ☎ 703/687–3166 or 800/237–6615).

IN THE U.K.

The **Association of British Insurers** (51 Gresham St., London EC2V 7HQ, ☎ 0171/600–3333; 30 Gordon St., Glasgow G1 3PU, ☎ 0141/226–3905; Scottish Provident Bldg., Donegall Sq. W., Belfast BT1 6JE, ☎ 01232/249176; call for other locations) gives advice by phone and publishes the free **"Holiday Insurance,"** which describes typical policy provisions and costs.

L

LODGING

APARTMENT AND HOUSE RENTALS

Among the companies to contact are **Hometours International** (Box 11503, Knoxville, TN 37939, ☎ 615/588–8722 or 800/367–4668), **Rent-a-Home International** (7200 34th Ave. NW, Seattle, WA 98117, ☎ 206/789–9377 or 800/488–7368), **Vacation Home Rentals Worldwide** (235 Kensington Ave., Norwood, NJ 07648, ☎ 201/767–9393 or 800/633–3284), and **Villas and Apartments**

Abroad (420 Madison Ave., Suite 1105, New York, NY 10017, ☎ 212/759–1025 or 800/433–3020). Members of the travel club **Hideaways International** ($99 annually; 767 Islington St., Portsmouth, NH 03801, ☎ 603/430–4433 or 800/843–4433) receive two annual guides plus quarterly newsletters and arrange rentals among themselves.

HOME EXCHANGE

Principal clearinghouses include **Intervac International** ($65 annually; Box 590504, San Francisco, CA 94159, ☎ 415/435–3497), which has three annual directories, and **Loan-a-Home** ($35–$45 annually; 2 Park La., Apt. 6E, Mount Vernon, NY 10552-3443, ☎ 914/664–7640), which specializes in long-term exchanges.

M

MONEY MATTERS

ATMS

For specific **Cirrus** locations in the United States and Canada, call 800/424–7787. For U.S. **Plus** locations, call 800/843–7587 and enter the area code and first three digits of the number you're calling from (or of the calling area for which you want an ATM).

WIRING FUNDS

Funds can be wired via **American Express MoneyGram** (☎ 800/926–9400 from the United States and Canada for locations and information) or

Western Union (☎ 800/325–6000 for agent locations or to send using MasterCard or Visa, 800/321–2923 in Canada).

N

NEWSPAPERS:
ORLANDO

The leading Orlando region newspaper is the **Orlando Sentinel** (Box 2833, Orlando, FL 32802, ☎ 407/420–5000).

P

PHOTO HELP

The **Kodak Information Center** (☎ 800/242–2424) answers consumer questions about film and photography.

R

RADIO NEWS:
ORLANDO

To get plugged into Orlando news, tune in to **WDBO-AM**, 58 on the AM dial.

RAIL TRAVEL

Amtrak (☎ 800/USA–RAIL) operates the *Silver Star* and the *Silver Meteor* to Florida. Both stop in Winter Park (150 Morse Blvd.), Orlando (1400 Sligh Blvd.), and Kissimmee (416 Pleasant St.).

S

SENIOR CITIZENS

Fairy Godmothers (☎ 407/277–3724) squires older travelers as well as youngsters around the theme parks.

EDUCATIONAL TRAVEL

The nonprofit **Elderhostel** (75 Federal St., 3rd Floor, Boston, MA 02110, ☎ 617/426–7788), for people 60 and older, has offered inexpensive study programs since 1975. The nearly 2,000 courses cover everything from marine science to Greek myths and cowboy poetry. Fees for programs in the United States and Canada, which usually last one week, run about $300, not including transportation.

ORGANIZATIONS

Contact the **American Association of Retired Persons** (AARP, 601 E St. NW, Washington, DC 20049, ☎ 202/434–2277; $8 per person or couple annually). Its Purchase Privilege Program entitles members to discounts on lodging, car rentals, and sightseeing, and the AARP Motoring Plan furnishes domestic trip-routing information and emergency road-service aid for an annual fee of $39.95 per person or couple ($59.95 for a premium version).

For other discounts on lodgings, car rentals, and other travel products, along with magazines and newsletters, contact the **National Council of Senior Citizens** (membership $12 annually; 1331 F St. NW, Washington, DC 20004, ☎ 202/347–8800) and **Mature Outlook** (subscription $9.95 annually; 6001 N. Clark St., Chicago, IL 60660, ☎ 312/465–6466 or 800/336–6330).

PUBLICATIONS

The 50+ Traveler's Guidebook: Where to Go, Where to Stay, What to Do, by Anita Williams and Merrimac Dillon ($12.95; St. Martin's Press, 175 5th Ave., New York, NY 10010, ☎ 212/674–5151 or 800/288–2131), offers many useful tips. **"The Mature Traveler"** ($29.95; Box 50400, Reno, NV 89513, ☎ 702/786–7419), a monthly newsletter, covers travel deals.

STUDENTS

GROUPS

Major tour operators include **Contiki Holidays** (300 Plaza Alicante, Suite 900, Garden Grove, CA 92640, ☎ 714/740–0808 or 800/466–0610).

HOSTELING

Contact **Hostelling International–American Youth Hostels** (733 15th St. NW, Suite 840, Washington, DC 20005, ☎ 202/783–6161) in the United States, **Hostelling International–Canada** (205 Catherine St., Suite 400, Ottawa, Ontario K2P 1C3, ☎ 613/237–7884) in Canada, and the **Youth Hostel Association of England and Wales** (Trevelyan House, 8 St. Stephen's Hill, St. Albans, Hertfordshire AL1 2DY, ☎ 01727/855215 and 01727/845047) in the United Kingdom. Membership ($25 in the U.S., C$26.75 in Canada, and £9 in the U.K.) gives you access to 5,000 hostels worldwide that charge $7–$20 nightly per person.

I.D. CARDS

For discounts on transportation and admissions, get the **International Student Identity Card** (ISIC) if you're a bona fide student or the **International Youth Card** (IYC) if you're under 26. In the United States, the ISIC and IYC cards cost $16 each and include basic travel-accident and illness coverage, plus a toll-free travel hot line. Apply through the Council on International Educational Exchange (*see below*). Cards are available for $15 each in Canada from Travel Cuts (187 College St., Toronto, Ontario M5T 1P7, ☎ 416/979–2406 or 800/667–2887) and in the United Kingdom for £5 each at student unions and student travel companies.

ORGANIZATIONS

A major contact is the **Council on International Educational Exchange** (CIEE, 205 E. 42nd St., 16th Floor, New York, NY 10017, ☎ 212/661–1450), with locations in Boston (729 Boylston St., Boston, MA 02116, ☎ 617/266–1926), Miami (9100 S. Dadeland Blvd., Miami, FL 33156, ☎ 305/670–9261), Los Angeles (1093 Broxton Ave., Los Angeles, CA 90024, ☎ 310/208–3551), 43 college towns nationwide, and the United Kingdom (28A Poland St., London W1V 3DB, ☎ 0171/437–7767). Twice a year, it publishes *Student Travels* magazine. The CIEE's Council Travel Service offers domestic air passes for bargain travel within the United States and is the exclusive U.S. agent for several student-discount cards.

Campus Connections (325 Chestnut St., Suite 1101, Philadelphia, PA 19106, ☎ 215/625–8585 or 800/428–3235) specializes in discounted accommodations and airfares for students. The **Educational Travel Centre** (438 N. Frances St., Madison, WI 53703, ☎ 608/256–5551) offers rail passes and low-cost airline tickets, mostly for flights departing from Chicago.

In Canada, also contact **Travel Cuts** (*see below*).

T
TOUR OPERATORS

Among the companies selling tours and packages to Walt Disney World, the following have a proven reputation, are nationally known, and have plenty of options to choose from.

GROUP TOURS

Escorted tours to Walt Disney World generally spend only a day or two at the park as part of a longer Florida itinerary. For deluxe motorcoach tours, contact **Maupintour** (Box 807, Lawrence, KS 66044, ☎ 913/843–1211 or 800/255–4266) and **Tauck Tours** (11 Wilton Rd., Westport, CT 06880, ☎ 203/226–6911 or 800/468–2825). Another operator, falling between deluxe and first-class, is **Globus** (5301 South Federal Circle, Littleton, CO 80123-2980, ☎ 303/797–2800 or 800/221–0090). In the first-class and tourist range, try **Collette Tours** (162 Middle St., Pawtucket, RI 02860, ☎ 401/728–3805 or 800/832–4656) and **Domenico Tours** (750 Broadway, Bayonne, NJ 07002, ☎ 201/823–8687 or 800/554–8687). For budget and tourist-class programs, contact Cosmos (*see* Globus, *above*).

PACKAGES

Contact **American Airlines Fly AAway Vacations** (☎ 800/321–2121); **Continental Airlines' Grand Destinations** (☎ 800/634–5555); **Delta Dream Vacations** (☎ 800/872–7786); **Globetrotters** (139 Main St., Cambridge, MA 02142, ☎ 617/621–9911 or 800/999–9696); **Kingdom Tours** (300 Market St., Kingston, PA 18704, ☎ 717/283–4241 or 800/872–8857); **United Vacations** (☎ 800/328–6877); and **USAir Vacations** (☎ 800/455–0123). **Funjet Vacations,** based in Milwaukee, Wisconsin, and **Gogo Tours,** based in Ramsey, New Jersey, sell Walt Disney World packages only through travel agents.

Regional operators specialize in putting together Walt Disney World packages for travelers from their local area. Arrangements may include charter or scheduled air transportation. Contact **Apple Vacations** (25 N.W. Point Blvd., Elk Grove Village, IL

60007, ☎ 708/640–1150 or 800/365–2775) and **Travel Impressions** (465 Smith St., Farmingdale, NY 11735, ☎ 516/845–7000 or 800/224–0022).

Disney Vacations land-only packages are available through Disney's Central Reservations Office (☎ 407/W–DISNEY). Disney's tend to be pricier, but they include more than packages sold by most other operators. Meals, use of sports facilities, and tips, as well as theme-park admissions, are included in the package price.

FROM THE U.K.➤ Tour operators offering packages to Walt Disney World and the Orlando area are **British Airways Holidays** (Astral Towers, Betts Way, London Rd., Crawley, West Sussex RH10 2XA, ☎ 01293/518022); **Jetsave Travel Ltd.** (Sussex House, London Rd., E. Grinstead, W. Sussex RH19 1LD, ☎ 01342/312033); **Key to America** (1–3 Station Rd., Ashford, Middlesex TW15 2UW, ☎ 01784/248777); **Kuoni Travel (Kuoni House, Dorking, Surrey** RH5 4AZ, ☎ 01306/742222); and **Premier Holidays** (Westbrook, Milton Rd., Cambridge CB4 1YQ, ☎ 01223/516688). Car rental is included in all Florida holidays.

Travel agencies that offer cheap fares to Orlando and Miami include **Trailfinders** (42–50 Earl's Court Rd., London W8 6FT, ☎ 0171/937–5400), **Travel Cuts** (295a Regent St., London W1R 7YA, ☎ 0171/637–3161; *see* Students, *above*), and **Flightfile** (49 Tottenham Court Rd., London W1P 9RE, ☎ 0171/700–2722).

ORGANIZATIONS

The **National Tour Association** (546 E. Main St., Lexington, KY 40508, ☎ 606/226–4444 or 800/682–8886) and **United States Tour Operators Association** (USTOA, 211 E. 51st St., Suite 12B, New York, NY 10022, ☎ 212/750–7371) can provide lists of member operators and information on booking tours.

PUBLICATIONS

Consult the brochure **"Worldwide Tour & Vacation Package Finder"** from the National Tour Association (*see above*) and the Better Business Bureau's **"Tips on Travel Packages"** (publication No. 24-195, $2; 4200 Wilson Blvd., Arlington, VA 22203.

TRAVEL AGENCIES

For names of reputable agencies in your area, contact the **American Society of Travel Agents** (1101 King St., Suite 200, Alexandria, VA 22314, ☎ 703/739–2782).

V

VISITOR

INFORMATION

For Walt Disney World, contact **Walt Disney World Information** (Box 10040, Lake Buena Vista, FL 32830, ☎

407/824–4321, TTY 407/827–5141); for reservations, contact the **Central Reservations Office** (for lodging and entertainment, ☎ 407/934–7639; TTY 407/345–5984; for dining, ☎ 407/939–3463). To be a member of the audience at a show being taped at Disney-MGM Studios, call **Production Information** (☎ 407/560–4651).

For information on other theme parks in the Orlando area, contact **Sea World** (7007 Sea World Dr., Orlando 32821, ☎ 407/351–3600), **Universal Studios Florida** (1000 Universal Studios Plaza, Orlando 32819–8000, ☎ 407/363–8000, TTY 407/363–8265), and **Busch Gardens** (Box 9158, Tampa 333674, ☎ 813/987–5283).

For Greater Orlando area information, contact the **Orlando/Orange County Convention and Visitors Bureau** (8445 International Dr., Orlando, FL 32819, ☎ 407/363–5871). Ask for the free *Discover Orlando* guidebook; it includes the Orlando Magicard, good for discounts on area attractions. For information about the Kissimmee area on U.S. 192, contact the **Kissimmee/St. Cloud Convention and Visitors Bureau** (1925 E. Irlo Bronson Memorial Hwy., Kissimmee, FL 34744, ☎ 407/847–5000 or 800/327–9159). For information about the tony suburb of Winter Park, contact the **Winter Park Chamber of Com-**

merce (Box 280, Winter Park, FL 32790, ☎ 407/644–8281).

For information on destinations outside the immediate Orlando-Kissimmee area, contact the **Florida Department of Commerce Division of Tourism** (126 W. Van Buren St., Tallahassee, FL 32399–2000, ☎ 904/487–1462).

In the U.K., also contact the **United States Travel and Tourism Administration** (Box 1EN, London W1A 1EN, ☎ 0171/495–4466). For a free USA pack, write the USTTA at Box 170, Ashford, Kent TN24 0ZX. Enclose stamps worth £1.50.

W

WEATHER

For current weather and forecasts, plus the local time and helpful travel tips, call the **Weather Channel Connection** (☎ 900/932–8437; 95¢ per minute) from a touch-tone phone.

SMART TRAVEL TIPS A TO Z

Basic Information on Traveling in Orlando and Savvy Tips to Make Your Trip a Breeze

The more you travel, the more you learn about how to make trips run like clockwork. To help make your travels hassle-free, Fodor's editors have rounded up dozens of tips from our contributors and travel experts all over the world, as well as basic information on visiting Walt Disney World, Universal Studios, and the other attractions of Central Florida. For names of organizations to contact and publications that can give you more information, *see* Important Contacts A to Z, *above.*

A

AIR TRAVEL

If time is an issue, **always look for nonstop flights,** which require no change of plane and make no stops. If possible, **avoid connecting flights,** which stop at least once and can involve a change of plane, although the flight number remains the same; if the first leg is late, the second waits.

CUTTING COSTS

The Sunday travel section of most newspapers is a good source of deals.

MAJOR AIRLINES➤ The least-expensive airfares from the major airlines are priced for round-trip travel and are subject to restrictions. You must usually **book in advance and buy the ticket within 24 hours** to get cheaper fares, and you may have to **stay over a Saturday night.** The lowest fare is subject to availability, and only a small percentage of the plane's total seats are sold at that price. It's good to **call a number of airlines, and when you are quoted a good price, book it on the spot**—the same fare on the same flight may not be available the next day. Airlines generally allow you to change your return date for a $25 to $50 fee, but most low-fare tickets are nonrefundable. However, if you don't use it, you can apply the cost toward the purchase price of a new ticket, again for a small charge.

CONSOLIDATORS➤ Consolidators, who buy tickets at reduced rates from scheduled airlines, sell them at prices below the lowest available from the airlines directly—usually without advance restrictions. Sometimes you can even get your money back if you need to return the ticket. Carefully read the fine print detailing penalties for changes and cancellations. If you doubt the reliability of a consolidator, **confirm your reservation with the airline.**

ALOFT

AIRLINE FOOD➤ If you hate airline food, **ask for special meals when booking.** These can be vegetarian, low-cholesterol, or kosher, for example; commonly prepared to order in smaller quantities than standard catered fare, these meals can be tastier.

SMOKING➤ Smoking is banned on all flights within the United States of less than six hours' duration and on all Canadian flights; the ban also applies to domestic segments of international flights aboard U.S. and foreign carriers. Delta has banned smoking system-wide; British Airways and Virgin Atlantic have banned smoking on most international flights.

AIRPORT TRANSFERS

BY BUS➤ Public buses operate between the airport and the main terminal of the Tri-County Transit Authority, in downtown Orlando. Though the cost is 75¢, other options are preferable because center-city Orlando is far from most of the hotels used by theme-park vacationers.

BY TAXI➤ Taxis take only a half hour to get from the airport to most hotels used by WDW visitors; they charge about $25 plus tip to the International Drive area, about $10 more to the U.S. 192 area. Depending on the number of people in your party, this will cost more or less than paying by the head for an airport shuttle.

B
BUS TRAVEL

If you are staying along International Drive, in Kissimmee, or in Orlando proper, you can ride public buses to get around the immediate area. To find out which bus to take, ask your hotel clerk or call the Tri-County Transit Authority Information Office (☎ 407/841–8240) for more information.

FROM THE HOTELS TO THE ATTRACTIONS

Scheduled service and charters linking just about every hotel and major attraction in the area are available. In addition, many hotels run their own shuttles especially for guests; to arrange a ride, all you have to do is ask your hotel's concierge, inquire at the front desk, or phone the operator directly.

When making your plans, remember that the bus schedule may not always coincide

with your schedule: Buses may not run to the places you want to see on the days or at the times you prefer, whether that's back to your hotel at midday or out to the theme parks in late afternoon. Some buses also pick up or drop off guests at several hotels, adding to your ride time and delaying your arrival at your destination.

One-way fares are usually $6–$7 per adult, a couple of dollars less for children 4–11, between major hotel areas and the Disney parks. Excursion fares to Busch Gardens and Cypress Gardens, which are more than a half-hour's drive, are $27 per person, including admission as well as round-trip fare.

C
CAMERAS, CAMCORDERS, AND COMPUTERS

LAPTOPS

Before you depart, **check your portable computer's battery,** because you may be asked at security to turn on the computer to prove that it is what it appears to be. At the airport, you may prefer to **request a manual inspection,** although security X-rays do not harm hard-disk or floppy-disk storage.

PHOTOGRAPHY

If your camera is new or if you haven't used it for a while, **shoot and develop a few rolls of film** before you leave. Always **store film in a**

cool, dry place—never in the car's glove compartment or on the shelf under the rear window.

Every pass through an X-ray machine increases film's chance of clouding. To protect it, carry it in a clear plastic bag and **ask for hand inspection at security.** Such requests are virtually always honored at U.S. airports. Don't depend on a lead-lined bag to protect film in checked luggage—the airline may increase the radiation to see what's inside.

VIDEO

Before your trip, **test your camcorder, invest in a skylight filter to protect the lens, and charge the batteries.** (Airport security personnel may ask you to turn on the camcorder to prove that it's what it appears to be).

Videotape is not damaged by X-rays, but it may be harmed by the magnetic field of a walk-through metal detector, so **ask that videotapes be hand-checked.**

CHILDREN AND TRAVEL

All the theme parks get high marks from young travelers. Hotel facilities for children range from okay to fabulous. The only problem is that the times when your kids are out of school are the times when every other child in the universe is out of school and every other parent is packing up the car to drive to Orlando as well. Preschoolers can find these crowds overwhelming. So if your children are of varying ages and those in school are good students, consider taking them out so you can visit in the less-congested off-season. Educational programs and the broadening experience of travel itself may persuade your children's teachers to excuse the absence. Teachers may also arrange special study assignments relating to the trip.

If your children cannot afford to miss school, try to take your vacation in late May or early June (as soon as the school year ends).

BABY-SITTING

Baby-sitting is widely available; **check with your hotel desk.**

At Walt Disney World, there are strong children's facilities and programs at the Contemporary, Dolphin, Grand Floridian, Polynesian Village, Wilderness Lodge, Yacht and Beach Clubs, and Swan; the Polynesian Village's Neverland Club will enchant you and your offspring with its Peter Pan–theme clubhouse and youngsters-only dinner show. Parents also rave about the Sand Castle Club at the Yacht and Beach Clubs. The Hilton, near Disney Village Marketplace, has a Youth Hotel where parents can leave their offspring until midnight for a night on the World; meals are served and there's even a dormitory.

Off-site, many hotels have supervised children's programs. Standouts are the camplike programs at the Stouffer Orlando Resort opposite Sea World (it's called Shamu's Playhouse); at the Hyatt Regency Grand Cypress near Disney Village (which has a separate teens-only evening program); the Westgate Lakes Resort; and the Holiday Inn at Lake Buena Vista and the Holiday Inn Maingate East. These have trained counselors and planned activities as well as attractive facilities; some even have mascots. The age range varies from 4 or 5 to 15; some accept children as young as 2, however. The Peabody Hotel has an evening program that allows you to drop off your youngsters while you dine in the hotel's restaurants; call ahead. *See also* Chapter 8, Lodging.

BABY SWAP

Parents with small children under the height limit for major attractions have to take turns waiting in the long lines, right? Wrong. In what's unofficially known as the Baby Swap, both of you queue up, and when it's your turn to board, one stays with the youngsters until the other returns; the waiting partner then rides without waiting again. (Universal Studios calls it a Baby Exchange and has Baby Exchange areas at most rides.)

CHARACTER MEALS

At special breakfasts, brunches, and dinners offered by many Walt Disney World restaurants, Mickey, Donald, Goofy, Chip 'n' Dale, and other favorite characters sign autographs and pose for snapshots. Reservations are not always necessary, but these early morning feeding frenzies are wildly popular, so **show up early if you don't like to wait.** *See* Chapter 7, Dining. Universal Studios has its own character meal, right in the park before official park-opening hours; Woody Woodpecker, the Flintstones, and other favorites are on hand, and you will be strategically positioned to head the stampede to Back to the Future . . . The Ride. Plan your character meal for toward the end of your visit, when your little ones will be used to seeing these large and sometimes frightening figures; they're also a good way to kill the morning on the day you check out. *See also* Chapter 3, Universal Studios, Sea World, and Beyond, *and* Chapter 7, Dining.

DINING

Many restaurants in the Orlando area have a special children's menu. And providing that reassuring taste of home, franchised fast-food eateries abound. The McDonald's on International Drive has an elaborate multilevel playground that seems almost bigger than the restaurant.

DRIVING

If you are renting a car, **arrange for a car seat**

when you reserve. Sometimes they're free.

EDUCATIONAL PROGRAMS

Be sure to reserve ahead for any of these behind-the-scenes tours.

WALT DISNEY WORLD➣ Walt Disney World offers its six-hour Wonders Program courses year-round for those ages 10–15; the cost is $79 per course. Your youngsters can sign up for Wildlife Adventure: Exploring the Environment, which visits Discovery Island and WDW's 7,500-acre conservation preserve, where several rare species have found refuge from encroaching development; Art Magic: Bringing Illusion to Life, which introduces students to animation, costuming, landscaping and set design in movies, stage shows, and theme parks; Showbiz Magic: The Walt Disney World of Entertainment, during which students get to meet the performers and technicians who create the Disney shows and get an understanding of how music, lighting, costumes, and timing all combine to beguile an audience; or Passport: Secret Mission to Other Lands, a scavenger hunt through Epcot Center's World Showcase. In summer there is also a separate four-hour Kidventure Program, which focuses on Discovery Island plants and wildlife and is open to students ages 8–14; it costs $30, including boat transportation.

SEA WORLD➣ Three year-round Sea Safari programs ($5.95 adults, $4.95 children 3–9) offer behind-the-scenes looks at park operations: Backstage Explorations and Animal Lover's Adventure are 90-minute guided tours of park facilities; Animal Training Discoveries consists of a 45-minute chat and demonstration with the park's trainers. For a wide selection of age-specific classes on wildlife and ecology, you'll have to wait for summer, when the calendar is chockablock with programs ranging from one day to one week in length; most cost $15–$60. In addition, the bring-your-own-sleeping-bag Education Sleepovers, offered exclusively to school groups in winter, are open to individual visitors. (How about bedding down in the shark exhibit at Terrors of the Deep? Or try Cool Nights with Penguins to see the nightlife of the tuxedoed masses.) There's even talk of conducting overseas trips that combine classes at the park with a few days in Belize or the Bahamas.

BUSCH GARDENS➣ Multiday Zoo Camps keep children learning here from June through October. There's a different program for each age group, from kindergartners through 10th graders, and each program lasts several days ($80–$100 per session). Youngsters can also sign up for classes that last just a few hours ($15–$20), from

a hands-on introduction to wildlife for toddlers to a night hike for preteens.

FLYING

On domestic flights, children under 2 not occupying a seat travel free, and older children currently travel on the "lowest applicable" adult fare.

BAGGAGE

In general, the adult baggage allowance applies for children paying half or more of the adult fare.

SAFETY SEATS➣ According to the FAA, it's a good idea to **use safety seats aloft.** Airline policy varies. U.S. carriers allow FAA-approved models, but airlines usually require that you buy a ticket, even if your child would otherwise ride free, because the seats must be strapped into regular passenger seats.

FACILITIES➣ When making your reservation, **ask for children's meals or a freestanding bassinet** if you need them; the latter is available only to those with seats at the bulkhead, where there's enough legroom. If you don't need the bassinet, **think twice before requesting bulkhead seats**—the only storage area for in-flight necessities is the inconveniently distant overhead bins.

LODGING

In all but the smallest motels there is little or no charge for children under 18 who share a room with an adult.

PLAYGROUNDS, GAME ROOMS, THEME POOLS

All hotels on Disney property and many others in the area have playgrounds and arcades with video games and pinball machines. The one in Disney's Contemporary Resort is, hands down, the biggest game room in any hotel in the area. Parrot Cay, a little island in the Caribbean Beach Resort's lagoon, is anchored by a winning little playground with soft white sand underfoot. Swimming pools—such as the one here (it has a pirate stronghold and a cannon that lets out periodic booms), the Stormalong Bay area between Disney's Yacht and Beach Club, and the lagoon at Disney's Dixie Landings Resort—are long on Disney charm.

STROLLER RENTALS

Stroller rentals are available in theme parks, but you may want to bring your own, since fees run $5–$6 per day (plus a deposit) and you will probably need a stroller in places where you can't rent one—to explore Orlando off the beaten track, to explore Orlando's malls, even just to get around your hotel, if it's big. No one rents double strollers, and the singles available in Walt Disney World are sturdy but unyielding, not optimal for infants.

If you do rent a stroller, there is always the possibility that it will be taken. A word to the wise: although it is tempting, **don't leave packages in strollers.** At the three Disney theme parks, you can arrange to have large packages sent to the gate, where you can pick it up upon leaving. Experienced park visitors suggest either taping a large card with your name to the stroller or leaving some small personal item to mark it, such as a bandanna, a T-shirt, even a clear plastic bag with diapers inside; the theory is that people who wouldn't think twice about purloining theme-park property that they will subsequently return hesitate to make off with something that belongs to a fellow parent. If your stroller does disappear, you can easily pick up a replacement; ask any park staffer for the nearest location.

CUSTOMS AND DUTIES

BACK HOME

IN THE U.K.➤ From countries outside the EU, including the United States, you may import duty-free 200 cigarettes, 100 cigarillos, 50 cigars or 250 grams of tobacco; 1 liter of spirits or 2 liters of fortified or sparkling wine; 2 liters of still table wine; 60 milliliters of perfume; 250 milliliters of toilet water; plus £136 worth of other goods, including gifts and souvenirs.

D

FOR TRAVELERS WITH DISABILITIES

Central Florida attractions are among the most accessible destinations in the world for people who have disabilities. The hospitality industry continues to spend millions on barrier-removing renovations. Though some challenges remain, most can be overcome with planning.

When discussing accessibility with an operator or reservationist, **ask hard questions.** Are there any stairs, inside *or* out? Are there grab bars next to the toilet *and* in the shower/tub? How wide is the doorway to the room? To the bathroom? For the most extensive facilities, meeting the latest legal specifications, **opt for newer facilities,** which more often have been designed with access in mind. Older properties or ships must usually be retrofitted and may offer more limited facilities as a result. Be sure to **discuss your needs before booking.**

The main park-information centers (*see* Chapters 2 and 3) can answer specific questions and dispense general information for guests with disabilities.

LOCAL TRANSPORTATION

Although there are some lift-equipped vans for rent and some shuttle service available, guests need to plan itineraries in advance. The exception is on Disney property: Every other Disney bus on each route is lift-equipped, so there's never more than a 30-minute wait for hotel-to-theme-park trips. Consult transportation companies for more information.

Designated parking is available for guests with disabilities. It's near the turnstile area for most parks. The Magic Kingdom's special lot is near the Transportation and Ticket Center, where ferries depart for the Magic Kingdom and monorails travel there and to Epcot Center. Monorail entrances are level, but the ramp up is quite steep.

LODGING

Hotels and motels here are continually being renovated to comply with the Americans with Disabilities Act. Call the Disabled Traveler's Helpline of Central Florida for up-to-the-minute information.

GUESTS USING WHEELCHAIRS➤ **Staying at Disney-owned resort hotels is particularly convenient,** since the Disney transportation system has dozens of lift-equipped vehicles. Most resorts here in every price range have rooms with roll-in showers or transfer benches in the bathrooms.

You will be comfortable at any number of on-property Disney resorts. Especially worthwhile and convenient is the Grand Floridian, a luxurious monorail resort, and Port Orleans, which has all the advantages of Dixie Landings but a much more intimate feel. One of the most accommodating off-site resorts is the Marriott Orlando World Center; its level

of commitment is especially apparent on Sunday mornings, when the Garden Terrace Restaurant hosts one of the most delicious and hospitable Sunday brunches in central Florida.

GUESTS WITH VISUAL IMPAIRMENTS➤ In most properties, only elevators are braille-equipped, but some have programs to help employees understand how best to assist guests with visual impairments. Particularly outstanding is the Buena Vista Palace on Hotel Plaza Boulevard at Walt Disney World Village; its Australian-themed Outback Restaurant even has a table-side storyteller who paints pictures with words. The Embassy Suites Resorts at Lake Buena Vista and International Drive offer services such as talking alarm clocks and braille or recorded menus.

GUESTS WITH HEARING IMPAIRMENTS➤ Most area properties have purchased the equipment necessary to accommodate guests with hearing impairments. Telecommunications devices for the deaf, flashing or vibrating phones and alarms, and closed captioning are common; an industry-wide effort to teach some employees sign language is under way. The Grosvenor Resort, on Hotel Plaza Boulevard, has excellent facilities but no teletype reservations line.

THEME PARKS

DISCOUNTS➤ Guests with disabilities can **take advantage of a wide variety of discounts:** 50% at Busch Gardens for wheelchair users and the visually or hearing impaired; at least 50% at Cypress Gardens and Sea World for guests with visual or hearing impairments; and 20% at Universal Studios for those with a disability that limits enjoyment of the park.

GUESTS USING WHEELCHAIRS➤ Accessibility in the area is constantly improving for people who use wheelchairs. At Walt Disney World, a new standard of access was set with the opening of the Disney-MGM Studios. All of its restaurants, shops, and attractions, except one thrill ride, can be enjoyed right from a wheelchair. Epcot Center comes in a close second; some of the rides have a tailgate that drops down to provide a level entrance to the ride vehicle. Though the Magic Kingdom, now in its third decade, was designed before architects gave consideration to access issues, renovation plans are under way. Even so, the 18 accessible attractions combine with the live entertainment around the park to provide a most memorable experience. For specific accessibility information, see the Access for Travelers with Disabilities section for each park.

Universal Studios and Sea World are both

substantially barrier-free. Universal has retrofitted its major attractions, with the exception of Back to the Future, for wheelchair accessibility. At Sea World, most shows are in stadiums or theaters and have always been barrier-free. Now guests can even take their wheelchairs on the Behind the Scenes tours. Cypress Gardens and Splendid China are accessible by guests with disabilities.

In some attractions, guests who use scooters may be required to transfer to a wheelchair. In others, guests must be able to leave their own wheelchair to board the ride vehicle (and must have a traveling companion assist them, as park staff cannot do so). Attractions with emergency evacuation routes that have narrow walkways or steps require additional mobility. Turbulence on other attractions poses a problem for some guests.

Rest rooms at all of these parks have standard accessible stalls. Yet more spacious facilities are available in First Aid stations.

GUESTS WITH VISUAL IMPAIRMENTS➤ WDW and Universal Studios have produced descriptive cassette tapes that can be borrowed, along with portable tape recorders (deposit required); Sea World has no cassette program but does offer a braille guidebook and a free tour. The other parks have no services for the visually impaired. Service animals, while welcome, must be leashed or in a harness; they may board many rides, but not all—usually not those with loud noises, pyrotechnics, and other intense effects.

GUESTS WITH HEARING IMPAIRMENTS➤ Walt Disney World publishes a special guidebook describing the theme and story of various attractions in the three parks. At Epcot Center, you can rent personal translator units that amplify the sound tracks of seven shows ($4 plus $40 deposit). There and in the Magic Kingdom (and in Disney-MGM Studios by special arrangement), four-hour guided tours in sign language are available. Advance reservations are a must; provide two-weeks' notice if possible ($5 for adults, $3.50 for children 3–9).

Both Universal Studios and Sea World can also provide guides fluent in sign language with advance notice; Universal also has scripts available for all its shows. Busch Gardens, Cypress Gardens, and Splendid China do not offer assistance in sign.

WHEELCHAIRS

Probably the most comfortable course is to bring your wheelchair from home. However, except in theater-style shows, access may be difficult if it's wider than 24½ inches and longer than 32 inches (44 inches for scooters); consult hosts and hostesses at the attrac-tion. Thefts of personal wheelchairs while guests are inside attractions are rare but have been known to occur; take the precautions you would in any public place.

Wheelchair rentals are available from area medical-supply companies that will deliver to your hotel and let you keep the chair for the duration of your vacation. You can also rent by the day in major theme parks ($6 a day for wheelchairs, $25–$30 daily for the limited number of scooters, plus a deposit; see Chapters 2 and 3 for specifics).

In Disney parks, since rental locations are relatively close to parking, it may be a good idea to send someone ahead to get the wheelchair and bring it back to the car; at day's end, a Disney host or hostess may escort you to your car and then return the wheelchair for you. Here and at the other major area theme parks, rented wheelchairs that disappear while you're in a ride can be replaced throughout the parks—ask any staffer for the nearest location. Attaching some small personal item to the wheelchair may prevent other guests from taking yours by mistake.

DISCOUNT CLUBS

Travel clubs offer members unsold space on airplanes, cruise ships, and package tours at as much as 50% below regular prices. Membership may include a regular bulletin or access to a toll-free hot line giving details of available trips departing from three or four days to several months in the future. Most also offer 50% discounts off hotel rack rates. Before booking with a club, **make sure the hotel or other supplier isn't offering a better deal.**

To get to the hotel areas from the airport, catch the Beeline Expressway (Rte. 528) west to International Drive, and exit at Sea World. Or stay on the Beeline to I–4, and head either west to Walt Disney World and U.S. 192/Kissimmee or east to downtown Orlando. Call your hotel for the best route.

The most important artery in the Orlando area is I-4. This interstate highway, which links the Atlantic Coast to Florida's Gulf of Mexico, ties everything together, and you'll invariably receive directions in reference to it. The problem is that I–4, though considered an east–west expressway in our national road system (where even numbers signify an east–west orientation and odd numbers a north–south orientation), actually runs north and south in the Orlando area. So when the signs say east, you are usually going north, and when the signs say west, you are usually going south. Think north–EAST and south–WEST.

Another main drag is

International Drive, a.k.a. I-Drive, which has many major hotels, restaurants, and shopping centers. You can get onto International Drive from I–4 Exits 28, 29, and 30B.

The other main road, U.S. 192, cuts across I–4 at Exits 25A and 25B. This highway goes through the Kissimmee area and crosses Walt Disney World property, taking you to the Magic Kingdom's main entrance. U.S. 192 is sometimes called by its former names, Spacecoast Parkway and Irlo Bronson Memorial Highway. Irlo Bronson was a prominent local developer.

G

GAY AND
LESBIAN TRAVEL

The Genesis Foundation has organized an annual Gay Day at Walt Disney World for the past five years. In 1995, the event was expanded to include an entire weekend's worth of activities, including a Lesbian and Gay Business Expo at the Orange County Convention Center.

GUIDED TOURS

IN THE
THEME PARKS

Guided tours are available in all the area's major theme parks (*see* Essential Information *in* the individual theme-park sections of Chapters 2 and 3).

AROUND ORLANDO

BALLOON RIDES➤
Quick, look up! Any morning in Orlando chances are fair to good

that you'll spot a bright-colored hot-air balloon floating through the skies. You don't have to have your own gear to experience these silent, beautiful craft. Several operators offer trips, which usually include a Continental-breakfast picnic with champagne or a gala restaurant meal. They'll take children as well as adults (though most discourage parents from bringing babies and toddlers, who may be frightened by the experience). The cost is about $150 per adult at **Balloons by Terry** (3529 Edgewater Dr., Orlando, ☎ 407/422–3529); **Aerial Adventures,** the Church Street Station Balloon team (also 3529 Edgewater Dr., Orlando, ☎ 407/841–UPUP); and **Rise & Float Balloon Tours** (5767 Major Blvd., opposite Universal Studios at the Mystery Fun House, Orlando, ☎ 407/352–8191), whose hot-air balloon is decorated with two hot-pink flamingos and a giant palm tree.

HELICOPTER RIDES➤
Seven different area tours, ranging from $20 to $399, are available from **Falcon Helicopter Service** (8990 International Dr., next to Caruso's Palace, Orlando, ☎ 407/352–1753; at the Hyatt Hotel at I–4 and U.S. 192, ☎ 407/396–7222; and at Howard Johnson's, 5071 W. Irlo Bronson Memorial Hwy., Kissimmee, ☎ 407/397–0228).

THE GOLD GUIDE / SMART TRAVEL TIPS

I

INSURANCE

Travel insurance can protect your investment, replace your luggage and its contents, or provide for medical coverage should you fall ill during your trip. Most tour operators, travel agents, and insurance agents sell specialized health-and-accident, flight, trip-cancellation, and luggage insurance as well as comprehensive policies with some or all of these features. Before you make any purchase, **review your existing health and homeowner's policies** to find out whether they cover expenses incurred while traveling.

BAGGAGE

Airline liability for your baggage is limited to $1,250 per person on domestic flights. On international flights, the airlines' liability is $9.07 per pound or $20 per kilogram for checked baggage (roughly $640 per 70-pound bag) and $400 per passenger for unchecked baggage. However, this excludes valuable items such as jewelry and cameras that are listed in your ticket's fine print. You can buy additional insurance from the airline at check-in, but first **see if your homeowner's policy covers lost luggage.**

FLIGHT

You should **think twice before buying flight insurance.** Often purchased as a last-minute impulse at the airport, it

pays a lump sum when a plane crashes, either to a beneficiary if the insured dies or sometimes to a surviving passenger who loses eyesight or a limb. Intended to supplement the airline's coverage described in the limits-of-liability paragraphs on your ticket, it's expensive and basically unnecessary. Charging an airline ticket to a major credit card often automatically entitles you to coverage and may also embrace travel by bus, train, and ship.

HEALTH

FOR U.K. TRAVELERS➤ According to the Association of British Insurers, a trade association representing 450 insurance companies, it's wise to **buy extra medical coverage when you visit the United States.** You can buy an annual travel-insurance policy valid for most vacations during the year in which it's purchased. If you go this route, make sure it covers you if you have a preexisting medical condition or are pregnant.

TRIP

Without insurance, you will lose all or most of your money if you must cancel your trip due to illness or any other reason. Especially if your airline ticket, cruise, or package tour is nonrefundable and cannot be changed, it's essential that you **buy trip-cancellation-and-interruption insurance.** When considering how much coverage you need, look for a policy that will cover the cost

of your trip plus the nondiscounted price of a one-way airline ticket should you need to return home early. Read the fine print carefully, especially sections defining "family member" and "preexisting medical conditions." Also **consider default or bankruptcy insurance,** which protects you against a supplier's failure to deliver. However, such policies often do not cover default by a travel agency, tour operator, airline, or cruise line if you bought your tour and the coverage directly from the firm in question.

M

MONEY AND EXPENSES

ATMS

Chances are that you can **use your bank card at ATMs** to withdraw money from an account and get cash advances on a credit-card account if your card has been programmed with a personal identification number, or PIN. Before leaving home, **check in on frequency limits** for withdrawals and cash advances.

On cash advances you are charged interest from the day you receive the money from ATMs as well as from tellers. Transaction fees for ATM withdrawals outside your home turf may be higher than for withdrawals at home.

TRAVELER'S CHECKS

Whether or not to buy traveler's checks depends on where you are headed; **take cash to** rural areas and small towns, traveler's checks to cities. The most widely recognized are American Express, Citicorp, Thomas Cook, and Visa, which are sold by major commercial banks for 1%–3% of the checks' face value—it pays to shop around. Both American Express and Thomas Cook issue checks that can be countersigned and used by you or your traveling companion.

WIRING MONEY

You don't have to be a cardholder to send or receive funds through MoneyGram℠ from American Express. Just go to a MoneyGram agent, located in retail and convenience stores and in American Express Travel Offices. Pay up to $1,000 with cash or a credit card, anything over that in cash. The money can be picked up within 10 minutes in cash or check at the nearest MoneyGram agent. There's no limit, and the recipient need only present photo identification. The cost, which includes a free long-distance phone call, runs from 3% to 10%, depending on the amount sent, the destination, and how you pay.

You can also send money using Western Union. Money sent from the United States or Canada will be available for pickup at agent locations in 100 countries within 15 minutes. Once the money is in the system, it can be picked up at any one of 25,000 locations. Fees range from 4% to 10%, depending on the amount you send.

O
OPENING AND CLOSING TIMES

Most major attractions, restaurants, hotels, and shops are open for business seven days a week year-round.

DAILY HOURS

Theme-park hours vary from season to season; daily hours are extended mornings and evenings in busy periods. Walt Disney World's Magic Kingdom, for instance, closes at 7 PM in November but stays open until 2 AM on New Year's Eve. Cypress Gardens is open 9:30–5:30 daily year-round.

HOLIDAYS

Some public and private establishments close on holidays—not only the traditional holidays of New Year's Day, Easter, Memorial Day, Fourth of July, Labor Day, Thanksgiving, and Christmas but also January 15 (Martin Luther King, Jr.'s, Birthday), February 19 (Presidents' Day), the third Monday in February (Robert E. Lee's Birthday), April 26 (Confederate Memorial Day), June 3 (Jefferson Davis's Birthday), and the second Monday in October (Columbus Day).

P
PACKAGES AND TOURS

Firms that sell tours and packages purchase airline seats, hotel rooms, and rental cars in bulk and pass some of the savings on to you. In addition, the best operators have local representatives to help you out at your destination.

If you want to spend most of your vacation at Walt Disney World, independent vacation packages are an easy way to pay one price for theme-park admissions, sightseeing, car rental, excursions, and accommodations. You can often get a room, in your choice of hotel, for dates that Walt Disney World's own Central Reservations Office indicates are sold out. When booking your package, ask whether hotels are on-site or outside Walt Disney World; you might pay a lower price for a package that includes an off-site hotel, but you'll be sacrificing convenience. Finally, make sure any theme-park tickets included in your package are not limited to certain days of the week.

A GOOD DEAL?

The more your package or tour includes, the better you can predict the ultimate cost of your vacation. Make sure you know exactly what is included, and beware of hidden costs. Are taxes, tips, and service charges included? Transfers and baggage handling?

Entertainment and excursions? These can add up.

Most packages and tours are rated deluxe, first-class superior, first-class, tourist, and budget. The key difference is usually accommodations. If the package or tour you are considering is priced lower than in your wildest dreams, **be skeptical.** The location of the accommodations the tour or package includes may be miles and miles away from the theme parks if the price is rock-bottom—a fact you need to take into consideration when you plan your days. Make sure that any media that are included do not limit you to certain days of the week. Also, **make sure your travel agent knows the hotels** and other services. Ask about location, room size, beds, and whether it has a pool, room service, or programs for children, if you care about these. Has your agent been there or sent others you can contact?

BUYER BEWARE

Each year consumers are stranded or lose their money when operators go out of business—even very large ones with excellent reputations. If you can't afford a loss, take the time to **check out the operator**—find out how long the company has been in business, and ask several agents about its reputation. Next, **don't book unless the firm has a consumer-protection program.** Members of the

United States Tour Operators Association and the National Tour Association are required to set aside funds exclusively to cover your payments and travel arrangements in case of default. Nonmember operators may instead carry insurance; look for the details in the operator's brochure—and the name of an underwriter with a solid reputation. Note: When it comes to tour operators, **don't trust escrow accounts.** Although there are laws governing those of charter-flight operators, no governmental body prevents tour operators from raiding the till.

Next, **contact your local Better Business Bureau and the attorney general's office** in both your own state and the operator's; have any complaints been filed? Last, **pay with a major credit card.** Then you can cancel payment, provided that you can document your complaint. Always **consider trip-cancellation insurance** (*see* Insurance, *above*).

BIG VS. SMALL➤ An operator that handles several hundred thousand travelers annually can use its purchasing power to give you a good price. Its high volume may also indicate financial stability. But some small companies provide more personalized service; because they tend to specialize, they may also be experts on an area.

USING AN AGENT

Travel agents are an excellent resource. In fact, large operators accept bookings only through travel agents. But it's good to **collect brochures from several agencies,** because some agents' suggestions may be skewed by promotional relationships with tour and package firms that reward them for volume sales. If you have a special interest, **find an agent with expertise in that area;** the American Society of Travel Agents can give you leads in the United States. (Don't rely solely on your agent, though; agents may be unaware of small niche operators, and some special-interest travel companies only sell direct.)

SINGLE TRAVELERS

Prices are usually quoted per person, based on two sharing a room. If you are traveling solo, you may be required to pay the full double-occupancy rate. Some operators eliminate this surcharge if you agree to be matched up with a roommate of the same sex, even if one is not found by departure time.

PACKING FOR ORLANDO

Comfortable walking shoes or sneakers are essential. The entire area is extremely casual, day and night, so men will need a jacket and tie in only a handful of restaurants. For sightseeing and theme-park visits, pack shorts, sundresses, cotton slacks or jeans, T-shirts, and a light sweater as protection against the sometimes glacial air-conditioning. Experienced theme-park visitors also suggest using a waist pouch ("fanny pack") rather than a tote bag or purse. And don't forget your sunglasses!

In winter, be prepared for a range of temperatures: Take clothing that you can layer, including a sweater and warm jacket. For summer, you'll want a sun hat, sunscreen lotion, and a poncho and folding umbrella in case of sudden thunderstorms (a daily occurrence during the summer months).

Bring an extra pair of eyeglasses or contact lenses in your carry-on luggage, and if you have a health problem, **pack enough medication** to last the trip. In case your bags go astray, **don't put prescription drugs or valuables in luggage to be checked.**

LUGGAGE

Toy guns, toy knives, and the like sold in Frontierland and Adventureland should be packed in checked luggage. Security may give you a hard time if you try to carry them on board.

Free airline baggage allowances depend on the airline, the route, and the class of your ticket; ask in advance. In general, on domestic flights you are entitled to check two bags—neither exceeding 62 inches, or 158 centimeters (length + width +

height), or weighing more than 70 pounds (32 kilograms). A third piece may be brought aboard; its total dimensions are generally limited to less than 45 inches (114 centimeters), so it will fit easily under the seat in front of you or in the overhead compartment. In the United States, the Federal Aviation Administration gives airlines broad latitude to limit carry-on allowances and tailor them to different aircraft and operational conditions. Charges for excess, oversize, or overweight pieces vary.

SAFEGUARDING YOUR LUGGAGE➤ Before leaving home, **itemize your bags' contents** and their worth, and label them with your name, address, and phone number. (If you use your home address, cover it so potential thieves can't see it.) Inside your bag, **pack a copy of your itinerary.** At check-in, **make sure your bag is correctly tagged** with the airport's three-letter destination code. If your bags arrive damaged or not at all, file a written report with the airline before you leave the airport.

PASSPORTS AND VISAS

CANADIANS

No passport is necessary to enter the United States.

U.K. CITIZENS

British citizens need a valid passport. If you are staying fewer than 90 days and traveling

on a vacation, with a return or onward ticket, you will probably not need a visa. However, you will need to fill out the Visa Waiver Form, 1-94W, supplied by the airline.

While traveling, **keep one photocopy of the data page** separate from your wallet and leave another copy with someone at home. If you lose your passport, promptly call the nearest embassy or consulate, and the local police; having the data page can speed replacement.

PLANNING YOUR VISIT

Careful planning is key to the most hassle-free visit to the Orlando area. The first step is to **figure out everything you want to see and do in the area.** Will you be staying put in the Orlando area, or do you want to spend some time at the beach? Once you've settled on your sightseeing priorities, you can figure out how long you want to stay, make reservations, and buy tickets.

HOW LONG TO STAY

There are a couple of ways to approach this question. If your objective is to enjoy the complete Walt Disney World resort experience, five days is a comfortable period to allow; this gives you time to see all of its major and minor parks, to sample the restaurants and entertainment, and to spend some time around the pool. Six days would be better. Figure on an additional day for every other area theme park you want to visit, and then add your travel time to and from home.

If you're coming to the area mostly to go on the rides and see the theme parks, allow one day per theme park (this supposes that you're willing to start out early every day, move quickly, breeze through shops, and hurry through meals). Then add your travel time to and from home.

In either case, **add time for visiting the minor theme parks,** for exploring Orlando off the beaten track, and for shopping in Orlando's flea markets and discount malls. In addition, **add an extra day or two if you're traveling with small children,** who may have limited patience for marathon touring; if you want to linger during your stays; if you're staying off Disney property or using local shuttle transportation rather than your own or a rental car (to accommodate the extra time you will spend just getting to and from your destinations); or if you're visiting during a busy period, when long lines will make it nearly impossible to see all the most popular attractions (unless you have a lot of stamina for long days on your feet and are willing to be on the go from early in the morning until park closing). You could easily spend two weeks in the area and still not see it all.

CREATING AN ITINERARY

Once you know what you want to see and do, the first step is to **lay out a day-by-day touring plan,** using the Strategies for Your Visit sections of our theme-parks sections in Chapters 2 and 3 and the italicized Crowds and Strategy information following each review. Don't try to plot your route from hour to hour; instead break the day up into morning, afternoon, and evening sections. Finally, **make a schedule for calling for any reservations** you will need. Put each day's plan on a separate index card, and carry the card with you as you explore.

WHAT TO SEE WHEN➤ First find out the busy days of the week in the parks you want to visit (usually Friday, Saturday, and Sunday are quietest, except during holiday weeks). Then, beginning with the dates on which you plan to visit, **decide which parks you will see on each day.**

Think creatively. If you're staying on Walt Disney World property in a not-too-busy period and have at least five days, **consider spending afternoons at one of the water parks,** at your hotel swimming pool, or at a spa or sports facility. If you buy a multiday pass, which is good for unlimited visits to WDW's major parks, you can also **visit two or more theme parks in a single day**—say, combine a visit to the Magic

Kingdom in the morning, when the park isn't crowded, with an afternoon in Epcot Center's Future World, that area's least busy time.

MAKING RESERVATIONS➤ Make a list of all the things you want to do that require reservations. Note on the list how far in advance you can book for each. (In this book, this information is usually in the italicized information following each review.) Then, based on your travel schedule, designate the date on which you should call for the reservations you want. Some reservations can be made as soon as you book your hotel; others will have to wait until you're in the area.

BUYING YOUR TICKETS

If you aren't signing up for an escorted tour or travel package, **buy your WDW** tickets as soon as your travel dates are definite. Prices typically go up two or three times a year, so you may just beat a price hike and save some money. Many local offices of the American Automobile Association (AAA) also sell tickets to WDW; you don't have to be a AAA member to buy these tickets.

Before you get your tickets for other Orlando-area attractions, check into various money-saving offers. The Orlando Magicard, available free from the Orlando/Orange County Convention and Visitor's Bureau, entitles you to discounts at restaurants, dinner shows, and sometimes even theme parks (though never WDW). AAA members can often qualify for 10%–20% discounts on non-Disney theme-park tickets; call your branch office for more information. If applicable, also *see* Travelers with Disabilities, *above,* and Senior-Citizen Discounts, *below,* for further discount information.

R
RENTING A CAR

Although public transportation in Orlando is practically nonexistent and taxis are expensive because of the distances involved, it is by no means absolutely necessary to rent a car when you are in Orlando. If you are staying at a Disney hotel or purchase a multiday passport instead of buying daily admission tickets to the Disney parks, your transportation within Walt Disney World is free. Outside Walt Disney World, just about every lodging is linked by private shuttle to area attractions. However, should you want to visit the major theme parks outside Walt Disney World, venture off the beaten track, or eat where most tourists don't, then a rental car is essential. Fortunately, Orlando offers some of the lowest rental-car rates in the United States.

CUTTING COSTS

To get the best deal, **book through a travel agent and shop around.** When pricing cars, **ask where the rental lot is located.** Some off-airport locations offer lower rates—even though their lots are only minutes away from the terminal via complimentary shuttle. You may also want to **price local car-rental companies,** whose rates may be lower still, although service and maintenance standards may not be up to those of a national firm. Also **ask your travel agent about a company's customer-service record.** How has it responded to late plane arrivals and vehicle mishaps? Are there often lines at the rental counter, and, if you're traveling during a holiday period, does a confirmed reservation guarantee you a car?

INSURANCE

When you drive a rented car, you are generally responsible for any damage or personal injury that you cause as well as damage to the vehicle. Before you rent, **see what coverage you already have** by means of your personal auto-insurance policy and credit cards. For about $14 a day, rental companies sell insurance, known as a collision damage waiver (CDW), that eliminates your liability for damage to the car; it's always optional and should never be automatically added to your bill.

SURCHARGES

Before picking up the car in one city and leaving it in another, **ask about drop-off** charges or one-way service fees, which can be substantial. Note, too, that some rental agencies charge extra if you return the car before the time specified on your contract. To avoid a hefty refueling fee, **fill the tank just before you turn in the car.**

FOR U.K. CITIZENS

In the United States you must be 21 to rent a car; rates may be higher for those under 25. Extra costs cover child seats, compulsory for children under 5 (about $3 per day), and additional drivers (about $1.50 per day). To pick up your reserved car, you will need the reservation voucher, a passport, a U.K. driver's license, and a travel policy covering each driver.

S
SENIOR CITIZENS

Bear in mind that school vacation times can spell ordeal rather than adventure if you have limited energy (or patience). What endurance you have will go farther if you arrive in the theme parks at opening time or even before. Do a little homework about your destination, and have a plan of action. Take in first those attractions that you most want to see. Spend the morning taking in the attractions so you can take it easy when the day warms up. Then relax in the shade, have a nice long lunch, see some shows in air-conditioned theaters, and maybe even go back to your hotel to relax around the pool, read, or nap. Refreshed, you can return to one of the theme parks, when they're open late, or explore Pleasure Island, Church Street Station, or Orlando's other after-dark options. Don't overdo it.

DISCOUNTS

Most hotels and restaurants in the area have senior-citizen discounts. Pick up brochures as you visit places, read the newspapers (especially the *Orlando Sentinel*), and don't be shy about asking for suggestions at your hotel.

To qualify for age-related discounts, **mention your senior-citizen status up front** when booking hotel reservations, not when checking out, and before you're seated in restaurants, not when paying your bill. Note that discounts may be limited to certain menus, days, or hours. When renting a car, **ask about promotional car-rental discounts**—they can net lower costs than your senior-citizen discount.

T
TAXIS

Taxi fares start at $2.45 and cost $1.40 for each mile thereafter. Sample fares: To WDW's Magic Kingdom, about $20 from International Drive, $11–$15 from U.S. 192. To Universal Studios, $6–$11 from International Drive, $25–$30 from U.S. 192. To Church Street Station, downtown,

$20–$25 from International Drive, $30–$40 from U.S. 192.

For information on getting to or from the airport by taxi, *see* Airport Transfers *in* Air Travel, *above.*

W
WHEN TO GO

Timing can spell the difference between a good vacation in the theme parks and a great one. During certain periods, the parks are oppressively crowded, with discouraging lines. At other times, you can step right into the major rides and attractions. During busy periods, the parks have longer hours, run all rides at full capacity, and add entertainment and parades (like Spectro-Magic in Disney's Magic Kingdom) that you can't see in quiet periods. If you have children, it's more fun to travel when you can count on there being plenty of other children around; if you prefer a more adult experience, you will be happier skipping school vacation periods.

CLOSED FOR REPAIRS?

Before you finalize your travel schedule, call the theme parks you plan to visit in order to find out about any planned maintenance that will close major attractions you want to see.

CROWDS

The most crowded times of the year in all of the Central Florida theme parks are when school is out. The single

busiest week is from Christmas through New Year's Day. All of the area's attractions are also packed around Easter. Memorial Day weekend is not only crowded but also hot and humid. Other busy periods are from mid-June through mid-August, Thanksgiving week in November, the week of Presidents' Day in mid-February, and the weeks of college spring break in late March.

Are crowds inescapable, then? Not at all. Particularly from early September until just before Thanksgiving, attendance is very light. Mid-afternoons will still feel busy, but you're not packed in body-to-body as during the most crowded seasons. The least crowded time of all is from just after the Thanksgiving weekend until the beginning of the Christmas holidays. Another excellent time is January and the first week of February. If you must go in summer, late August is best.

Cypress Gardens attracts older travelers, so it is busier during the winter.

CLIMATE

The following are average daily maximum and minimum temperatures for Orlando.

Climate in Orlando

Jan.	70F	21C	May	88F	31C	Sept.	88F	31C
	49	9		67	19		74	23
Feb.	72F	22C	June	90F	32C	Oct.	83F	28C
	54	12		74	23		67	19
Mar.	76F	24C	July	90F	32C	Nov.	76F	24C
	56	13		74	23		58	14
Apr.	81F	27C	Aug.	90F	32C	Dec.	70F	21C
	63	17		74	23		52	11

Orlando Area

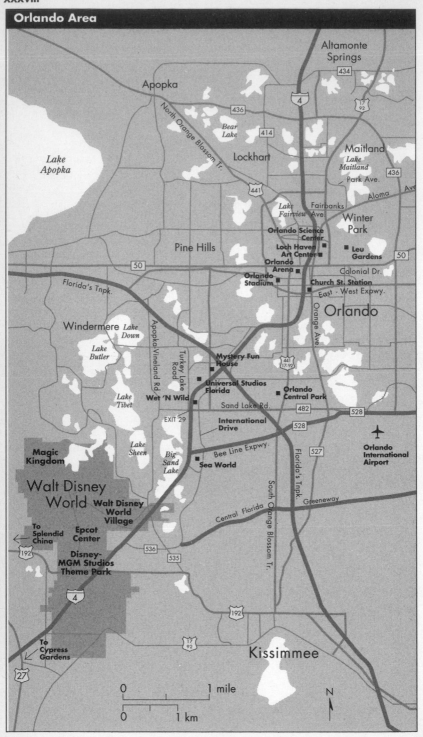

1   Destination: Walt Disney World®, Universal Studios and Orlando

READY, SET, DISNEY!

Everything You Need to Know about Getting Started at Walt Disney World: Our New Disney at-a-Glance Guide

AS DUSK FALLS on Walt Disney World, the sky over Cinderella Castle turns a perfect pink. It is the end of your first day in Never-Never-Land and you've racked up an Indiana Jonesworthy number of accomplishments. Suppressing the urge to squeeze *just one more* attraction into the day's itinerary, you beckon to your brood—who by now are moving like a trained corps de ballet—and all plunk down onto a bench. Voila! A flock of doves wheel from the marzipanned heights of the enchanted castle into the clouds overhead and you realize—with a deep sigh of contentment—that Once Upon a Time is happening this very moment.

Now it can be told: You're in Walt Disney World's "sweet zone"—where only children of all ages who have satisfied their yearning for wonderment can enter. The key to entering this sweet zone is a combination of canny strategizing, patience, and luck—and this special Disney-at-a-Glance guide is here to get you started. Walt Disney World can be tremendous, terrific, and delightful. But many visitors, especially first-time travelers, find WDW—to use the abbreviation for Walt Disney World—like a giant jigsaw puzzle that's blank on both sides. Flummoxed by the breadth of the choices, they don't know where to start. What are the must-dos? The must-sees? Where to stay? Where to eat? The 43-square-mile complex is, after all, double the size of Manhattan. The Magic Kingdom alone has 41 *major* adventures. Then there's Epcot Center—and it's twice the size of the Magic Kingdom—and Disney-MGM Studios and Typhoon Lagoon and Blizzard Beach and Discovery Island—you can get out of breath just trying to list them all—and still more.

For those with what feels like a million questions, this tell-all Disney Digest introduces each park step by step. You take it from there. Use our tips to design a manageable tour around all your priorities. Then let the kid inside you take over. And don't pout if you can't fit everything in—you'll have joined the ranks of the average How-come-I-can't-do-it-all Disney visitor.

Getting Oriented in Walt Disney World

The sheer scope of this Florida family entertainment capital makes the name Walt Disney *World* highly appropriate. But don't let its enormity stop you in your tracks.

THE BIG PICTURE➤ Basically, it's just Florida scrub sprinkled with hotel complexes, theme parks, and water parks—several of each genre. What most people imagine to *be* Walt Disney World, the **Magic Kingdom,** is actually just a small part of it. Similar to California's Disneyland, it's the wellspring of Mickeymania, a paradise for children of all ages, and the most popular individual theme park in the whole United States, welcoming more than 11 million visitors a year. **Epcot Center** is another theme park that's part of the show. Designed to make you adore learning, it's packed with multimillion-dollar fun-type science rides that are sure to turn on any family's curiosity quotient and ignite any child's Jurassic spark (Epcot Center covers everything from dinosaurs to nuclear energy). It's like a huge world's fair. The fabled glamour capital of the world known as Hollywood is long gone, but its ghosts linger at **Disney-MGM Studios,** WDW's third theme park, the home of a real-live movie studio and still more astonishing rides, including the Twilight Zone Tower of Terror. Then come the fabulous water parks: the spanking-new **Blizzard Beach,** along with **Typhoon Lagoon** and **River Country.** Finally, there's **Discovery Island**—a natural habitat for more than 200 species of animals who run the gamut from scary to sweet. You can see why staying at WDW much less than a week is like getting only half a serving of dessert.

THE FIRST DAY➤ Most people tackle the Magic Kingdom right away. Just take I–4 to the Magic Kingdom exit and follow the signs to the parking lot; then board the next tram (it'll be along soon) to the

Transportation and Ticket Center, a.k.a. the TTC (it's the only place the tram goes). There, you can buy your tickets (*see* Chapter 2), pick up an essential park map and entertainment flyer, and catch a paddle wheeler or the monorail to head into the park and start having fun.

The Magic Kingdom is Aptly Named

Packed with more fantasy per square foot than any other place on earth, the Magic Kingdom fulfills the promise of photographs and much, much more. Kids think they've found heaven on earth, and they may be right. And for adults—so many of whom have grown up with Cinderella, Peter Pan, Dumbo, Davey Crockett, and Pinocchio—it's one of those magical places "so full of echoes, allusions, and half-memories as to be almost metaphysical," to use a phrase of renowned travel writer Jan Morris.

WAGON WHEEL➤ For the four-year-old you're about to become, everything is very neatly organized, although the walkways through the park twist and turn so as to conceal the true layout—a wagon wheel with a hub and spokes. Passing through the park entrance turnstiles, you find yourself in Town Square, which segues into Main Street USA, a boulevard that runs due north, ending at Central Plaza, which is also known as the Hub. Main Street USA is the first of the Magic Kingdom's seven lands. The landmark Cinderella Castle anchors the Hub and is encircled by the rest of them: Adventureland, Frontierland, Liberty Square, Fantasyland, Mickey's Starland, and Tomorrowland. Rope Drop, as the ceremonial stampede that kicks off each day is called, occurs in the Magic Kingdom at the Central Plaza end of Main Street USA.

MAIN STREET USA➤ Tomorrow seems a century away in this gingerbread-trimmed, calliope-accented, pastel-candy-color valentine to turn-of-the-century America. Once past the Victorian-style station of the **Walt Disney World Railroad,** you're in Town Square, site of information central, better known as **City Hall.** Follow Main Street up to Central Plaza and Cinderella Castle. (Disney fact: Did you know that at the top of the castle is an apartment once intended for Walt Disney and his family?) While strolling, enjoy the antique automobiles oohga-oohga-ing, barbershop quartets, the

Penny Arcade, and the vintage Disney cartoons on view in the **Main Street Cinema.**

ADVENTURELAND➤ Bear left at the Hub and the view is of tangled tropical vegetation, and elephant calls, pounding drums, squawking parrots, and other jungle chatter fill the air. If you've ever wanted to stare a gigantic hippo in the eye, sail between the guns of two warring pirate ships, or be serenaded by a tiki god statue with blinking red eyes, then Adventureland is for you. It's home to such favorites as **Pirates of the Caribbean,** a cruise through the middle of a rowdy pirate battle; the **Swiss Family Treehouse,** the shipwrecked family's digs, complete with running water; and the "danger-filled" **Jungle Cruise,** where Audio-Animatronic headhunters and hippos immediately target you as "jungle bait." Meet Claude Birdbrain at the **Enchanted Tiki Birds,** one of the first Disney Audio-Animatronic achievements—corny but utterly delightful.

FRONTIERLAND➤ Keep to the main footpath and you'll notice a subtle change in the vegetation. Frontierland lies straight ahead. If you're accustomed to a morning run, you'll love the rope-drop dash to Disney's wettest attraction, **Splash Mountain**—more thrills per capita than almost any other in the Magic Kingdom: a flume ride peopled by Brer Rabbit and 67 Audio-Animatronic friends, culminating in a nail-biting 52½-foot drop, the flume world's longest and sharpest. Make sure you're wearing your Mickey Mouse rain poncho if you sit in the first or last rows! Ready for more? Climb aboard a runaway gold-rush mine train at the **Big Thunder Mountain Railroad,** then take in the sit-back-and-watch pleasures, the **Diamond Horseshoe Jamboree** and **Country Bear Jamboree.**

LIBERTY SQUARE➤ Disney's answer to Williamsburg lies next along your path. Centered around a 130-year-old live oak tree, hung with 13 lanterns representing the 13 original colonies, it's made up primarily of Early America–themed shops and eateries; the main draw for Disneyphiles is the **Haunted Mansion**—"Tomb, Sweet Tomb" to such characters as Manny Festation, Clare Voince, and Paul Tergyst. The **Hall of Presidents,** a multimedia tribute to the Constitution, features amazingly lifelike Audio-Animatronic figures of every American president. Nearby, you can cool down on a trip on a romantic side-wheeler, the **Liberty Square Riverboat** or the Gully-whumper, one of the **Mike Fink Keel Boats.**

FANTASYLAND➤ In "the happiest kingdom of them all," storybook dreams come true with a minimum of high-tech and a full load of fairy-tale charm. Seated in pirate ships, you soar above moonlit London (and a tick-tocking crocodile) on **Peter Pan's Flight;** get vertigo on the **Mad Tea Party** teacup ride; take in the toned-down **Snow White's Adventures;** hop on **Cinderella's Golden Carrousel** and **It's a Small World** (Arnold Schwarzenegger's favorite WDW ride); jump into the jump seat of Mr. J. Thaddeus Toad's runaway Model-T and career along the road to Nowhere in Particular on **Mr. Toad's Wild Ride;** and wind up at the "mane" attraction, a **Legend of the Lion King** stage show (featuring the music of Elton John). Fantasyland is *the* place for very young children (whose favorite ride is inevitably **Dumbo**).

MICKEY'S STARLAND➤ Home of America's favorite mouse, this land was built on the edge of Fantasyland in 1988 to celebrate the Mickster's 60th birthday. After a 35-minute show at **Mickey's Hollywood Theater,** the crowds jam **Mickey's Dressing Room** for an autograph and a photo-op with ol'-big ears. In other words, backstage passes for all! Don't forget to visit **Minnie Moo,** a placid Holstein cow whose distinctive black spots just happen to fall into an outline of the Mick's famous silhouette.

TOMORROWLAND➤ Fascinating mostly for its backward look at forward thinking, newly revamped Tomorrowland contains the must-do **Space Mountain,** a two-minute in-the-dark roller-coaster ride crammed with scary sights. (Hint: Hold on to your eyeglasses.) With the addition of the new **Alien Encounter,** this land has become, in the words of Disney Imagineers, "an intergalactic docking bay for extraTERRORestrials." Developed with *Star Wars* producer George Lucas, it makes use of computer simulations, lasers, and other electronic technology. Robin Williams is the voice of Timekeeper, the robot at Tomorrowland's other new attraction next door, the **Transportorium.**

Excellent Edutainment: Epcot Center

Epcot Center is that rare paradox, an *educational* theme park—and a very successful one. A subtle blend of the entertaining and the edifying, this enormous park encourages the brain to keep simmering even when the body is enjoying time-outs. The 40-acre World Showcase Lagoon separates its two main segments: **Future World**—anchored by the trademark 17-story silver geosphere known as **Spaceship Earth,** where pavilions focus on discoveries and the fascinations of science; and **World Showcase,** where you can see the world, minus jet lag, via a grand tour of exhibition pavilions representing 11 nations.

FUTURE WORLD➤ This Einstein among theme-park lands is made up of eight major attractions that, surprisingly, are not the least bit boring. **Universe of Energy,** which may sound stodgy and dull, puts you in the middle of a dinosaur-ridden primeval landscape where moonlight and erupting volcanoes illuminate a giant–sea snake attack—and that's only the beginning. In **Wonders of Life, Body Wars** has you zipping platelet-to-platelet through the human circulatory system; *The Making of Me,* a film, shows where babies come from, while **Cranium Command,** another movie, takes you inside the "Home of the Flying Endorphins," with celebrities doing the voices of body parts. The **Living Seas** introduces you to the aquatic splendors of a **Caribbean coral reef** through 18-foot-high aquarium windows; there's also **Sea Base Alpha,** which is supposed to look like a prototype undersea research facility but is actually just a series of pretty interesting exhibits. **The Land** pavilion has a boat ride, the new *Lion King* "Circle of Life" presentation, and **Food Rocks,** starring the likes of the Peach Boys and Chubby Cheddar. In **Journey into Imagination,** Disney touts **Honey, I Shrunk the Audience** as a "4-D" show. In the 100,000-square-foot **Innoventions,** top corporations roll out new products for techy tykes, teens, gizmoids, preteen prodigies, and their elders; the Sega room alone has more than 130 video games.

WORLD SHOWCASE➤ With your eyes closed, twirl the globe and aim your finger; it just might land on one of the countries featured in World Showcase, the equivalent of a gerrymandered international dateline, featuring the cultures and cuisines of 11 countries. Each pavilion is staffed by natives of the sponsoring country, but they all speak excellent English, so you can skip the phrase books. Even so, all the globe's citizenry understands oohs and ahs, probably the gist of your vocabulary while touring these parts. Buy a spinning doll at Der Teddybär in **Germany** or china in the **United Kingdom,** climb a mountain in **Canada,** eat tacos in **Mexico** or couscous in **Morocco** (while belly dancers gyrate), and see the Eiffel Tower in **France,** the Piazza San Marco in **Italy,** and Beijing's Temple of Heaven in **China**—all in a single day (they're all scaled-down models, of course). World Showcase also gives strong evidence of the universality of one common language: food, in the form of some of the finest dining in all of Florida (book ahead—these restaurants are very popular).

Reel Life: Disney-MGM Studios

With a cast that reads like the credits of the biggest blockbuster ever made—to Walt's name, add George Lucas, Stephen Spielberg, Jim Henson, plus the Duke, Bogie, and Marilyn—this is Disney's attempt to bring Hollywood to Florida. Here, more than a dozen top attractions marry movies to the latest in Disney-ride technology; grace notes are the fully operational film and television production center and nostalgia tours of the "Hollywood that never was and always will be." No need to scope out this sequins-and-sunglasses theme park for celebrities of note; the gimmick here is that *you're* the celebrity, given the full star treatment when a Grace Kelly look-alike comes asking for your autograph. Fancy yourself Clark Gable? Get a screen test at **La Cinema Storage,** then head to **Cover Story** to see that famous face—your own—on the covers of all the big magazines.

Of course, the park's amazing rides are the key to its success: there's that stunt artist's showcase, the **Indiana Jones Stunt Spectacular;** the peak thrillathon, the **Star Wars** simulator adventure; Jim Henson's **Muppet*Vision 3-D;** the **Great Movie Ride** (*the* greatest); and the **Art of Animation,** a behind-the-scenes look at Disney animators animating. (Disneyfact: Did you know that when they began working on *Snow White, Pinocchio,* and *Bambi* there was no Dopey, Jiminy Cricket, or Thumper planned?) For those who have always wished someone would tell them "You oughtta be in pictures," there's **Superstar Television,** a chance to costar in such TV shows as "I Love Lucy" and "The Golden Girls." Finally, this is home to the 199-foot-tall, 13-story **Twilight Zone Tower of Terror** (don't let the cheery name fool you), housed in WDW's tallest structure. Don't wait until the free-falling elevator plunges more than 160 feet toward terminal velocity to ask yourself if you're having fun yet.

The Wetter, the Better!

What could be better than an entire park devoted to water rides? How about three of them? Since the opening of the first of these, **River Country,** Disney has been uniting humans and water in a tumultuously semiamphibious state of cohabitation. **Typhoon Lagoon** came next, followed quickly by **Blizzard Beach.** And they're always jam-packed. The best—or is it the worst?—is the wild 55 mph dead-drop to a splashy landing from the **Summit Plummet,** the fastest water slide on the planet, a feature at Blizzard Beach. (This park has no fewer than 19 water slides and "icy" bobsled runs that stay warm and fast—including the Slush Gusher and Teamboat Springs.) In Typhoon Lagoon, a doozy known as **Keelhaul Falls** has you spiraling 400 feet downward, and **Humunga Kowabunga** sends you careening at 30 mph down a 50-foot-high slide. Then—oh, buoy!—there are Typhoon Lagoon's **Jib Jammer, Rudder Buster,** and **Stern Burner** storm slides and River Country's **Whoop 'n' Holler Hollow,** a pair of water slides down the side of an ersatz mountain.

If you have water babies in tow, look for Typhoon Lagoon's scaled-down **Ketchakiddie Creek,** Blizzard Beach's **Tike's Peak,** and its unnamed River Country counterpart. If you're a beach potato type, you'll get a charge out of the parks' amazing creativity. Typhoon Lagoon's centerpiece is **Mount Mayday,** a lively volcano that periodically tries to dislodge the *Miss Tilly,* a shrimp boat impaled on the top rim, with rip-roaring geysers.

Antarctica with waving palm trees, bikinis, and flip-flops confronts you at Blizzard Beach. The Imagineers envisioned a freak blizzard, whose heavy snowfall turned to melt before a planned ski resort could be completed. Left with the biggest Sno-Kone in the world, they transformed it into a slippery-when-wet water adventure whose ski and toboggan runs are the tallest, fastest, and most exhilarating in the world of water slides. The 90-foot-tall "snowcapped" Mt. Gushmore is the centerpiece.

You can easily get submerged without leaving your Disney hotel grounds, too: Almost every major swimming pool has a little something special going for it, even if it's just a water slide. The 790,000-gallon **Stormalong Bay** at the Yacht and Beach Club is a cousin of the Pacific. At Port Orleans's **Doubloon Lagoon,** a sea serpent–shape water slide runs the length of the lagoon.

What's New, What's Great

One reason 70% of WDW's guests are repeat visitors is that Disney's Imagineers are constantly devising new state-of-the-art attractions, spending many millions in the process. Just because they've created the theme-park world's eighth wonder of the world today doesn't mean they won't be working on a ninth wonder tomorrow.

You've already heard about Blizzard Beach, 66 acres of water park. The Magic Kingdom's revamped Tomorrowland will put to bed its old nickname, "Yesterdayland." The nondenominational **Fairy Tale Wedding Pavilion** can accommodate many of the 1,000 weddings that take place at WDW each year. The WDW bride can ride in a Cinderella coach, have rings borne to the altar in a glass slipper, and invite Mickey and Minnie to attend the reception. And then there's **Planet Hollywood,** not far from Pleasure Island. The vittles are as kitschily varied as the Hollywoodiana treasures on view. Don't forget to eat—which you might do once you spot Tom Hanks' *Forrest Gump* costume and the bus used in *Speed*.

Disney enters the world of learning vacations with the debut of the **Disney Institute,** near the Disney Village Resort, in February 1996. Want to perfect your slam-dunk under the guidance of basketball legend Bill Walton, acquire the animation secrets Tim Burton used in *The Nightmare Before Christmas*, or discuss the future of America with former Senate majority leader George Mitchell? These are just a few features of the institute's multiday themed discovery vacations for individuals, couples, and families with children ages 10 and up; the institute even has its own lodging and dining facilities.

The Bus Stops Here: Getting Around WDW

Walt Disney World operates a transportation system that most medium-size cities would envy. More than 110 buses cover about 8.5 million miles a year, shuttling visitors around the World. Add in the monorails and boats, and you have about 200,000 passenger trips per day.

HOW TO GET THERE FROM HERE➤ You don't have to be a rocket scientist to get anywhere. The transportation system is what urban planners would call multimodal—your kids will call it just plain fun, especially the boats and the monorails. Parking lots are there when you need them. So are Disney staffers, ready and willing to give directions. Many hotels have system maps. If you can't figure it out or find someone to ask, there's a number to call (☎ 407/824–4457). And transportation is free if you're staying in a Disney hotel or carrying a multiday passport; everyone else pays just $2.50.

WDW's fastest and most frequently used mode of transportation is the monorail; one loop shuttles between Epcot Center and the TTC, while the other connects the TTC with the Magic Kingdom and the Polynesian, Grand Floridian, and Contemporary resorts (but *not* the nearby Wilderness Lodge). Just follow the signs.

Boats ferry guests staying at the Polynesian, Grand Floridian, and Contemporary resorts and the new Wilderness Lodge to the Magic Kingdom and take WDW Swan and Dolphin guests to Epcot Center and Disney-MGM Studios.

And there is a huge network of buses, which run every 15 to 20 minutes, picking up and dropping off guests at the theme parks, the water parks, the hotels, and almost every other destination in Walt Disney World.

When the Going Gets Tough . . .

START EARLY➤ As Ben Franklin said, early to bed and early to rise makes you healthy, wealthy, and wise—it also gives you the chance to take WDW's most popular rides without waiting in line. By 10 or 11 AM, the parks are bursting at the seams and you wait everywhere in busy seasons. (How early? Note that though the Magic Kingdom, Epcot Center, and Disney-MGM officially open at 9 AM, visitors may enter at 8:30, and sometimes even at 8, with some special breakfasts beginning at 7:30.) For more information, *see* Opening and Closing Hours in Chapter 2.

In summer, another good reason to arrive early is that by noon the heat and humidity become a challenge and at 5 PM—count on it—it is almost guaranteed to rain. Weather dictates one other summer strategy: Do outdoor rides before noon, when the sun is almost sure to shine. Then in the afternoon, you can relax somewhere that's cool and dry—like a seat in Honey, I Shrunk the Audience.

GO WHERE—AND WHEN—THE CROWDS DON'T➣ To minimize time in line, go against the flow. In a Disney Olympics, the Gold should go to whomever runs past Spaceship Earth at Epcot Center's front door and heads past it to the Living Seas or Journey into Imagination. Circle back to Spaceship Earth later. Are we suggesting running up the down escalator at Macy's on Christmas Eve? Yes. (Unless, that is, you're one of the first guests through the Epcot Center entrance turnstiles, in which case the advice is different: Claim your Spaceship Earth ride vehicle before someone else beats you to it.)

Another way to hang-ten on the tidal wave of tourists: Have lunch at either 11:30 AM (if you arrived early) or around 2:30 PM (if you started late).

STOP THE WORLD, I WANT TO GET OFF➣ Chances are, toward midafternoon, you'll be tired of the whining, the pointing, and the childish behavior—and that's just on the part of the parents. Slow down to .00001 mph and give your unbionic feet a rest. Scattered throughout the parks are green oases made just for time-outs. In Epcot Center there's one just behind the Rose & Crown Pub in the United Kingdom; in the Magic Kingdom, Tom Sawyer's Island is wonderful for the weary.

DON'T SHOP TILL *AFTER* YOU'VE DROPPED➣ Do all your seeing, riding, and walking before hitting the souvenir shops—you can do that later in the afternoon when lines clog every attraction. (If you are staying at a Disney hotel or the Swan or Dolphin, remember that you can have purchases sent right to your hotel concierge or front desk.)

Checking In: Should You Be Mickey's Guest?

If you'll be spending most of your time at WDW theme parks, it makes sense to stay on the property. With 12 successful resorts in all but rock-bottom-budget price categories—and more on the way—it's clear that Disney's head honchos are used to winning those little red hotels in Monopoly. But they're major players in Florida's hotel stakes because their resorts, in addition to selling sleep, pack as much excitement as the WDW attractions: You can lodge in Polynesian, southwestern, Caribbean, even grand hotel style. Your favorite little leaguers can even bed down in the lee of a multistory baseball bat.

FOR BIG SPENDERS ONLY➣ Still, with more than 20,000 hotel rooms at WDW alone, it's easy to be thrown into a stall at decision time. If you feel you deserve the crème de la crème, there are the showplaces: the turn-of-the-century-style **Grand Floridian**—with a handkerchief-white beach and fine restaurants; the stunning new **Wilderness Lodge,** a Honey-I-Blew-Up-the-Log-Cabin-size national park–style hotel where you can "rough it"; the **Contemporary,** at which latter-day Judy Jetsons arrive in high style aboard the in-house monorail; the gorgeous **Polynesian,** where the only thing missing is a welcoming conch-shell fanfare; the **Yacht Club and Beach Club** resorts, which make boaties feel right at home with their turn-of-the-century New England nautical nuances; and if you're sweet on suites, the **Disney Village Resort** and Key West–style **Vacation Club Suites and Villas** (the latter the choice of Disney chairman Michael Eisner and family when in residence).

OPTIONS FOR TIGHTWADS➣ No longer are Disney hotels concentrated in the luxury price category. The moderately priced **Dixie Landings, Caribbean Beach,** and **Port Orleans** resorts and, in the economy range, the **All-Star Sports and Music resorts**—all offer rooms starting at $69 per night. (And if you can get by without a lobby, elevators, and bellhops, don't forget the Ft. Wilderness Campground.)

THE ACCESSIBILITY FACTOR➤ If convenient access is high on your list, note that the Contemporary, Polynesian, Grand Floridian, and Wilderness Lodge are closest to the Magic Kingdom, while the Caribbean Village, the Beach and Yacht Clubs, and the Michael Graves–designed Swan and Dolphin hotels are nearest to Epcot Center. (In fact, you can walk there from the Swan and Dolphin.) Dixie Landings, Port Orleans, and the Disney Village Resort and Vacation Club are 1½ miles west of Epcot Center and Pleasure Island. The economy-priced All-Star Resorts are closest to Disney-MGM Studios. Scheduled to open in 1996 are the Boardwalk Resort (near Epcot Center) and the Coronado Springs Hotel (north of Blizzard Beach on World Center Drive).

COMPROMISING POSITIONS➤ A fair compromise in terms of convenience and price can be found at any of the seven hotels that constitute Hotel Plaza, near the Disney Village Marketplace and Typhoon Lagoon. The biggies of the hotel-chain world are here, including Hilton, Travelodge, and Courtyard by Marriott. Note, however, that they do not offer many of the perks you would receive as a guest at a Disney-owned hotel.

WHY STAY ON-SITE?➤ Of course, you can still pay much less off-property, and if money is seriously an object, there's no real choice. But in most cases perks like early admission to theme parks, proximity, and guaranteed entry to all parks even when the turnstiles close to outsiders tip the balance in the dollars-versus-distance equation in favor of an on-property base. Benefits like these make it possible for you to see more each day—and even cut your visit short by a night, thereby saving plenty on your vacation bill.

WHEN TO STAY OFF-PROPERTY➤ If you need to save a serious bundle or if you plan to include Univeral Studios, Sea World, and Busch Gardens in your Central Florida itinerary, hotels outside WDW remain a viable choice. Because the local hotel scene is overbuilt, good deals abound—maybe even steals. Decent, safe, pleasant hotel rooms on International Drive and on U.S. 192 in Kissimmee can go for as little as $30 a night.

But remember, I-Drive is at least 20 minutes from WDW's gates, and that's when there's no traffic jam. As for transportation, although many hotels offer shuttle buses to and from WDW, you pay per head; if you're traveling with your family, it makes sense to rent a car—something you don't necessarily need if you're staying on Disney property. For other recommendations, *see* Chapter 8, Lodging.

Tips for Tots—and Their Parents

Breakfast with Tigger and Pooh. A paw autograph from Goofy. Ten twirls around on Cinderella's Golden Carrousel. It takes a tyke to truly appreciate some experiences at WDW. Here are a few tips on handling the very young and the restless.

QUEUING TACTIC➤ The wait times for major attractions are often posted, so if it's going to be more than 20 minutes to ride Dumbo, the Flying Elephant, send your favorite Power Rangers off for a power snack while you stand in line. If you suspect that your tot may want to a second whirl on Cinderella's Golden Carrousel, lurk at the very end of the line while your significant other rides a flashing steed.

CHARACTER BREAKFASTS➤ A must for most tots is breakfast à la Disney, where they can chow down on Mickey Mouse–shape waffles while engaging in a heart-to-heart with Disney characters. Ariel wanna-bes will choose the Under the Sea Breakfast at the Coral Reef restaurant in Epcot Center. Or have Breakfast with Pooh at the Disney Vacation Club or with Minnie Mouse at the Polynesian's Papeete Bay Verandah, or try the Once Upon a Time Breakfast at King Stefan's Banquet Hall in Cinderella Castle.

KIDS' NIGHT OUT➤ One of the better-thought-out programs for kids is the Polynesian's **Neverland Club.** Youngsters have 4–12 have a ball, beginning with a crawl out a window that leads into the world of Peter Pan. Then there's a dinner-show meal, with visiting Disney characters and Discovery Island animals, and Disney movies while Papa and Mama Bear enjoy a night of their own out at Pleasure Island. (You don't have to be a guest at the hotel to sign up your offspring.) Similar programs include **Camp Swan** and **Camp Dolphin** and the **Vacation Station** at the Hilton.

PARADES!➤ More fun for the kiddies comes in the shape of the Magic Kingdom parades, every one of them a winner. The real dazzler is the **SpectroMagic** parade, which involves Disney characters and lavish floats and costumes outlined with twinkling lights. This parade runs twice nightly during peak season, at 9 and 11 PM and during busy periods at other times of the year; the Cinderella Castle forecourt is one good place from which to watch, although if you want to make a quick exit afterward, a better choice is Town Square near the WDW railroad station underpass. If SpectroMatic is too late for your youngsters, there's always the 3 PM **Character Parade** (its specific theme changes from time to time); good vantage points are near the Sleepy Hollow Sandwich Shop and and Diamond Horseshoe Jamboree area (get there 20 minutes early to stake out a spot). One to three times a day, Disney-MGM Studios' Hollywood Boulevard has its own character parade, usually themed around the most recently released Disney animated film.

BABY SWAP➤ No, this does not refer to what you feel like doing with your offspring at the whining end of a full, rich Disney day. If a child is too small for a ride that's a must for you, tell an attendant you intend to baby-swap as you approach the boarding area. One parent waits at the starting point with the little tykes while the other enjoys the ride, then they swap positions so the waiting parent takes a turn.

PLACES & PARAPHERNALIA➤ Keep in mind that the **Baby Services** in each major park has rocking chairs and peace and quiet for nursing mothers, microwaves to heat up baby food, small toilets for toddlers, changing tables, and other thoughtful facilities for young families. Changing tables are in all women's rest rooms and some men's. Strollers are available for rent in every park (mark yours with a recognizable bit of clothing to prevent it from getting lost or removed when you leave it outside a ride's entrance).

EATS & TREATS➤ Many times in the course of a long, hot Disney day, kids want to know three things: Where do we eat? When do we eat? What are we eating? Since restaurant lines can be long, keep in mind that Disney security will not wrestle you to the ground if you carry a small backpack stocked with a candy bar and small plastic bottles that you can refill at water fountains. Brave souls have been known to bring in a sandwich and a juice box or two or three; there is no salami detector at the gates.

Beauty and the Feast

Let's eat! This familiar cry may not be prompted entirely by hunger at WDW; here it's not the food but the decor that does the dazzling. You can breakfast in Bora-Bora at **Minnie's Menehune** at the Polynesian, then have lunch in the Florida Keys (a.k.a. **Olivia's Cafe** at the Disney Vacation Club). In the afternoon, for a positively ducal English-tea-and-clotted-cream service, take a break at the **Grand Floridian.** For dinner, you might virtually munch your way around the world at the 11 ethnic restaurants of Epcot Center—Disney's bona fide dining capital. When the fare is as good as the fettuccine at Italy's **Alfredo di Roma** restaurant (with its beautiful faux marble and frescoes), you just might forget you're in Florida.

Rest assured: When you want to eat, there's always food nearby. And you're sure to find something that'll tickle your taste buds among the 6,000 menu items Disney offers at its more than 250 restaurants—from haute to healthy, hamburgers to nouvelle, from the varied fare at the food courts at the Caribbean Beach, Dixie Landings, and Port Orleans resorts to the creamy yogurt treats at Tomorrowland's **Anti Gravity's Galactic Goodies** and the expensive-but-worth-it dinners at the Grand Floridian's **Victoria and Albert;** don't forget the California Grille, high up in the Contemporary Hotel, *the* place for viewing fireworks over the Magic Kingdom. And no less than *Vogue* magazine raved about the **San Angel Inn** in Epcot Center's Mexico, where stars shimmer in a perpetual midnight sky and a simmering volcano casts a glow over diners.

In Disney-MGM Studios there are two don't-misses: At the **Prime Time Café,** waitresses act just like Mom—no dessert if you don't eat your meat loaf *and* your vegetables! The **Brown Derby** delivers nonstop Grace Kelly glamour and a pretty fair Cobb salad. For other dining recommendations, *see* Chapter 7, Dining.

So Much Disney, So Little Time
Those who want to give you the long and
short of it usually forget to give you the
short. We don't—just turn to our **Blitz
Tours** in Chapter 2, which show you how
to master Disney: The Challenge—doing
an entire Disney park in a single day. Pay
attention to our tips, and don't worry if
you miss a few attractions. It takes practice to see everything while remaining
stress-free. The payoff will come when you
make your magical second trip—your
first Disneyversary!

—*Robert I. C. Fisher*

WHAT'S WHERE

Universal Studios, Sea World, and Beyond

Universal Studios
With Disney-MGM Studios just down the
road, is Universal Studios Florida even
worth the visit? The answer is a resounding yes. Far from being a "me-too" version
of Disney, Universal is a theme park with
plenty of hip originality and a saucy, sassy
personality of its own. It doesn't hesitate
to invite comparisons with the competition
either; after a stunt man in the Wild, Wild,
Wild West Stunt Show falls down a well,
he emerges spouting water and shouting,
"Look, Ma, I'm Shamu!" Disney-MGM's
strolling actors are pablum compared with
the Blues Brothers' peeling rubber in the
Bluesmobile. And let's face it, even the
Muppets are matched by E. T., Tickli Moot
Moot, and the other inventions of Steven
Spielberg, Universal's genius-on-call.

While Disney has a goodly share of grav-
ity-challengers (especially the free-falling
Twilight Zone Tower of Terror ride) and
other white-knucklers, Universal is the
theme park that reverberates with really
bloodcurdling screams—usually your own.
Tops for terror is **Jaws**, where 40 feet of
teeth come in for the kill and almost wind
up in your lap. Then, in a manner of
speaking, head for Detonation Unknown
and assorted fires, floods, and explosions
at **Earthquake, Dynamite Nights Stuntacular,** and **Kongfrontation.** Careen past dinosaur mouths and lava showers in the

teeth-loosening **Back to the Future** ride. Not
all of Universal's attractions, of course, leave
your heart fluttering in the vicinity of
your tonsils. E. T. does, after all, go home
in **E.T. Adventure**—you feel the wind on
your face while pedaling him across the
moon and get a photo op in his closet. Then
you can rescue Elroy Jetson from inter-
galatic baddies in the **Funtastic World of
Hanna-Barbera** or fire up your Nutrana
Wand at **Ghostbusters.** And, on the biggest
backlot in the world, see sitcoms filmed
and make your own screen debut with Captain Kirk (don't count on an Oscar).

Power Rangers may have backed Barney
onto the gymboree set's B- list, but Universal has recently injected new energy into
the vaunted Purple One's life. The park's
newest attraction, **A Day in the Park with
Barney,** includes a boppin' musical revue
and a hands-on educational playground.
The rest of Universal Studios allows teens
to "ride the movies," but Barney makes
it possible for tykes to walk through a magical land of primary-color trees and indoor
clouds, bringing all their television fantasies
into action. Give the kids a break from high-
flying karate kicks long enough and they'll
love it.

Sea World
Sleek dolphins perform like Mary Lou
Retton, and orca whales sail through the
air like featherweight Nijinskys at the
aptly named 135-acre Sea World. The
world's largest zoological park is entirely
devoted to mammals, birds, fish, and reptiles that live in the ocean and its tributaries. Every attraction is designed to
teach visitors about the marine world and
its vulnerability to man's use. Yet the presentations are never pedantic, always enjoyable, and almost always memorable.
The park rivals Disney properties for
sparkly cleanliness, a smiley staff, and attention to detail.

The highlight is **Shamu Stadium,** where
you can see Shamu and his sidekicks,
Namu and Kandu, propel their trainers into
the air like Saturn missiles. Whales, as
you will learn, are right up there with
dolphins and chimpanzees as the Ein-
steins of the animal world; Unlike old
dogs, these orcas constantly beg to learn
new tricks. Don't forget that these guys
like to make a big splash: Wear rain gear
if you plan to sit within the first four

rows! Everything else goes swimmingly here, too. Friendly denizens await at **Penguin Encounter, Dolphin Community Pool,** and **Sea Lion & Otter Stadium.** The newest attraction is **Wild Arctic.** Part thrill ride, part environmental lesson, part zoo exhibit, it's Sea World's most ambitious creation to date. Cold air whips across your face as polar bears take center stage, cavorting among ice floes and boulders in 900,000 gallons of man-made sea water. Their nonstop antics, plus a thermostat set at 50 degrees, make this truly the coolest place in the park.

Busch Gardens

Now that you've enjoyed Sea World's seafari, why not head for the safari-in-a-day fun of the African-themed park that is Busch Gardens? Wildlife at its chest-thumping best is the specialty here, befitting Busch Gardens' claim to be one of America's leading legitimate zoos. Going eyeball-to-eyeball with a Western Lowland gorilla will please any family's budding Jane Goodall. You'll often feel you're on a Tarzan-movie set. Walking around the sights, however, might throw your personal gyroscope into a spin: In Timbuktu you'll find, of all things, a Dolphin Theater, and you experience the Serengeti Plain from a space-age monorail. The mightiest spins come on the roller coaster and the Congo River Rapids ride. Best of all is the 55-foot drop of the Tanganyika Tidal Wave, an outrageous way to test zero gravity.

Cypress Gardens

A botanic garden, amusement park, and water-skiing circus rolled into one, Cypress Gardens is uniquely Floridian. Here flowers bloom in colors so kitschy you'd think you were viewing vintage tinted postcards. A 45-minute drive from Walt Disney World, the park encompasses 233 acres and contains more than 8,000 varieties of plants gathered from 75 countries. Amid all these sylvan glades you discover a bevy of hoop-skirted southern belles, a mammoth walk-through butterfly conservatory, and the Water Ski Stadiums, home to those amazing aquatic revues. Even the cerise-and-cerulean sunsets look color-coordinated with the cypress-draped canals: for fans, this is Florida at its Technicolor best.

The Space Coast

Exploration of the last remaining frontier—outer space—first became a reality at the Kennedy Space Center, an hour's drive east of Orlando. Here the history of travel was rewritten when astronauts blasted off to the moon. Today the home-launch base of America's Space Shuttle program has become an out-of-this-world tourist attraction. Highlights include two-hour bus tours that offer camera stops near Space Shuttle Launch Pads, the massive Vehicle Assembly Building, a 365-foot Saturn V Moon Rocket, and an IMAX movie that will make you feel you're standing on the launch pad during a Space Shuttle take-off. For information on future launch schedules, phone 407/452–2121.

FODOR'S CHOICE

No two people agree on what makes a perfect vacation, but it's fun and helpful to know what others think. Here's a compendium compiled from the must-see lists of hundreds of Florida travelers. These special memories-in-the-making await you at three of the top Orlando attractions—WDW, Universal Studios, and Sea World. For detailed information about each entry, refer to the appropriate chapters in this guidebook.

Walt Disney World: Magic Kingdom

Looking like an illuminated page from a fairy-tale book, **Cinderella Castle** is the fulfillment of every child's dream. Everyone falls under its spell at dusk, when doves are released to circle the castle's cloud-borne towers.

With the steepest drop of any flume ride in existence, **Splash Mountain** makes you feel like Wily E. Coyote as you head over that final hang-onto-your-hat moment.

Get a paw autograph from Goofy, and feast on Mickey Mouse–shape pancakes at one of the **Disney Character breakfasts.**

Walt Disney believed we are all children at heart, and **It's a Small World** proves it. With hundreds of dancing babies—Dutch moppets in clogs, Russian balalaika players, tiny Tower-of-London guards, Polynesian hip-twitchers—even grumps exit grinning.

Join the magnificent Mr. Toad on his collision course with a runaway train on Fantasyland's **Mr. Toad's Wild Ride.**

The best 10-minute African safari in the world, the **Jungle Cruise** throws hyperactive hippos and hungry headhunters at you every step of the way. Beware of Old Smiley, the crocodile, who's always waiting for a handout—or, as the guide quips, "a foot out."

The portrait busts bespeak the world's greatest "ghost writers" at the **Haunted Mansion,** where ghoulish wit and Victorian decor add up to a delightful scarefest.

Have a heart-to-heart with you-know-who at **Mickey's Starland** in his dressing room.

"You can fly, you can fly, you can fly" over moonlit London at **Peter Pan's Flight.**

Stake out your place in the fun at Disney's lanai-by-the-lagoon, the **Polynesian Resort.**

At Tomorrowland's **Space Mountain,** you penetrate hyperspace by plummeting through the darkened abyss of the world's largest enclosed roller coaster.

Epcot Center

You'll need a chin wrap to keep your mouth closed at Epcot Center's **Spaceship Earth,** where you'll see Roman centurions building roads, Michelangelo painting the Sistine Chapel ceiling, and many other Audio-Animatronic wonders.

Breathe Mesozoic fog and ward off an attack by a prehistoric sea serpent while learning the fascinating story of energy at Epcot Center's **Universe of Energy.**

The funniest 3-D show in the world, **Honey, I Shrunk the Audience** is the newest sensation at Epcot Center's Journey into Imagination.

Dine under a perpetually starry purple sky within sight of a glowing volcano at Disney's dreamiest restaurant, Epcot Center's San Angel Inn.

Buy some not-to-be-believed **animal crackers** at the Süssigkeiten bakery at World Showcase's Germany pavilion.

Disney-MGM Studios

Flout every law of gravitation at the **Twilight Zone Tower of Terror,** a deserted hotel where you'd be better off taking the stairs if there were any. The elevator comes to a (dead) stop, then plunges so fast your stomach will be relocated close to your screechbox.

Will you be the one chosen to reenact *I Love Lucy*'s famous candy-factory scene at **Superstar Television**?

Take a behind-the-scenes look at the great animated cartoons at **Magic of Disney Animation.** (Disney fact: Did you know that Disney animators modeled the Tramp from *Lady and the Tramp* on an adorable mutt found at the local pound?)

Other Walt Disney World Delights

Celebrate New Year's Eve every day of the year at midnight on **Pleasure Island.**

Stomp your feet and chow down on all the fixin's at the **Hoop-Dee-Doo Revue,** Disney's most popular dinner show, staged at Fort Wilderness's rustic Pioneer Hall.

Land on your snowy butt after the wild 55-mph plunge on the Summit Plummet water ride at **Blizzard Beach.**

Make real sure your swimsuit is tied on tightly before tackling **Typhoon Lagoon**'s Humunga Kowabunga!

For a true "When You Wish Upon a Star" finale, cap it all off with the best Disney evening extravaganzas: the **IllumiNations** show in Epcot Center or (in busy seasons only) the dazzling **SpectroMagic** parade in the Magic Kingdom.

Universal Studios Florida

You saw Elliot save him in the movies and now it's your turn at **E.T. Adventure.** The little guy even thanks you personally (how he learns your name is a trade secret Universal won't reveal).

There are plenty of fish in the sea, but only one with Bruce's talents: Play Tooth or Consequences with him at **Jaws.**

Thrill zealots run to **Back to the Future . . . The Ride,** where Doc Brown captains a time-traveling trip covering everything from dinosaurs to the Wright Brothers at Kitty Hawk.

Sea World

Bed down with sharks, eels, and barracudas on the special bring-your-own-sleeping bag Education Sleepovers offered at Sea World's **Terrors of the Deep** aquarium.

Check out that polar-bear paradise, **Wild Arctic**—easily the coolest place in all Florida.

Pet and feed the spooky residents of **Stingray Lagoon.**

Don't forget to pick out a pair of neoprene **Aqua Socks** water shoes decorated in black and white, à la orca, at Fashionations.

FESTIVALS AND SEASONAL EVENTS

Scheduling a vacation to Orlando around one of the area's many festivals and seasonal events can add extra excitement to your trip. Top area events include the Florida Citrus Bowl on New Year's Day, the Walt Disney World Wine Festival in February and the Magic Kingdom's Eastertime Celebration during April, Light Up Orlando in November, and the Walt Disney World Christmas festivities. The following is the annual calendar of special events.

WINTER

DECEMBER➤ Early in the month, Orlando's Loch Haven Park stages a **Pet Fair & Winterfest** (☎ 407/ 644–2739). For Christmastime, Cypress Gardens mounts its annual **Poinsettia Festival** (☎ 813/324– 2111), featuring 48,000 multicolored blooms. For a **Disney Christmas,** Walt Disney World gears up by decorating Main Street in perfect Victorian style, complete with a magnificent Christmas tree in Town Square, strolling characters, special afternoon parades, and entertainment. A Nativity Pageant, *Mickey's Christmas Carol* stage show, and appearances by the North Pole's most important citizen take place at Disney Village Marketplace (☎ 407/824–4321). December 31 occasions the **Citrus Bowl Parade** in Orlando (☎ 407/629– 4944), a street party at

Church Street Station (☎ 407/422–2434), and a double fireworks display and extra-late hours in Walt Disney World's Magic Kingdom, which usually records some of the biggest crowds of the year for the event.

JANUARY➤ The **Comp USA Florida Citrus Bowl Football Classic** (☎ 407/423– 2476) takes place at the Orlando Citrus Bowl on January 1. At the end of the month, **Scottish Highland Games** are played at Orlando's Central Florida Fairgrounds (☎ 407/ 672–1682).

FEBRUARY➤ Early in the month, the **Walt Disney World Village Wine Festival** (☎ 407/934–6743) showcases the vintages of 60 participating wineries from all over the country, and the **National Championship Rodeo Finals** at the Orlando Arena (☎ 407/ 849–2020) give cowboys from all over a chance to compete. It's followed at the end of the month by Kissimmee's **Silver Spurs Rodeo** (☎ 407/847–5000), one of the oldest and largest events of its kind in the South, drawing cowboys from all over the United States and Canada. At about the same time, or early in March, the **Annual Central Florida Fair** is held at Orlando's Central Florida Fairgrounds (☎ 407/295–3247), with shows, rides, exhibits, and entertainment. **Pleasure Island Mardi Gras** (☎ 407/ 939–7814) is touted as the biggest, most authentic Mardi Gras festival outside New Orleans.

SPRING

MARCH➤ It's baseball spring-training time, with the **Houston Astros** at Osceola County Stadium in Kissimmee (☎ 407/ 933–5500) and the **Kansas City Royals** at Baseball City Stadium (☎ 813/424–2424). Cypress Gardens kicks off its **Spring Flower Festival** (☎ 813/324–2111), which runs through May and features extraordinary floral topiaries and a profusion of spring blossoms.

One weekend in early March, the **Kissimmee Bluegrass Festival** showcases bluegrass bands and gospel music at the SilverSprings Arena (☎ 407/856–0246). On March 17, the **St. Patrick's Day Street Party** encourages the "wearin' o' the green" at Church Street Station (☎ 407/422– 2434). Mid-month, the **Nestle Invitational,** a regular PGA Tour event, stops at Orlando's Bay Hill Club (☎ 407/876– 2888), and the **Winter Park Sidewalk Art Festival** (☎ 407/644–8281) draws thousands of art enthusiasts to trendy Park Avenue.

APRIL➤ From early April through early May, the **Orlando Shakespeare Festival** pays tribute to the Bard at Orlando's Lake Eola Amphitheater (☎ 407/423–6905). Also early in April, the **Dr. Pepper Annual Surf**

Festival (☎ 407/783–5813) draws professional and amateur surfers to Cocoa Beach. On Easter Sunday there are **Easter Sunrise Services** at Sea World's Atlantis Theater (☎ 407/351–3600) and an **Easter Parade** down Main Street during mid-April at Walt Disney World (☎ 407/939–7814). From the end of April until early May, the **Orlando International Fringe Festival** brings 200 artists and theater troupes to perform in downtown Orlando. Cypress Gardens' Spring Flower Festival also wraps up in early May. Leading into June, the annual **"Up, Up and Away" Airport Art Show** takes place at Orlando International Airport (☎ 407/826–2055).

SUMMER

JUNE➤ Late in the month and early in July is the **Silver Spurs Rodeo** (☎ 407/847–5000); there's another in early February.

JULY➤ The **Fourth of July** is a big day in and around Orlando. Walt Disney World's fireworks are legendary; recent years have brought record crowds (☎ 407/939–7814). In downtown Orlando, huge crowds gather around Lake Eola for the city's fireworks (☎ 407/363—5871). There are also fireworks in Kissimmee as part of its old-fashioned celebration in Lakefront Park, which also features games, rides, entertainment, and food (☎ 407/932–7223), and in Cypress Gardens, which mounts special ski shows as well (☎ 813/324–2111).

AUTUMN

SEPTEMBER➤ **Oktoberfest at Church Street Station** (☎ 407/422–2434) means oompah bands and German folk dancers, food, and beer.

OCTOBER➤ Early in the month, the **Universal Art Show** is held on Orlando's Central Florida Fairgrounds (☎ 407/295–3247). Midmonth is the season for the **Walt Disney World Oldsmobile Golf Classic,** played on three of Walt Disney World's 18-hole golf courses (☎ 407/824–2250); for Cypress Gardens' **Annual Mustang Roundup** (☎ 800/282–2123), which draws aficionados of that most famous Ford to exhibit and ogle models from 1965 to the present; and for the **Winter Park Autumn Art Festival** at Rollins College (☎ 407/644–8281). Later on is the **Pioneer Days Folk Festival,** with craftspeople and musicians on the grounds of the Folk Art Center on East Fairlane Avenue in suburban Pine Castle (☎ 407/855–7461). For **Halloween,** there's a street party at Church Street Station (☎ 407/422–2434).

NOVEMBER➤ Early in the month, the **American Indian Powwow** (☎ 407/295–3247) takes place at the Central Florida Fairgrounds. Midmonth is the **Festival of the Masters,** with 230 top artists exhibiting their creations at Disney Village Marketplace (☎ 407/934–6743). **Light Up Orlando** is a street party downtown with live entertainment (☎ 407/648–4010). Cypress Gardens hosts its monthlong **Chrysanthemum Festival** (☎ 813/324–2111).

2 Exploring Walt Disney World®

By Catherine
Fredman

Updated by
Marianne
Camas

MILLIONS OF VISITORS, even those who place Pirates of the Caribbean and Space Mountain among the wonders of the world, can't accurately define Walt Disney World. When you take a Walt Disney World exit off I–4 or U.S. 192 and begin traveling across empty land devoid of billboards or any other promotional materials, you're already on the grounds, even though there's no Cinderella Castle in sight. It's a very big place. And it's crammed with pleasures: from swooping above a starlit London in the Magic Kingdom's Peter Pan's Flight to just sitting under the shade of a Callary pear tree frosted with blooms in Epcot Center.

The sheer size of the property—27,400 acres near Kissimmee, Florida—suggests that WDW is more than a single theme park with a fabulous castle in the center and the most dazzling rides on earth. The property's acreage translates to 43 square miles—twice the size of Manhattan or Bermuda, 60 times larger than Monaco, and just a shade smaller than Nantucket or Liechtenstein. If you were to drive at 60 miles per hour from one side of the property to the other, it would take close to 45 minutes. On a tract that size, 98 acres is a mere speck, yet that is the size of the Magic Kingdom. When most people imagine Walt Disney World, they think only of those 98 acres, but there is much, much more.

More than 2,500 acres of the property is occupied by hotels and villa complexes, each with its own theme and each equipped with recreational facilities such as swimming pools and golf courses. Epcot Center, a little more than twice the size of the Magic Kingdom, is the second major theme park. A combination of a science exploratorium and a world's fair, Epcot offers visions of the future and celebrations of the world's cultural diversity. In 1989, the Disney-MGM Studios Theme Park, devoted to the doings of the film business, opened nearby. In addition, there are thousands of acres of undeveloped land—grassy plains and pine forests patrolled by deer, and swamps patched by thickets of palmettos and fluttering with white ibis—even now, 25 years after opening day.

As Disney himself decreed, WDW has never been completed; as one new confection welcomes its first guests, another begins construction and still others are under study. So read up before you go, call ahead to find out what's new, and make a plan. Then relax—and have a wonderful time.

ESSENTIAL INFORMATION

Important Numbers

Information

For **general information,** contact Guest Relations or Guest Services in any Disney theme park or hotel (☎ 407/824–4321) or the central WDW switchboard (☎ 407/824–2222). For **accommodations and shows,** call WDW Central Reservations (☎ 407/W–DISNEY). To inquire about **resort facilities,** call the individual property (*see* Disney Hotels in WDW *and* Other Hotels in WDW *in* Chapter 8, Lodging).

To get very specific information, call the attraction or department directly: **Blizzard Beach** (☎ 407/407/560–2316), **Discovery Island** (☎ 407/824–3784), **Disney Village Marketplace** (☎ 407/828–3058), **Fort Wilderness** (☎ 407/824–2900), **KinderCare** child care (in-room, ☎ 407/827–5444; drop-off, ☎ 407/827–5437), **learning programs** (☎ 407/354–1855), **Pleasure Island** (☎ 407/934–7781), **River Country**

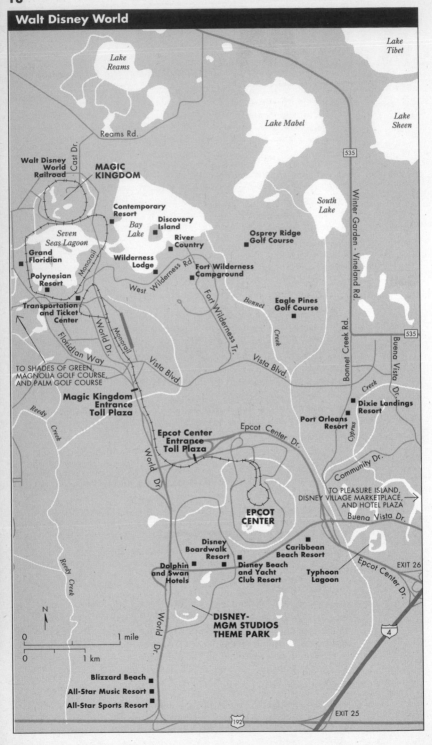

(☎ 407/824–2760), **Disney-MGM Studios TV-show tapings** (☎ 407/560–4651), **Typhoon Lagoon** (☎ 407/560–4141).

Reservations

To make reservations at restaurants in Walt Disney World, including the heavily booked **Epcot Center restaurants**, call 407/WDW–DINE. To reserve **golf tee times and lessons** (☎ 407/824–2270).

Financial Services

Fulfill your banking needs at either the **Sun Bank** branch in the Magic Kingdom (☎ 407/824–5767) or the one in Lake Buena Vista, across the street from the Disney Village Marketplace (☎ 407/828–6106). There are **automatic teller machines** located at the entrances to the Magic Kingdom, Epcot Center, Disney-MGM Studios and in Pleasure Island.

Lost and Found

There are same-day lost-and-found offices at **Epcot Center** (☎ 407/560–6166 or 407/560–6236), in the **Magic Kingdom** at City Hall (☎ 407/824–4521), and in **Disney-MGM Studios** (☎ 407/560–4668). After one day, all items are sent to the **Main Lost & Found** office at the Magic Kingdom's Ticket and Transportation Center (☎ 407/824–4245).

Getting There by Car

Walt Disney World has three exits off I–4. For the Magic Kingdom, Disney-MGM Studios, Fort Wilderness, and the rest of the Magic Kingdom resort area, take the one marked **Magic Kingdom–U.S. 192.** From here, it's a 4-mile drive along Disney's main entrance road to the toll gate, and another mile to the parking area; during peak vacation periods, be prepared for serious bumper-to-bumper traffic both on I–4 nearing the U.S. 192 exit and on 192 itself.

For access to Disney Village Marketplace, Pleasure Island, Typhoon Lagoon, the Crossroads Shopping Center, and the establishments on Hotel Plaza Boulevard, use the **Route 535–Lake Buena Vista** exit.

The **Epcot Center–Disney Village** exit is the one to use if you're bound for those destinations or for hotels in the Epcot Center and Disney Village resort areas; you can also get to Disney Village Marketplace and Disney-MGM from here.

Parking

Every theme park has a parking lot—and all are huge. (Disney prides itself on noting that the Magic Kingdom's parking lot, with its 12,000 parking spaces, is the second-largest lot in the universe, next to Houston's Astrodome.) Always write down exactly where you park and take the number with you. Although in theory Goofy 45 is unforgettable (sections of the Magic Kingdom lot are named for Disney characters; Epcot's are named after environments, such as Space Mountain; Disney-MGM Studios' are film genres), a day full of unforgettable experiences in the Disney parks may prove otherwise. Trams make frequent trips between the parking area and the parks' turnstile areas.

PARKING FEES

For each lot, admission is $5 for cars, $6 for RVs and campers (or free for Walt Disney World resort guests with ID). Save your receipt; if you want to visit another park the same day, you won't have to pay to park twice. Parking is free at Typhoon Lagoon and River Country.

Auto Needs

The gas islands at the **Disney Car Care Center** near the Magic Kingdom are open daily until 90 minutes after the Magic Kingdom closes.

Getting Around

Walt Disney World has its own transportation system that can get you wherever you want to go. It's fairly simple once you get the hang of it. All charges for transportation are now included in the price of your multiday passport; guests with a single-day admission ticket pay $2.50.

By Monorail

The elevated monorail serves many important destinations. It has two loops: one linking the Magic Kingdom, an area known as the Transportation and Ticket Center (TTC), and a handful of resorts, including the Contemporary, the Grand Floridian, and the Polynesian Village, and the other looping from the TTC directly to Epcot Center. Before this monorail line pulls into the station, the elevated track circles through Future World—Epcot Center's northern half—and circles the giant silver geosphere housing the Spaceship Earth ride to give you a preview of what you'll see.

By Boat

Motor launches connect WDW destinations located on waterways. Specifically, they operate between the Epcot Center resorts (except the Caribbean Beach) and Disney-MGM Studios and between Discovery Island—in Bay Lake—and the Magic Kingdom, Fort Wilderness, and the Polynesian, Contemporary, and Grand Floridian resorts.

By Bus

In addition, buses provide direct service from every on-site resort to both major and minor theme parks, and express buses go directly between the major theme parks. To Typhoon Lagoon, you can go directly from (or make connections at) the TTC, Disney Village Marketplace, Epcot Center, and the Epcot Center resorts (the Beach Club and Yacht Club, the Caribbean Beach Resort, the Swan, and the Dolphin).

By Tram

From the Epcot Center resort area, trams operate to the International Gateway of the park's World Showcase.

Hours

Monorail, launches, buses, and trams all operate from early in the morning until at least midnight. (Hours are shorter during early closing periods.) Check on the operating hours of the service you need if you plan to be out later than that.

Admission Fees

Visiting Walt Disney World is not cheap, especially if you have a child or two along. Everyone 10 and older pays adult price; reductions are available for children 3–9. No discounted family tickets are available.

Tickets

In Disneyspeak, "ticket" refers to a single day's admission to the Magic Kingdom, Epcot Center, or the Disney-MGM Studios. If you want to spend two or three days visiting the attractions, you have to buy a separate ticket each day. A ticket is good in the park for which you buy it only on the day you buy it; with tickets, you can't park-hop. If you buy a one-day ticket and later decide to extend your visit, you can apply the cost of it toward the purchase of any passport. Exchanges can be made at City Hall in the Magic Kingdom, at Guest Relations in Epcot Center, or at Guest Relations at Disney-MGM.

Passports

If you want to spend more than three days, you have several options. The **Four-Day Value Pass** allows admission to each of the three parks on any three days. You can then visit one of the parks again on one more day. You cannot visit more than one park on one day. There is a way to avoid this restriction: the **Four-Day Park Hopper,** a personalized photo ID pass that allows unlimited visits to the three parks on any four days. The **Five-Day World Hopper** is also a photo ID; it includes unlimited visits to the three theme parks over five days, plus seven consecutive days' admission (dated from first entry to WDW) to WDW's minor parks—Pleasure Island, Typhoon Lagoon, River Country, Blizzard Beach, and Discovery Island. Disney says it introduced the photo IDs as a way to prevent counterfeiting; however, these park-hopping passes were introduced after Disney weathered a storm of controversy over its decision to allow park-hopping only to guests registered at hotels on Disney property.

These three passes can save you money. In fact, if you plan to visit the minor parks or go to Typhoon Lagoon or Blizzard Beach more than once, it may pay to buy a Five-Day World Hopper Pass even if you're staying only four days. Each time you use a passport, the entry date is stamped on it; remaining days may be used even years in the future. A variety of annual passes are also available, at a cost only slightly more than a World Hopper Pass; if you plan to visit twice in a year, these are a good deal. Guests at Disney resorts can also purchase Length of Stay Passes, which are good from the time of arrival until midnight of the departure day. Length of Stay Passes may be purchased at the front desks of all resorts as well as in Guest Services at the three theme parks. Prices (not including tax) are based upon the number of room nights and range from $80 for a 1-night/2-day adult pass to $262 for 9-nights/10 days. The pass is good for all three theme parks, as well as the three water parks, Pleasure Island, and Discovery Island.

Prices

Disney changes its prices at least once a year and without any notice. At press time, WDW admission prices (including 6% tax) were as follows, but call as close as possible to the time of your trip for the most current information. Note that admission prices to Blizzard Beach and Typhoon Lagoon have now been combined into one **Water Park Hopper,** which entitles you to use both water parks in one day (separate admission is needed to River Country).

	ADULTS	CHILDREN
One-day ticket	$39.22	$31.80
Four-Day Value Pass	$131.44	$102.82
Four-Day Park Hopper	$145.22	$115.54
Five-Day World Hopper	$197.56	$156.88
River Country	$15.64	$12.19
Discovery Island	$10.60	$5.83
Combined River Country/ Discovery Island	$19.61	$14.05
Combined Blizzard Beach/ Typhoon Lagoon	$23.85	$18.02
Pleasure Island	$16.91	$16.91

Where to Buy Tickets and Passports

Tickets and passports to Walt Disney World, Epcot Center, and Disney-MGM Studios Theme Park can be purchased at admission booths at the TTC, in all on-site resorts (if you're a registered guest), and at the Walt Disney World kiosk on the second floor of the main terminal at Orlando International Airport. American Express, Visa, and MasterCard are accepted, as are cash, personal checks (with ID), and traveler's checks. Discounted tickets are also sold at many offices of the American Automobile Association. (Check with your local office before you leave home.)

By Mail

If you buy your Passports by mail, you'll be waiting at the turnstiles, ready to get a jump on the day, while everyone else is lining up at Guest Services in the Disney hotels or at the ticket booths at the theme parks. Send a check or money order to Ticket Mail Order Dept., Walt Disney World, Box 10000, Lake Buena Vista, FL 32830. Note that this is only for multiday admissions. Allow four–six weeks for processing.

Hand Stamps

If you want to leave the Magic Kingdom, Epcot Center, and Disney-MGM and return on the same day, be sure to have your hand stamped on the way out. You'll need your ticket *and* the hand stamp to be readmitted.

Opening and Closing Hours

Major Theme Parks

Operating hours for the **Magic Kingdom, Epcot Center,** and **Disney-MGM Studios** theme parks vary widely throughout the year and change for school and legal holidays. In general, the longest days are during the prime summer months and over the year-end holidays, when the Magic Kingdom is open until midnight (later on New Year's Eve); Epcot Center is open until 11 PM; and Disney-MGM is open until 9 PM.

At other times, Epcot Center and Disney-MGM are open until 8 and the Magic Kingdom until 7—but there are variations, so call ahead.

Note that though the Magic Kingdom, Epcot Center's Future World (Epcot's World Showcase opens at 11 AM), and Disney-MGM officially open at 9 AM, visitors may enter at 8:30, and sometimes at 8. The parking lots open at least an hour before the parks do. Arriving at the Magic Kingdom turnstiles before the official opening time, you can breakfast in a restaurant on Main Street, which opens before the rest of the park, and be ready to dash to one of the popular attractions in other lands at Rope Drop, the Magic Kingdom's official opening time. Arriving in Epcot Center or Disney-MGM Studios, you can make dinner reservations before the crowds arrive and take in some of the attractions and pavilions well before the major crowds descend, which is usually at about 10.

Note that guests who stay at an on-site Disney-owned hotel can enter one of the three parks (on alternating days) a full hour and a half before the official opening time of 9 AM. They can get a jump on some of the main attractions, which open for them at 8 AM (more information is included with the passport).

Minor Parks

Hours at **Discovery Island, River Country, Typhoon Lagoon,** and **Blizzard Beach** are 10–5 daily (until 7—occasionally 10—in summer).

Dining

Walt Disney World is full of places to snack and eat. The theme parks are chockablock with fast-food spots; all have full-service, sit-down restaurants, and in Epcot Center's World Showcase, these eating-and-drinking spots are part of the show. On-site hotels offer still other options, including buffeterias as well as full-service restaurants.

This book does not describe and rate every eating spot. Best bets for quick meals are described as Time Out in the theme park sections of this chapter, and top options for meals in full-service restaurants are in the theme parks' Dining sections. For reviews of restaurants in Disney hotels and at Epcot Center, *see* Chapter 7, Dining.

Fresh fruits, salads, steamed vegetables, and low-fat foods are more widely available than you might expect. In full-service restaurants, for instance, you can usually get skim milk, and many fast-food operations have low-fat milk.

Beer, Wine, and Spirits

The Magic Kingdom's no-liquor policy does not extend to the rest of Walt Disney World, and in fact, most restaurants and watering holes, particularly those in the on-site hotels, mix elaborate fantasy drinks based on fruit juices or flavored with liqueurs.

Important Tips for Your Visit

The order in which you tour each of the Disney parks has everything to do with your priorities, the time of year you visit (which is in turn related to the opening and closing hours and the size of the crowds), how long you're staying in Walt Disney World, and whether you're staying on or off WDW property. The "Strategies for Your Visit" section included for each of the various Disney theme parks assumes that you want to see that park in a single day and that you're traveling during a period of good-size crowds and long hours. The italicized "Crowds" and "Strategy" information that follows each attraction's review should help you draw up alternative plans. No matter where you go, you will have a smoother time of it if you follow certain basic rules.

- Arrive in the theme parks early—well ahead of the published opening times—so that you can check belongings into lockers, rent strollers, and otherwise take care of business before everyone else.

- See the three-star attractions either first thing in the morning, during a parade, or at the very end of the day.

- Whenever possible when you're visiting the theme parks, eat in a restaurant that takes reservations, or have meals before or after mealtime rush hours (from 11 AM to 2 PM and again from 6 to 8 PM). Or leave the theme parks altogether for a meal in one of the hotels. Early meals are particularly advantageous; you'll be resting up and cooling off while the rest of the world is waiting in line; while they're all waiting to order, you'll be walking right into many attractions.

- Spend afternoons in high-capacity sit-down shows or catching live entertainment—or leave the park entirely for a swim in your hotel pool.

- If you plan to take in Blizzard Beach or Typhoon Lagoon, go early in your visit (but not on a weekend). You may like it so much that you'll want to go again.

- If a meal with the characters is in your plans, save it for the end of your trip, when your youngsters will have become accustomed to these large, looming figures.

- If a meal at an Epcot Center World Showcase restaurant is in your plans, reserve in advance by calling 407/WDW–DINE. If you can only make reservations in person, try to get to Epcot Center's World Key Information booths as early in the day as possible (*see* Chapter 7, Dining).

- Familiarize yourself with all age and height restrictions—and don't let your younger children get excited about rides they're too short or too young to experience.

Entertainment

Live entertainment adds texture to visits to the Disney theme parks. Although the jokes may be silly, the humor broad, and the themes sometimes excessively wholesome, the level of professionalism is high and the energy of the performers unquestionable. Be sure to pick up a performance schedule on your way into the theme parks.

Ratings

Every visitor leaves the Magic Kingdom, Epcot Center, and Disney-MGM Studios with a different opinion about what was "the best." Some attractions get raves from all visitors, whereas others are enjoyed most by young children or older travelers. To take this into account, our descriptions rate each attraction with ★, ★★, or ★★★, depending on the strength of its appeal to the visitor group noted by the italics preceding the stars. A three-star attraction, standing out for its imaginative qualities or technical wizardry, elicits the most enthusiastic responses in that group; see it even if your time is limited.

At Epcot Center's World Showcase, the national pavilions are enjoyable by audiences of all ages; however, young children may consider such cultural fare less exciting than the fantasy-oriented attractions in the Magic Kingdom or Disney-MGM, and they may be exhausted by all the walking required.

Access for Travelers with Disabilities

Attractions in all the Disney parks typically have both a visual element that makes them appealing without sound and an audio element whose charm remains even without the visuals; many are accessible by guests using wheelchairs, and most are accessible by guests with some mobility. Guide dogs and service animals are often permitted.

At many rides and attractions, guests with mobility, hearing, and visual impairments do not use the main entrance and sometimes even bypass lines; to find out where to enter or if you have specific questions, ask any host or hostess.

WDW's **Guidebook for Guests with Disabilities** details many specific challenges and identifies the special disabled-guest entrances. In addition, story notes, scripts, or song lyrics are covered in the **Guidebook for Guests with Hearing Impairments.** Both publications are available at the main visitor information locations in every park, along with **cassette tapes** and **portable players** that provide audio narration for most attractions (no charge, but refundable deposit required). There are also **wheelchair rentals** in every park.

MAGIC KINGDOM

For most people, the Magic Kingdom *is* Walt Disney World. Certainly it is both the heart and soul of the Disney empire. The Magic Kingdom is comparable to California's Disneyland; it was the first Disney outpost in Florida when it opened in 1971, and it is the park that traveled, with modifications, to France and Japan.

For a park that wields such worldwide influence, the Magic Kingdom is surprisingly small: At barely 98 acres, it is the tiniest of Walt Disney World's Big Three. However, the unofficial theme song—"It's a Small World After All"—doesn't hold true when it comes to the Magic Kingdom's attractions. Packed into six different "lands" are nearly 50 major crowd pleasers, and that's not counting all the ancillary attractions: shops, eateries, live entertainment, cartoon characters, fireworks, parades, and, of course, the sheer pleasure of strolling through the beautifully landscaped and manicured grounds.

Many of the rides are geared to the young, but the Magic Kingdom is anything but a kiddie park. The degree of detail, the greater vision, the surprisingly witty spiel of the guides, and the tongue-in-cheek signs that crop up in the oddest places (for instance, in Fantasyland, the rest rooms are marked "Prince" and "Princess") all contribute to a delightful sense of discovery that's far beyond the mere thrill of a ride.

Essential Information

Getting Around
Once you're in the Magic Kingdom, distances are generally short, and the best way to get around is on foot; the Walt Disney World Railroad, the Main Street vehicles, the Skyway between Fantasyland and Tomorrowland, and the Tomorrowland Transit Authority (formerly the WEDway PeopleMover) do help you cover some territory and can give your feet a welcome rest, but they're primarily forms of entertainment, not transportation.

Tourist Information
City Hall (☎ 407/824–4521) is the principal information center. Here you can pick up the *Magic Kingdom Guide Book* and a schedule of daily events (if you haven't requested one by mail in advance), search for misplaced belongings or companions, and ask questions of the omniscient staffers.

Other cast members throughout the park can be helpful, too. In fact, providing information for visitors is part of the job description of the young men and women who sweep the pavement and faithfully keep litter in its place.

Reservations
One of the most frequently asked questions at City Hall is whether this is the place to make reservations for the Diamond Horseshoe Jamboree. (The answer is no. That's done across Town Square at Disneyana Collectibles.) In order to ensure reservations at the handful of other full-service restaurants, take advantage of the Disney reservation hot line, 407/WDW–DINE.

Services
BABY CARE
The Magic Kingdom's soothing, quiet Baby Care Center is next to the Crystal Palace at the end of Main Street. Furnished with rocking chairs, it has a low lighting level that makes it comfortable for nursing. There are toddler-size toilets, and the cast members have supplies such as **formula, baby food, pacifiers,** and **disposable diapers** for sale. You'll find **changing tables** here, as well as in all women's rooms and some men's rooms. You can also buy disposable diapers in the Emporium on Main Street. The Stroller Shop near the entrance to the Magic Kingdom (on the east side of Main Street) is the place for **stroller rentals** ($6 fee; $1 deposit required).

BARBERSHOP
Tucked in a corner just off Main Street, where the Emporium ends, the Harmony Barber Shop isn't just for show—it's a for-real place to get a **haircut** from Disney cast members dressed in 19th-century costumes.

CAMERAS AND FILM
Kodak's disposable Fun Saver cameras are widely available in shops throughout the theme parks and hotels. Or, at the Camera Center on Main Street, you can rent **35mm cameras** or **video camcorders** ($5 and $40, respectively; refundable $70–$600 deposit required). Multiple-day rentals of camcorders are available. Be advised that camcorders are full-size models.

For **minor camera repairs,** the Camera Center on Main Street is the place.

For **two-hour film developing,** look for the Photo Express sign throughout the park; drop your film in the container, and you can pick up your pictures at the Camera Center as you leave the park. Instant (almost) gratification.

FIRST AID
The Magic Kingdom's First Aid Center, staffed by registered nurses, is alongside the Crystal Palace.

GUIDED TOURS
A good way to get a feel for the layout of the Magic Kingdom and what goes on behind the scenes is to take the "Keys to the Kingdom" tour, a 3½- to 4-hour guided orientation tour ($25 adults and children 10 and up; no younger children allowed). Tours leave from City Hall daily between 9:15 and 9:30 AM and are on a first-come, first-served basis. Included are visits to some of the "backstage" zones: the parade staging area and parts of the underground "Tunnel," including the wardrobe area.

LOCKERS
You'll find them in an arcade underneath the Main Street Railroad Station (50¢). If what you need to store won't fit in the larger lockers, inquire at City Hall.

LOST CHILDREN AND ADULTS
If you're worried about your children getting lost, you can get them **name tags** at the Magic Kingdom (at City Hall or at the Baby Center next to the Crystal Palace). If your fears are realized, immediately ask any cast member and try not to panic; obviously lost children are usually taken to City Hall or the Baby Care Center, where lost children's logbooks are kept, and everyone is well trained to effect speedy reunions.

City Hall also has a computerized **Message Center,** where you can leave notes for your traveling companions, both those in the Magic Kingdom and in other parks.

LOST AND FOUND
City Hall is the place to report losses and finds (or call 407/824–4521). If nobody claims what you turn in, you may get to keep it.

MONEY
For cash or currency exchange, go to the Guest Relations window in the turnstile area, to City Hall, or to the Sun Bank branch in Town Square (open 9–4 daily), with an ATM nearby.

PACKAGE PICKUP
Ask the shop clerk to send any large purchase you make to Guest Relations in the Entrance Plaza so you won't have to carry it around all day. (Allow three hours.)

WHEELCHAIR RENTALS
Go to the gift shop to the left of the ticket booths at the Transportation and Ticket Center or the Stroller and Wheelchair shop inside the main entrance to your right ($6 plus $1 deposit); the latter also has motor-powered chairs ($30 plus $20 deposit). Electric scooters are available by reservation ($30 plus $20 deposit; ☎ 407/824–4321). If your rental needs replacing, ask a host or hostess.

Strategies for Your Visit

Arriving at least 30 minutes before Rope Drop is essential to get your bearings and explore the shops on Main Street. If you are staying at a Disney resort, check your passport to see whether you are entitled to early admission; this is vital, especially for parents with small children, who will be able to visit most of the Fantasyland rides before the park officially opens, thereby offering the option of an afternoon trip to Discovery Island.

Blitz Tours

WITH SMALL CHILDREN
Go directly to Fantasyland and start with a ride on **Dumbo, the Flying Elephant.** Then ride **Cinderella's Golden Carrousel** and, moving clockwise, the other attractions. Check the line at **Legend of the Lion King**; if it's moving briskly, join the crowd. You'll get into the next show. Leave **It's a Small World** until last; its continuously moving lines keep crowds shuffling along and it's a nice end to a Fantasyland visit.

Proceed to Liberty Square and have an early lunch at Liberty Tree Tavern. Take a postprandial tour of **Tom Sawyer Island** and follow it up with the next show at Frontierland's **Country Bear Jamboree.** By now it should be about time to find a place on the pavement to watch the three o'clock parade—Frontierland is one of the best places in the park in which to do it.

Upon exiting the Country Bear Jamboree, turn right (most people go left, to Splash Mountain and Big Thunder Mountain Railroad). Then make another right at Frontier Woodcarving at the end of the row of false-fronted shops and take the shortcut to Adventureland.

Proceed directly across the Adventureland plaza to the **Jungle Cruise.** If your arms and legs are up to it, scramble around the **Swiss Family Treehouse.** We don't really recommend the **Enchanted Tiki Birds** unless you're in need of an air-conditioned place to sit down or want to inoculate your children against terminal kitsch.

Now stroll through the rest-room arch next to Plaza del Sol Caribe by the **Pirates of the Caribbean** back to Frontierland, round the corner of Splash Mountain to the **Walt Disney Railroad** station. Take the train to **Mickey's Starland.** From here, depending on your stamina, either proceed to Tomorrowland for **Carousel of Progress** or hop back on board the train to Main Street.

If you're really determined to eke out every penny, leave the park (for Discovery Island, perhaps, or your hotel). Come back for dinner at the **Crystal Palace.** Many kids want to repeat the rides in Fantasyland, so now is a good time to do that. At about eight o'clock, claim a piece of pavement to watch the nine o'clock **SpectroMagic** parade.

Upon entering the gates of the Magic Kingdom, go right over to **Disneyana Collectibles** on the right side of Town Square and make reservations for a late-morning show of the **Diamond Horseshoe Jamboree.** Position yourself for the Rope Drop at the southwestern spur off the Hub that leads to Adventureland. Then sprint right over to **Splash Mountain** via the Adventureland plaza (it's marginally shorter than going through Frontierland, which is what everyone else is doing). From Splash Mountain, everyone naturally goes to **Big Thunder Mountain Railroad**; buck the trend and go instead to Adventureland. Here you can visit **Pirates of the Caribbean, Jungle Cruise,** and the **Swiss Family Treehouse** before the crowds, as well as knock off this relatively remotely located land.

Proceed to Frontierland through the exit near the **Enchanted Tiki Birds.** You should have just enough time to get oriented before going to the **Diamond Horseshoe Jamboree** (to your left as you enter Frontierland). Have a snack here—you'll be having a late lunch. At this point, everyone else is beginning to think about lunch—so it's a good time to visit the **Haunted Mansion.** If the lines look too daunting, backtrack to the **Hall of Presidents** and try again later.

From the Haunted Mansion or Hall of Presidents it's a quick slide over to Fantasyland. Hit one or two of the more accessible attractions while those with younger kids are at the feeding trough—you'll be back. When it looks as though the postlunch crowd is swelling, head out through **Cinderella Castle** and take a right to the Crystal Palace for your own relaxed, late lunch. You'll also be perfectly positioned to grab a piece of pavement for viewing the three o'clock parade.

Head straight across the Hub to Tomorrowland. Again, count on the fact that everyone else had an early lunch and therefore will need an early dinner—which is when you can ride **Space Mountain** and take in **Alien Encounter.** Whet your appetite in the meantime, and take a little break on the **Tomorrowland Transit Authority, AstroOrbiter,** or **Carousel of Progress,** and the **Metropolis Science Centre.**

Hop on the **Skyway** right outside of Space Mountain for a journey back to Fantasyland. By now, it should be getting on in the day—a good time to visit some more attractions, now that tired children are being taken home. Wander back to Liberty Square for dinner at the Liberty Tree Tavern, give yourself time to digest—the **Country Bears Jamboree** is a good spot for this—and then head over to **Big Thunder Mountain Railroad** for a nighttime ride. After that, it's time to find a place to watch the **SpectroMagic** parade, which wends its way up Main Street, around the Hub and—how fortuitous!—into Frontierland.

You've still got about an hour or so before the fireworks. This is a good time to visit attractions that were just too mobbed earlier (like Alien Encounter or Space Mountain, if you missed one during your first pass) or attractions that are easy on the adrenaline and light on the mood (like **Cinderella's Golden Carrousel** or **It's a Small World**). Again, you'll want to stake out a place to view the fireworks about 30 minutes before ignition—the southwest corner of the Hub is good because you can see over the trees and get a great view of Tinkerbell as she wafts along her wire to tomorrow and tomorrow and Tomorrowland. (Or try the central court of Fantasyland, where you can watch sitting down, nursing a soft-ice-cream sundae from one of the stands.)

Rainy Days

If you visit during a busy time of year, pray for rain. Rainy days dissolve the crowds here. Unlike those at Disney-MGM and Epcot Center, however, many of the Magic Kingdom's attractions are outdoors. If you don't mind getting damp, pick up a bright yellow poncho on Main Street ($4.25 adults, $3.75 children) and soldier on.

Exploring the Magic Kingdom

Numbers in the margin correspond to points of interest on the Magic Kingdom map.

The park is laid out on a north–south axis, with Cinderella Castle at the epicenter and the various lands surrounding it in a broad circle. Upon passing through the entrance gates, you immediately discover yourself in Town Square, a central connection point containing City Hall, Sun Bank, Tony's Town Square Café, and Disneyana Collectibles. Town Square directly segues into Main Street, a boulevard filled with Victorian-style stores and dining spots. Main Street runs due north and ends at the Hub, a large tree-lined circle, known as Central Plaza, located in front of Cinderella Castle. Rope Drop, the ceremonial stampede that kicks off each day, occurs at various points along Main Street and the Hub.

As you move clockwise from the Hub, the Magic Kingdom's different lands start with Adventureland—home of Pirates of the Caribbean, the Jungle Cruise, and the Swiss Family Robinson Treehouse. Next come Frontierland and Liberty Square, containing Splash Mountain, Big Thunder Mountain Railroad, and the Haunted Mansion. Fantasyland is located directly behind Cinderella Castle—in the castle's courtyard, as it were. Mickey's Starland is set off the upper right-hand corner (that's northeast, for geography buffs) of Fantasyland. And Tomorrowland, directly to the right of the Hub, rounds out the circle.

Main Street

With its pastel Victorian buildings, antique automobiles oohga-oohga-ing as they stop to offer you a lift, sparkling sidewalks, and atmosphere of what one writer has called "almost hysterical joy," Main Street is more than a mere conduit to the other enchantments of the Magic Kingdom. It is where the spell is first cast.

Like Dorothy waking up in a technicolor Oz or Mary Poppins jumping through the pavement painting, you emerge from the tunnel beneath the Walt Disney World Railroad Station into a realization of one of the most tenacious American dreams. The perfect street in the perfect small town in a perfect moment of time is burnished to jewellike quality thanks to a ⅝-scale reduction, nightly cleanings with a fire hose, and constant repainting; neither life-size nor so small as to appear toylike, the carefully calculated size is meant to make you feel as though you're looking through a telescope into another world.

Everyone's always happy in this world, their spirits kept sunny thanks to outpourings of music: Dixieland jazz, barbershop quartets, brass-band parades, and scores of Disney films and American musicals played over loudspeakers. Old-fashioned horse-drawn trams and omnibuses—horns a-tootle—chug along the street. Street vendors in Victorian-era costumes sell balloons and popcorn. And to complete the illusion of the perfect dream, Cinderella Castle floats at the end of Main Street: the Holy Grail that is for once within reach.

❶ On your left as you enter Town Square is **City Hall,** information central, and opposite, in the bright yellow, Victorian gingerbread building **❷** that used to house the Walt Disney Story, is the home of **Disneyana Collectibles,** a trivia buff's delight of animation art and other memorabilia.

30

The Magic Kingdom

Fort Sam Clemens

Rivers of America

WDW Railroad Frontierland Depot

Columbia Harbour House

Aunt Polly's Landing

FRONTIERLAND

LIBERTY SQUARE

Liberty Tree Tavern

Caribbean Plaza

Adventureland Bazaar

Crystal Palace

First Aid Station

ADVENTURELAND

Automatic Tellers

Newsstand

Monorail

N

KEY

🍴 Restaurants

🚻 Restrooms

—— Rail Line

••••• Skyride

—••— Monorail

FANTASYLAND

Fantasy Faire

Skyway

25

21

28

26

27

King Stefan's

20

Cinderella Castle

Castle Forecourt Stage

Central Plaza

Plaza Restaurant

Mickey's Hollywood Theatre

WDW Railroad Mickey's Starland Depot

30

Grandma Duck's Farm

Skyway

37

TOMORROWLAND

33

31 32

34

35

38

39

36

Tomorrowland Theatre

MAIN STREET U.S.A.

5

4

Emporium

Kodak Camera Center

Town Square

2

Tony's Town Square Café

3

Lockers

Stroller Shop

Entrance Turnstiles

Guest Relations

Seven Seas Lagoon

Ferry Landing

Although attractions with a capital "A" are minimal on Main Street, there are plenty of inducements to spend more than the 40 minutes most visitors usually take. The stores that most of the structures contain range from the **House of Magic,** complete with trick-showing proprietors; to the **Harmony Barber Shop,** where you can have yourself shorn; to a milliner's emporium stocking Cat-in-the-Hat fantasies; to all sorts of snacks and souvenirs. (If the weather looks threatening, head for the **Emporium** to purchase those signature mouse-eared umbrellas and bright yellow ponchos with Mickey emblazoned on the back.) The best time to shop is midafternoon, when the lines at the rides resemble a malevolent anaconda taking a nap. During the afternoon parade, store clerks have actually been seen twiddling their thumbs; if you're looking for a hard-to-find item, this is the time to ask for sales assistance. If you go at the end of the day, you'll be engulfed by the rush-hour crowds.

Main Street is also full of in-jokes for those in the know. For instance, check out the proprietors' names above the shops: Crystal Arts honors Roy Disney, Walt's brother; the Shadow Box—nod, nod, wink, wink—is the domain of Dick Nunis, chairman of Walt Disney Attractions; at the House of Magic, Card Walker—the "Practioner of Psychiatry and Justice of the Peace"—is the company's former chairman of the Executive Committee. At last glance, today's Head Mouseketeer, Michael Eisner, still doesn't have his own shop.

3 Step right up to the elevated platform above the Magic Kingdom's entrance for a ride on living history, the **Walt Disney World Railroad.** Walt Disney was a railroad buff of the highest order—he constructed a ⅛-scale train in his backyard and named it *Lilly Belle,* after his wife. Another *Lilly Belle* rides the rails here, as do *Walter E. Disney, Roy O. Disney* (named for Walt's brother), and *Roger Broggie* (named for a Disney Imagineer and fellow railroad aficionado). All the locomotives date from 1928, coincidentally the same age as Mickey Mouse. Disney scouts tracked them down in Mexico, where they were used to haul sugarcane in the Yucatán, brought them back, and completely overhauled them to their present splendor. And splendid they are, with their striped awnings, brightly painted benches, authoritative "choo-choo," and hissing plume of steam. They are also quite useful. Their 1½-mile track runs along the perimeter of the Magic Kingdom, through the woods and past Tom Sawyer Island and other attractions; stops are in Frontierland and Mickey's Starland. It's a great introduction to the layout of the park and a much-welcome relief for tired feet and dragging legs. The four trains run at five- to seven-minute intervals. *Duration: 21 min. Crowds: Can be substantial beginning in late morning through late afternoon. Strategy: Go in midafternoon if you don't see a line; otherwise, skip on a first-time visit. Audience: All ages. Rating:* ★

4 Six screens run continuous vintage Disney cartoons in the cool, air-conditioned quiet of the **Main Street Cinema,** halfway up Main Street on the right. It's a great opportunity to see the genius of Walt Disney and to meet the endearing little mouse that brought Disney so much fame. *Steamboat Willie,* the first sound cartoon, was also the first chance America had to meet Mickey Mouse, who, in his silver-screen debut, meets Minnie and is inspired to serenade her by using a cow's udder. Disney said that he loved his creation more than any woman (one wonders how Lilly Belle felt about this, especially since it was she who convinced her husband to change the character's name from Mortimer). Standing room only and the lure of other attractions farther inside the park keep Main Street Cinema from ever being too crowded, and in fact you can sit on the raised platform in the center of the screening room and still see all the films—all of them silents, without dialogue, screened with organ music. *Duration: Stay as long as you like. Crowds: Negligible. Strategy: A refuge on hot, crowded afternoons. Audience: All ages. Rating:* ★★

Electronic-games rooms are de rigueur, it seems, at most theme parks, and even the Magic Kingdom is not immune. Located on the left side **⑤** of Main Street, just before you reach Central Plaza, the **Penny Arcade** is nonetheless a game room with history. Sure, there are a few contemporary quarter-eaters, but most are the sort of amusements that parents in *The Music Man* would have worried about if they hadn't been so concerned about the dangers of pool. There are manual Mute-o-scopes and their automatic successors, Cail-o-scopes, an early version of a moving picture in which images are drawn on a stack of cards that is quickly flipped to animate the image. (Interestingly, the Disney animation department produces its films based on the same principle.) Most of the short stories are slapstick comedy, of the sort later popularized by Mack Sennet and his Keystone Kops: In "Yes, We Have No Bananas," a suitor slips on a fateful banana peel; "Oh Teacher" describes the antics of a teacher's pet; and "Expecting" details the trials and tribulations of people waiting in line—something you should expect to do a lot of during the course of a visit. There are also several fortune-telling machines with marionette-like seers—the type that got Tom Hanks into such *Big* trouble. *Duration: Up to you. Crowds: Moderate but seldom oppressive except at parade time. Strategy: A good place to while away the busy part of a day, but bring a pocketful of change. Audience: All ages. Rating:* ★★

Adventureland

From the scrubbed brick, manicured lawns, and meticulously pruned trees of the Central Plaza, an artfully dilapidated wooden bridge leads to Adventureland, Disney's version of jungle fever. The landscape artists went wild here: South African Cape honeysuckle droops, Brazilian bougainvillea drapes, Mexican flame vines cling, spider plants clone, and three different varieties of palm trees sway, all creating a seemingly spontaneous mess. The bright, all-American, singalong tunes that fill the air along Main Street and Central Plaza are replaced by the recorded repetitions of trumpeting elephants, pounding drums, and squawking parrots. The architecture is an eclectic mishmash of the best of Thailand, the Caribbean, Africa, and Polynesia, arranged in an inspired disorder that recalls comic-book fantasies of far-off places. The message is that though the natives may be restless, the kids are all right.

Adventureland surrounds its own oblong central plaza. To the right as you cross the bridge is the **Adventureland Bazaar,** whose six shops have names like Bwana Bob's, Traders of Timbuktu, Zanzibar Shell Company, and Elephant Tales; they sell exotic—and generally quite affordable—safari-theme clothing, sharks'-teeth jewelry, elephant-hair bracelets, and other trinkets from the erstwhile Dark Continent as well as a menagerie's worth of life-size tropical critters. To the left are the spreading branches of the Swiss Family Robinson's banyan tree. Continuing around the plaza are the entrances to the Jungle Cruise, the Pirates of the Caribbean, and the Polynesian greathouse containing the Enchanted Tiki Birds.

In the far end of the plaza is another conglomeration of shops, the **Caribbean Plaza,** selling treasures inspired by the Pirates of the Caribbean: tropical clothing, costume jewelry (how about some pineapple earrings?), pirates' swords, hats embroidered with skull and crossbones, and in a surprising lapse in kitsch, delicate crystal and blown glass. (Be advised that many of these crystal items are also for sale in the King's Gallery inside the archway of Cinderella Castle.) At **Lafitte's Portrait Deck,** you can stick your head through a pirate cutout and bring home a picture of yourself as the Scourge of the Spanish Main.

6 Few New York City apartments can boast the light, the airiness, the number of rooms, and all the services of the **Swiss Family Treehouse,** the first attraction on your left (the camouflaged entrance is *way* over to the left). In fact, the only thing lacking is an elevator. Based on the classic novel by Johann Wyss about the adventures of a family shipwrecked on the way to America, the treehouse shows what you can do with a big banyan and a lot of imagination. The rooms are furnished with patchwork quilts and mahogany furniture. Disney detail abounds: The kitchen sink is made of a giant clamshell; the boys' room, strewn with clothing, has two hammocks instead of beds; and an ingenious system of rain barrels and bamboo pipes provides running water in every room (German visitors seem especially fascinated by this). Small wonder that in the 1960 film, when offered the chance to leave their island, all but one Robinson decided to stay on. As you clamber around the narrow wooden steps and rope bridges that connect the rooms in this split-level dwelling, take a look at the Spanish moss. It is real, but the tree itself— some 90 feet in diameter, with more than 600 branches—was constructed by the props department. The 800,000 leaves are made of vinyl and cost $1 per leaf in the early 1970s. It all adds up to a species of tree unofficially called *Disneyodendron eximus,* or "out-of-the-ordinary Disney tree." *Duration: Up to you. Crowds: Artfully camouflaged so you may not see them—and the lines move slowly. Strategy: Go first thing in the morning or after dark. Audience: All ages; toddlers unsteady on their feet may have trouble with the stairs. Rating:* ★★

7 Register your geographical switch from the Caribbean to the jungle by playing bongo drums on the grinning fetish statues that separate the Robinsons' idyllic condo and the **Jungle Cruise.** During this ride, you cruise through three continents and along four rivers: the Congo, the Nile, the Mekong, and the Amazon. The canopied launches pack in visitors tighter than sardines, the safari-suited guides make a point of checking their pistols, and the *Irrawady Irma* or *Mongala Millie* is off for another "perilous" journey. The guide's spiel is surprisingly funny, with just the right blend of cornball humor and the gently snide; unfortunately, some guides' tendencies to imitate the unintelligible Chuck Yeager drawl patented by airline pilots is all too successful, and you can't understand half of what they're saying. Nitpicking aside, you'll encounter animals of the African veldt, elephants bathing, slinky pythons, an irritated rhinoceros, a bunch of hyperactive hippos (good thing the guide's got a pop pistol), and a tribe of hungry headhunters. Then there's Old Smily, the crocodile, who's always waiting for a handout—or, as the guide quips, "a foot out." Kids who might be terrified by the Pirates of the Caribbean will love this ride, and adults love the patter and all the detail (listen for what's playing on the radio of the overturned Jeep). *Duration: 10 min. Crowds: Huge, from late morning until supper time. Strategy: Go first thing in the morning or during the daily parade, but not after dark—you'll miss a lot. Audience: All ages. Rating:* ★★★

TIME OUT Among the fast munchies here, some of the best are the fresh pineapple spears at Adventureland's **Aloha Isle.**

8 "Avast, ye scurvy scum!" is the sort of greeting your kids will proclaim for the next week—which gives you an idea of the impact of the stellar **Pirates of the Caribbean.** This boat ride is Disney at its best: memorable vignettes, incredible detail, a gripping story, and catchy music whose relentless "Yo-Ho!"-ing can only be eradicated by "It's a Small World."

The gracious arched entrance soon gives way to a dusty dungeon, redolent of damp and of a spooky, scary past. Lanterns flicker as you board the boats and a ghostly voice intones, "Dead men tell no tales." (Usually, at this point, a much higher, younger voice quavers, "Mommy, can we get off?") A deserted beach, strewn with shovels, a skeleton, and a disintegrating map indicating buried treasure, is the preface to this story of greed, lust, and destruction.

Emerging from a pitch-black time tunnel, you're literally in the middle of a furious battle. A pirate ship, cannons blazing, is attacking a stone fortress. Cannonballs splash into the water just off your bows, and Audio-Animatronic pirates hoist the Jolly Roger while brave soldiers scurry to defend the fort—to no avail. Politically correct nerves may twinge as the women of the town are rounded up and auctioned. "Strike your colors, ye brazen wench, no need to expose your superstructure!" shouts one pirate, but the scene is terrific: pirates chasing chickens, ducking the town mayor in the well, and collapsing into a snoring stupor with a couple of pigs. Check out the hairy legs of the two carousers straddling the wall. The wild antics of the pirates result in a conflagration, the town goes up in flames, and all go to their just reward amid a chorus of "Yo-ho! Yo-ho! A pirate's life for me." There's a moral in there somewhere, if you want to look for one—or you can just enjoy the show. *Duration: 10 min. Crowds: Waits seldom exceed 30 min, despite the ride's popularity. Strategy: A good destination even during the busy afternoon hours. Audience: All ages. Rating:* ★★

Don't expect much when your preshow host is a mechanical toucan called Claude Birdbrain. Inside the blessedly air-conditioned Polynesian longhouse that houses the **Enchanted Tiki Birds,** the avian intelligence quotient doesn't improve markedly, and ethnic stereotyping runs rampant. Four parrots run the joint—Pierre, José, Fritz, and Michael (the Irish one—need we add that his plumage is green?)—each of which has an appropriately ethnic accent. "Tropical Serenade" is sung and whistled by hundreds of Audio-Animatronic figures: exotic birds, swaying flowers, and Tiki god statues with blinking red eyes. Toddlers love the repetition of the song "In the Tiki, Tiki, Tiki, Tiki, Tiki Room." Older folks tend to roll their eyes along with the statues. This was Disney's first Audio-Animatronic attraction and the animatronics still hold up fine, but the audio could use an update. *Duration: 17 min. Crowds: Waits seldom exceed 30 min. Strategy: Go when you need to sit in an air-conditioned room. Audience: All ages. Rating:* ★

From Adventureland, you can go on to Frontierland or to Liberty Square. For the latter, continue around to the left as you exit the Tiki House, into the passageway between the Sunshine Tree Terrace and the Tiki Tropic shop. For Frontierland—and a shortcut to Splash Mountain—look for the rest rooms in the Caribbean Plaza as you exit the Pirates of the Caribbean. They open onto a tiled arcade that divides the two lands. Note, however, that rest room patrons get easily confused upon exiting and end up in the wrong land. In other words, this is a prime place to misplace your children or your partner, so station someone *right* outside the rest rooms in the arcade to keep watch.

Frontierland

Frontierland, in the northwest quadrant of the Magic Kingdom, invokes the American frontier. The period seems to be the latter half of the 19th century, and the West is being won by Disney staffers dressed in checked shirts, leather vests, cowboy hats, and brightly colored neck-erchiefs. Banjo and fiddle music twang from tree to tree.

The screams that periodically drown out the string-sawing are not the result of a cowboy surprising an Indian. They come from one of the Magic Kingdom's big guns, Splash Mountain, an elaborate water flume. Opened in October 1992, it quickly eclipsed all the other attractions in popularity. Big Thunder Mountain Railroad, one of the park's two roller coasters, also gives vocal cords a workout. Other Frontierland attractions are somewhat tamer: Tom Sawyer Island, an enormous landscaped playground perfect for games of hide-and-go-seek; the Frontierland Shooting Arcade, an electronic shooting arcade that pleases even the sulkiest adolescent; and two musical revues—the Country Bear Jamboree and the Diamond Horseshoe Jamboree.

The rust-red rock spires of Thunder Mountain and Splash Mountain serve as local landmarks and set a landscaping tone best described as "Arid, Extra Dry." In contrast to the lush vegetation of Adventureland, Frontierland is planted with mesquite, twisted Peruvian pepper trees, slash pines, and many varieties of cactus. The unpainted buildings and wooden sidewalks have a ramshackle quality, and even though you know that no dust is allowed in Walt Disney World, the setting evokes dusty thoughts.

Shops and eateries are along the avenue bordering the southern curve of a lake that, because it variously represents the Mississippi and Missouri rivers and their tributaries, is called Rivers of America. (It still looks like a lake.) Emporia here are generally referred to as "posts," as in the Frontierland Trading Post and Prairie Outpost, which sell sheriff badges, leatherwork, cowboy hats, and southwestern, Indian, and Mexican crafts. Then there's Big Al's, for genuine Davy Crockett coonskin hats. Yee-haw!

The Walt Disney World Railroad makes a stop at Frontierland. It tunnels through Splash Mountain and drops you off between Splash Mountain and Thunder Mountain.

⑩ At Rope Drop, the hordes hoof it to **Splash Mountain.** Based on the animated sequences in Disney's 1946 film *Song of the South,* it features Audio-Animatronic creations of Brer Rabbit, Brer Bear, Brer Fox, and a menagerie of Brer beasts (including Brer Frog and a Heckle-and-Jeckle duo of Brer Crows). No matter what time you get there, you *will*, repeat, *will* wait in line. So the Disney folks have made the waiting area here as entertaining and comfortable as possible, with lots of large shade trees, little critters in tiny houses, and toe-tappin' country music wafting from speakers hidden in rocks. When you finally do settle into the eight-person hollowed-out logs, Uncle Remus's voice growls, "Mark mah words, Brer Rabbit gonna put his foot in Brer Fox's mouth one of these days." And this just might be the day.

As the boat carries you through a lily pond (just bopping with Brer Frogs merrily singing the ride's theme song, "Time to Be Moving Along") past signs for Brer Fox's lair and Brer Bear's den, Brer Rabbit's silhouette hops along in front, always just ahead of you. Every time some critter makes a grab for the bunny, the log boats drop out of reach. But Brer Fox has been studying his book *How to Catch a Rabbit,* and our lop-eared friend looks as if he's destined for the pot. Things don't look so good for the flumers either, as the boats creak up and up the mountain, past a pair of pessimistic crows. You get one heart-stopping pause at the top—just long enough to grab the safety bar—and then the boat plummets down the world's longest and sharpest flume drop right into a gigantic briar patch. (In case you want to know what you're getting into, the drop is 52½ feet tall—that's about five stories—at a 45-degree angle, enough to reach speeds of 40 miles per hour and make you feel weightless.) From the boat—especially if you are in the front seat—it looks truly as if you are going to be impaled on those enormous spikes. Try to smile through your clenched teeth: As you begin to drop, a flash-bulb pops, so you can purchase a photographic memento of the experience before exiting the ride. Brer Rabbit escapes—and so do you, wet and exhilarated—to the tune of "Zip-a-Dee-Doo-Dah," whose bouncy melody has become something of a Disney theme song. If you want to get really wet—and you will get splashed from almost every seat—ask the ride attendant to seat you in the front row.

Knowing how much we all like to watch people getting the pants scared off them, Disney constructed the flume so that spectators can see the plunge into the briar patch from the footbridge between Splash Mountain and Thunder Mountain. In an especially neat touch, it looks as if the log boats disappear into the pond below the briar patch with a giant splash—leaving only bubbles in their wake. *Duration: 11 min. Crowds: Yes! Strategy: If you're not in line by 9:45, your only hope is during meals or a parade. Audience: All except very young children. No pregnant women or guests wearing back, neck, or leg braces; minimum height 44". Rating:* ★★★

Now that your blood is up, scoot across the footbridge to another classic Disney ride, **Big Thunder Mountain Railroad.** As any true roller-coaster lover can tell you, this three-minute ride is a tame one; despite the posted warnings, you won't stagger off, you won't throw up, and you won't vow never to subject yourself to the experience again. The thrills are there, however, thanks to the intricate details and stunning scenery along every inch of the 2,780-foot-long wooden track.

Set in gold-rush days, the runaway train rushes and rattles past 20 Audio-Animatronic figures—including donkeys, chickens, a goat, and a grizzled old miner surprised in his bathtub—$300,000 of genuine antique mining equipment, tumbleweeds, a derelict mining town, hot springs, and a flash flood.

The ride was 15 years in the planning and took two years and close to $17 million to build (a price tag that, give or take a few million, equaled the entire cost of California's Disneyland in 1955). The 197-foot mountain is based on the monoliths of Utah's Monument Valley, and thanks to 650 tons of steel, 4,675 tons of cement, and 16,000 gallons of paint, it closely resembles the real thing. *Duration: 4 min. Crowds: Large. Strategy: Thunder Mountaineers swear that the ride is even better at night, when you can't anticipate the curves and the track's rattling sounds as if something's about to give. But then you'd miss the scenic details. The solution—go twice. Audience: All except young children. No pregnant women or guests wearing back, neck, or leg braces; minimum height 40". Rating:* ★★★

Head back across the footbridge past Splash Mountain, and bear left along Frontierland's main drag to the landing stage for the rafts to **Tom Sawyer Island.** (These rafts are not to be confused with the Mike Fink Keel Boats or the Liberty Square Riverboat, both of which also ply Rivers of America but dock in Liberty Square.)

An artfully misspelled sign, signed by Tom Sawyer, conveys the island's attractions: "If'n you like dark caves, mystry mines, bottomless pits, shacky bridges 'n' big rocks, you have came to the best place I know." Aunt Polly would have walloped Tom for his orthography, but she couldn't have argued with the truth. The 6-mile-long island—actually two islands connected by an old-fashioned swing bridge—is a natural playground, all hills and trees and rocks and shrubs. Other guidebooks suggest that parents sit this one out on the porch of Aunt Polly's Landing, sipping lemonade; we say, why let the kids have all the fun?

Most of the attractions are on the main island, where the boats dock and where Aunt Polly's Landing and the rest rooms are. These include the mystery cave, a pitch-black (almost) labyrinth where the wind wails in a truly spooky fashion; Injun Joe's cave, all pointy stalactites and stalagmites and endowed with lots of columns and crevices from which to jump out and startle younger sisters and brothers; Harper's Mill, an old-fashioned grist mill (nothing scary here); and, in a clearing at the top of the hill, a rustic playground. As you explore the shoreline on the dirt paths, keep an eye out for the barrel bridge—every time someone takes a step, the whole contraption bounces.

On the other island is Fort Sam Clemens, a log fortress from which you can fire air guns (with great booms and cracks) at the soporific passengers on the Liberty Square Riverboat. It's guarded by an equally soporific Audio-Animatronic sentry, loudly snoring off his last bender. Both islands are sprinkled with lookouts for great views to Thunder Mountain and Frontierland, as well as nice natural niches—often furnished with benches and water fountains. *Duration: Up to you. Crowds: Seldom overwhelming, but it wouldn't matter—here, the more the merrier. Strategy: Try it as a refreshing afternoon getaway. Audience: All ages. Rating:* ★★

Back on the main street, a row of barns, false-fronted buildings, and other structures straight out of Dodge City house shops, eateries, and
⓭ two theaters. The first one on your right is home to the **Country Bear Jamboree,** a stage show in which wisecracking, cornpone Audio-Animatronic bears joke, sing, and play country music and 1950s rock and roll. The show stars Henry, the massive but debonair master of ceremonies; the robust Trixie, the Tampa Temptation, who laments a love lost while perched in a swing suspended from the ceiling; Bubbles, Bunny, and Beulah, harmonizing on "All the Guys That Turn Me Down Turn Me On"; and Big Al, a cult figure who has inspired postcards, stuffed animals, and his own shop next door. *Duration: 16 min. Crowds: Large, considering the relatively small theater. Strategy: Visit before 11 AM, during the daily parade, or after most small children have left for the day. Stand to the far left in the anteroom where you wait to end up in the front rows; to the far right if you want to sit in the last row, where small children can perch on top of the seats to see better. Audience: All ages. Rating:* ★★★

⓮ The **Frontierland Shootin' Arcade** is a classic shooting arcade but with laser beams subbing for bullets and an 1850s frontier-town theme. Genuine Hawkins 54-caliber buffalo rifles have been refitted to emit electronic beams. When they strike, tombstones spin and epitaphs change, ghost riders gallop out of clouds, and skulls pop out of graves, accompanied by the sounds of howling coyotes, creaking bridges, and the cracks of the rifles blasted over the digital audio system. *Cost: 25¢ per 5 shots. Strategy: Bring a pocketful of change. Audience: Older children and adults. Rating:* ★★

"Knock, knock." "Who's there?" "Ya." "Ya who?" "Yaaahooo!" And they're off, with another riproaring, raucous, corny, nonstop,
⓯ high-kicking, elbow-jabbing, song-and-dance-and-fiddling **Diamond Horseshoe Jamboree,** staged in a re-creation of an Old West saloon. The show features a sextet of dance-hall girls and high-spirited cow-

boys; Sam, the stagestruck and lovelorn saloon keeper; and Lily, a shimmying, feather-boa-toting reincarnation of Mae West, whose throaty version of "A Good Man Is Hard to Find" brings down the house. (At other times, Lily switches around the hall, tickling noses with her boa and uttering such lines as "Watch it, honey, this is Frontierland, not Fantasyland!") The cowboys leap from the balconies and swing around columns, Lily's Girls perform an exuberant cancan, and everyone has a hand-clapping good time. Seating begins half an hour before curtain time, and snacks and light refreshments may be purchased at your table. *Showtimes: 10:45, 12:15, 1:45, 3:30, and 4:45; reservations essential. Duration: 30 min. Crowds: Full house for most performances. Strategy: Book in early morning at Disneyana Collectibles (12:15 show fills up first) or show up 30 min before showtime to wait for cancellations. But give it a miss if you're on a tight schedule and have plans to see the Hoop-Dee-Doo Revue in Fort Wilderness. Audience: All except young children. Rating:* ★★

Liberty Square

The weathered siding gives way to neat clapboard and solid brick, the mesquite and cactus are replaced by stately oaks and masses of azalea, and the rough-and-tumble western frontier gently slides into Colonial America. Liberty Square picks up where Frontierland leaves off, continuing around the western shore of Rivers of America and forming the eastern boundary of Fantasyland.

The theme is Colonial history, which northerners will be happy to learn is solid Yankee. The small buildings, topped with weather vanes and exuding comfortable prosperity from every rosy brick and every spiffy shutter, are pure New England, and in a delightful literary wink, the silversmith shop lists as its proprietor J. Tremaine (hero of the Esther Forbes novel about the Revolutionary War that's required reading in most junior high schools). There's even a **Liberty Tree,** a 130-year-old live oak actually found on Walt Disney World property and moved to the Magic Kingdom. Just as the Sons of Liberty hung lanterns on trees as a signal of solidarity after the Boston Tea Party, the Liberty Tree's branches are decorated with 13 lanterns representing the 13 original colonies.

After the crowds in Frontierland, Liberty Square seems relaxed and peaceful—perhaps because its attractions tend to be sedentary. There's the Hall of Presidents, an Audio-Animatronic view of the history of the United States; Mike Fink Keel Boats and Liberty Square Riverboat—two ways to waste time on the Rivers of America; and the Haunted Mansion, Disney's ne plus ultra spook show. The shops in this area tend to sell more arts than kitsch; in addition to the silversmith shop, there's Olde World Antiques's one-of-a-kind objects and reproductions as well as custom-blended perfumes; the Yankee Trader's gourmet food and cooking items; the Silhouette Cart's profiles, hand-cut and framed while you wait; and the Umbrella Cart, whose personalized products are sure to come in handy during the daily summer afternoon thundershower. There are plenty of tree-shaded tables for picnicking and plenty of carts and fast-food eateries supplying the goods. Liberty Tree Tavern, a gracious, table-service restaurant that could have been airlifted from Colonial Williamsburg, is one of the best at the Magic Kingdom; reservations are essential.

Disney could probably patent its winning combination of movie and computerized robots and sound-and-light show, for Disney invented it, refined it, and has kept it state-of-the-art. The **Hall of Presidents,** a multimedia tribute to the Constitution, caused quite a sensation when it opened, because it was here that the first refinements of the Audio-

Animatronic system could be seen. Now surpassed by Epcot Center's American Adventure, it's still well worth attending, as much for the two-part show as for the spacious, air-conditioned theater.

It starts with a film, narrated by writer Maya Angelou, that discusses the Constitution as the codification of the spirit that founded America. Visitors learn about threats to the document, ranging from the 18th-century Whiskey Rebellion to the Civil War, and hear such famous speeches as Benjamin Franklin's plea to Continental Congress delegates to ratify it and Abraham Lincoln's fear that "a house divided cannot stand." The shows conveying Disney's brand of patriotism may be ponderous, but they're always well researched and lovingly presented; this film, for instance, was revamped in 1994 to replace a lingering subtext of Cold War paranoia with the more progressive assertion that our democracy is a work in progress, that liberty and justice still do not figure equally in the lives of all Americans.

The second half is a roll call of all 42 U.S. presidents. Each chief executive rises and responds with a nod—even those who blatantly attempted to subvert the Constitution. The detail is lifelike, right down to the brace on Franklin Delano Roosevelt's leg. And because Disney humor will out, the robots can't resist nodding, fidgeting, and even whispering to each other while waiting for their names to come up. The last to be called is Bill Clinton, who, unlike other contemporary presidential robots, has a speaking part. Audio-Animatronic Clinton's speech was written for Disney by *Lion King* lyricist Tim Rice (he of *Jesus Christ Superstar* and *Evita*) in collaboration with the President's chief speechwriter; the audio was provided—in one take—by human Bill Clinton himself. *Duration: 30 min. Crowds: Usually moderate. Strategy: Go in the afternoon, when you'll appreciate the air-conditioning. Audience: Older children and adults. Rating:* ★★

TIME OUT   **Liberty Square Market** carts sell fresh fruit—a welcome change from the Magic Kingdom's ubiquitous french fries and burgers.

A real old-fashioned steamboat, the *Richard F. Irvine* (named for a key Disney designer) is authentic, from its calliope whistle and the gingerbread trim on its three decks to the boilers that produce the steam that drives

17 the big rear paddlewheel. In fact, this **Liberty Square Riverboat** misses authenticity on only one count: There's no mustachioed captain to guide it during the ride around the Rivers of America. That task is taken care of by an underwater rail. The trip is slow and not thrilling, except, perhaps, to the kids getting shot at by their counterparts at Fort Sam Clemens on Tom Sawyer Island. But it's a relaxing break for all concerned, and some lucky parents can take a load off on the few chairs scattered around the upper deck while their offspring explore the boat. *Duration: 15 min. Crowds: Moderate, but capacity is high so waits are seldom trying. Strategy: Go when you need a break from the crowds. Audience: All ages. Rating:* ★

18 The **Mike Fink Keel Boats,** plying the same waters as the Liberty Square Riverboat, are short and dumpy and you have to sit on a bench, wedged tightly between fellow visitors, and listen to a heavy-handed, noisy spiel about those roistering, roustabout days along the Missouri. And the Tom Sawyer Island crowd doesn't even bother to shoot you. Just for that we're going to tell you the answer to the guide's extraordinarily lackluster joke: "Firewood." So there—make our day. *Duration: 10–15 min. Crowds: Lines move slowly because of boats' low passenger capacity. Strategy: Skip this on your first visit. Audience: All ages. Rating:* ★

⑲ The repository of special effects known as the **Haunted Mansion** is a howl. Or do we mean a scream? You are greeted at the creaking iron gates of this Hudson Gothic mansion by a lugubrious attendant (this must be the only job at Walt Disney World for which smiling is frowned upon, except, of course, for the occasional sinister smirk) and ushered into a spooky picture gallery. A disembodied voice echoes from the walls: "Welcome, foolish mortals, to the Haunted Mansion. I am your ghost host." A scream shivers down and you're off on one of the best attractions at Walt Disney World.

Part walk-through, part ride on a "doom buggie," the Haunted Mansion is scary but not terrifying, and the special effects are phenomenal. Catch the glowing bats' eyes on the wallpaper—a riveting twist in interior decorating; the suit of armor that comes alive; the shifting walls in the portrait gallery (are they moving up or are you moving down?); the strategically placed gusts of damp, cold air; the marble busts of the world's greatest ghost writers in the library; the wacky inscriptions on the tombstones as you wait in line; the spectral xylophone player who enlivens the graveyard shift with bones instead of mallets; and, of course, the chattering head of the woman in the crystal ball (psst, she's a hologram). Just when you think the Imagineers have exhausted their bag of ectoplasmic tricks, along comes another one. They've saved the best for last, as you suddenly discover that your doom buggie has gained an extra passenger. As you approach the exit, your ghoulish guide intones, "Now I will raise the safety bar and the ghost will follow you home." Thanks for the souvenir, pal.

An interesting piece of Disney trivia: One of the biggest jobs for the maintenance crew here is not cleaning up but keeping the 200-odd trunks, chairs, harps, dress forms, statues, rugs, and other knickknacks appropriately dusty. Disney buys its dust in 5-pound bags and scatters it throughout the mansion from a special gadget resembling a fertilizer spreader. According to local lore, enough dust has been dumped since the park's 1971 opening to completely bury the mansion. Where does it all go? Perhaps the voice is right in saying that something will follow you home. *Duration: 8 min. Crowds: Substantial, but high capacity and fast loading usually keep lines moving. Strategy: Go early, late, or during the nighttime parade; at any other time, check line and go back later if it's long. Audience: All except young children, who may be frightened. Rating:* ★★★

Photographers will want to take advantage of one of the least-traveled byways in the Magic Kingdom. Just before exiting Liberty Square, turn left at the Sleepy Hollow snack shop. Just past the outdoor tables you'll find a shortcut to Fantasyland that provides about the best unobstructed ground-level view of Cinderella Castle. It's a great spot for a family photo.

Fantasyland

You know you're in Fantasyland because the rest rooms are designated "Prince" and "Princess." And even though the thrones are plebeian and the crowds pedestrian, you can't help feeling special in this area. Walt Disney called this "a timeless land of enchantment," and Fantasyland does have the aura of having been sprinkled with pixie dust. Perhaps that's because Fantasyland's fanciful gingerbread houses, gleaming gold turrets, and, of course, its rides based on Disney-animated movies are what the Magic Kingdom is all about.

With the exception of the slightly spooky Snow White's Adventures and Mr. Toad's Wild Ride, the attractions here are imaginative rather than thrilling. Like the animated classics on which they are based, rides that could ostensibly be classified as kiddie rides are, in fact, packed with enough delightful detail to engage adults. While the kids are awed by the bigger picture, their parents are amused by the road signs at Mr. Toad's Wild Ride or enchanted by the view of moonlit London in Peter Pan's Flight.

You can enter Fantasyland on foot from Frontierland or by skyway from Tomorrowland, but the classic introduction is through the Cinderella Castle. To set yourself up for the magic—and to provide yourself with a cooling break—turn left immediately after you exit the castle's archway. Here you'll find one of the most charming and most overlooked touches in Fantasyland: Cinderella Fountain, a lovely brass casting of the castle's namesake, who's dressed in her peasant togs and surrounded by her beloved mice and bird friends. Water splashing from the fountain provides a cooling sensation on a hot day—as do the very welcome brass drinking fountains at the statue's base. Don't forget to toss in a coin and make a wish; after all, you're in Fantasyland, where dreams do come true. Straight ahead from the castle you'll find Cinderella's Golden Carrousel. The land's other attractions are arranged around it in a somewhat bulging circle.

Fantasyland is always the most heavily trafficked area in the park, and its rides are almost always crowded. Luckily, its rides sometimes open early for guests at WDW-owned resorts. Or you can take your chances during the afternoon parade. Visitors without children should save Fantasyland for evening, when a sizable number of the little ones will have departed for their own private dreamland.

㉒ The royal blue turrets, gold spires, and glistening white towers of the **Cinderella Castle** are every child's fairy-tale castle come true. It was inspired by the castle built by the mad Bavarian king Ludwig at Neuschwanstein as well as by drawings prepared for Disney's animated film of the classic French fairy tale. Although often confused with Disneyland's Sleeping Beauty Castle, at 180 feet this castle is more than 100 feet taller, and with its elongated towers and lacy fretwork, it is immeasurably more graceful. It's easy to bypass the elaborate murals on the walls of the archway as you rush toward Fantasyland, but they are worth a stop. The five panels, measuring some 15 feet high and 10 feet wide, were created by Disney artist Dorothea Redmond and realized in a million bits of multicolored Italian glass, real silver, and 14-karat gold by mosaicist Hanns-Joachim Scharff. Following the images drawn for the Disney film, the mosaics tell the story of the little cinder girl from pumpkin to prince and happily ever after.

The fantasy has feet, if not of clay, then of solid steel beams, fiberglass, and 500 gallons of paint. Instead of dungeons, there are service tunnels for the Magic Kingdom's less-than-magical quotidian operations (the same tunnels that honeycomb the ground under much of the park). And upstairs does not hold, as rumor has it, a casket containing the cryogenically preserved body of Walt Disney but instead mundane broadcast facilities, security rooms, and the like.

Within the castle's archway, on the left as you face Fantasyland, is the **King's Gallery,** one of the Magic Kingdom's finest (and priciest) shops. Here you'll find exquisite hand-painted models of carousel horses, delicate crystal castles, and other symbols of fairy-tale magic, including Cinderella's glass slipper in a variety of colors and sizes.

㉑ The whirling, musical heart of Fantasyland—and maybe even of the entire Magic Kingdom—the antique **Cinderella's Golden Carrousel** encapsulates the Disney experience in 90 prancing horses and then hands it to you on a 60-foot platter. Seventy-two of the dashing steeds date from the original carousel built in 1917 by the Philadelphia Toboggan Company; 12 additional mounts were made of fiberglass. All are meticulously painted—at a rate of about 48 hours per horse—and like real horses, each one is completely different. One steed sports a collar of bright yellow roses, another a quiver of Indian arrows, and yet another, for some completely mysterious reason, a portrait of Eric the Red. They gallop ceaselessly beneath a wooden canopy, gaily striped on the outside and muraled on the inside with 18 panels depicting scenes from Disney's 1950 film *Cinderella*. As the platter starts to spin, the mirrors sparkle, the fairy lights glitter, and the rich notes of the band organ— no calliope here—play favorite tunes from Disney movies. If you wished upon a star, it couldn't get more magical than this. *Duration: 2 min. Crowds: Lines during busy periods. Strategy: Go early, during the daily parade, or in the evening. Audience: All ages. Rating:* ★★

㉒ The first attraction on the left as you enter Fantasyland is **Legend of the Lion King,** an elaborate stage show featuring an advanced form of puppeteering, further boosted by special effects and Elton John's lyrical music. It brings to vivid life Simba, Mufasa, Scar, and the rest of the characters from Disney's 32nd animated feature. Unlike many of the stage shows in the Magic Kingdom, this one showcases "humanimals," Disneyspeak for bigger-than-life-size figures that are manipulated by human "animateers" hidden from the audience's view. (The adult Simba, for instance, is nearly 8 feet tall.) The preshow consists of the opening "Circle of Life" overture from the film. It's a perfect stage-setter for the fun and drama to come. *Duration: 15 min. Crowds: Rendered insignificant by large theater capacity. Strategy: Save this for mid- or late-afternoon, when you want to sit down and cool off. Audience: All ages. Rating:* ★★

㉓ Moving clockwise through Fantasyland brings you to **Peter Pan's Flight,** a truly fantastic indoor ride inspired by Sir James M. Barrie's story about the boy who wouldn't grow up (Disney animated it in 1953). You board two-person magic sailing ships, whose brightly striped sails catch the wind and soar into the skies above London en route to Never-Never-Land. Along the way, you watch as Wendy, Michael, and John are sprinkled with pixie dust while Nana barks below, wave to Princess Tiger Lily, meet the evil Captain Hook, and cheer for the ticktocking, clock-swallowing crocodile who's breakfasted on Hook's hand and is more than ready for lunch. Despite the lack of '90s high-tech special effects, kids love this ride. Adults will especially enjoy the dreamy views of London by moonlight, a galaxy of twinkling yellow lights punctuated by Big Ben, London Bridge, and a moonlit Thames River. There's so much to see that the ride seems much longer than it is. *Duration: 2½ min. Crowds: Always heavy, except in the evening and early morning. Strategy: Go early, during the daily parade, or in the evening. Audience: All ages. Rating:* ★★

㉔ Visiting Walt Disney World and *not* stopping for **It's a Small World**— why, the idea is practically un-American. Disney raided the remains of the 1964–65 New York World's Fair for this exhibit (sponsored, as anyone over 35 will remember, by Pepsi-Cola long before soft drinks were "It" or "The Right One, Baby, Uh-Huh") and then appropriated the theme song of international brotherhood and friendship for its own.

This ride strains the patience more than the adrenal glands. Moving somewhat slower than a snail, the barges inch through several barnlike rooms, each crammed with musical moppets, all madly singing the theme song, "It's a Small World After All." It's the revenge of the Audio-Animatrons, you think, as rather simplistic dolls differentiated only by their national costumes—Dutch babies in clogs, Spanish flamenco dancers, German oompah bands, Russian balalaikas, sari-wrapped Indians waving temple bells, Tower of London guards in scarlet beefeater uniforms, yodelers and goatherds, Japanese kite fliers, and juvenile cancan dancers, to name just a few—parade past, smiling away and wagging their heads in time to The Song. But somehow by the time you reach the end of the ride, you're grinning and wagging too. You just can't help it—and small children can't wait to ride it again. By the way, there is only one verse to The Song and it repeats incessantly, tattooing itself indelibly into your brain. Now all together: "It's a world of laughter, a world of tears. It's a world of hope and a world of fears . . ." *Duration: 11 min. Crowds: Steady, but lines move fast. Strategy: Look for the line to the left—it's usually the shorter of the two. Go anytime but mid-afternoon. Audience: All ages. Rating:* ★★

㉕ A tribute to the 1941 Disney animated film *Dumbo*, **Dumbo the Flying Elephant** is one of Fantasyland's most popular rides. While the story has one baby elephant with gigantic ears who accidentally downs a bucket of champagne and learns he can fly, the ride has 16 jolly Dumbos flying around a central column, each pachyderm packing a couple of kids and a parent. A joystick controls each of Dumbo's vertical motions, so you can make him ascend or descend at will. Alas, the ears do not flap. *Duration: 2 min. Crowds: Perpetual, except in early morning. Strategy: If accompanying small children, make a beeline here at Rope Drop; otherwise, skip it, especially on a first visit. Audience: Young children. Rating:* ★

㉖ A staple in carnivals (where it's known as "Tubs o' Fun"), the **Mad Tea Party** is for the vertigo addict looking for a fix. The Disney version is based on the 1951 film *Alice in Wonderland,* in which the Mad Hatter hosts a tea party for his un-birthday. You hop into oversize, pastel-colored teacups and whirl around a giant platter. Add your own spin to the teacup's orbit with the help of the steering wheel in the center. If the centrifugal force hasn't shaken you up too much, check out the soused mouse that pops out of the teapot centerpiece and compare his condition to your own. *Duration: 2 min. Crowds: Steady from late morning on, with slow-moving lines. Strategy: Skip this on your first Magic Kingdom visit. Rating:* ★

㉗ **Mr. Toad's Wild Ride,** based on the 1949 Disney release *The Adventures of Ichabod and Mr. Toad* (itself derived from Kenneth Grahame's classic children's novel *The Wind in the Willows*), puts you into the jump seat of the speed-loving amphibian's flivver as he floors the accelerator on a jolting, jarring jaunt through the English countryside. At the entrance, notice the ride's two lovingly adhered-to mottoes (*Toadí Acceleratío* and *Semper Absurda*), and inside keep an eye out for such whimsical touches as signposts indicating "Worcestershire" and "Notsoshire" as well as your own destination, "Nowhere in Particular." Along the way you'll crash through walls, scatter chickens, nearly get clobbered by a falling suit of armor, go hurtling through haystacks, and end up on a collision course with a freight train. *Duration: 3 min. Crowds: Steady from late morning until evening. Strategy: Go very early, during the daily parade, or after dark. Audience: All ages. Marginally less scary than Snow White's Adventures; may startle young children. Rating:* ★★

What was previously an unremittingly scary three-minute indoor spook-house ride reopened in December 1994 as a kinder, gentler ㉘ **Snow White's Adventures.** Where once the dwarves might as well have been named Anxious and Fearful, the new ride—now with six-passenger cars and a mini-version of the movie—has been tempered. There's still the evil queen, her nose wart, and her cackle, but joining the cast at long last are the prince and Snow White herself. The trip is still packed with plenty of scary moments, but an honest-to-goodness kiss followed by a happily-ever-after ending might even get you heigh-ho-ing on your way. *Duration: 3 min. Crowds: Steady from late morning until evening. Strategy: Go very early, during the daily parade, or after dark. Audience: All ages; may frighten young children. Rating:* ★★

29 The **Skyway to Tomorrowland** takes off on its one-way aerial trip to Tomorrowland from an enchanted attic perched above the trees in the far left corner of Fantasyland (this is also the terminus for those taking the Skyway from Tomorrowland to Fantasyland). You soar above the turquoise lagoon dotted with Captain Nemo's weird boats, the striped canopy of Cinderella's Golden Carrousel, the crowds thronging around Fantasyland, the Grand Prix Raceway at the edge of Tomorrowland, and the extraordinarily mundane tar-paper rooftops of the buildings that house the magic. Although this is a quick shortcut to Tomorrowland, it's actually more fun to take it in the other direction. That way you'll preview the sights of Fantasyland, hear the happy music ascending, and then alight in the attic terminus, in the mood for magic. *Duration: 5 min. Crowds: Moderate from late morning until evening but usually not a problem. Strategy: Bypass this on a first visit until you've seen the major attractions. Audience: All ages. Rating:* ★

For a company that owes its fame to a certain endearing big-eared little fellow, Walt Disney World is astonishingly mouse-free. Until, that **30** is, you arrive at **Mickey's Starland,** a concentrated dose of adulation built in 1988 to celebrate Mickey Mouse's 60th birthday. Rarely crowded, the 3-acre niche set off to the side of Fantasyland is like a scene from a cartoon, and everything is child size. The attractions are in the imaginary town of Duckburg (yes, Donald and Huey, Dewey, and Louie are all here, along with a cast of other Disney characters), whose pastel houses are positively Lilliputian, with miniature driveways, toy-size picket fences, and signs scribbled with finger paint. The best way to arrive is on the Walt Disney World Railroad, the old-fashioned choo-choo that also stops at Main Street and Frontierland.

It looks as if the Mickster himself has just left mustard-colored clapboard **Mickey's House** (note the whimsical address). Sad to say, despite Minnie's ministrations, her mate is a slob—to say nothing of a pack rat. Mickey's red pants are carelessly tossed over a chair, his slippers and golf clubs lie nearby, he leaves the radio on when he's not here (tuned to Disney songs), and his diet, to judge from the shopping list tacked to the fridge, is decidedly one-dimensional. Check out the mouse-ear-shaped andirons in the fireplace.

You can visit with Minnie in the kitchen, then slip out the back to tour her own neat and separate dwelling, as well as Donald Duck's houseboat and Goofy's ramshackle abode. Though this is primarily a children's attraction, adults will get a kick out of the imaginative architecture and the Disney attention to detail.

Mickey's Starland Show and Hollywood Theater, held under a yellow-and-white-striped big top, presents the television stars of "The Disney Afternoon" in a cheerful sing-along musical comedy that kids adore. There are Chip and Dale, Scrooge McDuck, the ever-bumbling Launchpad McQuack, and Gadget of the "Rescue Rangers." A video cartoon of pop star Cyndi Lauper singing "Hey Mickey, You're So Fine" kicks off the performance in high gear. Afterward, all the kids dash around backstage to **Mickey's Dressing Room,** where the star graciously signs autographs and poses for pictures with his adoring public.

Diagonally across the street from Mickey's House you'll find a delightful play area. Here the kids can climb, jump, slide, explore, and have a plain good old time in **Mickey's Treehouse** and **Minnie's Doll House** while Mom and Dad take a rest on benches that have a clear view of the climbing areas. For toddlers and preschoolers, there's the **Mouse-Ka-Maze,** a scaled-down version of the maze from *Alice in Wonderland.*

Next to the play area at **Grandma Duck's Farm**—a petting zoo with real live animals—the star is Minnie Moo, a placid Holstein cow whose distinctive black splotches just naturally arranged themselves into Disney's mouse logo. Like the rest of Mickey's Starland, the animals are pint-size, too, and a more cuddly bunch of baby chicks, sheep, calves, rabbits, pigs, and goats couldn't be imagined. How Walt Disney World manages to keep this imaginative barnyard so spick-and-span is completely beyond us. *Duration: Up to you. Crowds: Moderate and seldom a problem. Strategy: Go anytime. Audience: Young children, mainly. Rating:* ★★

Tomorrowland

A brand-new Tomorrowland began to make its long-awaited debut in late 1994. The stark, antiseptic future forecasted by the original design had become embarrassingly passé: Bare concrete and plain white walls, plus such outdated rides as Star Jets and Mission to Mars, said more about Eisenhower-era aesthetics (or lack thereof) than third-millennium progress. To revitalize what had become the least appealing area of the Magic Kingdom, Disney artists and architects created new facades, restaurants, and shops for an energized Future City, which is more similar in mood to the themed villages of other lands. And this time around the creators showed that they had learned their lesson: Rather than predict a tomorrow destined for obsolescence, they focused on "the future that never was"—the future envisioned by sci-fi writers and moviemakers in the '20s and '30s, when space flight, laser beams, and home computers belonged in the world of fiction, not fact.

With two completely new attractions—Alien Encounter and Transportarium in the Metropolis Science Centre—an overhauled version of the StarJets (now reincarnated as AstroOrbiter), and an updated Carousel of Progress, Tomorrowland is certain to be high on the list of returning Disneyphiles as well as first-timers. Eateries here have also been revamped inside and out; however, while the menus and decor may have changed, they're still heavy on the fast-food side of things. In addition to all the new goodies, this land is home to one of the park's perennial favorites, the Space Mountain roller coaster, so count on lines at just about all hours of the day and night.

㉛ Disney Imagineers have pulled out the stops on the **Transportarium in the Metropolis Science Centre.** Combining CircleVision 360 filmmaking with Audio-Animatronic figures, this attraction, which replaces the CircleVision 360 "American Journeys," takes visitors on a time-traveling adventure to the past and on into the future. Don't plan on a relaxing voyage, however; there are no seats in the theater—only lean rails. Hosted by Time Keeper, a C-3PO clone whose frenetic personality is given voice by Robin Williams, and Nine-Eye, a slightly frazzled droid, time-travelers meet famous inventors and visionaries of the machine age. *Duration: 20 min. Crowds: Moderate; moves steadily since theater capacity is nearly 900. Strategy: Go when the lines at Alien Encounter are long. All ages. Rating:* ★★

③② There's almost never a wait at **Delta Dreamflight,** which should put your suspicions on red alert. It's in the same building complex as the Transportarium, and, in fact, the entrances can be easily confused—Dreamflight is farther along and to the right. Sponsored by Delta Airlines, this ride takes a look at the adventure of flying by showing a series of scenes of pop-up figures and photos of Delta's destinations. The idea is cute, but the execution—surprising given Disney's experience with special effects—falls far short of thrilling. At its best, the attraction screens special 70mm film segments showing barnstorming wing walkers performing such stunts as hanging off the wing and picking a ribbon off the ground and then sends you through a jet engine (you can ride past the rest of the plane's body at Disney-MGM's Backstage Studio Tour). At its worst, the photography looks as if it came from the local tourist information bureau. *Duration: 4½ min. Crowds: Light. Strategy: Go in the afternoon when everything else is crowded. Audience: All ages. Rating:* ★

③③ Despite a disappointing lack of truly special effects, **Alien Encounter** is still certain to become one of the Magic Kingdom's most popular new attractions, since the show provides a welcome change from its stodgy predecessor, Mission to Mars. (Old-time Disneyphiles will note, though, that the room in which the "encounter" takes place is in exactly the same circular configuration as the Mars misadventure.) Playing on Tomorrowland's new Future City theme, this attraction has guests enter what is ostensibly the city's convention center to watch a test of a new teleportation system. Representatives from the device's manufacturer, an alien corporation called XS-Tech (pronounced *excess*; their motto: "If something can't be done with XS, it can't be done at all."), try to transport the company's CEO from their planet to Earth to demonstrate the product. The attempt fails, however, and the resulting catastrophe consists of a close encounter with an "extraTERRORrestrial" creature. *Duration: 20 min. Crowds: Expect lines. Strategy: Go first thing in the morning, during the afternoon parade, or during the evening fireworks. Audience: Not suitable for small children. Rating:* ★★

③④ At the center of Future City is the **AstroOrbiter,** whose gleaming superstructure of revolving planets will most likely come to symbolize the new Tomorrowland as much as Dumbo represents Fantasyland. The ride itself, however, hasn't changed much from its previous life as StarJets. Ride vehicles—now looking more like Buck Rogers toys than space shuttles—sail past the whirling planets during a swing through space where you control the altitude if not the velocity. *Duration: 2 min. Crowds: Humongous, and line moves slowly. Strategy: Skip on your first visit if time is short, unless there's no line. Audience: All ages. Rating:* ★★

③⑤ Just past AstroOrbiter, you'll find the **Tomorrowland Transit Authority** (TTA). A reincarnation of the WEDway PeopleMover, the TTA takes a nice, leisurely ride around the perimeter of Tomorrowland, circling the AstroOrbiter and eventually gliding through the middle of Space Mountain. (Some faint-hearted TTA passengers have no doubt chucked the notion of riding the roller coaster after being exposed first-hand to the screams emanating from the mountain—it sounds worse than it really is, though.) Disney's version of future mass transit is smooth and noiseless, thanks to an electromagnetic linear induction motor that has no moving parts, uses little power, and emits no pollutants. *Duration: 6 min. Crowds: Not one of the park's popular attractions, so lines are seldom long. Strategy: Go to preview Space Mountain, but skip on a first-time visit until you've been through all the major attractions. Audience: All ages. Rating:* ★

③⑥ Walt Disney's **Carousel of Progress** has only been in Tomorrowland since 1974, but it was the first attraction to be given a major face-lift in the recent renovation. Originally seen at the 1964–65 World's Fair in New York, this revolving theater traces the impact of technological progress on the daily lives of Americans from the turn of this century into the near future. In each decade, there's an Audio-Animatronic family that sings the praises of the new gadgets that technology has wrought. (Fans of the holiday film *A Christmas Story* will recognize the voice of its narrator, Jean Shepard, who injects his folksy, all-American humor as the father figure through the decades.) A new pre-show, seen on overhead video monitors while you're waiting to enter the theater, details the design of the original carousel and features Walt himself singing the theme song. Speaking of which, gone is the irritating theme of years' past, "The Best Time of Your Life"; it's been replaced by the ride's original ditty, "There's a Great Big Beautiful Tomorrow"—very fitting for the new Tomorrowland. *Duration: 20 min. Crowds: Moderate. Strategy: Skip on a first-time visit. Audience: All ages. Rating:* ★

Set off to the extreme left corner of Tomorrowland opposite the land's
③⑦ main block of shops and restaurants, **Grand Prix Raceway** is one of those rides that incite instant addiction among kids and immediate antipathy among parents. The reasons for the former are easy to figure out: the brightly colored Mark VII model gasoline-powered cars that swerve around the four 2,260-foot tracks with much vroom-vroom-vrooming. Like real sports cars, the vehicles are equipped with rack-and-pinion steering and disc brakes; unlike the real thing, these run on a track. However, the track is so twisty that it's hard to keep the car on a straight course—something the race car fanatics warming the bleachers love to watch. If you're not a fanatic, the persistent noise and pervasive smell of high-test on a muggy central Florida afternoon can quickly rasp your nerves into the danger zone. Furthermore, there's a lot of waiting: You wait to get on the track (it can take up to an hour), you wait again for your turn to climb in a car, then you wait one more time to return your vehicle after your lap—all this for a ride in which the main thrill is achieving a top speed of 7 miles per hour. *Duration: 5 min. Crowds: Steady and heavy from late morning to evening. Strategy: Go in the evening or during a parade; skip on a first-time visit until you've been through all the major attractions. Audience: Older children. Minimum height for drivers 52". Rating:* ★

③⑧ The needlelike spires and gleaming white concrete cone of **Space Mountain** are almost as much of a Magic Kingdom landmark as Cinderella Castle. Towering 180 feet high, the structure has been called "Florida's third-highest mountain." Inside is arguably the world's most imaginative roller coaster. Although there are no loop-the-loops, gravitational whizbangs, or high-speed curves, the thrills are amply provided by Disney's masterful brainwashing as you take a trip into the depths of outer space—in the dark.

The mood for your space shot is set in the waiting area (long lines are inevitable, so milk the mood for all it's worth). A dim blue light reflects off the mirror-and-chrome walls, while above planets and galaxies and meteors and comets whirl past, strobe lights flash, and the fluorescent panels on the six-passenger rockets streak by leaving phosphorescent memories. Screams and shrieks echo in the chamber, piercing the rattling of the cars and the various otherworldly beeps and buzzes. Meanwhile, you can't help overhearing gossip about how earrings have been known to be ripped out of earlobes by the centrifugal force, pocketbooks shaken open and upended, and so on. Although it's a good idea to stow personal belongings securely, Disney staffers in a control booth constantly monitor the ride on a battery of closed-circuit televisions; at the first sign of any guest having trouble, the ride can be stopped.

That rarely happens. Instead, you wedge yourself into the seat. The blinking sign in front switches from "boarding" to "blast off," and you do. The ride lasts only 2 minutes and 38 seconds and attains a top speed of 28 miles per hour, but the devious twists and invisible drops, and the fact that you can't see where you're going, make it seem twice as long and many more times as thrilling. People of all ages adore this ride; there is, however, a bail-out area just before boarding in case you have second thoughts. *Duration: 3 min. Crowds: Large and steady, with long lines from morning to night despite high capacity. Strategy: Go either at the end of the day, during a parade, or at Rope Drop (in which case wait at the Plaza Restaurant rather than at the top of Main Street to get a 120-yd head start on the crowd). Audience: All except young children. No pregnant women or guests wearing back, neck, or leg braces; minimum height 44".* Rating: ★★★

⟨39⟩ The brightly colored cable cars of the one-way **Skyway to Fantasyland** can be picked up at the station right outside Space Mountain for the commute to the far western end of Fantasyland. Not only a great short-cut, the open-air cars offer magnificent views of Cinderella Castle and many of the Fantasyland rides; that is, you can scope out the lines from above and plan your strategy accordingly. Last but not least, those aerial tramlets provide one of the few opportunities for a little peace and quiet among the madding crowd. If you can time things right, there's no better way to view the 10 PM fireworks. *Duration: 5 min. Crowds: 10- to 20-min wait, except in early morning and during parades. Strategy: Skip this on your first visit. Audience: All ages.* Rating: ★

Dining

Alas, the gustatory offerings are mostly fast food—and mundane fast food at that. Every land has its share of restaurants serving burgers, hot dogs, and nachos, with chef's salad thrown in as the token "health food" for the on-the-go crowd. In addition, the walkways are peppered with carts dispensing popcorn, ice cream, lemonade, and soda.

Full-Service Restaurants

There are three full-service restaurants in the Magic Kingdom; reservations are essential and can be made at all restaurants.

LIBERTY SQUARE

Liberty Square's **Liberty Tree Tavern** is hands-down the best of the group. Decorated in lovely Williamsburg colors, with Early American antiques and lots of brightly polished brass, it's a pleasant place even when jammed to the gills. The menu is all-American, with the oversize salads and assorted sandwiches a good bet at lunch, and fresh fish, prime rib, and chicken the best choices at dinner. You can also order a full Thanksgiving turkey feast with all the trimmings—even in July. But then you'd miss out on the idiosyncratic garnish that decorates the sandwiches: a slice of watermelon cut to resemble Mickey Mouse's profile, ears and all.

FANTASYLAND

No Magic Kingdom visitor can consider dining in the park without contemplating **King Stefan's Banquet Hall.** The food covers the basic choices of seafood salad or roast beef sandwiches at lunch, with chicken or seafood or prime rib at dinner. But the real attraction is that you get to eat inside Cinderella Castle in an old mead hall, where Cinderella herself is sometimes on hand and serving wenches whisk around in long medieval gowns and 13th-century-style wimples. How they prevent their veils from dragging in the mayonnaise is one of those secrets revealed only to the adepts.

MAIN STREET
The third full-service restaurant of the trio is **Tony's Town Square Café,** named after the Italian restaurant in *Lady and the Tramp* where Disney's most famous canine couple share their first kiss over a plate of spaghetti. (The video plays on a TV in the restaurant's waiting area.) Lunch and "Da Dinner" menus offer pasta, of course, along with seafood, steak, and chicken.

Cafeteria

The cafeteria service at the **Crystal Palace,** just to the left of the Hub, makes for as pleasant a dining experience as the full-service places do. The offerings in this glass-roofed conservatory are varied, generous, and surprisingly good (the black bean soup is especially noteworthy, as are the burritos and the herb-roasted chicken), and there's a sizable choice of pasta dishes and hearty salads. The place is huge, but its barn-size dimensions are softened by numerous nooks and crannies, comfortable banquettes, cozy cast-iron tables, and lots of sunlight. It's also one of the few places in the Magic Kingdom that serve breakfast.

Entertainment

Daytime

Particularly along Main Street, you'll come upon all sorts of shows and happenings: a **barbershop quartet, ragtime pianist, brass bands, banjo pickers.** Every day just after 5, homing pigeons wing their way to Cinderella Castle from Town Square as part of a **flag ceremony.** There are usually **song-and-dance revues** in the Cinderella Castle forecourt and in Fantasyland and Tomorrowland as well.

Still, **Disney characters** are the main event, especially if you're traveling with children (but even if you're not). They sign autographs and pose for snapshots throughout the park—line up at City Hall for your turn to pose for a picture, or snag Mickey's autograph in the star's own dressing room in the Hollywood Theater in Mickey's Starland. You can get another eyeful at the 30-minute-long **daily parade** that proceeds down Main Street through Frontierland beginning at 3; it shows off floats, balloons, cartoon characters, dancers, singers (usually lip-synching to music played over the public-address system), and much waving and cheering. It's as good as the Macy's Thanksgiving Day Parade—and the streets are cleaner. There's usually some thematic rubric attached; recently, it's been billed as Mickey Mania, with oversize mouse-ear icons covering floats, costumes, toys, clocks, and balloons. Note that lines at popular attractions often disappear during the parade.

After Dark

The former Main Street Electrical Parade was shipped overseas to France and replaced by **SpectroMagic,** a 30-minute extravaganza of battery-lighted floats, sequined costumes, sparkling decorations, and twinkling trees. (This parade runs only during peak holiday periods and during the summer.) There are staffers dressed as dragonflies, carrying battery packs that light up their emerald-and-sapphire wings. Shimmering, oversize Christmas-tree ornaments roll down the street. Mickey Mouse and Minnie—in silver sequins—ride an ornate peacock, and Cinderella's coach is outlined in hundreds of fairy lights.

Speaking of fairies, let's not forget **Fantasy in the Sky,** the Magic Kingdom fireworks display. Heralded by a dimming of all the lights along Main Street, the camouflaged loudspeakers play "When You Wish upon a Star." A single spotlight illuminates the top turret of the Cinderella Castle and—poof!—Tinkerbell emerges in a shower of pixie dust. Thanks to an invisible guy wire, she appears to fly over the treetops and the crowds, on her way to a Never-Never-Land touchdown located, appropriately enough, in Tomorrowland. Her disappearance signals the start of the fireworks, which fill the sky with some pixie dust of their own. It's a magical way to end an enchanted idyll.

Shopping

Everywhere you turn there are shops and stalls urging you to take home a little piece of the magic. The big daddy of all shops in the Magic Kingdom is the enormous **Emporium,** which stocks thousands upon thousands of Disney character products, from keychains to T-shirts to stuffed animals. Although perpetually crowded (and absolutely mobbed at closing time), the Emporium is, hands down, one of the best places in which to find souvenirs, especially for hard-to-buy-for Aunt Tilly. Hang on to the kids in here; they're likely to wander away as they discover new delights. Within other sections of the park, you'll find trinkets and treasures that are theme-related to their home base. Here are some of the all-time best Magic Kingdom souvenirs: pirate hats, swords, and plastic hooks-for-hands sold at the **House of Treasure** just outside Pirates of the Caribbean in Adventureland; creepy-crawly rubber snakes and lizards, just the sort of thing to spook a younger sibling, sold at **Bwana Bob's** kiosk next to the entrance to the Jungle Cruise in Adventureland; Davy Crockett coonskin hats, personalized sheriff badges, and Big Al memorabilia at **Big Al's** across from the Country Bear Jamboree in Frontierland; a fairy princess upside-down-ice-cream-cone hat with a gauze veil, at the **King's Gallery** inside Cinderella Castle; children's clothing with Disney characters at **Tinkerbell's Treasures** in Fantasyland; all things Winnie-the-Pooh at the **Briar Patch** next door to Splash Mountain; and last but not least, distinctive canary yellow umbrellas with black mouse ears on top and the signature yellow ponchos adorned with a smiling Mickey on the back—a bargain at $4.51.

Access for Travelers with Disabilities

Attractions

MAIN STREET

To board the **Walt Disney World Railroad** at the Main Street Station, you must transfer from your wheelchair, which can be folded to ride with you or left in the station. Alternatively, board at Frontierland or Mickey's Starland. The **Main Street Cinema** is barrier free for guests using wheelchairs—a definite miss for visually impaired guests, since the cartoons are silents, played without dialogue, and set to theater organ music. The **Main Street Vehicles** can be boarded by guests with limited mobility who can fold their wheelchair and climb into a car. In the **Penny Arcade,** the machines may be too high for guests using wheelchairs and not of much interest for some guests with visual impairments. There are curb cuts or ramps on each corner.

ADVENTURELAND

The **Swiss Family Robinson Treehouse,** with its 100 steps and lack of narration, gets low ratings among those with mobility and visual impairments. At the **Jungle Cruise,** boarding requires that a guest step down into the boat; those who can lip-read will find the skippers' punny narration, delivered with a handheld mike, difficult to follow, though you can try (ask for a seat up front). Boarding **Pirates of the Caribbean** requires transferring from a nonfolding to a folding wheelchair, available at the entrance; the flume drop may make the attraction inappropriate for those with limited upper-body strength or who wear neck or back braces, and because of gunshot and fire effects, service animals should stay behind. The theater-style **Enchanted Tiki Birds** is barrier free for guests using wheelchairs.

FRONTIERLAND

To ride **Big Thunder Mountain Railroad** and **Splash Mountain,** you must be able to step into the ride vehicle and walk short distances (in case of emergency evacuation); those with limited upper-body strength should assess the situation on site, and those wearing back, neck, or leg braces should not ride. (Ditto for service animals.) **Tom Sawyer Island,** with its stairs, bridges, inclines, and narrow caves, is not negotiable by those using a wheelchair. The **Diamond Horseshoe Jamboree** and the **Country Bear Jamboree** are completely wheelchair accessible; if you lip-read, ask to sit up front (especially at the Diamond Horseshoe, whose script is not in the guide for guests with hearing impairments). The **Frontierland Shootin' Gallery** has two guns at wheelchair level. Frontierland is the only area of the park, aside from Main Street, that has sidewalk curbs; there are ramps by the Mile Long Bar and east of Frontierland Trading Post.

LIBERTY SQUARE

The **Hall of Presidents** is completely barrier free for guests using wheelchairs. The **Liberty Square Riverboat** is completely wheelchair accessible; to ride the **Mike Fink Keel Boats,** guests must negotiate two steep steps. At the **Haunted Mansion,** guests using wheelchairs must transfer to the "doom buggies" and take one step; however, if you can walk as much as 200 feet, you will enjoy the great preshow as well as the sensations and eerie sounds of the rest of the ride. **Mickey's Starland** is completely accessible.

FANTASYLAND

Boarding the **Skyway** is impossible for guests who use a wheelchair unless they can transfer to the ride cabins. Go for the round-trip, because stairs are a chief feature of the Tomorrowland Station. And if you're visually impaired, don't waste your time; there's no narration, and the panoramic view is the ride's chief raison d'être. The stage show **Legend of the Lion King** has wheelchair seating; for guests with visual impairments, the chief attraction is the music by Elton John. **It's a Small World** can be boarded without leaving your wheelchair, but only if it's a standard-size one; guests using a scooter or an oversize chair must transfer to one of the attraction's standard chairs, available at the ride entrance. To board **Peter Pan's Flight, Dumbo the Flying Elephant, Cinderella's Golden Carrousel, the Mad Tea Party, Mr. Toad's Wild Ride,** and **Snow White's Adventures,** guests using wheelchairs must transfer to the ride vehicles. Mr. Toad's, Dumbo, and Peter Pan's are inappropriate for service animals.

TOMORROWLAND

Alien Encounter, Transportarium, and **Carousel of Progress** are barrier free for those using wheelchairs. To board **Delta Dreamflight, AstroOrbiter,** and the **Tomorrowland Transit Authority,** you must be able to walk several steps and transfer to the ride vehicle. The TTA has more appeal to guests with visual impairments, Dreamflight greater charm for those with hearing impairments. To drive **Grand Prix Raceway** cars, you must have adequate vision and be able to steer, press the gas pedal, and transfer into the low car seat. The cautions for Big Thunder Mountain Railroad and Splash Mountain (*see* Frontierland, *above*) also apply to **Space Mountain.**

Shops and Restaurants
All restaurants and shops throughout the park have level entrances or are accessible by ramps.

Information
See Access for Travelers with Disabilities *in* Essential Information, *above.*

EPCOT CENTER

Walt Disney World was created because of Walt Disney's dream of EPCOT, an "Experimental Prototype Community of Tomorrow." Disney envisioned a future in which nations coexisted in peace and harmony, reaping the miraculous harvest of technological achievement. He suggested the idea as early as October 1966, saying, "EPCOT will be an experimental prototype community of tomorrow that will take its cue from the new ideas and new technologies that are now emerging from the creative centers of American industry." He wrote of the never completed, always improving Epcot, "Epcot . . . will never cease to be a living blueprint of the future . . . a showcase to the world for the ingenuity and imagination of American free enterprise."

But with Disneyland hemmed in by development, Disney had to search for new lands in which to found his new world. He found it in central Florida. Many of the technologies incorporated into the Walt Disney World infrastructure were cutting-edge at the time. But the permanent community that he envisioned has not yet come to be. Instead, we have Epcot Center—which opened in 1982, 16 years after Disney's death—a showcase, ostensibly, for the concepts that would be incorporated into the EPCOTs of the future. Then, as now, it was composed of two parts: **Future World,** where the majority of its 10 pavilions are sponsored by major U.S. corporations and demonstrate their technological advances, and **World Showcase,** where 11 exhibition areas each represent a different country.

Epcot Center today is both more and less than Walt Disney's original dream. Less because some of the Future World pavilions are stuck in a 1965 World's Fair mentality, their driving vision, like the companies that sponsored them, eerily out of touch with today's values. Less because World Showcase presents idealized views of its countries, as an Epcot guide put it: "as Americans perceive them." Less because the missionary zeal that infuses the park backfires occasionally; young children get bored and adults start to wonder if they have to take a short test at the exit.

But these are minor quibbles in the face of the major achievement: Epcot is that rare paradox—an educational theme park—and a very successful one, too. The amount of imagination concentrated in its 230 acres is astounding and can't help rubbing off on the visitors. Through ingenious architecture, intriguing exhibits, amusing and awe-inspiring movies, and lively rides, Epcot Center inspires curiosity, rewards discovery, and encourages the creative spark in each of us.

Although rides have been added over the years to amuse young 'uns, the thrills are mostly in the mind. Consequently, because it helps to have a well-developed intelligence that one can exercise, Epcot is best for older children and adults.

Essential Information

Getting Around

It's a big place; a local joke suggests that Epcot is an acronym for "Every Person Comes Out Tired." But still, the most efficient way to get around is to walk. Just to vary things, you can cruise across the lagoon in one of the air-conditioned, 65-foot water taxis that depart every 12 minutes from World Showcase Plaza at the border of Future World. There are two docks: Boats from the one on the left zip to the Germany pavilion, from the right to Morocco. In World Showcase, you can board the slow-moving double-decker buses that depart every 5–8 minutes and stop in front of every other pavilion.

If you think the huge distances involved may be a problem, start out by renting a stroller or wheelchair (*see* Services, *below*).

Tourist Information

Earth Station, underneath Spaceship Earth, is the principal information center, the place to pick up schedules of live entertainment, park brochures, and the like. The computerized WorldKey Information System kiosks, in Earth Station and in World Showcase near Germany, are another resource. Using the touch-sensitive screens, you can obtain detailed information about every pavilion, leave messages for companions, and get answers to almost all of your questions. If the computer can't give you the answer, you can request the assistance of a host or hostess.

Reservations

Lunch or dinner reservations for Epcot Center full-service restaurants may be made in advance by calling 407/WDW–DINE or in person at the WorldKey terminals at the park (only on the day of the meal) or at the restaurants themselves when they open for lunch at 11 AM. For complete information, *see* Reservations at Epcot Center *in* Chapter 7, Dining, or call Guest Relations (☎ 407/824–4321).

Services

BABY CARE

Epcot Center has a Baby Care Center as peaceful as the one in the Magic Kingdom; it's near the Odyssey Restaurant in Future World. Also furnished with rocking chairs, it has a low lighting level that makes it comfortable for nursing, and cast members have supplies such as **formula, baby food, pacifiers,** and **disposable diapers** for sale. You'll find **changing tables** here, as well as in all women's rooms and some men's rooms. You can also buy disposable diapers near the park entrance at Baby Services. For **stroller rentals** ($6 a day; $1 deposit required), look for the special stands on the east side of the Entrance Plaza and at World Showcase's International Gateway.

CAMERAS AND FILM

Kodak's disposable Fun Saver cameras are widely available. Or you can borrow a Kodak **disk camera** (you just have to buy the film) or rent **35mm cameras** or **video camcorders** ($5 and $40, respectively; refundable $70–$600 deposit required); sources include the Kodak Camera Center, in the Entrance Plaza; the lagoon's-edge World Traveler, at the end of the promenade between Future World and World Showcase; and Cameras and Film at Journey into Imagination.

For **two-hour film developing,** look for the Photo Express signs throughout the park (at the Kodak Camera Center and Cameras and Film at Journey into Imagination in Future World, and in World Showcase at Northwest Mercantile in Canada, World Traveler at International Gateway, Heritage Manor Gifts in the American Adventure, at the booth on the right as you enter Norway, and Artesanias Mexicanas in Mexico); drop your film in the container, and you can pick up your pictures at the Kodak Camera Center as you leave.

FIRST AID
The park's First Aid Center, staffed by registered nurses, is near the Odyssey Restaurant in Future World.

GUIDED TOURS
Reserve up to three weeks in advance for the two 4-hour behind-the-scenes tours, led by knowledgeable Disney cast members and open to guests 16 and older (☎ 407/560–6150; $20 plus park admission). Both offer up-close views of the phenomenal detail involved in the planning and maintenance of Epcot Center. **Hidden Treasures of World Showcase** (Sun., Wed., and Fri.; times vary) tells you everything from the provenance of the boulders in Japan's garden to the number of bricks in the U.S. pavilion. **Gardens of the World** (Mon., Tues., and Thurs.; times vary) explains World Showcase's realistic replicas of exotic plantings.

LOCKERS
You'll find them to the west of Spaceship Earth; outside the Entrance Plaza; and in the Bus Information Center by the bus parking lot (50¢). If what you need to store won't fit into the larger lockers, go to Guest Relations in the Entrance Plaza or at Earth Station.

LOST CHILDREN AND ADULTS
If you're worried about your children getting lost, get them name tags at either Earth Station or the Baby Care Center. If the worst happens, immediately report it to any cast member and try not to panic; the staff here is experienced at reuniting families, and there are lost-children logbooks at Earth Station and the Baby Care Center.

Earth Station also has a computerized Message Center, where you can leave notes for your traveling companions, both those in the Magic Kingdom and other parks.

LOST AND FOUND
Go to the west edge of the Entrance Plaza. If nobody claims what you turn in, you may get to keep it.

MONEY
For cash and currency exchange, go to the Sun Bank branch at Epcot Center (open daily 9–4), the Guest Relations window, or Earth Station. There is an American Express ExpressCash machine on the left side of the Entrance Plaza.

PACKAGE PICKUP
Ask the shop clerk to forward any large purchase you make to Guest Relations in the Entrance Plaza so that you won't have to carry it around all day. (Allow three hours.)

WHEELCHAIR RENTALS
You'll find them inside the Entrance Plaza on the left, to the right of the ticket booths at the Gift Stop, and at World Showcase's International Gateway. Standard models are available ($6 plus $1 deposit); you can also reserve an electric scooter (☎ 407/824–4321; $30 plus $20 deposit).

Strategies for Your Visit

Epcot Center is now so vast and varied that a dedicated visitor really needs two days to explore it all. However, if you want to attempt the whole thing in a day, the first rule is: Don't sleep late. Not only are there so many attractions, but you'll want to arrive early to beat the lines and make reservations at the restaurants. The second rule is: Don't spend time eating. Instead, have a big breakfast and tote a snack to tide you over so that you can have a late lunch. The third rule is: Walk fast, see the shows when the park is empty, and slow down and enjoy the shops and the live entertainment when the crowds thicken.

Blitz Tour

When you arrive at Epcot Center, your first task is to send the speediest member of your party ahead to the WorldKey Information System terminals at Guest Relations to make reservations for a 5:30 dinner (if you haven't already made advance bookings using 407/WDW–DINE), because after your marathon day, you'll be ready to sit down. Thus, dining early will give you time to zip through the attractions you've missed while everyone else is dawdling over dinner. Reservations made, you can smugly proceed to **Spaceship Earth** with nothing more on your mind than to have it expanded. Everyone else will also be lining up at Spaceship Earth, but the first-thing-in-the-morning lines move along snappily, and this attraction really is the best introduction to Future World.

Upon leaving Spaceship Earth, everyone else will head for the first pavilion they see: either Universe of Energy or the Living Seas. Skip 'em, we say, and go directly to the **Wonders of Life.** Once here, stay to your left; if the lines are minimal, you can segue from Body Wars to *The Making of Me* to Cranium Command with barely a pause.

Then head to Future World's western pavilions. Visit **Journey into Imagination** first; while most other visitors are breathing Mesozoic fog at Universe of Energy, you can meet Dreamfinder on the ride and then, with a little good luck and timing, walk right into *Honey, I Shrunk the Audience*. Don't linger in the Image Works—you can always come back.

Now enter **The Land**; take the boat ride and see Circle of Life and Food Rocks. By this time there may be a line at Living Seas, but if there isn't, go on in and stay as long as you like. Outside, things should be getting crowded. Head counterclockwise into World Showcase, toward **Canada.** (Everyone else will be hoofing it toward Mexico.) Then see **France** and the **American Adventure.** If there are lines at **Norway** by the time you get there, head for **Innoventions** and the **Image Works.**

After dinner, see any World Showcase attractions you missed, plus the **Universe of Energy, Horizons,** and **World of Motion**; lines are practically nonexistent then, and because rides are continuous at the last two pavilions, you can literally run from one to another, detouring at the **Wonders of Life** for a fruit-yogurt smoothie. World Showcase empties after 5, and there's a truly magical quality to the lush plantings at dusk.

If you have a day and a half or two days, plan to do just the opposite of what most visitors do: Explore World Showcase in the late morning, Future World in the early evening.

Exploring Epcot Center

Epcot Center is divided into two distinct areas separated by the 40-acre World Showcase Lagoon. The northern half, which is where the monorail drops you off and which is considered the official entrance, comprises Future World, whose pavilions honoring technological achievements are sponsored by major U.S. corporations. The southern half, at whose International Gateway the trams from the Dolphin and Swan hotels and Disney's Yacht Club and Beach Club resorts drop you off, comprises World Showcase, whose 11 exhibition areas, each spotlighting the culture of a different country, are sponsored by foreign governments and corporations.

Future World

Future World is made up of two concentric circles of pavilions. The inner core is composed of the Spaceship Earth geosphere and, just beyond it, the new Innoventions exhibit and Innoventions Plaza. The large Fountain of Nations serves as a dividing point between the inner core and the pavilions beyond.

Seven pavilions compose the outer ring of the circle. On the east side they are, in order, Universe of Energy, Wonders of Life, Horizons, and World of Motion. With the exception of the Wonders of Life, the pavilions present a single, self-contained ride and an occasional post-ride showcase; a visit rarely takes more than 30 minutes, but it depends on how long you spend in the post-ride area. On the west side there's the Living Seas, The Land, and Journey into Imagination. Like the Wonders of Life, these blockbuster exhibits contain both rides and interactive displays; count on spending at least 1½ hours per pavilion—and wanting to stay longer.

SPACESHIP EARTH

Balanced like a giant golf ball waiting for some celestial being to tee off, the multifaceted silver geosphere of Spaceship Earth is to Epcot Center what the Cinderella Castle is to the Magic Kingdom. As much a landmark as an icon, it can be seen on a clear day from an airplane flying down either coast of Florida.

Everyone likes to gawk at the golf ball, but here are some truly jaw-dropping facts: It weighs 1 million pounds, measures 164 feet in diameter and 180 feet in height (aha! you say, it's not really a sphere!), and encompasses more than 2 million cubic feet of space. It's balanced on six pylons sunk 100 feet into the ground. The anodized aluminum sheath is composed of 954 triangular panels, not all of equal size or shape. And, last, because it is not a geodesic dome (which is only a half sphere), the name "geosphere" had to be invented; no other like it existed when it was built.

Spaceship Earth contains both the Spaceship Earth ride and Earth Station, the principal source of Epcot Center information.

Hands-down the most popular ride at Epcot Center, as much for its subject matter and execution as for its proximity to the entrance, Spaceship Earth explores human progress and the continuing search for better forms of communication. Scripted by science fiction writer Ray Bradbury and now narrated by Jeremy Irons (who replaced Walter Cronkite as the disembodied voice of the past, present, and future), the journey begins in the darkest tunnels of time, proceeds through history, and ends poised on the edge of the future, including a dramatic look at a "virtual reality" classroom.

Audio-Animatronic figures present in astonishing detail Cro-Magnon man daubing mystic paintings on cave walls, Egyptian scribes scratching genuine hieroglyphics on papyrus, Roman centurions building roads, Islamic scholars mapping the heavens, and 11th- and 12th-century Benedictine monks hand-copying ancient manuscripts in order to preserve the wisdom of the past (one monk, not as tireless as history would have us believe, is conked out at his carrel, his candle smoking in the gusts of his snores). As you move into the Renaissance, Michelangelo paints the Sistine Chapel, Gutenberg invents the printing press, and in rapid succession, the telegraph, radio, television, and computer

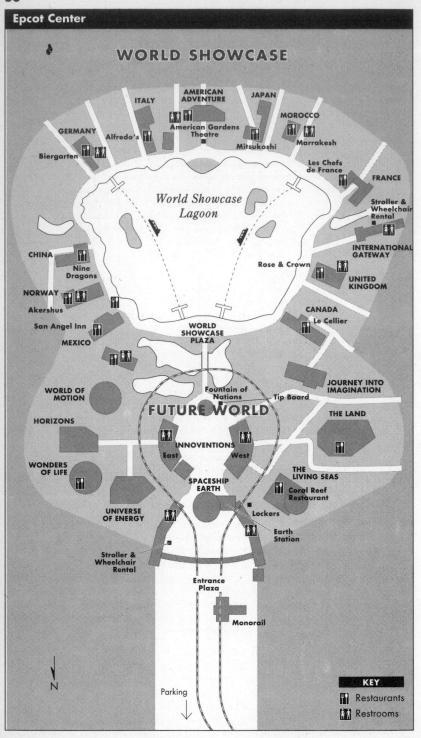

WORLD SHOWCASE

ITALY

AMERICAN ADVENTURE

JAPAN

MOROCCO

GERMANY

Alfredo's

American Gardens Theatre

Mitsukoshi

Marrakesh

Biergarten

Les Chefs de France

FRANCE

World Showcase Lagoon

Stroller & Wheelchair Rental

CHINA

Nine Dragons

Rose & Crown

INTERNATIONAL GATEWAY

NORWAY

Akershus

UNITED KINGDOM

San Angel Inn

CANADA

Le Cellier

MEXICO

WORLD SHOWCASE PLAZA

WORLD OF MOTION

Fountain of Nations

Tip Board

JOURNEY INTO IMAGINATION

FUTURE WORLD

THE LAND

HORIZONS

INNOVENTIONS

East   West

WONDERS OF LIFE

THE LIVING SEAS

SPACESHIP EARTH

Coral Reef Restaurant

Lockers

UNIVERSE OF ENERGY

Earth Station

Stroller & Wheelchair Rental

Entrance Plaza

Monorail

N

Parking

KEY

🍴 Restaurants

🚻 Restrooms

come into being. The pace speeds up, you're bombarded with images from our communication age, and, just as you begin to think you can't absorb another photon, you're shot through a tunnel of swirling lights into serene space, its velvety darkness sparkling with thousands of stars, and in one corner, hanging like the jeweled toy envisioned by Milton in *Paradise Lost,* is our own Earth as photographed by the astronauts on one of the *Apollo* moon shots. It's breathtaking. Toward the conclusion of the ride, visitors arrive in a "Global Neighborhood" that ties all of the peoples of the earth together through an interactive global network. Special effects, animated sets, and audience-enclosing laser beams are used to create the experience. *Duration: 15 min. Crowds: Longest during the morning and shortest just before park closing time. Strategy: Ride first thing in the morning or just before leaving. Audience: All ages. Since a portion of the ride is in total darkness, Disney recommends that persons who experience anxiety in dark, narrow, or enclosed spaces do not ride. Rating:* ★★★

INNOVENTIONS

Disney's latest addition to Future World is Innoventions, a two-building, 100,000-square-foot attraction situated at the center of the complex. (Repeat visitors will remember this attraction as Communicore East and West.) Live stage demonstrations, interactive hands-on displays, and exhibits highlight new technology that affects daily living. Each major exhibition area is presented by a leading manufacturer. **Innoventions East** will appeal more strongly to adults, with manufacturers such as General Electric, Hammacher Schlemmer, and Honeywell displaying products for the home of the not-too-distant future. There's also a hands-on display of Apple computer software that will keep your kids entertained—provided they can get to a PC. **Innoventions West** is hugely popular with pre-teens, and no wonder. It features an enormous display of Sega toys and games. One of the most popular is an eight-car Formula-One Grand Prix race in which you get to drive a full-size car through a turn-filled course that's projected onto a huge screen in front of each vehicle. You'll be hard-pressed to pull the kids out of here. *Duration: Up to you. Crowds: Largest around the popular computer displays. Strategy: Go first thing in the morning or during the evening IllumiNations laser show. Audience: All ages, although young children will tend to be bored. Rating:* ★★★

TIME OUT Two large fast-food emporiums dominate the Innoventions Plaza area. In Innoventions East you'll find the **Electric Umbrella.** The fare here is chicken sandwiches, burgers, and salads. If you hit this side of Innoventions later in the day, you might want to check out the snacks offered at **Desserts & Things.** (Those who are tempted by things high in calories will be happy to note that this treatery is open only during peak seasons.) Innoventions West offers the **Pasta Piazza Ristorante.** As its name suggests, it's heavy on the Italian side, with pizza, pasta, and salads. It's also one of the few places in Epcot that serve breakfast. On certain days, breakfast with Disney characters is on the menu. Morning fare includes omelets and the Sunrise Scramble, a tasty Egg McMuffin clone. Adjacent to the Sunrise Terrace is **Fountainview Expresso,** a café with freshly ground coffees, scrumptious croissants, fruit tarts, crème brulée, and éclairs. You can eat at the circular counter or perch on a chair at one of the high tables. There's also a patio with tables and umbrellas that offers a fine view of the fountain. In the afternoon, this is a great place to sip wine and watch the Fountain of Nations Walter Ballet Show without having to stand in the blazing sun and crane your neck.

UNIVERSE OF ENERGY

Two large topiary dinosaurs stand guard over Universe of Energy. The first of the pavilions on the left, or east, side of Future World, it occupies a large, lopsided pyramid, sheathed in thousands of mirrors, which serve as solar collectors to power the ride and films within. One of the most technologically complex shows at Epcot Center, the exhibit combines one ride, two films, the largest Audio-Animatronic animals ever built, 250 prehistoric trees, and enough cold, damp fog to make you think you've been transported to the inside of a defrosting refrigerator. "We don't want to go through that fog again," one child announced after emerging from a particularly damp vision of the Mesozoic era. About the rest of the ride, however, he had few qualms.

The 10-minute preshow film about the different forms of energy—nuclear, solar, electric, mechanical, and thermal—takes place in an enormous, standing-only (or sitting-on-the-floor) antechamber. There's a twist, however: The 14-by-90-foot projection surface is made up of 100 separate screens, which rotate according to complicated computerized directions to form what their creator, Czech filmmaker Emil Radok, described as a "kinetic mosaic." Here you are also serenaded for the first of many times with the jingle peculiar to this particular pavilion: "Hear the flow, see it grow, it's the Universe of Energy." If you say so.

Everyone then files into an adjoining area, which resembles a drive-in theater, complete with seats arranged in blocks. This is the setting for a five-minute animated film depicting the eras in which today's fossil fuels originated. No cute Disneyesque dinosaurs populated this earth; these animals are hulking, shadowy figures, lumbering across a steamy landscape of volcanoes, lush plants, and eerie insects. Even more eerie is the moment at the conclusion of the movie when the blocks of seats shift and rotate, then break up, and move forward into the ride.

The ride lurches into the forest primeval—and do we ever mean primeval. Huge trees loom out of the mists of time, ominous blue moonbeams waver in the fog, sulfurous lava burbles up, and the air smells distinctly of Swamp Thing. Through this unfriendly landscape brontosauruses wander trailing mouthfuls of weeds, a tyrannosaurus fights it out with a triceratops, pterodactyls swoop through the air, and a truly nasty sea snake emerges from the swamp to attack the left side of the tram. It's a view of the past that makes you glad to live in the present. In fact, it's almost a relief to hear the familiar "Hear the flow, see it grow . . ."

The ride concludes with another film, this one a 12-minute description of the search for alternative forms of energy. Dramatic shots of North Sea drilling platforms and a space-shuttle blastoff sequence so unusual that even NASA requested a copy serve to underline rather than mask the message. An interesting fact here: The 96-passenger, 30,000-pound "traveling theaters" are guided along the concrete floor by a wire only ⅛-inch thick and are powered by the 80,000 solar cells on the roof so that you have been, as they say, "riding on sunshine." *Duration: ½ hr. Crowd: Steady but never horrible; 600 people enter every 15 min. Strategy: To be at the front of the ride (and have your experience of the primeval landscape unspoiled by rows of modern heads in front of you), sit in the seats to the far left and front of the theater. Audience: All ages. Rating:* ★★★

WONDERS OF LIFE

A towering statue of a DNA double helix outside the gold-crowned dome of the Wonders of Life welcomes you to one of Epcot Center's most popular attractions. Truly one of the wonders of Epcot Center, it takes an amusing but serious and educational look at health, fitness, and modern lifestyles. One improvisational theater revue, two films, and dozens of interactive gadgets that whiz, bleep, and blink make up the Fitness Fairground. Walt Disney World's first flight simulator—Body Wars—takes visitors on a bumpy platelet-to-platelet ride through the human circulatory system. And the entertaining multimedia presentation, Cranium Command, reveals the workings of the mind of a typical 12-year-old boy during the course of an ordinary day.

The flight-simulator technology that is used to train commercial and military pilots adapts perfectly to thrill rides. By synchronizing the action on a movie screen with the movement of the capsule, the simulator tricks your mind into thinking that you're experiencing a wild ride without your ever leaving your seat. Probably the mildest flight simulator in central Florida, **Body Wars** still offers a thrilling ride, thanks to the fascinating film and the ingenious idea. You and your fellow scientists enter a capsule (the simulator chamber) that, like something out of *Honey, I Shrunk the Kids,* will be miniaturized and injected into the body's bloodstream. "How's the weather in there?" calls out one of the specialists on the screen. "Clear and warm, temperature about 98.6," comes the reply from within. And in a couple of seconds, you experience it yourself: shooting through the heart, wheezing through the lungs, and picking up a jolt of energy in the brain. *Duration: 5 min. Crowds: Sometimes discouraging, with occasional 45-min waits. Strategy: Go as soon as the park opens, during the hour before closing, or between 6 and 7 PM, the peak dinnertime in World Showcase. Audience: All but young children. Not recommended for pregnant women or guests who have neck or back injuries, heart problems, or motion sickness. Rating:* ★★★

Showtimes are staggered to pick up as soon as another lets out, so with a little luck you can segue right into **The Making of Me,** a valuable film on human conception and childbearing. Starring Martin Short as a man who, in search of his origins, journeys back in time to his parents' childhood, youth, marriage, and, eventually, their decision to have him, the film uses both animation and actual footage from a live birth to explain where babies come from. Some scenes are explicit, but all the topics are handled with gentle humor (as when the sperm race for the egg to the tune of "The Ride of the Valkyries") and (as when his parents make the big decision) with great delicacy. Children tend to be dumbstruck; many adults find the film affecting enough to get out the handkerchiefs for a quick swipe at overflowing eyes. *Duration: 14 min. Crowds: Long lines all day because the theater is so small. Strategy: Save this one for after 6 PM. Audience: All ages. Rating:* ★★★

Luckily the theater housing **Cranium Command** seats 200 at a shot. Combining a fast-paced movie with an elaborate set, this engaging show looks at how the cranium manages to make the heart, the uptight left brain, the laid-back right brain, the stomach, and an ever-alert adrenal gland all work together as their host, a 12-year-old boy, surmounts the slings and arrows of a typical day. The star is Buzzy, a bumbling Audio-Animatronic Cranium Commando for whom adolescent boys are the last chance before being consigned to run the brain of a chicken. Buzzy's is not an easy job; as the sign on the way to the theater warns, you are entering "The Home of the Flying Endorphins." As Buzzy's 12-year-old wakes up late, dashes off without breakfast, meets the new girl in school, fights for her honor, gets called up before the principal, and, finally, returns home (and has a much-needed snack), Buzzy attempts to coordinate a heart (operated by *Saturday Night Live*'s muscle-team Hans and Franz), a stomach (run by George Wendt, formerly of *Cheers,* in a sewer worker's overalls and rubber boots), and all the other body parts. He succeeds—barely. And the show is so well done that we'd almost like to see Buzzy fail, so we could watch him run the life of a typical chicken. *Duration: 20 min. Crowds: Long lines, but the big theater can quickly erase 'em. Strategy: Go when everyone else is at Body Wars. Audience: All ages. Rating:* ★★★

The rest of the Wonders of Life pavilion is taken up by the **Fitness Fairground,** an educational playground that teaches both adults and children about good health. There are games in which you can test your golf and tennis prowess, pedal around the world on a stationary bicycle while watching an ever-changing view on video, and guess your stress level at an interactive computer terminal. "Goofy about Health," an eight-minute multiscreen montage, follows Goofy's conversion from a foul-living dog to a fun-loving guy. The Anacomical Players Theater, seating 100 people, is a corny but funny improvisational show with lots of audience participation. The Frontiers of Medicine, the only completely serious section of the pavilion, demonstrates leading-edge developments in medicine. *Duration: Up to you. Crowds: Shifting, but they don't affect your visit. Strategy: Hang loose and take turns. Audience: All ages. Rating:* ★★★

TIME OUT **Pure & Simple,** a food stall offering healthful snacks and full meals, proves that nutritious can also be delicious. While cholesterol addicts pig out on basic burgers and fries, those who take the Wonders of Life message to heart can sample the venison chili spiked with fresh herbs, the salads with a choice of zippy dressings (including the beta-carotene salad with tomato-basil vinaigrette), and sandwiches that for once are better than what you'd make at home, all followed by a slice of angel food cake or a fruit or yogurt smoothie. The whole-wheat waffles with berry toppings are somewhat overrated but a nice touch. The prices won't give you a heart attack either, although overhearing the Anacomical Players ask—and answer—as you eat, "Why do some people pick their nose?" may give you pause.

HORIZONS

Horizons is a relentlessly optimistic look at the once and future future. After being enjoined to "live your dreams," you ride a tram past visions of the future, where former great minds imagine what the world might have been like in a hundred years or so. There's the 19th-century French artist Albert Robida's vision of Paris in the 1950s, with dirigible taxis, and Jules Verne's picture of spaceships as bullets with microscopic portholes. Visitors slathered with sunscreen will get a kick out of the 1930s view of the 1990s home, which includes personal tanning centers where you could choose between Hawaiian, Floridian, or Bahamian shades of brown. The tram then moves past a series of tableaus of life in a future space colony. This pavilion was built more than a decade ago, and the magnetic levitation trains it envisioned are now being tried out in Japan. Who knows whether the holographic telephones will soon be marketed? Visitors who have already gone through Living Seas and The Land will find Mesa Verde's future farming sequence and the Sea Castle section especially interesting; at Horizons you get the idea of what innovations are being imagined and then you see them being tested in other pavilions. The Omega Centuri tableau, portraying a free-floating space colony, prefigures virtual reality, with its games of zero-gravity basketball and simulated outdoor sports. *Duration: 15 min. Crowds: Often large because of its location near Innoventions, but the only time the wait exceeds 15 min is when the megaride at the nearby Universe of Energy lets out, and usually swift-moving trams keep wait times down.*

Strategy: Keep an eye on the line, and if it's long, just go back later. Audience: All ages. Rating: ★★

WORLD OF MOTION

Shaped like a wheel, World of Motion features the TransCenter—a 33,000-square-foot exhibit and auto showroom displaying new models from General Motors—and the **World of Motion ride,** which is essentially a dippy, feel-good frolic through scenarios depicting the history of human attempts to get somewhere else faster. Despite the 20-odd elaborate sets and more than 140 Audio-Animatronic characters, sophisticated this ain't. Broad humor rules as humanity tries out ostrich-power and zebra-power before harnessing horse-power, invents the wheel, rolls up the magic carpet, and experiments with flying machines, balloons, steam carriages, riverboats, stagecoaches, airplanes, automobiles, and a host of Rube Goldberg contraptions. Genuine antiques, such as old-fashioned autos and a 150-year-old Wells Fargo stagecoach, lend verisimilitude. Kids love this, as well as the addictive jingle, "It's Fun to Be Free." Adults may feel the same way when the ride ends. *Duration: 15 min. Crowds: Large, but this high-capacity, continuously loading ride can handle the numbers. Strategy: Go anytime, and don't be daunted by lines—they move quickly. Audience: All ages. Rating: ★★*

What's fascinating about the **TransCenter** is not just the latest models from GM, or the assembly line robot, or even the wind tunnel demonstrating the principles of aerodynamic drag, but the display of all the experimental automobiles that provide faster, cheaper, more ecologically sound alternatives to what clogs up our roads nowadays. You also see short presentations on milestones in 20th-century transportation and the quality tests GM uses to ensure it doesn't raise lemons.

TIME OUT Handsome, hexagonally shaped **Odyssey** restaurant looks like a pleasant sit-down eatery, but the food comes a lot faster.

LIVING SEAS

On Epcot Center's western outer ring is the first satellite pavilion, Living Seas, a favorite among children. Epcot Center is known for its imaginative fountains; the one at Living Seas flings surf in a never-ending wave against a rock garden beneath the stylized marquee. Time and technology have caught up with the 5.7-million-gallon aquarium at the pavilion's core, thrilling when it first opened, so that what was once revolutionary has now been equaled by top aquariums around the country and at Sea World. Still, the three-minute **Caribbean Coral Reef Ride** encircling the acrylic tank may be too short. Sometimes you'll catch sight of a diver, testing out the latest scuba equipment, surrounded by a cloud of parrot fish while scattering a mixture of dry dog food, chicken's laying pellets, amino-acid solution, and B-complex vitamins or carefully placing a head of lettuce within reach of a curious sea turtle.

After the ride, you may want to circumnavigate the tank at your own speed on an upper level, pointing out barracudas, stingrays, parrot fish, sea turtles, and even sharks, before exploring the two levels of **Sea Base Alpha,** a prototype undersea research facility that is a typical Epcot Center playground. Each of its six modules is dedicated to a specific subject: the history of robotics, ocean exploration, ocean ecosystems, dolphins, porpoises, and sea lions. Fully interactive, these contain films, touchy-feely sections, miniaquariums, and video quizzes; there's even a deep-sea diving suit that visitors can try on. *Duration: 45 min and up, including the 3-min ride, depending on how long you leer at angelfish and play Diver Dan at the modules. Crowds: Large, all day* *long. Strategy: Stop in first thing in the morning or after 5. Audience: All but young children. Rating:* ★★★

THE LAND

Shaped like an intergalactic greenhouse, the enormous skylighted The Land pavilion dedicates 6 acres and a host of different attractions to everyone's favorite topic: food. You can easily spend two hours exploring here. The main event is the **Listen to the Land** boat ride. Piloted by an informative, overalls-clad guide, you cruise through three biomes (rain forest, desert, and prairie ecological communities) and into an experimental greenhouse that demonstrates how food sources may be grown in the future, not only on the planet but also in outer space. Sunshine bass, tilapia, pacu—the piranha's vegetarian cousin—and shrimp are raised in controlled aquacells, and tomatoes, peppers, and squash thrive in the Desert Farm area through a system of drip irrigation that delivers just the right amount of water and nutrients to their roots. Gardeners will be interested in the section on integrated pest management, which relies on "good" bugs like ladybugs to control insect predators. Many of the growing areas are actual experiments-in-progress, in which Disney and the U.S. Department of Agriculture have joined forces to produce, say, a sweeter pineapple or a faster-growing pepper. Interestingly, while the plants and fish in the greenhouse are all quite real—and are regularly harvested for use in The Land's restaurants—those in the biomes are artful fakes, manufactured by Disney elves out of flexible, lightweight plastic. The grass is made out of glass fibers and is implanted into rubber mats—a useful deterrent to barefooted trespassers, perhaps. *Duration: 14 min. Crowds: Large, all day. Strategy: Go during mealtimes. Audience: Teens and adults. Rating:* ★★★

The terminally cute singing fruits and vegetables of the Kitchen Kaberet Revue have been replaced with a new musical extravaganza, **Food Rocks**. It's a rowdy concert where recognizable rock 'n' roll performers take the shape of favorite foods and sing about the joys of nutrition. There are performances by the Peach Boys, Chubby Cheddar, and Neil Moussaka, among others. *Duration: 20 min. Crowds: A large theater erases them. Strategy: Go when the line at Listen to the Land is too long. Audience: Children. Rating:* ★

The newest attraction at The Land is the **Circle of Life** presentation, a film featuring three stars of *The Lion King*—Simba the lion, Timon, the meerkat, and Pumbaa, the waddling warthog—in a powerful message about protecting the world's environment for all living things. Part animation, part *National Geographic*–like film (using spectacular 70mm live-action footage), *Circle of Life* tells a fable about a "Hakuna Matata Lakeside Village" that Timon and Pumbaa are developing by clearing the African savanna. Simba cautions them about mistreating the land by telling a story about a creature who occasionally forgets that everything is connected in the great Circle of Life. "That creature," he says, "is man." The lilting accompaniment, of course, is Elton John's award-winning song. *Duration: 20 min. Crowds: Large, all day. Strategy: Hit this first at The Land. Audience: Enlightening for children and adults but a nap opportunity for some toddlers. Rating:* ★★

Still hungry? Guided **Greenhouse Tours** of the greenhouses and aquacell areas cover the same topics as the boat ride but in much more detail—and you have the chance to ask questions. Reservations are essential and can be made on the lower floor, in the corner opposite the boat ride entrance, behind Broccoli and Co., a delightful shop stocking hydroponic plants, gardening books, vegetable refrigerator magnets, place mats, and cheerful aprons. *Duration: 45 min; available daily* *every ½ hr 9:30–4:30. Strategy: Reserve ahead. A good activity for busy times of day—late morning through afternoon. Audience: Adults and budding horticulturists. Rating:* ★★

TIME OUT Talk about a self-contained ecosystem: The pavilion grows its own produce and houses the **Farmer's Market** food court, composed of a dozen or so stands—a soup-and-salad stand, bakery (with great jumbo-size cinnamon rolls and corn muffins before 11 AM and brownies and cheesecake afterward), barbecue store, sandwich stand, ice cream stand, potato store, and beverage house, which bolsters the usual soft drinks with milk shakes, buttermilk, vegetable juice, and exotic fruit nectars. The brownies are legendary, and Epcot staffers have been known to make a special trip to pick up some of the bakery's chocolate chip cookies. Just remember that at this pavilion, you must eat all your vegetables.

JOURNEY INTO IMAGINATION

The last of the big three pavilions on the west side, Journey into Imagination, sets your mind spinning. We'd say that it's a fitting climax to an Epcot Center visit except for the fact that you want to be as alert and sparkling as possible to enjoy the clever Journey into Imagination ride through the creative process, the 3-D film *Honey, I Shrunk the Audience,* and the Image Works, a computer-enhanced creative playground. Don't miss the quirky fountains outside: the Jellyfish Fountains, which spurt streams of water that flatten at the top into their namesake shape, and the Serpentine Fountains, whose random squirts arc from one garden bed to another, over paths and—most of the time—over the people standing on them. Count on spending at least 1½ hours here, more if you become addicted to the Stepping Tones section of the Image Works.

The stars of the pavilion are a jolly red-headed, full-bearded, top-hatted professorial type called Dreamfinder and his sidekick, the ever-inquisitive, pop-eyed purple dragon, Figment (who often show up outside the pavilions to welcome visitors). They also guide you on the **Journey into Imagination,** a dreamy exploration of how creativity works. It begins with Dreamfinder's creating this Figment of his imagination, by combining a lizard's body, a crocodile's nose, a goat's horns, two big yellow eyes, two small wings, and an ineffable sense of wonder. Your most important stop is the Dreamport, which stores data collected by the senses for use by the imagination. Subsequent scenes show the data being spun into dreams that influence all areas of life, from science and technology to literature and the performing arts. Laser beams zing back and forth, lightning crackles, letters leap out of a giant typewriter, and an iridescent painting unfolds across a wall. Smile when you see flashing lights (about ¾ of the way through the ride)—you're on candid camera. You'll see the results at the end of the ride. *Duration: 13 min. Crowds: Steady during crowded periods. Strategy: Go early or late. Audience: All ages. Rating:* ★★★

No other theme park has anything that compares with the **Image Works,** an electronic funhouse crammed with interactive games and wizardry that will give your imagination a real workout. There's the Electronic Philharmonic (best done with a partner), in which you can take turns conducting an orchestra; you wave your hands over a console to increase or decrease the sound of an indicated batch of musical instruments. These, in turn, are spotlighted on a giant screen so that everyone can tune in. At the Magic Palette, you can use an electronic paintbrush to paint video images and washes of color that resemble psychedelic northern lights. Jumping up and down on the magic carpet at the Stepping Tones produces lights and music; each hexagonal splotch of colored light corresponds to a sound—a drumroll, a harp throb, a choral blast—and with a little bit of fancy dancing, you can create an étude. Though it's lots of fun to try out all the activities, it's equally entertaining to watch other people, too. *Duration: Allow at least ½ hr. Crowds: Thick in late morning and afternoon, but there's plenty of room. Strategy: Go during busy periods; because there's a separate entrance, you don't have to enter through the Journey into Imagination ride. Audience: All ages. Rating:* ★★★

Honey, I Shrunk the Audience replaced *Captain EO,* the longtime favorite featuring Michael Jackson, in 1994. It has quickly become one of the most popular attractions in Epcot, and it's not hard to understand why. This 3-D adventure utilizes the futuristic "shrinking" technologies demonstrated in two hit films that starred Rick Moranis. Moranis reprises his role as Dr. Wayne Szalinski, who is about to receive the Inventor of the Year Award from the Imagination Institute. While Dr. Szalinski is demonstrating his latest shrinking machine, though, things go really, really wrong. It'll cut into your fun too much if we give anything else away, but be prepared to laugh and scream your head off, courtesy of the special in-theater effects, moving seats, and 3-D film technology. *Duration: 14 min. Crowds: Large theater capacity should mean a relatively short wait, but the ride's popularity can make for big crowds. Strategy: Go first thing in the morning or just before closing. Audience: All but the youngest children. Rating:* ★★★

World Showcase

The 40-acre World Showcase Lagoon is 1⅓ miles around, but in that space, you circumnavigate the globe, or at least explore it, in pavilions representing 11 different countries in Europe, Asia, North Africa, and the Americas. In these, native food, entertainment, art and handicrafts, and usually a multimedia presentation showcase the culture and people; architecture and landscaping re-create well-known landmarks. France has a scaled-down model of the Eiffel Tower, America's display is housed in Liberty Hall, Japan glories in a pagoda, Italy has a reproduction of Venice's Piazza San Marco, and Morocco's minaret is practically a landmark of its own. Impressive as they are by day, the structures are truly fantastical at night, when they are outlined in literally miles of tiny lights. Instead of amusement park rides, you have breathtaking films at the Canadian, Chinese, French, and Norwegian pavilions; several art exhibitions; and the chance to chat in the native language of the friendly foreign staff, all of whom are part of a Disney exchange program. Live entertainment is an integral part of the pavilions' presentations.

The focal point of World Showcase is the American Adventure. The pavilions of other countries fan out from both sides, encircling the lagoon. Counterclockwise from World Showcase Plaza as you enter from Future World are Canada, the United Kingdom, France, Morocco, Japan, the American Adventure, Italy, Germany, China, Norway, and Mexico.

CANADA

"Oh, it's just our Canadian outdoors," said a typically modest native guide upon being asked the model for the striking rocky chasm and tumbling waterfall that represent just one of the high points of Canada. The beautiful formal gardens do have an antecedent: Butchart Gardens, in Victoria, British Columbia. And so does the Hôtel du Canada, a French Gothic mansion with spires, turrets, and a mansard roof; anyone who's ever stayed at Quebec's Château Frontenac or Ottawa's Château Laurier will recognize the imposing style favored by architects of Canadian railroad hotels. Like the size of the Rocky Mountains and the Great Canadian North, the scale of the structures seems immense; unlike the real thing, it's managed with a trick called forced perspective, which exaggerates the smallness of the distant parts to make the entire thing look humongous. Another bit of design legerdemain: The World Show-case Rockies are made of chicken wire and painted concrete mounted on a movable platform similar to a parade float. Ah, wilderness!

The top attraction is the CircleVision film *O Canada!* And that's just what you'll say after the stunning opening shot of the Royal Canadian Mounted Police literally surrounding you as they circle the screen. From there, you whoosh over waterfalls, saunter through Montreal and Toronto, sneak up to bears and bison, mush behind a husky-pulled dog sled, and land pluck—or, should we say, puck—in the middle of a hockey game. This is a standing-only theater, with lean rails. *Duration: 17 min. Crowds: Can be thick in late afternoon. Strategy: Go in the morning or evening. Audience: All ages (but no strollers permitted and toddlers have to be held aloft to see). Rating:* ★★★

Canada also contains shops selling maple syrup, lumberjack shirts, and other trapper paraphernalia to help you survive in the Far North or even the Deep South.

TIME OUT Le Cellier, a buffeteria with some style—vaulted stone ceilings and a cozy subterranean air—serves hearty fare such as pork pie, poached fresh salmon, and bread custard with maple sauce.

UNITED KINGDOM
Never has it been so easy to cross the English Channel. A pastiche of there-will-always-be-an-England architecture, the United Kingdom rambles between the elegant mansions lining a London square to the bustling, half-timbered shops of a village High Street to the thatched-roof cottages from the countryside (their thatch made of plastic broom bristles in consideration of local fire regulations). And of course there's a pair of the scarlet phone booths that used to be found all over the United Kingdom, now on their way to being historic relics. The pavilion has no single major attraction. Instead, you can wander through shops selling tea and tea accessories, Welsh handicrafts, Royal Doulton figurines, and woolens and tartans from Pringle of Scotland; Lords and Ladies sells fragrances, bath accessories, and heraldic plaques (only the British would see a connection between these three). Outside, the strolling Old Globe Players coax audience members into participating in their definitely low-brow versions of Shakespeare.

TIME OUT Revive yourself with a pint of the best—although you'll be hard put to decide among the offerings—at **Rose & Crown Pub,** which also offers traditional afternoon tea on the outside terrace. The adjacent dining room serves more substantial fare (reservations required; *see* Chapter 7, Dining).

FRANCE
You don't need the scaled-down model of the Eiffel Tower to tell you that you've arrived in France, specifically Paris. There's the poignant accordion music wafting out of concealed speakers, the trim sycamores pruned in the French style to develop signature knots at the end of each branch, and the delicious aromas surrounding the Boulangerie Pâtis-serie bakeshop. This is the Paris of dreams, a Paris without the prob-lems of parking, the numerous dogs, and all those irascible French people. (We can understand how Disney remedied the parking situation but still can't figure out where they found such a collection of pleasant, helpful, English-speaking natives who retain their inherited pertness.) It's a Paris of La Belle Epoque, "the beautiful age" just before World

War I, when solid mansard-roofed mansions were crowned with iron filigree, when the least brick was drenched in romanticism. Here's a replica of the conservatorylike Les Halles—the iron-and-glass-barrel-roofed market that no longer exists in the City of Light; there's an arching footbridge, and all around, of course, there are shops. You can inspect artwork, Limoges porcelain, and crystal sold in the exquisite Plume et Palette, buy decorated writing paper Proust would have envied and a pen to match at La Signature, pick up a baking pan to make those famous madeleine cookies at Tout pour le Gourmet, and acquire a bottle of Bouzy Rouge to wash it down with at La Maison du Vin, where wine tastings are frequently held (there's a small charge).

The intimate Palais du Cinema, inspired by the royal theater at Fontainebleau, screens the film *Impressions de France,* a homage to the glories of the country. Shown on five screens spanning 200° in an air-conditioned, sit-down theater (no uncivilized lean bars here!), the film takes you to vineyards at harvesttime, Paris on Bastille Day, the Alps, Versailles, Normandy's Mont-St-Michel, and the stunning châteaus of the Loire Valley. The musical accompaniment also hits high notes, with familiar segments from Offenbach, Debussy, and Saint-Säens, all woven together by longtime Disney musician Buddy Baker. *Duration: 18 min. Crowds: Considerable from late morning through late afternoon. Strategy: Come before noon or after dinner. Audience: Adults. Rating:* ★★★

TIME OUT   Stop in for a snack at **Boulangerie Pâtisserie** or **Au Petit Café,** a Parisian-style sidewalk café that serves sandwiches and omelets. *See also* Chapter 7, Dining.

MOROCCO

You don't need a magic carpet to be instantaneously transported into an exotic culture—just walk through the pointed arches of the Bab Boujouloud gate into Morocco. A gift from the kingdom of Morocco, they are ornamented with beautiful wood carvings and encrusted with intricate mosaics made of 9 tons of handmade, hand-cut tiles; 19 native artisans were sent to Epcot Center to install them and to create the dusty stucco walls that seem to have withstood centuries of sandstorms. Look closely and you'll see that every tile has a small crack or some other imperfection, and no tile depicts a living creature—in deference to the Muslim belief that only Allah creates perfection and life.

Koutoubia Minaret, a replica of the prayer tower in Marrakesh, acts as Morocco's landmark. Traditional winding alleyways, each corner bursting with carpets, brasses, leatherwork, and other North African craftsmanship, lead to a beautifully tiled fountain and lush gardens. You can take a guided tour of the pavilion (inquire of any cast member), check out the ever-changing exhibit in the **Gallery of Arts and History,** and entertain yourself examining the wares at such shops as Casablanca Carpets, Jewels of the Sahara, Brass Bazaar, and Berber Oasis.

JAPAN

A brilliant vermilion torii gate, derived from the design of Hiroshima Bay's much-photographed Itsukushima shrine, frames the World Showcase Lagoon and epitomizes the striking yet serene mood that pervades Japan. Disney horticulturists deserve a hand here for their achievement in constructing out of all-American plants and boulders a very Japanese landscape, complete with rocks, pebbled streams, pools, and hills. At sunset, or during a rainy dusk, the sharp edges of the evergreens and twisted branches of the corkscrew willows frame a perfect Japanese view of the five-story winged pagoda that is the heart of the pavilion. Based on the 8th-century Horyuji Temple in Nara, the brilliant blue pagoda has five levels, symbolizing the five elements of Buddhist belief—earth, water, fire, wind, sky. As you wander along the twisting paths, listen for the wind chimes and the soothing clack of the water mill, and watch a fiery sunset—Walt Disney World seems 5,000 miles away.

The peace is occasionally disturbed by performances on drums and gongs by the **Genroku Hanamai players.** Other entertainment is provided by demonstrations of traditional Japanese crafts such as kite making or snipping brown rice toffee into intricate shapes; these take place outdoors on the pavilion's plaza or in the **Bijutsu-Kan Gallery,** where there are also changing art exhibitions. Mitsukoshi department store, an immense three-centuries-old retail firm known as "Japan's Sears," carries everything from T-shirts to kimonos and row upon row of Japanese dolls.

TIME OUT   Westerners with a yen for Japanese tastes will be satisfied here at **Yaki-tori House,** which serves broiled chicken and beef on skewers (a sort of Japanese shish kebab) and batter-fried seafood and vegetables, as well as such Japanese specialties as clear soup and pickled ginger. Despite the fact that this is basically a gussied-up fast-food place, the food tastes authentic and is reasonably priced. *See also* Chapter 7, Dining.

AMERICAN ADVENTURE

At the American Adventure, housed in a scrupulous reproduction of Philadelphia's Liberty Hall, Disney's Imagineers prove that their kind of fantasy can beat reality hands-down. The 110,000 bricks, made by hand from soft pink Georgia clay, sheathe the familiar structure, which acts as a beacon for Epcot Center visitors across the lagoon. Talk about symbolism. And when those colored lights start flashing and the lasers zing from Spaceship Earth to Liberty Hall during the sound-and-light-and-fireworks IllumiNations show after dark, it's difficult not to feel patriotic.

The pavilion's superlative attraction is a 100-yard dash through history called the **American Adventure.** To the music of a piece called the "Golden Dream," performed by the Philadelphia Orchestra, it combines evocative sets, the world's largest rear-projection screen (72 feet in width), enormous movable stages, and 35 Audio-Animatronic players, which are some of the most lifelike ever created—Ben Franklin even climbs up stairs. Beginning with the arrival of the Pilgrims at Plymouth Rock and their grueling first winter, Ben Franklin and a wry, pipe-smoking Mark Twain narrate the episodes—both praiseworthy and shameful—that have shaped the American spirit. Disney detail is so painstaking that you never feel rushed and, in fact, each speech and each scene seems polished like a little jewel. You feel the cold at Valley Forge and the triumph when Charles Lindbergh flies the Atlantic; are moved by Nez Perce Chief Joseph's forced abdication of Native American ancestral lands and by women's rights campaigner Susan B. Anthony's speech; laugh with Will Rogers's aphorisms and learn about the pain of the Depression through an affecting radio broadcast by Franklin Delano Roosevelt; and recognize such popular figures as John Wayne, Lucille Ball, Muhammed Ali, and, yes, Mickey Mouse, epitomizing the American spirit. *Duration: 30 min. Crowds: Large, but the theater is huge, so you can almost always get into the next show. Strategy: Go when everything else is busy and you want to sit down and cool off. Audience: All ages. Rating:* ★★★

While waiting for the show to begin, be sure to read the quotes on the walls of the Hall of Presidents. They include thought-provoking comments from Wendell Wilkie, Jane Addams, Charles Lindbergh, Ayn Rand, Archibald MacLeish, and Thomas Wolfe, and they offer far from standard patriotic pablum. Directly opposite the pavilion, on the edge of the lagoon, is the **American Gardens Theatre.** Until recently this was the venue for concerts and shows of the Yankee Doodle Dandy variety; it now hosts the **Magical World of Barbie,** a high-spirited song-and-dance-review about the world's most famous doll and her travels and adventures around the world (aha! the Epcot connection!). Barbie and her pals Ken and Skipper also make a daily appearance near the entrance to World Showcase.

TIME OUT   **Liberty Inn,** a counter-service restaurant, serves burgers, sandwiches, apple pie, and other all-American fare.

ITALY

Saunter around the corner into the replica of Venice's Piazza San Marco and it's as if you've moved to the land of *la dolce vita.* In Italy, the star is the architecture: a reproduction of Venice's Doge's Palace that's true right down to the gold leaf on the ringlets of the angel perched 100 feet atop the Campanile; the seawall stained with age to whose barbershop-striped poles two gondolas are tethered; and the Romanesque columns, Byzantine mosaics, Gothic arches, and stone walls that have all been carefully "antiqued" to look historical. Mediterranean plantings such as cypress, kumquat, and olive trees add to the verisimilitude. Inside, shops sell Venetian beads and glasswork, leather purses and belts, and Perugina cookies and chocolate "kisses."

GERMANY

Germany, a make-believe village that distills the best folk architecture from all over that country, is so jovial that you practically expect the Seven Dwarfs to come heigh-ho-ing out to meet you. Instead, you'll hear the hourly chimes from the specially designed glockenspiel on the clock tower, musical toots and tweets from multitudinous cuckoo clocks, folk tunes from the spinning dolls and lambs sold at Der Teddybär, and the satisfied grunts of hungry visitors chowing down on hearty German cooking. Other than the four-times-a-day oompah band show in the Biergarten restaurant (*see* Chapter 7, Dining), Germany doesn't offer any specific entertainment, but it does boast the most shops of any pavilion. Our favorites: Die Weinachts Ecke, for nutcrackers and other Old World Christmas ornaments; Süssigkeiten, for cookies and not-to-be-believed animal crackers; and Volkskunst, whose folk crafts collection includes cuckoo clocks that range from hummingbird scale to the size of an eagle.

TIME OUT   The **Sommerfest** pretzel-and-bratwurst cart is one of the rare snacking options in this part of the World.

CHINA

At China, a shimmering red-and-gold, three-tiered replica of Beijing's Temple of Heaven towers over a serene Chinese garden, an art gallery displaying treasures from the People's Republic, a spacious emporium devoted to Chinese goods, and two restaurants. The garden, planted with rosebushes native to China, a 100-year-old mulberry tree, and water oaks (whose twisted branches look Asian but are actually Florida homegrown), is one of the most peaceful spots in the World Showcase, with its piped-in traditional Chinese music.

Think of the Temple of Heaven as an especially fitting movie theater for showings of the **Wonders of China,** a sensational panorama of the land and people dramatically portrayed on a 360° CircleVision screen. The only drawback is that the theater has no chairs; lean rails are provided. *Duration: 19 min. Crowds: Steady from late morning through late afternoon, but the theater's high capacity means you can usually get into* *the next show. Strategy: Go anytime. Audience: All ages (but no strollers permitted and small children have to be held aloft to see). Rating:* ★★★

TIME OUT **Lotus Blossom Café** has egg rolls and stir-fries that you can wash down with cold TsingTao beer. The food is a nonthreatening introduction for Occidental tastes, but more sophisticated palates will find it bland—and overpriced at that.

NORWAY

In Norway there are rough-hewn timbers and sharply pitched roofs (so the snow will slip right off), softened and brightened by bloom-stuffed window boxes, figured shutters, and lots of smiling, blond and blue-eyed young Norwegians, all eager to speak English and show off their country. The pavilion complex contains a 14th-century stone fortress that mimics Oslo's Akershus, cobbled streets, rocky waterfalls, and a wood stave church, modeled after one built in 1250, with wood dragons glaring from the eaves. The church houses an exhibit called "To the Ends of the Earth," which tells the story of two early 20th-century polar expeditions by using vintage artifacts. It all puts you in the mood to handle beautifully embroidered woolen sweaters (which sell briskly despite Florida's heat), wood carvings, and glass artworks in the pavilion's shops.

Norway also has a dandy boat ride: **Maelstrom.** Visitors pile into 16-passenger, dragon-headed longboats for a voyage through time that, despite its scary name and encounters with evil trolls, is actually more fascinating than frightful. The journey begins in a 10th-century village where a boat, much like yours and the ones used by Eric the Red, is being readied for a Viking voyage. You glide steeply up through a mythical forest populated by trolls, who cause the boat to plunge backward down a mild waterfall, then cruise amid the grandeur of the Geiranger fjord, experience a storm in the North Sea, and, as the presence of oil rigs signals a return to the 20th century, end up in a peaceful coastal village. Disembarking, you proceed into a theater for a quick and delightful film about Norway's scenic wonders, culture, and people. *Duration: 10 min. Crowds: Steady, with slow-moving lines from late morning through early evening. Strategy: Go in the evening. Audience: All ages. Rating:* ★★

TIME OUT Open-face sandwiches can be washed down with Norwegian Ringnes beer at **Kringla Bakeri og Kafe.** Go early or late for speediest service. *See also* Chapter 7, Dining.

MEXICO

Housed in a spectacular Mayan pyramid surrounded by a tangle of tropical vegetation, Mexico contains the El Río del Tiempo boat ride, an exhibit of pre-Columbian art, a restaurant, and, of course, a shopping plaza, where you can unload many, many pesos.

True to its name, **El Río del Tiempo** takes you on a trip down the river of time. Your journey from the jungles of the Yucatán to modern-day Mexico City is enlivened by video images of feathered Toltec dancers, by Spanish-colonial Audio-Animatronic dancing puppets, and by film clips of the cliff divers in Acapulco, the speed boats in Manzanillo (ah, progress!), and snorkeling around Isla Mujeres. The puppets are garish and reprise "It's a Small World," without the brain-numbing ditty. But this ride is still one of the major attractions in World Showcase. *Duration: 9 min. Crowds: Long, slow-moving lines from late morning through late afternoon. Strategy: Skip this one on a one-day first-time visit. Audience: All ages. Rating:* ★

Modeled on the *mercado* (market) in the town of Taxco, **Plaza de los Amigos** is well named: There are lots of friendly people—the women dressed in off-the-shoulder ruffled peasant blouses and bright skirts, the men in white shirts and dashing sashes—all eager to sell you trinkets from a cluster of canopied carts. The perimeter is rimmed with stores with tiled roofs, wrought-iron balconies, and window boxes drooling flowers. What to buy? Brightly colored paper blossoms, sombreros, baskets, pottery, leather goods, and colorful papier-mâché piñatas, which are so popular that Epcot Center imports them by the truckload.

TIME OUT   For burritos and margaritas, go outside to the counter-service **Cantina de San Angel.** *See also* Chapter 7, Dining.

Dining

In World Showcase every pavilion sponsors at least one and often two or even three eateries. Where there's a choice, it is between a full-service restaurant with commensurately higher prices, a more affordable ethnic fast-food spot, and carts and shops selling snacks ranging from French pastries to Japanese ices—whatever's appropriate to the pavilion. Reservations are essential at the formal restaurants (*see* Reservations, *above, and* Chapter 7, Dining).

Future World is not bursting with eateries. You won't starve here, but you do need to plan ahead. In addition to the counter-service spots, your options include **The Land Grille Room** in The Land pavilion, a revolving restaurant that serves solid American food, and **Coral Reef,** a seafood restaurant in the Living Seas with a windowed wall onto the pavilion's enormous aquarium. For other Epcot Center sit-down dining options, *see* Chapter 7, Dining.

Entertainment

Above the Lagoon

First there are the all-out spectaculars we've come to expect at the Disney parks. Figuring "Why waste a perfectly good lagoon?" Walt Disney World uses its watery stage for the spectacular **IllumiNations** show every night a half hour before closing. Be sure to stick around. Lasers, lights, fireworks, fountains, and music from every host nation fill the air over the lagoon; the show is so over the top that it's got to be seen to be believed. Although there's generally good viewing from all around the lagoon, the best spots are on the bridge between France and the United Kingdom, the promenade in front of Canada and Norway, and the bridge between China and Germany, which will give you a clear shot, unobstructed by trees. A sweet touch after the show: Concealed loudspeakers play the theme from "It's a Small World" manipulated into salsa, polka, waltz, and even—believe it or not—Asian rhythms. Talk about a total experience.

At the Pavilions

Some of the most enjoyable entertainment takes place outside the national pavilions in their courtyards and along the promenade by the lagoon. Live shows with actors, dancers, singers, mime routines, and demonstrations of folk arts and crafts are presented at varying times of day; get times from the WorldKey terminals in Earth Station or look for signs posted outside the pavilions. Italy's farcical **Commedia di Bologna,** France's **Theatre du Fromage,** and the United Kingdom's **Old Globe Players** each enlist audience members as heroes and villains, princes and princesses, to the hilarity of all. Near American Adventure, on the new America Gardens Stage, the **Magical World of Barbie** is a 30-minute musical that follows Barbie and her friends on a whirlwind tour of four continents. The humorous show features 18 singers and dancers and is performed five times a day, Wednesday through Sunday.

Shopping

Frankly, it's difficult to spend money at Future World. True, there are all sorts of kitchen- and garden-related knickknacks at The Land's **Green Thumb Emporium** and marine merchandise at Living Seas, but after that the pickings are slim indeed. The standard range of Epcot Center logo souvenirs is available at the **Centorium,** and you can pick up an aid to healthy living, including sweats emblazoned with Disney characters working up a sweat, at **Well & Goods Limited** in the Wonders of Life. But we suggest you save your shekels for the souks of World Showcase.

World Showcase is nothing if not crammed with souvenirs, because each pavilion shelters shops galore (most of them described in the pavilion's text). Many of their wares are also sold in shop branches and department stores around the United States. But among the more exotic items are leather belts and purses from Morocco's **Tangier Traders,** beautiful writing paper from **Plume et Palette** in France, heraldic plaques at **Lords and Ladies** in the United Kingdom, Inuit and Native American crafts at **Northwest Mercantile** in Canada, nutcrackers at **Die Weinachts Ecke** in Germany, piñatas at **Plaza de los Amigos** in Mexico, and kimonoed and obi-sashed dolls at **Mitsukoshi** in Japan.

If your shopping time is more limited, check out the two shops at the entrance to World Showcase: **Disney Traders,** as its name suggests, features Disney character dolls (dressed in the national costumes of the World Showcase participants) and the requisite T-shirts and sweatshirts. Kids love the flags from around the world. Also sold here—and only here—is a great keepsake for youngsters: a World Showcase Passport ($7.95). At each pavilion, kids can present their passports to be stamped—it's a great way to keep their interest up in this more adult area of Epcot. At **Port of Entry,** there are products from around the world; a recent shopping expedition there revealed a new theme, "Preserve and Protect," with ecologically sound products. In keeping with the green theme, our favorite item was the small topiary Mickey Mouse.

Access for Travelers with Disabilities

Accessibility standards in this park are high. Many attractions and most restaurants and shops are fully wheelchair accessible. Not only does the *Guidebook for Guests with Hearing Impairments* give scripts and story lines for all Epcot Center attractions with sound tracks; personal translator units can be rented ($4 plus $40 deposit) to amplify sound in some of the theater shows.

Attractions

FUTURE WORLD

To ride the **Spaceship Earth ride,** you must be able to walk four steps and transfer to a ride vehicle; in the unusual case that emergency evacuation may be necessary, it is by way of stairs. Service animals are not appropriate. Although much of the enchantment is in the visual details, the narration is interesting as well. The Epcot Discovery Center here is wheelchair accessible. **Innoventions** is completely wheelchair accessible. **Universe of Energy** is accessible to guests using standard wheelchairs and those who can transfer to them; especially because this is one of the attractions whose sound tracks are amplified by rental personal translator units, it is slightly more interesting to those with hearing impairments than to those with visual impairments. In **Wonders of Life,** Cranium Command, *The Making of Me,* Goofy about Health, and the Anacomical Theater are all totally wheelchair accessible, with special seating sections for guests using wheelchairs. Guests with visual impairments may wish to skip Goofy about Health; Cranium Command and *The Making of Me* are both covered in the guidebook for guests with hearing impairments. To ride the turbulent Body Wars, you must transfer to a ride seat; those who lack upper-body strength should request extra shoulder restraints. It's inappropriate for service animals. **Horizons** is accessible by guests who can walk three paces and step up one step. Service animals should not ride. **World of Motion** requires guests using oversize wheelchairs or scooters to transfer to Disney chairs; lock your brakes. In **Living Seas,** guests using wheelchairs typically bypass the three-minute ride and move directly into the SeaBase Alpha and aquarium area—the best part of the pavilion. In **The Land,** the Harvest Theater, Food Rocks, and the Greenhouse Tour are completely wheelchair accessible. Rental personal translator units amplify sound in the Harvest Theater film *Symbiosis,* and those who can read lips will enjoy the Greenhouse Tour. As for the Listen to the Land boat ride, guests using an oversize wheelchair or a scooter must transfer to a Disney chair. At **Journey into Imagination,** the ride requires guests to take three steps and step up into a ride vehicle. The Magic Eye theater, home to *Honey, I Shrunk the Audience,* is completely accessible. The hands-on activities of Image Works are wheelchair accessible; there's something for everyone in here.

WORLD SHOWCASE

Most people stroll about Epcot Center, but there are two forms of transportation here: Friendship boats, which require guests using oversize wheelchairs or scooters to transfer to Disney chairs, and the omnibuses that chug along the promenade, which require guests to walk up four steps and have a folding wheelchair. The **American Adventure, France, China,** and **Canada** are all wheelchair accessible; personal translator units amplify the sound tracks here. **Germany, Italy, Japan, Morocco,** and the **United Kingdom** all have live entertainment, most with strong aural as well as visual elements; the plaza areas where the shows are presented are wheelchair accessible. In **Norway,** you must be able to step down into and up out of a boat to ride the Maelstrom, and an emergency evacuation would require the use of stairs; service animals should not ride. In **Mexico,** the El Río del Tiempo boat ride is accessible to guests using wheelchairs, but those using a scooter or oversize chair must transfer to a Disney model.

Entertainment
Certain areas along the lagoon's edge at Showcase Plaza, the United Kingdom, and Italy are reserved for guests using wheelchairs during IllumiNations.

Shops and Restaurants
With a few exceptions, all are wheelchair accessible. In both the Land Grille Room and Living Seas' Coral Reef Restaurant, only one level is accessible to guests using wheelchairs, and France's Bistro de Paris is accessible only via staircase.

Information
See Access for Travelers with Disabilities *in* Essential Information, *above.*

DISNEY-MGM STUDIOS THEME PARK

When Walt Disney company chairman Michael Eisner opened Disney-MGM Studios in May 1989, he welcomed visitors to "the Hollywood that never was and always will be." Inspired by southern California's highly successful Universal Studios tour (an even more successful version of which is just down I–4), Disney-MGM combined Disney detail with MGM's motion-picture expertise in an amalgamation that blends theme park with fully functioning movie and television production center, breathtaking rides with instructional tours, nostalgia with high-tech wonders.

The rosy-hued view of the moviemaking business takes place in a dreamy stage set from the 1930s and 1940s, amid sleek Art Moderne buildings in pastel colors, funky diners, kitschy decorations, and sculptured gardens populated by roving actors playing, well, roving actors. Thanks to a rich library of film scores, Disney-MGM is permeated with music, all familiar, all happy, all evoking the magic of the movies and all constantly burbling through the camouflaged loudspeakers at a volume just right for humming along. And watching over all, like the penthouse suite of a benevolent genie, is the Earfful Tower, a 13-story water tower adorned with giant mouse ears.

Although some of the attractions will interest young children, Disney-MGM is really best for teenagers old enough to watch old movies on television and catch the cinematic references. Not quite as fantasy oriented as the Magic Kingdom or as earnestly educational as Epcot Center, Disney-MGM could almost be said to have attitude. Not a lot, mind you, but enough to add a little sizzle to the steak.

Lights, camera, aaaaand action!

Essential Information

Getting Around

Inside Disney-MGM Studios Theme Park, distances are small and walking is the optimal way to get around.

Tourist Information

The **Crossroads of the World** kiosk in the Entrance Plaza dispenses maps, entertainment schedules, brochures, and the like. Take specific questions to **Guest Relations,** inside the turnstiles on the left side of the Entrance Plaza.

The **Production Information Window** (☎ 407/560–4651), also in the Entrance Plaza, is the place to find out what's being taped when and how to get into the audience.

At the corner where Hollywood Boulevard intersects with Sunset Boulevard is the **Studios Tip Board,** a large chalkboard with constantly updated information about attractions' wait time—reliable except for those moments when everyone follows the "See It Now!" advice and the line immediately triples. Studio staffers are on hand.

Reservations

Make dining reservations at the Hollywood Junction kiosk, located just to the right of the Studio Tip Board at the intersection of Hollywood and Sunset boulevards. If you're staying at one of the Disney hotels, you can make reservations from one to three days in advance (☎ 407/824–4321). Reservations are also required for the popular Aladdin's Breakfast Adventure, held each morning from 8:30 AM to 10:30 AM at

Aladdin's Soundstage Restaurant (☎ 407/824–4321). Disney resort guests can reserve seats through their hotel's guest services desk.

Services

BABY CARE

At the small Baby Care Center, you'll find facilities for nursing as well as **formula, baby food, pacifiers,** and **disposable diapers** for sale. There are **changing tables** here and in all women's rooms and some men's rooms. You can also buy disposable diapers in the Guest Services building. Oscar's, just inside the entrance turnstiles and to the right, is the place for **stroller rentals** ($1 rental fee; $6 deposit required).

CAMERAS AND FILM

If you want something more than a disposable Kodak Fun Saver camera, walk through the aperture-shaped door of the Darkroom on Hollywood Boulevard, and rent a **35mm camera** or **video camcorder** ($5 and $40, respectively; refundable $70–$600 deposit required). Be advised that camcorders are full-size models only.

For **minor camera repairs,** the Darkroom is the place.

Drop off your film at the Darkroom for **one-hour film developing** or at any Photo Express container (look for signs) for two-hour film developing; you can pick up your pictures at the Darkroom or have them delivered to your hotel if you're staying on-site.

FIRST AID

It's in the Entrance Plaza adjoining Guest Services.

LOCKERS

You'll find them alongside Oscar's Classic Car Souvenirs, to the right of the Entrance Plaza after you pass through the turnstiles.

LOST CHILDREN AND ADULTS

If you're worried about your children getting lost, get them name tags at Guest Services. If you do get separated, ask any cast member before you panic; lost children's logbooks are kept (at Guest Services).

Guest Services also has a computerized Message Center, where notes can be left for traveling companions not only at Disney-MGM but also at other parks.

LOST AND FOUND

Report your loss or find at Guest Services in the Entrance Plaza. If nobody claims what you turn in, you may get to keep it.

MONEY

There is an ATM near the Production Information Window, outside Disney-MGM's Entrance Plaza. Currency exchange is available at the Guest Relations window.

PACKAGE PICKUP

Ask the shop clerk to forward any large purchase you make to Guest Services in the Entrance Plaza so you won't have to carry it around all day. (Allow three hours.)

WHEELCHAIR RENTALS

Go to Oscar's, to your right in the Entrance Plaza ($6 plus $1 deposit); Oscar's also has motor-powered chairs ($25 plus $20 deposit). No electric scooters are available in this park. If your rental needs replacing, ask a host or hostess.

Strategies for Your Visit

Blitz Tour

Pick up an entertainment schedule on your way into the park. Then run, do not walk, right up Hollywood Boulevard, hang a right at Sunset Boulevard, and dash to MGM's newest attraction, the 13-story **Twilight Zone Tower of Terror.** (You won't be the only one with this plan, so if the lines look too awful, consider swinging back during the quieter evening hours.) Next, head back to the Chinese Theater for the **Great Movie Ride.** It'll put you in the mood for a day at the Disney-MGM Studios like nothing else—and help you brush up on the songs pouring out of the hidden speakers. There's nothing like having a bunch of tunes to whistle while standing in line. So suitably armed, head to the **Backstage Studio Tour** and spend the rest of the morning backstage and **Inside the Magic.**

Beat the crowds to an early lunch at one of the lakeside beaneries. Keep your eyes tuned to the Indiana Jones Epic Stunt Spectacular and SuperStar Television schedules. As soon as they have magnetized enough people, take your cue and zip over to the **Monster Sound Show.** Nothing like some simple arithmetic to realize that 2,000 seats in the Indiana Jones amphitheater and 1,000 seats at SuperStar Television won't fit into the 270 seats at the Monster Sound Show without one humongous line, right? This way, you avoid it. *Then* you can go to **SuperStar Television.** However, save Indiana for later—it's especially dramatic at night.

Instead, amble over to **Jim Henson's Muppet*Vision 3D,** checking the lines at **Star Tours** on the way. If you can't see a line, nip in now. If the line looks appalling, the Muppets are a great consolation prize. Especially because Muppet*Vision lets out in a back corner and while everyone is milling around and thinking of wandering up New York Street, *you* can whip right back to Star Tours for a second try.

You'll need a little downtime after Star Tours. Take the opportunity to explore **Sunset Boulevard** (the shops here sell much of the same merchandise as those on Hollywood Boulevard and they're much less crowded), grab a healthful snack at the Anaheim Produce Company, and try to catch a late-afternoon performance of **Beauty and the Beast** at the **Theater of the Stars.** That will put you in the right mood for the **Magic of Disney Animation,** and the time will be right, too—the crowds here will have begun to thin but the animators won't have gone home yet. Spend all the time you want but make sure that you catch the last show at the **Indiana Jones Epic Stunt Spectacular.** We love the way the idol's eyes glow in the dusk, and the gobs of flame from the exploding truck make you understand just why this attraction is called "spectacular." Then there's the music, which will carry you all the way back to the parking lots. Remember to turn at the gate for one last look at the Earfful Tower, whose perky appendages are outlined in gold lights.

Exploring Disney-MGM Studios Theme Park

Disney-MGM Studios is divided into six sightseeing clusters. Hollywood Boulevard is the main artery to the heart of the park: the glistening red-and-gold, multiturreted replica of Grauman's Chinese Theater, home of the Great Movie Ride. Encircling it in a roughly counterclockwise fashion are Sunset Boulevard, which features the Twilight Zone of Terror; the Studio Courtyard, which houses the entrance to the Backstage Studio Tour, the Inside the Magic special effects and production tour, and the Magic of Disney Animation; the Backlot, which has Jim Henson's Muppet*Vision 3D and *Honey, I Shrunk the Kids* Movie Set Adventure playground; the Backlot Annex, containing the

Indiana Jones Epic Stunt Spectacular and Star Tours; and—adjoining Hollywood Boulevard—Lakeside Circle, whose principal attractions include SuperStar Television and the Monster Sound Show.

Surprisingly, the entire park is rather small—only 110 acres, ¼ the size of Universal Studios—with barely a dozen major attractions, as opposed to 45 in the Magic Kingdom and 23 in Epcot Center. When the lines are minimal, the park can be easily covered in a day with time for repeat rides. And even when the lines seem to stretch clear to Epcot Center, a little careful planning should allow you to see everything on one ticket.

Hollywood Boulevard

With its palm trees, pastel buildings, and flashy neon, Hollywood Boulevard paints a rosy picture of Tinseltown in the 1930s. The sense of having walked right onto a movie set is enhanced by the art-deco storefronts, strolling brass bands, and roving actors dressed in costume and playing everything from would-be starlets to nefarious agents. They are frequently joined by characters from Disney movies new and old, who pose for pictures and sign autographs. *Beauty and the Beast*'s Belle is a favorite, as are Jafar, Princess Jasmine, and the Genie from *Aladdin*.

Hollywood Boulevard, like Main Street, is crammed with souvenir shops and memorabilia collections. Oscar's Classic Car Souvenirs & Super Service Station is crammed with fuel pump bubble-gum machines, photos of antique cars, and other automotive knickknacks. At Sid Cahuenga's One-of-a-Kind antiques and curios, you might find (and acquire) Brenda Vaccaro's shawl, Liberace's table napkins, or autographed stars' photos. Down the street at Cover Story, don the appropriate costume and have your picture put on the cover of a major magazine. Next door, check out the movie memorabilia crammed into the Celebrity 5 & 10. At the end of the street, at the corner of Sunset Boulevard, you'll find loads of kid-size character clothing at L.A. Cinema Storage. The 40-something crowd will also appreciate this shop's collection of old Mickey Mouse Club black-and-white production stills.

TIME OUT   For a sweet burst of energy, snag a cinnamon swirl at **Starring Rolls Bakery,** near the Brown Derby. Or try the croissants, the turnovers, or the almost-authentic bagels.

Numbers in the margin correspond to points of interest on the Disney-MGM Studios map.

❶ At the head of Hollywood Boulevard is the fire-engine-red, pagodaed replica of Grauman's Chinese Theater, which houses the **Great Movie Ride.** Disney-MGM pulls out all the stops on this tour of great moments in film.

The lobby, really an ingenious way to spend time standing in line, slots you past such icons as Dorothy's ruby slippers from *The Wizard of Oz,* a carousel horse from *Mary Poppins,* and the piano played by Sam in *Casablanca.* You then shuffle into the preshow area, an enormous screening room with continuously running clips from *Mary Poppins, Raiders of the Lost Ark, Singin' in the Rain, Fantasia, Footlight Parade,* and, of course, *Casablanca.* (As the segment from *Raiders of the Lost Ark* comes on, kids who have already caught the Indiana Jones Epic Stunt Spectacular but not the original movie can be heard to say, "Say, that's the guy we saw today, right?") The line continues snaking through the preshow, which itself is so much fun that you almost resent that you'll miss favorite clips once the great red doors swing open and it's your turn to ride.

Disney cast members dressed in 1920s newsboy costumes usher you onto open trams and you're off on a tour—through Audio-Animatronics, scrim, smoke, and Disney magic—of cinematic climaxes. First comes the world of musical entertainment, with Gene Kelly clutching that immortal lamppost in one hand and a useless umbrella in the other as he sings the title song from *Singin' in the Rain* and Mary Poppins (with *her* umbrella) and her sooty admirers reprising "Chim-Chim-Cher-ee," among others. The lights dim and you move into gangsterland, with James Cagney snarling in *Public Enemy*. Then it's on to a western shootout à la John Wayne as Calamity Jane tries to rob the Miners' and Cattlemen's Bank and hijack the tram—and succeeds.

Nothing like a little time warp to bring justice. With pipes streaming fog and alarm klaxons whooping, the tram meets some of the slimier characters in *Alien* (look up for truly scary stuff) and then eases into the cobwebby, snake-ridden (and slithering) set of the Temple of Doom, where Calamity Jane attempts to bluff an idol threat—and gets vaporized.

Each time you think you've seen the best scene, the tram moves into another set: Tarzan yodels and swings on a vine overhead, then Bogey toasts Bergman in front of the plane to Lisbon. The finale has hundreds of robotic Munchkins cheerily enjoining you to "Follow the Yellow Brick Road," despite the cackling imprecations of the Wicked Witch of the West (check out Dorothy's tornado-tossed house—those on the right side of the tram can just spot the ruby slippers). The tram follows the Yellow Brick Road and there it is: Emerald City.

As icing on the cake, there's one more movie presentation with three screens all going at once to display yet more memorable moments, including great kisses ranging from Rhett Butler and Scarlett O'Hara embracing to Roger and Jessica Rabbit engaging in an animated smooch. Then the lights come up and the announcer calls you for the final scene: The Exit. *Duration: 22 min. Crowds: Steady and large all day long; when the inside lines start spilling out the door, expect at least a 25-min wait. Strategy: Go first thing in the morning or at the end of the day (then if the lines still look long, ask before you slink away discouraged—Disney staffers often "stack" people up outside to clear up the crowds inside and to prepare for closing). Audience: All but young children (for whom it may be too intense). Rating:* ★★★

Sunset Boulevard

This newest of Disney-MGM's theme avenues pays tribute to famous Hollywood monuments with facades derived from the Cathay Circle, the Beverly Wilshire Theatre, and other City of Angels landmarks. The Theater of the Stars, for example, is reminiscent of the famed Hollywood Bowl; rather than hosting rock acts, however, the 1,500-seat covered amphitheater is home to a musical production called **Beauty and the Beast—Live on Stage.** As guests turn onto Sunset Boulevard from Hollywood Boulevard, first stop for the hungry hordes is Hollywood Junction Station, where reservations can be made for restaurants throughout the park. Starstruck shoppers should find something to feed their fandom at Legends of Hollywood, which brims with books, videos, and posters of classic films, while the young at heart should stop by Once upon a Time, which showcases displays of vintage character toys.

TIME OUT   Sunset Boulevard features three fast-food eateries: **Rosie's Red Hot Dogs, Catalina Eddie's Frozen Yogurt,** and, for a healthful snack, the **Anaheim Produce Company.**

Disney-MGM Studios Theme Park

KEY

🍴 Restaurants
🚻 Restrooms

N

Catastrophe Canyon

Residential Street

New York Street

Sci-Fi Drive-In Diner

Mickey Avenue

50's Prime Time Cafe

Echo Lake

Earffel Tower

Hollywood & Vine Cafeteria

Studios Tip Board

Brown Derby

Hollywood Junction Restaurant Reservations

Guest Relations

Hollywood Boulevard

Entrance Plaza

Lockers

Studio Courtyard

Main Entrance

Automatic Teller

Sunset Boulevard

Theater of the Stars

Backstage
Studio Tour, **4**
Great Movie Ride, **1**
*Honey, I Shrunk the
Kids* Movie Set Adventure, **8**
Indiana Jones Epic
Stunt Spectacular, **10**

Inside the Magic Special Effects and Production Tour, **7**
Jim Henson's Muppet*
Vision 3D, **9**
Magic of Disney Animation, **3**

Making of
The Lion King, **6**
Monster Sound
Show, **13**
Star Tours, **11**
SuperStar
Television, **12**
Twilight Zone Tower
of Terror, **2**

Voyage of the Little
Mermaid, **5**

All the crowds, however, are most likely looking for the park's newest
② excuse for an adrenaline rush: the **Twilight Zone Tower of Terror.** Omi-
nously overlooking Sunset Boulevard is a 13-story structure that's re-
putedly the now-deserted Hollywood Tower Hotel. (It's especially
spooky at night.) You take an eerie stroll through the dimly lighted lobby
and decaying library to the boiler room before boarding the hotel's giant
"elevator." As you head upward past seemingly deserted hallways,
ghostly former residents appear around you, until suddenly—faster than
you can say "Where's Rod Serling?"—the creaking vehicle abruptly
plunges downward in a terrifying, 130-foot free-fall drop! *Duration:
10 min. Crowds: Yes! Strategy: Go early or, even better, wait until the
evening dinner hours when the crowds thin out. Audience: Older children and adults. No pregnant women or guests with back, neck, or
heart problems. Rating:* ★★★

Studio Courtyard

As you exit Sunset Boulevard, veer right through the high-arched gateway to the Studio Courtyard. You're now at one end of Mickey Avenue, and straight ahead are the Magic of Disney Animation, the
Backstage Studio Tour, and the Voyage of the Little Mermaid, often
combined with Inside the Magic at the other end of Mickey Avenue
for a two-hour whiz-bang revelation of cinematic secrets.

TIME OUT The Studio Courtyard also houses **Catwalk Bar** and **Soundstage
Restaurant,** a food court in an aptly named barn of a building with an
attic's worth of furniture dangling from the ceiling. This stuff would be a
great source of conversation—if you could hear anything. Burgers, fajitas, chef's salads, and the like are on the menu.

❸ The **Magic of Disney Animation,** a self-guided tour through the Disney
animation process, is one of the funniest and most engaging attractions
at the park. More than any backstage tour, more than any revelation
of stunt secrets, this tour truly takes you inside the magic as you follow the many steps of animation from concept to charisma.

Although you can move at your own pace, the staff tries to keep
crowds to a minimum, so groups assemble in a lobby. Take the opportunity to check out the collection of drawings and original cels, the
clear celluloid sheets on which the characters were drawn for *Snow
White, Fantasia,* and other Disney classics. Here, too, are the Academy
Awards that Disney has won for its animated films.

From the lobby, you segue into the Disney Animation Theater for a
hilarious eight-minute film in which Walter Cronkite and Robin
Williams explain animation basics. A *Peter Pan* sequel called *Back to
Neverland,* with Walter Cronkite as Walter Cronkite and Robin
Williams as a Little Lost Boy (the irrepressible Robin really wants it
to be called *Peter Pan: First Blood*), it was almost impossible to film
because the steadfast, avuncular Cronkite kept cracking up. You might,
too, if you suddenly discovered Tinkerbell in your jacket pocket. Robin
Williams discovers the potential range of animation ("Hey," he proclaims as he's redrawn into a familiar rodent, "I can be a corporate
symbol!") while we learn about cel making, layout artists, background
artists, cleanup artists, sound effects, and more.

From the theater, you follow walkways with windows overlooking the
working animation studios, where you see salaried Disney artists at
their drafting tables doing everything you just learned about. Their desks
are strewn with finished drawings of Simba, Scar, Aladdin, Genie, and

other famous characters, and you can peer over their shoulders at soon-to-be-famous characters. This is better than magic—this is real.

Meanwhile, Robin and Walter continue their banter on overhead monitors, explaining the processes as you saunter from story room, where animators develop story lines; to the drawing boards, where ideas metamorphose from sketch to colorful characters; to the cleanup room, the special effects area, and the special camera that transfers drawings to cels. To produce one 24-minute film, the 70-plus members of the animation team must create 34,650 drawings and add scenes from at least 300 background paintings. No wonder everyone wears headphones, although one doubts they're listening to "Whistle While You Work."

The penultimate stop is a continuously running video, *Animators on Animation*. "You believe the character *is* alive," confesses one of the geeky-looking animators who so identify with their characters that they can take on their personalities. Watching a low-key, pleasant Asian man become the blowsy, evil Ursula from *The Little Mermaid* right before your eyes makes you wonder if pixie dust is in the air.

Disney knows how to make an exit, and with a valedictory quip from Robin Williams, you head into the Disney Classics Theater for a presentation of the best moments from animated films. It's fascinating to see the evolution of the art from the bright colors and straightforward drawings in *Snow White* and *Pinocchio* to the rainbow hues and complex panoramas of *Beauty and the Beast, Aladdin,* and *The Lion King.* Best of all, you know that here the characters always will live happily ever after. *Duration: Usually around 30 min. Crowds: Steady all day. Strategy: Go in the morning or late afternoon, when you can get in with less waiting and still see the animators at work (they leave by 6 and are not always around on weekends). Audience: All but toddlers. Rating:* ★★★

❹ The **Backstage Studio Tour,** a combination tram ride and walking tour, takes you on a tour of the back-lot building blocks of movies: set design, costumes, props, lighting, and the de rigueur Catastrophe Canyon. Disney-MGM outdoes Universal Studios on this ride because it's got an ace in the hole: a real moviemaking environment. You literally ride through working offices, peering through windows as Foley artists mix sound, lighting crews sort cables, costumers stitch seams, and so on. The motor pool boasts the usual bunch of beat-up automobiles, including a series of old blue Plymouths from *Who Framed Roger Rabbit?* The greens department is a gardener's delight, with its elephant topiaries, trellised roses, and the faux tree trunk used in *Honey, I Shrunk the Kids;* most of the greens are used to camouflage unsightly parts of movie sets, so the next time you see a particularly verdant tree on film, think about what's behind it.

The residential street gives new meaning to the term "open house," as the tram winds past false fronts in styles ranging from Frank Lloyd Wright to generic suburban. New Yorkers will get the usual kick out of seeing the litter-free, graffiti-free depiction of their fair city on New York Street. The tram rumbles past the boneyard, where the helicopter from *Blue Thunder* and the orange-and-red Pacific Electric trolley car used in *Who Framed Roger Rabbit?* are permanently parked; an egret (live, not animated) now uses the trolley car as its perch.

Then it's on to Catastrophe Canyon. The tram's announcer swears that the film that's supposedly shooting in there is taking a break. Not! The next thing you know, the tram is bouncing up and down in a simulated earthquake, an oil tanker explodes in gobs of smoke and flame, and a water tower crashes to the ground, touching off a flash flood, which douses the oil tanker but threatens to drown the tram. Although the earthquake is more like a shimmy, the water and fire provoke genuine screams. As the tram pulls out, you see the backstage workings of the catastrophe: The canyon is actually a mammoth steel slide wrapped in copper-colored cement, and the 70,000 gallons of flood water—enough to fill 10 Olympic-size swimming pools—is recycled 100 times a day, or every 3½ minutes.

Let your heartbeat slow down as the tram takes another pass through the Big Apple. This time you're close enough to see that brownstones, marble, brick, and stained glass are actually expertly painted two-dimensional facades of fiberglass and Styrofoam. Grips can slide the Empire State and Chrysler buildings out of the way anytime. Note the storefronts carefully; you'll encounter them again in a Bette Midler film on the Inside the Magic tour.

Hop off the tram and walk through the **Studio Showcase,** a continually updated exhibit of film and television memorabilia, including models from such Disney TV programs and films as *The Nightmare Before Christmas* and *The Santa Clause*. Then follow Roger Rabbit's pink footsteps to the **Loony Bin,** where kids can have their picture taken in front of the directional signs indicating Thisaway and Thataway, or open all the Pandora's boxes of such sound effects as boinks, toots, squeaks, chugs, clunks, and speeding trains. Roger Rabbit souvenirs are sold here, as are palm buzzers and other magic tricks. *Duration: 25 min. Crowds: Steady through the afternoon, but lines seem to move quickly. Strategy: As you enter the tram, remember that people sitting on the left get seared and wet; people on the right get crushed as the people on the left leap into their laps. Go early. Closes at dusk. Audience: All but young children. Rating:* ★★★

5 A boxy building on Mickey Avenue invites you to join Ariel, Sebastian, and the underwater gang in the **Voyage of the Little Mermaid** stage show, which condenses the movie into a marathon presentation of the greatest hits. In an admirable effort at verisimilitude, a fine mist sprays the stage; visitors sitting in the front rows will get refreshed. *Duration: 15 min. Crowds: Perpetual. Strategy: Go first thing in the morning or wait until the stroller brigade's exodus after 5. Audience: All ages. Rating:* ★★★

Tucked behind the Voyage of the Little Mermaid, inside the Walt Disney Theater, is a fascinating behind-the-scenes look at Disney's latest **6** smash hit. The **Making of The Lion King** was originally produced for the Disney Channel and is now running for the masses at half-hour intervals. Narrated by Robert Guillaume (the voice of Rafiki, the film's psychic baboon), the film traces the making of the animated classic from concept to final scenes. Although small children may be bored during the "talking head" sequences of the directors and producers, there's enough footage from the film to keep them entertained. For adults, there's the chance to sit down in a blissfully air-conditioned theater and watch Jeremy Irons and James Earl Jones work their vocal magic behind the microphone. *Duration: 30 min. Crowds: Rendered insignificant due to theater size and relatively remote location. Strategy: Go in the afternoon when other lines are too long. Audience: All ages. Rating:* ★★★

TIME OUT The **Studio Catering Company Commissary** here will provide you with sustenance for the next tour: hot dogs, burgers, pizza, and fries.

❼ The **Inside the Magic Special Effects and Production Tour,** a walking tour, explains how clever cameramen make illusion seem like reality through camera angles, miniaturization, matte backgrounds, and a host of other magic tricks. While you're waiting in line, Goldie Hawn and Martin Short appear on overhead video screens. They host a humorous overview of the processes you're about to see. Then you're off to the first stop, an outdoor special-effects water tank. Here two willing, if unwary, members of the audience don bright yellow slickers. One gets to play the skipper of the ill-fated SS *Miss Fortune,* while the other unsuspecting soul assumes the role of submarine commander "Captain Duck," about to pilot his craft into battle. As the audience watches, the skipper nearly gets drowned in a thunderstorm, and the doughty Duck gets strafed, torpedoed, and doused with 400 gallons of water from a depth charge while a video records the scenario and plays it back with music and background.

To show how miniature props are filmed to look life-size, two children from the audience climb up on a hairy bumblebee to shoot a scene from *Honey, I Shrunk the Kids*. A matte, blue screen background is used to combine their scene with realistic shots of the bee's flight, and the audience sees the end result on overhead monitors.

Three soundstages are used for filming the *Mickey Mouse Club, Ed McMahon's Star Search,* and assorted movies. Specially soundproofed catwalks let visitors eavesdrop as overhead video monitors explain what goes on. It takes five hours to shoot a 30-minute episode of the *Mickey Mouse Club*; most of the taping takes place in the afternoon and evening. *Star Search,* on the other hand, tapes two or three shows a day from summer through Thanksgiving.

Then it's on to the sets of a complicated and hilarious sequence from *The Lottery,* a short film in which Bette Midler chases a pigeon that has stolen her winning $1-million lottery ticket. (Now New Yorkers can feel aggrieved at the graffiti-covered subway car, since no one else around the country realizes that the subways are now mostly graffiti-free.) The actual sequence is subsequently shown on overhead video screens. The 2½-minute scene took five days and 100 people to create; the work was done exclusively at Disney-MGM Studios, and you may recognize many of the scenes from the Backstage Studio Tour.

In the Post-Production area, George Lucas, aided by R2D2 and C-3PO, explains how computers are used for editing, and Mel Gibson and Pee-Wee Herman switch voices in a lecture on sound tracks. *Duration: 1 hr. Crowds: Large but constantly moving. Strategy: Don't assume that crawling into the tour guide's back pocket will give you the best view: Stay in the middle to remain in the center of the action, and aim for the right if you want a front-row view and the left if you want to stay dry. Audience: Older children and adults. Rating:* ★★★

The Backlot

A rather amorphous area built around New York Street, the Backlot merges so seamlessly into the Post-Production area that it's almost easier to consider it a post-post-production area rather than a separate section. In addition to New York Street sets that can be toured on foot as long as crews aren't filming—and are worth it, for the wealth of detail to be seen in the store windows—the Backlot also comprises a stage show by the Teenage Mutant Ninja Turtles, another by the Muppets, Jim Henson's Muppet*Vision 3D, and the *Honey, I Shrunk the Kids* Movie Set Adventure, a playground.

Take a left at the corner of Mickey Avenue and New York Street and

(8) let the kids run free in the **Honey, I Shrunk the Kids Movie Set Adventure,** a state-of-the-art playground based on the movie about Lilliputian kids in a larger-than-life world. They can slide down a gigantic blade of grass, crawl through caves, climb a mushroom mountain, inhale the scent of a humongous plant (and have it spit water back in their face), and dodge sprinklers set in the resilient flooring, which is made of ground-up tires. All the requisite playground equipment is present: net climbs, ball crawls, ingenious caves and slides, and so on. Because this is an enclosed area, there's often a line to get in, which seems rather restrictive for a playground. *Duration: Up to you. Crowds: Steady. Strategy: Come early or come back when there's no line. Audience: Children and those who love them. Rating:* ★★★

(9) You don't have to be a Piggyphile to get a kick out of **Jim Henson's Muppet*Vision 3D,** a combination of 3-D movie and musical revue. In the waiting area, Muppet movie posters advertise Miss Piggy in *Star Chores* ("She swore she'd never sign another autograph") and *To Have and Have More* ("Here's looking at you, pig"), and Kermit the Frog in an Arnold Schwarzenegger parody, *Kürmit the Amphibian* (starring Kürmit der Frög, "so mean, he's green"). The theater was constructed especially for this show, with special effects built into the walls. All the Muppet characters make an appearance, with Miss Piggy in the role of the Statue of Liberty. Guided by a new character, Waldo, the spirit of 3-D, the technology is at its best here. In fact, the 3-D effects are coordinated with other sensory stimulation so you're never sure what's coming off the screen and what's being shot out of vents in the ceiling and walls. An equal-effect theater, the house has no bad seats. *Duration: 10-min preshow, 20-min show. Crowds: Steady from morning through late afternoon, and because the waiting area is carefully hidden, you don't know how long the line is until you've waited for too long. Strategy: Go early or late. Audience: All ages. Rating:* ★★★

Just past the Miss Piggy Statue of Liberty you'll find the **Studio Arcade,** Disney-MGM's collection of video games, which replaced the collection of movie and TV props now in the Studio Showcase. Older kids will enjoy a stop here, perhaps while adults browse in nearby shops.

Backlot Annex

Segue from the Backlot into the Backlot Annex, more of an offshoot of Lakeside Circle. You can be sure the crowds are not swarming for the fast-food Backlot Express, which is nothing special. No, the attractions are two of the park's most high-powered: the Indiana Jones Epic Stunt Spectacular and Star Tours.

The rousing theme music from the Indiana Jones movies blares out like

(10) a clarion call, summoning visitors to see the **Indiana Jones Epic Stunt Spectacular,** featuring the stunt choreography of veteran coordinator Glenn Randall (*Raiders of the Lost Ark, Indiana Jones and the Temple of Doom, E.T.,* and *Jewel of the Nile* are among his credits). Presented in a 2,200-seat amphitheater, the show starts with a series of near-death encounters in an ancient Mayan temple. Clad in his signature fedora and looking cute enough for front-row viewers to consider painting "Love You" on their eyelids just like Professor Jones's adoring student did in *Raiders of the Lost Ark,* Indiana slides down a rope from the ceiling, dodges spears that shoot up from the floor, avoids getting chopped by booby-trapped idols, and snags a forbidden gemstone, setting off a gigantic boulder that threatens to render him two-dimensional.

It's hard to top that opener, but Randall and his pals do just that with the help of 10 audience participants ("Okay, I need some rowdy people," the casting director calls). While the lucky few demonstrate their rowdiness, behind them the set crew casually wheels off the entire temple (two people roll the boulder like a giant beach ball) and replaces it with a Cairo street, circa 1940. Nasty Ninja-Nazi stuntmen roll out a mat and bounce around performing flips and throws in the background. This is one of those times when it's better to be in the audience.

The scene they're working up to takes place on a busy Cairo street, down which saunter Indy and his redoubtable girlfriend, Marian Ravenwood, portrayed by a Karen Allen look-alike. She is to be kidnapped and tossed in a truck while Indy fights his way free with bullwhip and gun and bad guys tumble from every corner and cornice. Motorcycles buzz around, the street becomes a shambles, and as a stunning climax, the truck carrying Marian flips and bursts into flame. Viewers sitting up front can feel the heat.

Randall et al. do a great job at explaining the stunts. The audience sees how they are set up, watches the stars practice them in slow motion, and learns how cameras are camouflaged behind imitation rocks for trick shots. Only one stunt remains a secret: How do Indy and Marian escape the explosion? That's what keeps 'em coming back. *Duration: 30 min. Crowds: Large, but the theater's high capacity means that everyone who wants to get in usually does. Strategy: Go at night, when the idols' eyes glow red. Audience: All but young children. Rating:* ★★★

TIME OUT   At the **Backlot Express,** you don't need a reservation to chow down on the burgers, fajitas, and chef's salads.

⓫ While everyone else is heading to the stunt show, make tracks for **Star Tours,** the hands-down showstopper flight simulator. Flight simulators, on which many of the latest theme park rides are based, were once used simply to train military and commercial airline pilots. But when their film is synchronized to movement, as of a ride vehicle in theme parks, guests truly feel what they see. Guarded by an otherworldly metallic monster, Star Tours is inspired by the *Star Wars* films. "May the force be with you," says the attendant on duty, " 'cause I won't be!" Piloted by *Star Wars* characters R2D2 and C-3PO, the 40-passenger Star-Speeder that you board is supposed to take off on a routine flight to the moon of Endor. But with R2D2 at the helm, things quickly go awry: You shoot into deep space, dodge giant ice crystals and comet debris, innocently bumble into an intergalactic battle, and attempt to avoid laser-blasting fighters as you whiz through the canyons of some planetary city before coming to a heart-stopping halt.

Although the technology is the same as that of Body Wars in Epcot Center's Wonders of Life pavilion, the presentation is wittier and the ride is wilder. You don't "go" anywhere, as you do on a roller coaster; however, because your imagination and vision are engaged as you are tossed around, the experience is all-encompassing. Simply put, there's nothing like it—until, we have to say, you go on Back to the Future . . . The Ride, at Universal Studios. But that's almost too much for a first-timer, and this is just right. *Duration: 7 min. Crowds: Legendary, with near-perpetual 40- to 60-min waits. Strategy: Try shortly before closing time. Although you can always get in first thing in the morning, it'll spoil you for the rest of the park. When you line up to enter the simulation chamber, keep to the right to sit in the back rows (where you'll get a rougher ride), to the far left to sit up front (closer to the screen and therefore getting more realistic sensations). Audience:*

Older children and adults. No pregnant women, children under 3, or guests with motion sickness or neck, back, or heart problems; children under 7 must be accompanied by an adult. Rating: ★★★

Lakeside Circle

Set off to the left, or west side, of Hollywood Boulevard, Lakeside Circle is an idealized California. In the center is cool blue Echo Lake, an oasis fringed with trees and benches and ringed with landmarks: pink and aqua restaurants trimmed in chrome (with sassy waitresses and television sets at the tables); Min and Bill's Dockside Diner, which offers fast food in a shipshape atmosphere; and Gertie, a Sinclair gas station dinosaur that dispenses ice cream, Disney souvenirs, and the occasional puff of smoke in true magic-dragon fashion. Look for Gertie's giant footprints in the sidewalk. On the north side of the pond are Lakeside Circle's two attractions: SuperStar Television and the Monster Sound Show.

⑫ "I need a woman over 21 who can tell a guy off," the **SuperStar Television** casting director proclaims, and at least 25 candidates scream for attention. Twenty-eight are chosen and through judicious dubbing appear to play the starring roles on shows from *I Love Lucy* to *Gilligan's Island.*

While the volunteers are led off to makeup and costume, the audience files into a 1,000-seat theater reminiscent of the days of live television broadcasting. Most important, eight 6-foot-wide monitors hang in front of a stage that has three movable sets. Through blue-screen electronic techniques, the onstage action appears on the screen to have merged with clips from classic shows.

The pace is fast and furious, and a good director can make all the difference, coaching the volunteer actors with words and body language, then running on to the next skit. Soap opera fans get a special kick from a love-triangle scene in *General Hospital.* Then a woman volunteer, outfitted in white apron and tall white chef's hat, desperately tries to wrap chocolates on an ever-speedier assembly line in one of the best-known episodes from *I Love Lucy.* Other scenes include the "Vonzells" singing "Da Doo Run Run" on *The Ed Sullivan Show,* an extremely young New York Yankee (this role almost always goes to cute little kids, especially girls with pigtails) getting interviewed by Howard Cosell after hitting a grand slam homer, and Neil Armstrong landing on the moon and reading his famous "One step for a man, one giant step for mankind" line from a placard held by yet another volunteer.

Each show is flavored differently by the volunteer cast. It's not easy to get chosen—only about 12 out of 1,000 make it. To even the odds, arrive 15–30 minutes before starting time, go to the front of the waiting area, and let a staffer know that you would *love* to be in the show. Dressing outrageously and having a loud cheering section helps. By the way, unlike Indiana Jones volunteers, SuperStar actors can watch the action on monitors. *Duration: 30 min. Crowds: Large, but the large theater keeps waiting minimal. Audience: All but young children. Rating:* ★★

TIME OUT   **Min & Bill's Dockside Diner** is the spot for sandwiches—step right up to the counter. Be sure to save room for "Ice Cream of Extinction" at **Gertie's.**

⑬ Despite its name, the **Monster Sound Show** is anything but scary. Rather, it's a delightful, multifaceted demonstration of the use of movie sound effects. The show features many of the gadgets created by soundmaster Jimmy Macdonald, who became the voice of Mickey Mouse during the 1940s and invented some 20,000 sound effects during his 45 years at Walt Disney Studios. Most qualify as gizmos—a metal sheet that, when rattled, sounds like thunder; a box of sand for footsteps on gravel; and other noises made from nails, straw, mud, leather, and other ordinary components.

The 270-seat theater is small enough for volunteer Foley artists (the movie name for sound effects specialists, named for Jack Foley, the man who created the system) to be seen as they dash around trying to coordinate their sound effects with the short movie being shown simultaneously. The audience sees the scene—a hilariously klutzy Chevy Chase playing an insurance man on a visit to a haunted house—three times: once with the original sounds, once without any sound as the Foleys-for-a-day try to fill in, and then once more with the volunteer product. Somehow the boinks and bangs never seem to come in on time. Gonnng!

The postshow is a treat consisting of hands-on exhibits called **Sound-Works.** There are buttons that go boing and knobs you push to alter your voice. Earie Encounters lets you imitate flying-saucer sounds from the 1956 film *Forbidden Planet*. At Movie Mimics, you can try your chords at dubbing Mickey Mouse, Roger Rabbit, and other Disney heroes.

Soundsations is a "3-D audio" experience in which you enter a sound-proofed room, don a pair of earphones, and . . . you're a movie executive on the first day of work at Walt Disney Studios. A face-to-face chat with Mickey Mouse is just one thrill; wait until you meet the studio barber. It's literally hair-raising. *Duration: as long as you're interested. Crowds: Steady. Audience: All ages. Rating:* ★★★

Dining

Full-Service Restaurants

Although the glow often gets tarnished at mealtime, Disney-MGM's full-service restaurants are so much fun that the magic continues. Once you're inside, that is. Unfortunately, visitors never seem to want to leave their tables—after all, would you if you could watch television monitors airing '50s sitcoms while chowing down on veal-and-shiitake-mushroom meatloaf? Consequently, the lines can be enormous and reservations are routinely late.

With its staff in black tie and its airy, palm-fronded room positively exuding suave, the 235-seat **Brown Derby** is one of the nicest places to eat in the park. (It's also one of the most expensive.) The Cobb Salad, a conglomeration of salad greens, tomato, bacon, turkey, egg, blue cheese, and avocado—invented at the restaurant's Hollywood namesake—is alive and well here, as you can see from the numerous orders getting tossed tableside. The all-California wine list is wide-ranging enough to keep an oenophile happy. And the butter comes in molds shaped like miniature derby hats. Patrons seated in booths can even have a '40s-style dial telephone brought to their tables.

You'll certainly want to spend a leisurely lunch at the **'50s Prime Time Café,** whose video screens constantly show sitcoms, whose place mats pose television trivia quizzes, and whose waitresses play "Mom" with convincing enthusiasm. The menu is what your own mom might have made were she a character on one of those video screens—meatloaf, broiled chicken, pot roast, hot roast beef sandwich—all to be washed down with root beer floats and ice cream sodas. Don't go to Star Tours immediately afterward—the time warp might be too much to endure.

If you don't mind zombies leering at you while you slurp up sloppy joes, more meatloaf, chef's salad, and the like, then head for the **Sci-Fi Dine-In Theater,** a re-creation of an actual drive-in. All the tables (which are contained within candy-colored '50s vintage convertibles) face a large screen, where a 45-minute reel of the best and worst of science fiction trailers plays in a continuous loop. Only here would popcorn be considered an appropriate appetizer.

To replace the energy you've no doubt depleted by miles of theme park walking, load up on carbs at **Mama Melrose's Ristorante Italiano.** The menu features pasta, chicken, steak, and seafood dishes, as well as pizza baked in a gourmet brick oven.

RESERVATIONS

Reservations are required at all the full-service restaurants and, for popular seating times, must be made in person at the restaurant or first thing in the morning at Hollywood Junction Restaurant Reservations, just to the right of the Studios Tip Board, at the intersection of Hollywood and Sunset boulevards.

Cafeteria

The usual menu of upscale fast foods—baby back ribs, roasted chicken, and tortellini at lunch, prime rib, veal chops, and mesquite-grilled pork chops at dinner—constitutes the fare at **Hollywood & Vine Cafeteria of the Stars.** The usual complement of downscale fast-food spots is also available.

Entertainment

Parades? Disney characters? Eccentric actors? You never know what will turn up around the next bend, so pick up an entertainment schedule on your way into the park.

The Theater of the Stars has a new home on Sunset Boulevard. Like its predecessor, it's modeled after the famed Hollywood Bowl; unlike its predecessor, it has more seats. At press time, the Theater of the Stars was presenting the extremely popular and long-running **Beauty and the Beast—Live on Stage,** a skillful condensation of the animated film. The show is almost always crowded; queue up at least 30 minutes prior to show time for good seats, especially if you're with children.

About 12 times a day, a bright-yellow buggy comes roaring up Mickey Avenue on the Backlot, and out scramble the **Teenage Mutant Ninja Turtles**—Raphael, Michelangelo, Leonardo, and Donatello—to be welcomed by a horde of screaming kids. They deliver a 15-minute song-and-dance show, shout "Cowabunga, dude!" every 90 seconds or so, and sign autographs. If you want a good view, get to the staging area about 15 minutes before show time. Usually by the time you hear the first "Cowabunga!" it's too late.

Aladdin's Royal Caravan, a parade that marches down Hollywood Boulevard each day at 1 PM (twice daily during peak periods), is one of this park's most popular attractions. Parade-goers start staking out spots on the curb along the route up to 45 minutes before the parade begins. Prince Ali, the Genie, and their friends come to life in oversize characters complemented by marching bands, dancers in brightly colored costumes, and imaginative floats depicting scenes from the hit movie. Watch out for the water-spitting camels.

The **fireworks** here may be Disney's best. Revisiting Mickey as he appeared in the "Sorcerer's Apprentice" in *Fantasia,* they feature a giant balloon of the great star, floating amid the starbursts and chrysanthemums raining down on Grauman's Chinese Theater. Traditionally these are presented on Friday and Saturday nights (nightly in summer and during year-end holidays).

Shopping

Budding animators can hone their talents with Paint-a-Cel, a kit with two picture cels ready to be illustrated. It's sold at the **Animation Gallery** in the Animation Building. For movie memorabilia, there's the cleverly named **Movieland Memorabilia** located to the left of the park entrance. Also check out the **Celebrity 5 & 10** along Hollywood Boulevard and **Legends of Hollywood** on Sunset Boulevard. Strategically positioned shops and pushcarts adjacent to Voyage of the Little Mermaid, the Beauty and the Beast stage show at the Theater of the Stars, and the Making of *The Lion King* will satisfy the kids' lustings for character merchandise from these wildly popular films. Genuine Indiana Jones bullwhips and fedoras are sold at the **Indiana Jones Adventure Outpost** next to the stunt amphitheater. All sorts of Roger Rabbit magic tricks are just waiting to buzz, explode, squish, and trick you at the **Loony Bin.** At the conclusion of Star Tours, **Endor Vendors** stocks Darth Vader and Wookie masks as well as other out-of-this-world paraphernalia. For Disney-themed Christmas ornaments, try **It's a Wonderful Shop,** which is tucked in a corner near the Muppets on Location. The **Costume Shop,** near one of the entrances to the New York Street, features getups of Disney villains and villainesses, including favorite outfits of *Sleeping Beauty*'s wicked Maleficent and *101 Dalmatians'* Cruella DeVil. And who could resist a pair of Mickey Mitts, an easy-to-pick-up last-minute gift sold at **Legends of Hollywood** on Hollywood Boulevard. Use them to wave at the Earfful Tower on your way out.

Access for Travelers with Disabilities

Almost everything in this park is wheelchair accessible.

Attractions

Disney-MGM attractions are wheelchair accessible, with certain restrictions on the Star Tours thrill ride and Twilight Zone Tower of Terror.

SUNSET BOULEVARD

To board the **Twilight Zone Tower of Terror** you must be able to walk unassisted to a seat on the ride and have full upper-body strength. The ride's free-falls make it inappropriate for service animals. The **Theater of the Stars** is completely accessible to guests using wheelchairs.

HOLLYWOOD BOULEVARD

To board the **Great Movie Ride,** you must transfer to a Disney wheelchair if you use an oversize model or a scooter; the gunshot, explosion, and fire effects make the attraction inappropriate for service animals.

STUDIO COURTYARD

The **Voyage of the Little Mermaid** show, the **Magic of Disney Animation,** and the **Making of the Lion King** are all wheelchair accessible, with terrific entertainment value for all guests with disabilities. The **Backstage Studio Tour** is also wheelchair accessible. Guests with hearing impairments who lip-read should request a seat near the tour guide. The earthquake, fire, and water effects of the Catastrophe Canyon scene make the attraction inappropriate for some service animals. The **Inside the Magic Special Effects and Production Tour** are similarly accessible by those in wheelchairs.

<u>THE BACKLOT</u>

The *Honey, I Shrunk the Kids* **Movie Set Adventure** is barrier free for most guests using wheelchairs, although the uneven surface may make maneuvering difficult. Jim Henson's Muppet*Vision 3D is also completely wheelchair accessible. Guests with hearing impairments may request a personal audio link that will amplify the sound here.

<u>BACKLOT ANNEX</u>

The **Indiana Jones Epic Stunt Spectacular** is completely wheelchair accessible. Explosions and gunfire may make it inappropriate for service animals. **Star Tours,** a turbulent ride, is accessible by guests who can transfer to a ride seat; those lacking upper-body strength should request an extra shoulder restraint. Service animals should not ride.

<u>LAKESIDE CIRCLE</u>

SuperStar Television is completely wheelchair accessible. So is the **Monster Sound Show.** However, the entertainment value there is derived from the timing of different sound effects, so guests with hearing impairments may decide to skip this one.

Entertainment

Live entertainment locations, including those used at press time for the **Teenage Mutant Ninja Turtles** show and **Beauty and the Beast—Live on Stage,** are completely wheelchair accessible. Certain sections of parade routes are always reserved for guests with disabilities. **Tapings** of television shows are wheelchair accessible, but none of the sound stages currently have sign-language interpreters.

Restaurants and Shops

All are fully wheelchair accessible, but there are no braille menus or sign-language interpreters.

Information

See Access for Travelers with Disabilities *in* Essential Information, *above.*

DISCOVERY ISLAND

Originally conceived as a re-creation of the setting of Robert Louis Stevenson's *Treasure Island,* complete with wrecked ship and Jolly Roger, Discovery Island evolved gradually into its contemporary status as an animal preserve and member of the American Association of Zoological Parks and Aquariums, where visitors can see and learn about some 100 different species of exotic birds and animals amid 11½ lushly landscaped acres. Its long, white-sand beaches, its hills, and its hidden groves were sculpted and planned by Disney Imagineers, who brought in 15,000 cubic yards of sandy soil, added 1,000 tons of boulders and trees, and planted 20 types of palm trees, 10 species of bamboo, and dozens of other plants whose original habitats ranged from Argentina, Trinidad, and Costa Rica to the Himalayas and South Africa. Despite all that work, Discovery Island remains the least artificial attraction in Walt Disney World. Although it is barely a 15-minute boat ride from the dock at the Magic Kingdom, surprisingly few visitors take the time to explore it.

Although it's possible to "do" Discovery Island in less than an hour, anything more than a stop-and-start saunter would do it injustice. You can wander along the shady boardwalks at your own pace, stopping to inspect the bougainvillea or visit with a rhinoceros hornbill. You can picnic on the beach or on one of the benches in the shade and watch trumpeter swans glide by. You can simply sit and read without being disturbed by the ecstatic screams of thrill riders. The only thing you may not do is go swimming—the Water Sprites and motor launches on Bay Lake come just too close for safety.

Essential Information

Getting Around
Boardwalks and well-beaten paths wind through the island's lush vegetation.

Tourist Information
Disney hosts and hostesses at the entrance kiosk can answer most questions you may have and can give you maps and show schedules.

Guided Tours
Reserve ahead for **Discovery Island Kidventures,** four-hour guided tours for children aged 8–14 (☎ 407/824–3784; $32, including lunch, transportation, craft materials, and a souvenir photo), offered Wednesday and Sunday in summer, but Wednesday only the rest of the year.

Access
All paths and boardwalks are accessible by wheelchair. No signage is in braille, and no signing is available.

Wheelchairs
Available for rent throughout Walt Disney World, wheelchairs are available here on loan—with no charge.

Exploring Discovery Island

Pick up a map and a schedule of bird shows at the entrance kiosk and then start exploring. It's truly impossible to get lost, because the boardwalks, however twisty and no matter how many detours, essentially trace a circle around the island. It may take a while, but you'll always get back to your starting place.

Just past the first right-hand bend in the boardwalk is the **Discovery Island Bird Show,** where aviary "Animal Encounters" shows are presented in an open amphitheater equipped with benches and numerous perches. "Feathered Friends" features macaws and cockatoos, including the tricky green trio of Larry, Curly, and Moe. "Birds of Prey" demonstrates the behaviors of such predatory birds as owls, hawks, and king vultures. There's usually a show every hour from 11 to 4; most last about 15 minutes.

Large and airy enclosures holding additional birds and animals are set along the boardwalk throughout the island. More animals are allowed to roam free, so you're likely to surprise a male peacock spreading his iridescent fan in an attempt to woo an unimpressed female or you can watch 500-pound Galápagos tortoises inch along the beach. Informative signs explain the animal's characteristics and point out particularly interesting plants.

The island menagerie also contains areas dedicated to specific species. **Monkey Point** is home to a family of golden-lion tamarins from South America. **Avian Way,** one of the largest walk-through aviaries in the world, houses both a colony of scarlet ibis, whose brilliant color is enhanced by a special carotene-rich diet, and a bunch of blush-colored roseate spoonbills. It's especially amusing to watch the spoonbills scoop up fish in their lagoon—as well as to eavesdrop on the peanut gallery. More carotene helps the Caribbean flamingos in **Flamingo Lagoon** keep their characteristic tropical coral color. Dainty demoiselle and gold-crested African crowned cranes delicately pick their way around **Crane's Roost** while alligators loll about in slothful splendor in the **Alligator Pool.** The pool also hosts another Animal Encounter: "Reptile Relations" looks at the habits of snakes and alligators. And what would Florida be without pelicans? You don't have to imagine, thanks to a protected flock in **Pelican Bay.**

TIME OUT   Sandwiches, hot dogs and burgers, ice cream sandwiches and bars, frozen juice bars, and both beer and soft drinks are sold at the **Thirsty Perch,** at the entrance dock.

TYPHOON LAGOON

According to Disney legend, Typhoon Lagoon was created when the quaint, thatched-roof, lushly landscaped Placid Palms Resort was struck by a cataclysmic storm. It left a different world in its wake: Surfboards sundered trees, once-upright palms imitated the Leaning Tower of Pisa, a great buoy crashed through the roof of one building, a small boat was blown through the roof of another, and part of the original lagoon was cut off, trapping thousands of tropical fish—and a few sharks. Nothing, however, topped the fate of *Miss Tilly,* a shrimp boat from "Safen Sound, Florida," which was hurled high in the air and became impaled on Mount Mayday, a magical volcano that periodically tries to dislodge *Miss Tilly* with huge geysers of water.

Ordinary folks, the legend continues, would have been crushed by such devastation. But the resourceful residents of 56-acre Placid Palms were made of hardier stuff—and from the wreckage they created Typhoon Lagoon, the self-proclaimed "world's ultimate water park."

Four times the size of River Country, Typhoon Lagoon offers a full-day's worth of activities: bobbing in 4-foot waves in a surf lagoon the size of two football fields, speeding down arrow-straight water slides and around twisty storm slides, bumping through rapids, and snorkeling. More mellow folks can float in inner tubes along the 2,100-foot Castaway Creek, rubberneck from specially constructed grandstands as human cannonballs are ejected from the storm slides, or merely hunker down in one of the many hammocks or lounge chairs and read a book. A children's area replicates adult rides on a smaller scale. It's Disney's version of a day at the beach—complete with lifeguards in spiffy red-and-white-striped T-shirts.

Essential Information

Tourist Information

The **Guest Relations** window just outside the entrance turnstiles, to your left, can answer many questions. Inside, a chalkboard gives water temperature and surfing information, and all rides and attractions are marked with red nautical pennants indicating the thrill level: One pennant equals "laid back," two means "radical," three means "hot stuff," and four equals "awesome." Because the semantical differences between "radical" and "awesome" are minimal, assume that one and two pennants means you can keep your sunglasses on, and three or four pennants suggests that you should hand them to someone for safekeeping and then secure the knot on your swimsuit.

Services and Facilities

DRESSING ROOMS, LOCKERS, AND REST ROOMS

Men's and women's thatch-roofed **dressing rooms** and two sizes of full-day **lockers** ($5 and $7) are in two areas—to the right of the entrance and near Typhoon Tilly's Galley & Grog Shop. The latter area is usually less crowded. You can also rent **towels** (50¢ at the stand to the right of the main entrance), but they're a little skimpy; bring your own beach towel or buy one at Singapore Sal's (*see below*). The Typhoon Lagoon Imagineers thoughtfully placed **rest rooms** in every available nook and cranny. Most are equipped with showers, and they are much less crowded for clothes-changing than the main dressing rooms are.

FIRST AID
The small first-aid stand is left of the entrance, not far from the Leaning Palms food stand.

INNER TUBES, RAFTS, AND SNORKELS
The rental **rafts** concession, the building with the boat sticking through the roof to the left of the entrance, past the Leaning Palms food concession, rents **inner tubes.** You need to rent tubes only for the lagoon; they are provided for Castaway Creek and all the white-water rides. You can borrow **snorkels and masks** at Shark Reef, and **life vests** are available at High and Dry Towels (25¢ deposit). You may not bring your own equipment into Typhoon Lagoon.

LOST THINGS OR PEOPLE
Ask after your misplaced people or things at the Guest Relations window just outside the entrance turnstiles, to your left.

SUPPLIES
Singapore Sal's, to the right of the main entrance, is the place to acquire sunscreen, hats, sunglasses, and other beach paraphernalia.

Access
Wheelchair rentals are available in the entrance turnstile area (free with ID). All of the paths that connect the different areas of Typhoon Lagoon are wheelchair accessible. Guests who use a wheelchair can also float in Typhoon Lagoon and on Castaway Creek, provided it's possible to transfer to a raft or inner tube. The park is head and shoulders above River Country in the accessibility department.

Picnicking
Picnicking is also permitted. Tables are set up at Getaway Glen and Castaway Cove, near Shark Reef. Bring a box lunch from your hotel—and you'll eat well without having to line up with the masses.

Strategies for Your Visit

There's really only one problem with Typhoon Lagoon—it's popular. In the summer and on weekends, the park often reaches capacity (7,200 people) by midmorning, by which time Castaway Creek is a bank-to-bank carpet of tangled arms and legs, Typhoon Lagoon resembles the Times Square subway station at rush hour, and the lines for Humunga Kowabunga, the storm slides, and Shark Reef can top an hour. In that time, you could have driven to the Atlantic Ocean. Now that Blizzard Beach has opened, however, crowds will be able to breathe more freely here.

If you must go during the summer, go for a few hours during the dreamy late afternoons or when the weather clears up after a thundershower. (Typically, rainstorms drive away the crowds, and lots of people simply don't come back.) If you plan to make a whole day of it, avoid weekends—Typhoon Lagoon is big among locals as well as tourists. Instead, visit on a Monday, or on Sunday morning, when the locals are in church. Arrive 30 minutes before opening time so you can park, buy tickets, rent towels, and snag inner tubes before the hordes descend. Set up camp and hit the slides, white-water rides, and Shark Reef first. Then bobble along Castaway Creek and save the lagoon itself for later.

If you're visiting at a relatively unpopulated time of year, go in the afternoon, when the day will have warmed up a bit. Do Castaway Creek first to get a sense of the park.

There are plenty of lounge chairs, a number of hammocks, and definitely not enough beach umbrellas. If you crave shade, commandeer a spot in the grassy area around Getaway Glen on the left side of the park just past the raft-rental concession. If you like lots of action, people-watching, and sand in your face, go front and center at the surf pool. For sand and relative quiet, head for the coves and inlets on the left side of the lagoon.

Exploring Typhoon Lagoon

Numbers in the margin correspond to points of interest on the Typhoon Lagoon map.

The layout is so simple that it is truly impossible to get lost—trust us. The eponymous wave and swimming lagoon is at the center of the park; the waves break on the beaches closest to the entrance and are born in Mount Mayday at the other end of the park. Castaway Creek encircles the lagoon. Anything requiring a gravitational plunge—storm slides, speed slides, and raft trips down rapids—starts around the summit of Mount Mayday. Shark Reef and Ketchakiddie Creek flank the head of the lagoon, to Mount Mayday's right and left, respectively.

❶ The heart of the park is, of course, **Typhoon Lagoon,** a swimming area that spreads out over 2½ acres and contains almost 3 million gallons of clear, chlorinated water. It's scalloped by lots of little coves, bays, and inlets, all edged with white-sand beaches—spread over a base of white concrete, as body surfers will soon discover when they try to slide into shore. Ouch! The main attraction is the waves. Twelve huge water-collection chambers hidden in Mount Mayday dump their load with a resounding "whoosh" into trap doors to create waves large enough for Typhoon Lagoon to host amateur and professional surfing championships. A piercing hoot from *Miss Tilly* signals the start and finish of wave action: Every even hour, for 10 minutes on and 10 minutes off, 4-foot-plus waves issue forth every 90 seconds; every odd hour is devoted to moderate bobbing waves. Even during the big-wave periods, however, the waters in Blustery Bay and Whitecap Cove are protected enough for timid swimmers.

❷ Circular, 15-foot-wide, 3-foot-deep **Castaway Creek** is everyone's water fantasy come true. Snag an inner tube and float along the creek that winds around the entire park, a wet version of the Magic Kingdom's Walt Disney World Railroad. You pass through a rain forest that showers you with mist and spray (don't think you can put your ankles up and read a book, tempting though it may sound), you slide through caves and grottos, you burble by overhanging trees and flowering bushes, and you get dumped on at the Water Works (whose "broken" pipes the Typhoon Lagooners never got around to fixing). The current ambles at 2½ feet per second; it takes about 30 minutes to make a full circuit. There are exits along the way, where you can hop out and dry off or do something else—and then pick up another inner tube and jump right back in.

③ Follow Castaway Creek up toward Mount Mayday, and at the head of the lagoon, veer right for **Shark Reef.** Anyone who wanted to leap onto the stage at Disney-MGM's Voyage of the Little Mermaid or jump into the tank at Epcot Center's Living Seas will make tracks for this 360,000-gallon snorkeling tank. The coral reef is artificial, but the 4,000 tropical fish—including black-and-white striped sergeant majors, sargassum trigger fish, yellowtail damselfish, and amiable nurse and bonnet-head sharks—are quite real. So are the southern stingrays that congregate in the warmer, shallower water by the entrance (to prevent algae growth, Shark Reef is kept at a brisk 72°, which is 18° colder than the rest of Typhoon Lagoon). A sunken tanker divides the reef; its portholes give landlubbers access to the underwater scene and let them go nose to nose with snorkelers. Unless the reef is practically deserted—almost never—you are supposed to swim in a counterclockwise circle around the tanker; one circuit takes about 15 minutes. Go first thing in the morning or at the end of the day if you want to spend more time. Chilly air and water temperatures close the reef from November through April.

④ There's no time to scream on **Humunga Kowabunga,** but you'll hear just such vociferous reactions as the survivors emerge from the catch pool opposite Shark Reef. The basic question is: Want to get scared out of your wits in three seconds flat—and like it enough to go back for more? "Do that?" asked one observer. "I'm not crazy!" The two side-by-side Humunga Kowabunga speed slides rightly deserve their four-pennant designation, as they drop more than 50 feet in a distance barely four times that amount. (For nonmathematicians, that's *very steep.*) Oh yes, and then you go through a cave. In the dark. Awesome, indeed. The average speed is 30 miles per hour; however, you can really fly if you lie flat on your back, cross your ankles, wrap your arms around your chest, and arch your back. Just remember to smile for the rubberneckers on the grandstand at the bottom—and to readjust your bathing suit before leaving the water. *No pregnant women or guests with back or heart problems or other physical limitations.*

⑤ It's a long and twisty-turny schlep up the right side of Mount Mayday and a short but even more twisty-turny ride down on the **Jib Jammer, Rudder Buster,** and **Stern Burner storm slides.** Each of these three body slides is about 300 feet long and snakes in and out of rock formations, through caves and tunnels, and under waterfalls, but each has a slightly different view and offers an idiosyncratic twist (we'll only say that the one in the middle has the longest tunnel; the others' secrets you'll have to discover for yourself). Maximum speed is about 20 miles per hour and the trip takes about 30 seconds.

⑥ What goes down can also go up—and up and up and up and up. "It's like climbing Mount Everest," wailed one teenager about a climb that seems a lot steeper than the 85-foot peak of **Mount Mayday** would warrant. However, it's Mount Everest with hibiscus flowers, a shivering rope bridge, stepping-stones set in plunging waters, and—remember that seminal typhoon?—a broken canoe scattered over the rocks near the top. The view encompasses the entire park.

Mayday Falls, Keelhaul Falls, Gangplank Falls—white-water raft rides that you experience in oversize inner tubes—plunge down the left side of Mount Mayday. Like the storm slides, they feature caves and waterfalls and intricate rock work but add some extra elements. The 460-

❼ foot slide over **Mayday Falls,** in blue inner tubes, is the longest and generally acclaimed the bumpiest; it's a straight slide over the falls into a catchment area, which gives you just enough time to catch your breath

❽ before the next plunge. The spiraling, 400-foot **Keelhaul Falls** ride, in yellow inner tubes, takes a more roundabout trip, and the speed seems

❾ faster than the purported 10 miles per hour. **Gangplank Falls** was designed for groups and families, who ride in four-person, 6½-foot inner tubes down 300 feet of rapids.

❿ **Ketchakiddie Creek,** located just to the right of the white-water ride exits, sports scaled-down versions of the big people's rides. There are slides, minirapids, squirting whales and seals, bouncing barrels, waterfalls, sprinklers, and all the other ingredients of splash heaven. The bubbling sand ponds, in which kids can sit in what seems like an enormous Jacuzzi, are special favorites. *All adults must be accompanied by a child under 4 ft (and vice versa).*

TIME OUT Standard fast-food beach fare—burgers, dogs, chef's salads, and, of course, ice cream and frozen yogurt—is what's cooking at **Leaning Palms,** to the left of the entrance, and **Typhoon Tilly's Galley & Grog Shop,** on the right just south of Shark Reef. Tilly's grog is mostly carbonated, but she also sells Davy Jones lager. **Let's Go Slurpin',** a beach shack on the edge of Typhoon Lagoon, dispenses frozen margaritas as well as wine and beer. Food carts purveying lemonade, soda, ices, and snow cones are scattered around the park.

BLIZZARD BEACH

The newest entry in the Disney water park universe is a real chiller—literally and figuratively. With its oxymoronic name, Blizzard Beach promises the seemingly impossible—a seaside playground with an Alpine theme. As with its older cousin, Typhoon Lagoon, the Disney Imagineers have created an entire legend around the park's origin. In the case of Blizzard Beach, the story goes like this: After a freak winter storm dropped snow over the western side of Walt Disney World property, entrepreneurs decided to create Florida's first snow-ski resort. The plan, alas, was short-lived: The snow melted as Central Florida's weather returned to its usual sauna-like temperatures. Just as the resort's operators were ready to close up shop, however, they spotted a playful alligator sliding down the "liquid ice" slopes. The realization that the melting snow had created the tallest, fastest, and most exhilarating water-filled ski and toboggan runs in the world gave birth to the ski-resort/water-adventure park.

With that premise in mind, the Disney Imagineers have gone all-out to create the paradox of a ski resort in the midst of a tropical lagoon. Playing with the snow-in-Florida water motif, there are lots of verbal puns and sight gags. Most of the park's attractions have names that playfully follow through on the beach-ski theme. The park's centerpiece is Mt. Gushmore, which features the 120-foot-high Summit Plummet, as well as other toboggan and water sled runs with names such as Teamboat Springs (a white-water raft ride), Toboggan Racer, Slush Gusher, and Runoff Rapids. Swim-skiiers can also ride an actual chairlift converted from ski-resort to beach-resort use (with umbrellas and snow skis on their undersides) over the face of Mt. Gushmore,

Typhoon Lagoon

KEY

🍴 Restaurants

🚻 Restrooms

N

Miss Tilly

6

7

4

5

8

9

3

10

Low Tide Lou's

Beach Area

Typhoon Lagoon

Typhoon Tilly's

2

1

Rain Forest

Rain Forest

2

Raft Rentals

Beach Area

Slurp's Up

High & Dry Towels

Castaway Creek

Leaning Palms

Singapore Sal's Saleable Salvage

First Aid

Entrance

Castaway Creek, **2**

Gangplank Falls, **9**

Humunga Kowabunga
Speed Slide, **4**

Keelhaul Falls, **8**

Ketchakiddie Creek, **10**

Mayday Falls, **7**

Mount Mayday, **6**

Shark Reef, **3**

Storm Slides, **5**

Typhoon Lagoon, **1**

las and snow skis on their undersides) over the face of Mt. Gushmore, from its seaside base to its summit.

Essential Information

Tourist Information

Disney staffers at the **Guest Relations** window, located to the left of the ticket booth, can answer most of your questions. Unlike Typhoon Lagoon, there's no rating system for the slides; however, the two speediest slides, Summit Plummet and Slush Gusher, have a minimum height requirement of 48 inches.

Services and Facilities

DRESSING ROOMS, LOCKERS, AND REST ROOMS

Dressing Rooms (for "Sleigh Belles" and "Snowmen"—get it?) are located in the Village area, just past the main entrance. Here you'll find showers and rest rooms as well. **Lockers** can be found in two strategic locations: near the entrance—next to Snowless Joe's Rentals—and near Tike's Peak, the children's area (which could prove to be more convenient for adults with little swimmers in tow). Get locker keys at Snowless Joe's. Rentals for lockers are $5 for small and $7 for large, but you'll receive $2 back at the end of the day when you turn in your key (small lockers only are available at Tike's Peak). **Rest rooms** are conveniently located throughout the park; there are facilities in the Village area (near the entrance), in Lottawatta Lodge, at the Ski Patrol Training Camp, and just past the Melt Away Bay Beach Area. **Towels** are also available for rent at Snowless Joe's ($1) but they aren't beach towel size. Bring your own if you can.

FIRST AID

The first aid stand is in the Village, between Lottawatta Lodge and the Beach Haus.

LIFE PRESERVERS AND INNER TUBES

Personal flotation devices (life jackets) for both children and adults are available free of charge at Snowless Joe's. A refundable deposit is required—either $25 or the photo ID of a Disney multiday passport; credit card imprints are also taken. No inner tubes are available for rent; you'll find tubes provided at the various rides in the park.

LOST THINGS OR PEOPLE

Get reunited with lost children at Snowless Joe's.

SUPPLIES

Sundries, including sunglasses, sunscreen, bathing suits—even waterproof disposable cameras—are available at the **Beach Haus,** located within the Village. Check out the ski equipment hanging from the ceiling. Not surprisingly, a large variety of Blizzard Beach logo merchandise is available here as well.

Access

A limited number of wheelchairs are available for rent near the park entrance. Most of the paths in the park are wheelchair accessible. Guests who use a wheelchair can also float in Cross-Country Creek, provided they can transfer to a large inner tube. Some guests with limited mobility might also be able to use the inner tubes at some of the park's tamer slides.

Picnicking

Picnicking is allowed, but don't bring in any alcoholic drinks or glass containers in your cooler. There are several areas that lend themselves to picnicking, most notably the terrace outside Lottawatta Lodge and its surrounding environs.

Strategies for Your Visit

Chances are that Blizzard Beach will become just as popular as Typhoon Lagoon—and even more crowded, since it's the new kid on the block. As with every other mecca, your best bet is to get there early, before the gates fling open. Expect long lines at the major attractions, such as the Summit Plummet. If you go during the summer, try to arrive in the late afternoon, just after the daily thunderstorm. The air will be hot and humid, but you'll be cool as a cucumber because the hoards will have already departed for indoor pursuits. If thrill rides aren't your top priority, though, there's plenty of room in Melt-Away Bay's wave pool. A relaxing inner tube ride on Cross-Country Creek is a cool alternative as well.

Exploring Blizzard Beach

The park centers on **Mt. Gushmore,** a 90-foot "snow-capped" mountain. Here, "skiers" slide down the face of the mountain, tackling moguls, slalom courses, and toboggan and water-sled runs. At the base of the mountain, there's a sandy beach featuring the de rigueur wave pool, a lazy river, and play areas for both young children and pre-teens.

Mt. Gushmore's big gun is **Summit Plummet,** which Disney bills as "the world's tallest, fastest free-fall speed slide." From Summit Plummet's "ski jump" tower, it's a wild 55-mph plunge straight down to a splash landing at the base of the mountain. From far, far below, park visitors can see the first part of this "run." It looks almost like a straight vertical drop. If you're watching from the beach below, you can't hear the yells of the participants, but rest assured, they're screaming their heads off.

Next to Summit Plummet is **Slush Gusher,** a speed slide that drops through a snow-banked mountain gully. It's shorter and less severe than Summit Plummet but gives quite a rush nonetheless. *Must be 48" to ride.*

Teamboat Springs is a "white-water raft ride" in which six-passenger rafts zip along a twisting 1,200-foot series of rushing waterfalls.

Toboggan Racer sends guests down an eight-lane water slide over Mt. Gushmore's "snowy" slopes.

No water park would be complete without a flume ride, and Blizzard Beach has one: **Snow Stormers** is actually three flumes that descend from the top of Mt. Gushmore. Riders follow a switchback course through ski-type slalom gates.

For the slightly less adventurous, there's **Runoff Rapids,** an inner tube run where guests can slide down three different twisting, turning flumes.

If you're waterlogged, take a ride on the **Chair Lift,** which takes visitors from the beachfront base of Mt. Gushmore up over its face and on to the summit. While most riders will probably want to body-"ski" down via one of the water slides, you can opt to take the lift back to the beach. Few do, however.

The beach portion of the park has its share of attractions as well. Since Disney is never one to leave the kids out of the fun, there's **Tike's Peak,** a junior-size version of Blizzard Beach that features scaled-down elements of Mt. Gushmore. A snow-castle fountain play area is here as well. Kids can also swing across a pool via an overhead rope while stepping across floating icebergs.

Melt-Away Bay is the park's main pool, a 1-acre oasis that's constantly fed by "melting snow" waterfalls. The waves in the pool are man-made, of course, and create the desired ocean-like effect. If you're not a strong swimmer, though, stay away from the far end of the pool, where the waves emanate. You can get temporarily "stuck" in a pocket—a feeling not unlike getting caught in an ocean's undertow—even if your head is still above water.

Cross-Country Creek is similar to Typhoon Lagoon's Castaway Creek; circling the entire park, it lets guests float on inner tubes. Along the way, guests will encounter a bone-chilling ice cave, where they're splashed with "melting ice" from overhead—pure heaven on a steamy Florida day!

The pre-teens in your crowd will probably want to spend most of their time at the **Blizzard Beach Ski Patrol Training Camp.** Here they can use bungee-cord slides, a T-bar drop, and culvert slides. In addition, there's a chance to challenge Mogul Mania, a wide-open slide area filled with wet and slippery moguls.

TIME OUT **Lottawatta Lodge**—a North American ski lodge with a Caribbean accent—is the park's main food emporium (offerings here are of the fast-food variety) and, as such, has long lines at peak feeding times.

You can also satisfy your food cravings at **Avalunch,** where hot dogs, snow cones, and ice cream are offered. The **Warming Hut** has Italian sausage heroes, popcorn, and ice cream. In addition, stands around the park sell ice cream, soft drinks, bottled water, and beer.

RIVER COUNTRY

Imagine a mountain in Utah's red-rock country. Put a lake at the bottom, and add a verdant fuzz of maples and pines here and there on the sides. Then plant some water slides among the greenery, and call it a "good ole fashion' swimmin' hole." That's River Country.

It was the first of Walt Disney World's water parks. Whereas larger, glitzier Typhoon Lagoon is balmy and tropical, this one is rustic and rugged. Some of the activities are the same, but the mood is different. River Country is smaller and in many ways has more charm. Appropriately enough, it's the only one that gives visitors an unobstructed view of Sleeping Beauty's Castle. It's quite lovely to lie on a chaise longue and gaze at this icon glinting in the sunlight.

Essential Information

Tourist Information

The **Guest Services** window, at the entrance turnstiles, can answer most of your questions. It's also the spot to take finds and report losses.

Services and Facilities

DRESSING ROOMS AND LOCKERS

There are **dressing rooms** for men and women near the entrance, with coin-op **lockers** (50¢) and **towel rentals** ($1). Bring quarters to avoid having to wait in line for change, and bring your own towel (the ones here are skimpy). You'll also need your own beach towel.

FIRST AID

It's in the white building next to the guest pay phone, but it's open only during Easter break and in summer. At any other time, go to Guest Services.

Obviously lost youngsters are usually taken to the towel window and then walked around until they spot their folks. River Country is small enough for that system to work fine.

Access

Wheelchairs are available at Guest Services at no charge (with ID as deposit), but very little of the park is wheelchair accessible; you're better off at Typhoon Lagoon.

Tips

Go early in the morning to avoid the crowds that sometimes close River Country altogether on busy days. Alternatively, in summer, wait until 4 and take advantage of the reduced-price admission ticket.

Exploring River Country

Walking from the dressing rooms brings you to the 330,000-gallon swimming pool, bright blue and concrete paved, like something out of a more modern Midwest. There are a couple of short, steep water slides here. Beyond that is **Bay Cove,** the roped-off corner of Bay Lake that's the main section of River Country. Rope swings hang from a rustic boom, and there are various other woody contraptions from which kids dive and cannonball. The main event, however, consists of the two big water slides—100 and 260 feet long—that descend from **Whoop 'n' Holler Hollow** down the side of the mountain. Look for the boardwalk and stairway. A more leisurely trip down can be taken via **White Water Rapids,** a series of short chutes and swirling pools that you descend in a jumbo inner tube. Laughs, not thrills, are what this one is all about, as your tube gets caught in the pool's eddies and you spin around, stuck, until someone slides down and bumps you out.

Off to the edge of the property is a **nature trail** that skirts the shore of Bay Lake.

TIME OUT   You can pick up burgers, hot dogs, and fries at **Pop's Place** or, in summer and over Easter break, buy nachos, ice cream, soda, and beer at the **Watering Hole.** Picnicking is permitted.

ELSEWHERE IN THE WORLD

Walt Disney World is much more than theme parks. You can play tennis or golf, go boating or fishing, ride a bike, take a hike, or even work out in a health club (*see* Chapter 6, Sports and the Outdoors). Colorful restaurants and dinner shows abound, and children love having breakfast, lunch, or dinner with the Disney characters (*see* Chapter 7, Dining). And far from shutting down at night, this family entertainment spot gets a second wind when the sun goes down: You can sip a drink and listen to music in any number of night spots, take in a movie in a state-of-the-art theater, watch fireworks, and lots more (*see* Chapter 9, After Dark).

3 Universal Studios, Sea World, and Beyond

By Catherine
Fredman

Updated by
Mary Meehan

THEME PARKS GROW SO WELL in the sandy central Florida soil that one might almost imagine a handful of seeds, scattered across the fertile I–4 belt, waiting for the right combination of money and vision to nurture them into the next . . . Walt Disney World. WDW is, in fact, something of an up-start latecomer. Long before the strains of "It's a Small World" echoed through the palmetto scrub, other theme parks tempted visitors away from the beaches into the scruffy interior of central Florida.

None was anywhere near the scale of today's megaparks. I–4 hadn't even been built when Dick and Julie Pope created Cypress Gardens, which now holds the record as central Florida's oldest continuously running attraction. Busch Gardens was founded a quarter-century later, in 1959, as an exotic-animal sideshow attached to a brewery and beer garden.

But when the Magic Kingdom opened on October 1, 1971, and was immediately successful, the central Florida theme park scene went from mom-and-pop operations to big business. Sea World filled its tanks two years later. Epcot Center debuted in 1982. Disney-MGM Studios Theme Park threw down the movie gauntlet in 1989; Universal Studios answered the challenge one year later. Splendid China joined the fray in 1993. And meanwhile, Busch Gardens has steadily expanded, spawning the Busch Entertainment Corporation (BEC), which, with the 1989 acquisition of Cypress Gardens and Sea World, became the second-largest theme park owner and operator in the world. Its neighbor down the interstate remains number one.

Growth engendered more growth. Whereas it used to be that you could do a whole park—any park—in about six hours, a thorough visit now can barely be contained in a day—and a full day, too. As competition sharpened and tastes grew more sophisticated, a sort of me-too mentality became prevalent. If one park has a flight simulator, then all parks must have one (the best are Disney-MGM's Star Tours and Universal Studios' Back to the Future . . . The Ride). Ditto Broadway-style music-and-dance shows, distinguished for their professional presentation, snazzy costumes, high-kicking dancers, and completely forgettable plots. A blessing for parents, every park now has a sophisticated children's play area; ball crawls, four-story net climbs, bouncing rooms, water tricks, and twisty slides—all designed to match a preconceived theme—are de rigueur. So, too, thankfully, are lighter gustatory offerings that, though not exactly heart-healthy, are a welcome alternative to the usual greasy burnt offerings.

Prices have risen accordingly, with Universal Studios and Walt Disney World topping the scales at nearly $40 for a full-day adult ticket. Busch Gardens, Sea World, and Cypress Gardens match Walt Disney World's combined pass system with discounts on tickets to BEC parks that are purchased at another BEC attraction.

The problem for visitors with a tight schedule or a slim wallet is that each of the parks is worth a visit. But if you're staying in the Orlando area, a decision can be made on the basis of distance. Busch Gardens is 75 miles away, a good 90-minute commute each way; Cypress Gardens is a little closer, but the 60-minute drive through the dusty citrus groves seems to take forever. Coincidentally, these two parks offer few high-tech, gasp-producing spectacles. If you want to take in a park that has more cultural substance than blockbuster style, try Splendid China; this new attraction is only a few miles from WDW, but the emphasis here is on expert craftsmanship, not astounding effects. In any case, Sea World and Universal Studios are not to be missed. Universal Studios is best seen after visiting Disney-MGM; it definitely gilds Mickey's lily.

UNIVERSAL STUDIOS FLORIDA

Film fans know that Disney has no copyright on movie magic. Universal Studios has worked celluloid wizardry since 1915, and it wasn't long afterward that it offered visitors behind-the-scenes tours of what was to become the world's biggest and busiest motion picture and television production studio—that of Universal Studios Hollywood. So it wasn't surprising that Orlando's entertainment park expansion should pique the interest of that other candidate from California. Universal Studios Florida opened in June 1990.

Far from being a me-too version of Disney-MGM Studios, Universal Studios Florida is a theme park with plenty of personality of its own. And its personality can be summed up in one word: attitude. It's saucy, sassy, and hip—and doesn't hesitate to invite comparisons with the competition. Where Disney-MGM has the Muppets trilling "Great Balls of Fire," Universal's Beetlejuice Graveyard Revue, a new take on the Grateful Dead, sports a transfunkified Dracula belting "I'm Gonna Wait 'til the Midnight Hour" and a miniskirted Frankenstein's Bride getting down to "You Make Me Feel Like a Natural Woman." Disney-MGM's strolling actors are pabulum compared to the Blues Brothers peeling rubber in the Bluesmobile. And let's face it, even the Muppets are matched by E.T., Tickli Moot Moot, and other inventions of Steven Spielberg, Universal's genius-on-call. Universal's even figured out a way to keep people entertained while they wait in line: From arcade games at Nickelodeon to news shows on overhead screens in the *Jaws* line, Universal makes the most of its video connection.

In short, Universal Studios is the bad boy of central Florida entertainment parks. It's come a long way from the public relations nightmare of its opening days, when almost none of the highly touted rides functioned. Now they do, and so-called blockbuster rides such as Kongfrontation, Back to the Future . . . The Ride, E.T. Adventure, Earthquake—The Big One, and even the much-maligned Jaws (so glitch-haunted in its early days that it had to be closed for two years for repairs) are running and—judging from the delighted shrieks and groans issuing forth—running just fine. Universal Studios Florida is now the third most popular entertainment park in the United States, after Walt Disney World (with its three theme parks) and Disneyland; Universal Studios Hollywood, by the way, is a close fourth. Look forward to further expansion as Universal takes advantage of its Hollywood connections and opens rides and exhibits that tie in with hit movies. In 1994, a *Jurassic Park* exhibit opened. Could a ride be far behind?

The lofty adult ticket prices raise expectations very high indeed. They are met most of the time, but resentment can set in if you're confronted by too many long lines and the movie theater–like price gouging at ubiquitous concession stands and snackeries. We know, we know, it's a free country.

With Disney-MGM just down the road, is Universal worth the visit? Absolutely—they're not the same thing: If Disney-MGM is the introductory course, Universal Studios is graduate school. As such, the attractions are geared more to older kids than the stroller set. If your party is prepared for some loud and scary entertainment, then you should have a wonderful time.

Essential Information

Tourist Information

Contact Universal Studios (1000 Universal Studios Plaza, Orlando 32819-7610, ☎ 407/363–8000, TTY 407/363–8265).

Stop by **Guest Relations,** in the Front Lot to the right after you pass through the turnstiles, for brochures, maps, and a schedule of the day's entertainment, tapings, and filmings.

Studio Information Boards in front of Studio Stars Restaurant and Mel's Drive-In provide up-to-the-minute ride and show operating information—including the length of lines in minutes at the Studios' major attractions.

If you want to watch a production filming or taping, consult the Production Schedule at the entrance turnstiles or stop in at Guest Relations. Attendants at the Nickelodeon studio can tell you how to get studio audience tickets.

Reservations

Reservations at the Universal Studios restaurants that accept them (*see below*) can be made as far in advance as you want to make them; just call the restaurant or go there in person first thing in the morning.

Getting There

Universal Studios is about ½ mile north of I–4 Exit 30B (Kirkman Rd., or Rte. 435), near the intersection of I–4 and the Florida Turnpike. Be warned, however, that getting from the 30B/Kirkman exit to the park is confusing—you have to drive past the entrance gates and then loop back. It's much easier to reach Universal Studios if you get off I–4 at Exit 29, which is slightly south of the park. From Exit 29, directions are as follows: If traveling westbound on I–4, make a right onto Sand Lake Road and another right onto Turkey Lake Road; if traveling eastbound, make a left onto Sand Lake Road and then a right onto Turkey Lake Road. Numerous billboards and signposts mark the way.

PARKING

The cost is $5 for cars, $7 for campers. Valet parking is also available for $11.

Admission

Tickets, excluding tax, cost $37 for one day, $55 for two days; $30 and $44, respectively, for children 3–9. They're available in advance by mail through TicketMaster (☎ 800/745–5000).

DISCOUNTS

Making your purchase at the Orlando/Orange County Convention and Visitors Bureau ticket office at the Mercado International Market (8445 International Dr.) will save you about $4 per adult ticket ($3 on children's prices). When you buy your ticket at the gate, you can save $2.50 by using the Orlando Magicard, available free on request (☎ 800/551–0181) or in person at the Mercado. Card-carrying AAA members can receive a 10% discount at the park; the discount may be higher at an AAA office.

HAND STAMPS

If you want to leave the park and come back the same day, have your hand stamped when you leave, and show your hand and your Studio Pass when you return.

TICKET UPGRADES
If you decide that one day is not enough, buy your next day's ticket at
Guest Relations just inside the Main Entrance *before* you leave the park,
and you'll pay only the two-day ticket price.

Hours
Universal Studios is open 365 days a year, from 9 to 7, with hours extended as late as 10 during summer and holiday periods.

Services
BABY CARE
There are **diaper-changing tables** in both men's and women's rest rooms;
there are **nursing facilities** at Guest Relations just inside the Main Entrance and to the right, as well as at First Aid, adjoining Louie's Italian
restaurant between San Francisco and New York. No **diapers** are sold
on the premises; instead, they're complimentary—to guests in need—at
Animal House, Doc's Candy Store, the Universal Studios Store, and other
locations (ask!). You will find **strollers** (which look like Jurassic Park Jeeps)
for rent in Amity and just inside the Main Entrance to the right, next to
the First Union National Bank (singles $6, doubles $12; no deposit required). No formula or baby food is sold on the premises; the nearest
sources are Kmart on Sand Lake Road, Walgreen's on Kirkman Road,
and Publix supermarkets on Sand Lake and Kirkman roads.

BABY EXCHANGE
All rides have Baby Exchange areas, so that one parent or adult party
member can watch a baby or toddler while the other enjoys the ride
or show. The adults then change roles, and the former caretaker rides
without having to wait in line all over again.

CAMERAS AND FILM
At the Lights, Camera, Action shop in the Front Lot, just inside the
Main Entrance, you'll find **rental video cameras** ($29.95 per day; de-
posit or credit-card imprint required) and **loaner cameras.** You must
show a valid driver's license and a major credit card.

For **minor camera repairs,** go to the Dark Room on Hollywood
Boulevard.

For **one-hour film developing,** the Dark Room is the spot.

CAR CARE
You can fill 'er up at the '40s-vintage Texaco station at the Turkey Lake
Road entrance. If you need a battery jump, raise your hood and speak
to the nearest employee.

FIRST AID
Universal Studios' First Aid Center is between New York and San
Francisco, next to Louie's Italian Restaurant.

GUIDED TOURS
Universal has two VIP tours, which offer what's called "back-door admission" or, in plain English, the right to jump the line. No other theme
park has anything like this, which we suppose is the ultimate capitalist
fantasy. In any case, they're definitely worthwhile if you're in a hurry, if
the day is crowded, and if you have the money to burn—from $90 for
an individual four-hour VIP tour (including park admission) to $900 for
an eight-hour tour for up to 15 people (again including park admission).

LOCKERS
They're across from Guest Relations (*see above;* 50¢).

If you lose your children or traveling companions, speak up immediately at Guest Relations or at Security (behind Louie's, between New York and San Francisco).

Misplaced possessions go to Guest Relations near the Main Entrance.

The First Union National Bank, just inside the Main Entrance, cashes traveler's checks, makes cash advances on credit cards, and exchanges foreign currency. There's one ATM at the bank and another outside the Main Entrance, to the right of the Guest Relations window; they're linked to Plus, Honor, Cirrus, Visa, and MasterCard.

Wheelchairs ($5 a day) and electric wheelchairs ($25 a day) can be rented in Amity and just inside the Main Entrance, to the right, next to the First Union National Bank. You must leave a valid driver's license or $25 as a deposit. If the wheelchair breaks down, disappears, or otherwise needs replacing, speak to any shop attendant.

Strategies for Your Visit

When to Go

As in the Disney parks, Mondays through Wednesdays are the busiest days of the week. The pace slows down on Thursdays and Fridays and builds again over the weekend. Saturdays and Sundays are usually busy, but especially during holiday weeks.

Blitz Tour

Universal estimates that 14 hours are needed to experience the entire park. So if you want to at least attempt seeing everything in one day, arrive early so that you can take care of business and see the fabled attractions before the park gets very crowded.

Don't be distracted by the faux Hollywood streets, don't be lured into those shops calling to you as you go through the gate. Walk past all those inviting doorways straight back to **E.T. Adventure.** (Vacations require discipline.) After flying to alien worlds, zip over to **Back to the Future . . . The Ride,** and streak through Hill Valley, the town where the movie was set. Catch the animal show, then traipse over to Amityville, where the terrifying star of **Jaws** will try to catch you. Mosey over to the **Wild, Wild, Wild West Stunt Show.** Next, get a healthy dose of disaster with **Earthquake—The Big One** and **Kongfrontation,** see if the Blues Brothers are performing, and then have a little lunch. Skitter over to **Ghostbusters** in New York, then take the short walk to **Production Central,** tour **Nickelodeon,** catch **"Murder, She Wrote" Mystery Theater,** dodge the birds in **Hitchcock's 3-D Theatre,** and zoom through a cartoon world at the **Funtastic World of Hanna-Barbera.**

You will have made a circle around the park. Now, with all those people who didn't read this guide still standing in line to hit the big rides, you can enjoy **Lucy: A Tribute,** *Jurassic Park*: **Behind the Scenes,** the **Gory, Gruesome & Grotesque Horror Make-Up Show,** and **AT&T at the Movies.** And now, with the day waning, you can shop. If Hard Rock souvenirs beckon, let the kids play at **Fievel's Playland** or **A Day in the Park with Barney** while you stand in line to get into the store. This will put you in a good position to find a prime spot for the **Dynamite Stuntacular,** which allows you to end your day with a bang.

On Rainy Days

Except during Christmas week, rainy days are less crowded—even though the park is in full operation. (Only a couple of street shows get canceled.)

Other Tips

The strategies that stand you in good stead in the Disney parks also prevail here.

- Call the day before your visit to get official park hours.

- Arrive in the parking lot 30–45 minutes early and see the biggest attractions first.

- Lunch before 11 and dine at 5. Or have a filling snack at 10:30, lunch after 2, and dinner at 8 or later. Or lunch on the early side at a place that takes reservations (Lombard's Landing and Studio Stars are good bets). Be sure to make your reservations ahead of time (or, at the very least, when you enter the park).

- If you're traveling with small children, avoid backtracking. Universal is just too big.

- Set up a rendezvous point at the start of the day, just in case you and your companions get separated.

- Be sure to mark your parking location by some permanent landmark. Universal Studios' parking lots do not have overhead signs designating parking areas.

Exploring Universal Studios Florida

The 444 acres of Universal Studios are a bewildering conglomeration of stage sets, shops, reproductions of New York and San Francisco, and anonymous soundstages housing theme attractions as well as genuine moviemaking paraphernalia. On the map, these sets are neatly divided into six neighborhoods: the Front Lot, Production Central, Hollywood, New York, Expo Center, and San Francisco/Amity, which lazily wend their way around a huge blue lagoon, the setting for the Dynamite Nights Stunt Spectacular. On foot, it's a different story. There is no prominent central edifice by which to orient yourself, and the street names change depending on which "neighborhood" you're in. In other words, expect to get lost early and often. Rather than trying to figure out whether you're on Sunset Boulevard, Hollywood Boulevard, or Rodeo Drive (the answer is "yes"), look for official staffers; their snappy, surprisingly classy pink-and-white-striped oxford-cloth shirts and white walking shorts stand out.

The Front Lot

Like Disney-MGM's Hollywood Boulevard, Universal Studios' Front Lot is essentially a scene-setter, a mood manipulator, the first of many opportunities to squander the contents of your savings account on merchandise or snacks, and the place to find many services. The main drag, the Plaza of the Stars, stretches from the marble-arched entrance gateway straight down to the other end of the lot, affording a great trompe-l'oeil view of New York City's public library painted on a wall in the New York neighborhood. One thousand miles in as many yards—how's that for magic?

Hollywood

Angling off to the right of Plaza of the Stars, Rodeo Drive stretches from the Front Lot to the lagoon (turning into Hollywood Boulevard along the way). The street forms the backbone of Hollywood, which contains such attractions as Lucy: A Tribute, the Gory, Gruesome & Grotesque Horror Make-Up Show, and *Jurassic Park*: Behind the Scenes, as well as more shops and nosheries.

Numbers in the margin correspond to points of interest on the Universal Studios map.

① As the first attraction you meet after promenading through the grandiose gateway, **Lucy: A Tribute** occupies a prime corner at Rodeo Drive and Plaza of the Stars. A walk-through collection of Lucy's costumes, accessories, and other memorabilia; trivia quizzes; and 20-second spots from the series shown on overhead video screens, the exhibition doesn't quite match the value of the real estate. Fans of the ditzy redhead may want to reminisce over every item, however. *Duration: About 15 min. Crowds: Seldom a problem. Strategy: Save this for a peek on your way out or for a hot afternoon. Audience: Adults. Rating:* ★

② Farther along the street, just past the bend where Rodeo Drive turns into Hollywood Boulevard, the **Gory, Gruesome & Grotesque Horror Make-Up Show** is especially appreciated by young children and teens, showing as it does what goes into and oozes out of the most mangled monsters in movie history. There's a delicious irony in the fact that you settle into comfortable seats in an air-conditioned theater to find out how an actor's mouth turned into a roach motel in the movie *Creep Show,* how man-to-wolf transmogrification is effected in *American Werewolf in London,* and, of course, the secret of the famous spinning-heads scene in *The Exorcist*. The Horror Make-Up Show demystifies without disillusioning—although you never do learn the exact proportions of shrimp sauce, oatmeal, and red dye that go into making a gallon of blood and guts. *Duration: 25 min. Crowds: Not daunting. Strategy: Go in the afternoon or evening. Audience: All but young children, who may be frightened; older children eat up the blood-and-guts stories. Rating:* ★★

③ From the make-up show, walk out front to *Jurassic Park*: **Behind the Scenes.** This collection of memorabilia from the largest-grossing movie ever is surprisingly small given the film's blockbuster status. Nonetheless, it's worth dropping by if only to see the triceratops lying in the entryway. The rest of the exhibit includes some Jurassic Jeeps, costumes, and stills from the production process. Although park officials aren't promising anything, look for an accompanying dinosaur-themed thrill ride sometime in the near future. *Duration: 10–15 min. Crowds: Not a problem. Strategy: Go anytime. Audience: All ages. Rating:* ★★

TIME OUT   At the corner of Hollywood Boulevard and 8th Avenue (which, just for the sake of confusion, turns into Sunset Boulevard along the bottom shore of the lagoon) is **Mel's Drive-In,** a flashy '50s eatery with a menu and decorative muscle cars straight out of *American Graffiti*. For burgers and fries, this is one of the best choices in the park. It's complete with roving doo-wop group, and—unlike at the Hard Rock Café, which serves a similar menu—the decibel level allows normal conversation. You're on vacation—go ahead and have that extra-thick shake.

Production Central

Marked in green on the park map, Production Central spreads over the entire left side of the Plaza of the Stars and practically encircles Hollywood, too. It contains six huge warehouses with working soundstages, as well as such attractions as Hitchcock's 3-D Theatre, the Funtastic World of Hanna-Barbera, the "Murder, She Wrote" Mystery Theatre, Nickelodeon Studios, and Universal Studios' trademark Production Tram

Tour. Home to such shows as the syndicated *SeaQuest,* there is a chance of glimpsing some real stars.

Nickelodeon Way leads off to the left of the Plaza of the Stars opposite Lucy: A Tribute. Past the Green Slime Geyser welcoming you to
④ Nickelodeon Studios is the embarkation point for the **Production Tram Tour,** an updated version of the old Hollywood Glamortram that takes you on a nonstop ride around the park on which you can gloat at folks wearing out the soles on their Reeboks. The guide is full of nifty trivia about movies filmed on the giant soundstages (for instance, check out the continuity glitch in *Parenthood,* when Steve Martin extols the joys of living in St. Louis while driving past a sign that reads "Florida's Turnpike, 6 miles"), or props now slowly rusting in the boneyard—yes, this is where *Jaws*'s dorsal fin washed up—but the ride neither orients you nor takes you inside any of the soundstages. *Duration: 20 min. Crowds: Ebb and flow. Strategy: Go in the morning to get a feel for the place and mentally mark must-visit shops and photo-ops. Try to nab a seat in the front; exhaust fumes perfume the rear cars. Audience: All ages. Rating:* ★

The Production Tram Tour lets you off right back where you started, where the Green Slime Geyser is still going strong, enticing visitors into
⑤ **Nickelodeon Studios.** This tour, showing how a television show is produced, is akin to Disney-MGM's Inside the Magic. About 90% of Nickelodeon's original programming is produced on the soundstages you'll walk through. The banks of lights, concrete floors, and general-warehouse feel go a long way toward demystifying movie magic, but it's exactly that behind-the-scenes perspective that makes the tour interesting. You may even end up in the taping of a pilot. You'll get a peek at wardrobe and make-up studios, as well as a tour of the kitchen where Slime is made. The tour winds up in the **Game Lab,** an even wackier version of the interactive wonders in the Image Works at Epcot Center's Journey into Imagination. Kids of all ages who watch Nick will love it. *Duration: 30 min. Crowds: Steady, long lines. Strategy: Skip it on a first-time visit or if no shows are taping. Audience: All ages but especially grade-schoolers. Rating:* ★★

⑥ The **Funtastic World of Hanna-Barbera,** a combination ride-video-interactive display at the corner of Nickelodeon Way and Plaza of the Stars, is Universal's answer to Disney-MGM's Animation Building and one of the most popular attractions at Universal Studios. Before the show, Yogi Bear appears on overhead video monitors to explain how cartoons are constructed. The "dynamically aggressive ride," as the park puts it, puts you inside a *Jetsons* cartoon in a hint of what you might expect at the Back to the Future . . . The Ride flight simulator. But the best part is the interactive electronic magic booths at the end of the attraction, in which you provide the studio voice for a *Flintstone* cartoon, paint Pebbles's hair green with a computerized brush, and twirl dials and push buttons to mix up a sound-salad of boinks, splats, and plops. *Duration: 8 min. Crowds: Usually stunning, despite high capacity. Strategy: Go as soon as the gates open or at night. Audience: All ages; frightening for some toddlers. Young children can opt for stationary seats in the front of the theater. No pregnant women or guests with motion sickness or heart, neck, or back problems; must be 40" tall to ride. Rating:* ★★★

"Have you ever had a premonition?" asks the superbly cultured and ever-so-slightly spooky voice of Alfred Hitchcock, the star of the high-
⑦ capacity **Alfred Hitchcock's 3-D Theatre,** located across the Plaza of the Stars from Hanna-Barbera. It starts off a dandy multimedia tribute to

Universal Studios

SAN FRANCISCO/
AMITY

The Embarcadero

Lombard's
Landing

The
Lagoon

13

14

15

Amity Ave.

16

Exposition Blvd.

Sunset Blvd.

17

International
Food Bazaar

EXPO CENTER

Exit to
Hard Rock
Café

18

19

20

Hard Rock
Café

21

KEY

Restaurants

Restrooms

TO VINELAND RD. →

the master of suspense, who made 53 films for Universal Studios. Thanks to 3-D glasses, you learn what it's like to be a citizen of Bodega Bay on a day of abnormal avian activity. Audience participation reveals the secret of *Psycho*'s famous shower scene as well as some previously unseen 3-D footage from *Dial M for Murder*. As in any good Hitchcock film, this attraction engages your mind as well as your adrenaline—and has a characteristic twist of an ending. *Duration: 40 min. Crowds: Sizable but fairly fast moving because of the theater size. Strategy: Try to negotiate seats in the middle of the theater for best 3-D viewing. Audience: All but young children, who may be frightened. Rating:* ★★★

⑧ A harried TV producer gives you the rundown on the premise of **"Murder, She Wrote" Mystery Theatre** during one of Universal's patented pre-shows. The crew is running out of time and, well, you know Hollywood—there have been some artistic differences on the set. So now, you're in charge. Armed with any manager's key phrase—NO, ABSOLUTELY NOT—you try to beat the clock. (Or is that another network?) Using footage of senior super-sleuth Jessica Fletcher, it's no mystery why this is one of the best shows in the place. It's more than learning that lip-to-hand contact makes a better sound than the lip-to-lip variety. (More suction. Go ahead, try it.) The rows of screaming, laughing tourists make this big fun. When they ask for volunteers, raise your hand and help them make some joyful noise. *Duration: 40 min. Crowds: Substantial, but waits are seldom discouraging. Strategy: Go in the afternoon, when you feel like sitting down and cooling off. Audience: Older children and adults. Rating:* ★★★

⑨ Friends of Frostbite Falls follow the call of the moose around the back of the "Murder, She Wrote" soundstage to **"The Adventures of Rocky & Bullwinkle,"** a musical revue starring Bullwinkle the Moose, his faithful friend Rocky Squirrel, the dashing and ineffably dense Canadian Mountie Dudley Doright, and those two Russian no-goodniks, Boris Badenov and his slinky sidekick, Natasha. The action takes place on an animated set at the edge of Universal's New York backlot and involves lots of songs, corny jokes, and trademark explosions when Boris and Natasha's nefarious plot backfires. Kaboomski. *Duration: 15–20 min. Crowds: Never a problem. Strategy: Shows every hr, usually beginning around 11; go anytime. Audience: All ages. Rating:* ★★

New York

The New York backlot—like the San Francisco and Amity neighborhoods elsewhere in the park—has been rendered with surprising detail, right down to the cracked concrete and slightly stained cobblestones. Only two things are missing: potholes and litter. The Blues Brothers Bluesmobile regularly cruises the neighborhood, and musicians hop out to give impromptu performances at 70 Delancey. (These shows are really worth catching. Check the signs near Guest Services for performance times.) Every corner opens onto a trompe-l'oeil view of, say, Park Avenue or Gramercy Park. Designated photo-op spots place you with just the right backdrop.

⑩ New York is also home to **Ghostbusters,** those paranormal problem-solvers first introduced in the 1984 movie. The pre-show, which takes place in a stand-up theater designed as a cluttered store, is a sales pitch for a Ghostbusters franchise, with some hands-on lessons in slime control from volunteers from the audience. (Don't worry, the stuff slides right off your clothes without leaving any stains.) Then everyone files into the ectoplasmic containment chamber (that is, a large sit-down theater) for an equipment demonstration—suitably mismanaged to send spooks slithering through the auditorium. All the movie favorites—even the Stay Puft Marshmallow Man—are here amid ghostly explosions and arcing lasers, and the climax (we're not giving anything away when we say it involves the sprinkler system) is breathtaking. *Duration: 15 min. Crowds: Steady, but the auditorium can hold almost everyone. Strategy: A good bet for crowded periods; check show times at Guest Relations before you enter the park. Audience: Older children and adults. Rating:* ★★★

⓫ Keep up the thrill quotient at **Kongfrontation,** a Universal powerpunch just down 5th Avenue from Ghostbusters. The waiting area reproduces a New York subway station, complete with graffiti. (One former New York mayor objected to the set on the grounds that it painted a picture of a much-bruised Big Apple.) As you board the trams for the escape from the ape-threatened city to Roosevelt Island, police radios crackle with news of Kong-sightings. Then you round a corner and . . . you're in the middle of mayhem. King Kong grabs the tram, helicopter gunships swoop in for a shot, everyone's screaming joyously, and the distinctive odor of banana-breath fills the air. Somehow you escape, but the quavering voice of the tram operator implies that the beast still lurks, waiting for a second chance. *Duration: 5 min. Crowds: Lines ebb and flow throughout the day and move slowly because of the ride's small capacity. Strategy: Go early or late; if your time is limited, opt for Jaws and Earthquake, because they provide more thrill for the time spent in line. Audience: Older children and adults; Kong is too realistic for youngsters. No pregnant women or guests with motion sickness or heart, back, or neck problems; must be 40″ tall to ride alone. Rating:* ★★

San Francisco/Amity

From Gotham City, it's just a few yards to San Francisco, thanks to Universal Studios' magical geography. The structures here imitate the wharves and warehouses of the Embarcadero and Fisherman's Wharf district, with the distinctive redbrick Ghirardelli chocolate factory, cable-car tracks cut through the middle of the street, and rusty "No Fishing" signs written in Chinese. It's hard to know just where San Francisco segues into Amity, the New England fishing village terrorized by the shark in *Jaws.* But suddenly, you're definitely back on the East Coast, amid Cape Cod cottages and win-a-stuffed-animal game stall honky-tonks. At the center of town, a towering scaffold displays a 24-foot great white shark, complete with spiked teeth and nasty expression. One would think it would be safe to go back into the water, but . . . Universal Studios doesn't make money from movie sequels for nothing.

⓬ First, though, ease your transcontinental switch at **Beetlejuice's Graveyard Revue,** a live sound-and-light spectacle in an open-air amphitheater in which the ghoul with groove transfunkifies a group of scary monsters into a rhythm-and-blues band. Based on the 1991 movie starring Michael Keaton, it has a graveyard rock-and-roll call that includes a hot, earring-wearing Dracula, Frankenstein playing bass guitar, and his miniskirted bride street-dancing. The amplification is enormous, and what with the noise, the smoke, and the monsters, kids often seem confused, if not downright scared. But adults will enjoy the music and the high-energy performances. *Duration: 25 min. Crowds: Steady, but high capacity of amphitheater means no waiting. Strategy: Go when rides' lines are at capacity or after dark on hot days. Audience: Older children and adults. Rating:* ★★★

⓭ Just next door in what could easily be called Adrenaline Alley is another headliner, **Earthquake—The Big One.** The pre-show is almost as good as the main attraction; using audience volunteers, matte paintings, and video cameras, it reproduces choice scenes from the movie *Earthquake*. ("This is not a happy disaster, so no smiling," cautions the staffer running the show, as tourists shake and tremble in a mock tremor.) Suitably glum, everyone troops onto Bay Area Rapid Transit subway cars (Universal Studios seems determined to do in the urban public transportation systems) to ride out an 8.3 Richter scale tremor and its consequences: fire, flood, blackouts. Unlike in Disney-MGM's Disaster Canyon, there are no "safe" seats on this ride; catastrophe strikes from every angle (including above and below), so everyone gets a few months shaved off his or her life. This ride is a technological marvel that resets itself in a matter of minutes. *Duration: 20 min. Crowds: Heavy. Strategy: As with most blockbuster rides, if you want to ride it you will have to wait. The pre-show helps ease the tedium. Audience: All but young children. No pregnant women or guests with motion sickness or heart, neck, or back conditions; those under 40" must ride with an adult. Rating:* ★★★

⑭ Stagger out of San Francisco into Amity for **Jaws,** Universal's second attempt at this terror-filled boat-ride (the first incarnation had an embarrassing tendency to get stuck midattack). Bide your time watching Amity TV (WJWS) piped into the waiting line, complete with commercials for used recreational vehicles and candied blowfish. (Just the treat for the holidays!!!) Just when you think it's safe to go back into the water, along comes the finny fiend attempting to turn you into saltwater taffy. This time your boat is under attack, with concomitant explosions, noise, and shaking, in addition to the gnashing of sharp shark teeth. Don't think you're safe when the boat escapes into the boathouse, either. The special effects on this ride really shine, especially the fire and electrical explosions that allow you to feel the heat. *Duration: 7 min. Crowds: Lines are long most of the day, but nothing like those at Back to the Future. Strategy: Go early or after dark for an even more terrifying experience—you can't see the attack but can certainly hear and feel it. For the shortest lines, cast off for Jaws during the stunt show. Audience: All but young children, who will be frightened. No pregnant women or guests with motion sickness or heart, neck, or back conditions. Rating:* ★★★

⑮ Last but not least on the "can-you-top-this" parade is the **Wild, Wild, Wild West Stunt Show,** presented in a covered amphitheater at the very end of Amity Avenue. The sign "Square Dance and Hanging, Saturday Night," lets you know what kind of town you've moseyed into. Repeated playing of the theme from *Bonanza* confirms your hunch. The show involves trapdoors, fistfights, bullwhips (take that, Indiana!), water gags, explosions, shoot-outs, horseback riding, and one tough mama who proclaims, "Listen, poptart, I've been falling off barns since I was three," and then demonstrates her inimitable style by hurling herself off the ridgepole. By the end of the show, the set is in shambles and every other theme park in central Florida has been skewered in jokes and snide remarks ("Look, Ma, I'm Shamu," yells one sopping stuntman as he emerges, spitting water, from a well). The panting stuntpeople take time out from rebuilding the set for photographs, autographs, and questions. They will not, however, explain how you can replicate the stunt at home. *Duration: 16 min. Crowds: Large, but its 2,000-seat amphitheater means no waiting. Strategy: On hot days go after dark, when it will be cooler in the amphitheater. Audience: All ages. Rating:* ★★★

⑯ You're now at the end of the lagoon that's the setting for **Dynamite Nights Stunt Spectacular,** presented nightly at 7. This is a shoot-'em-up stunt show with a difference: It's performed on water skis and in motorboats and at night. As far as theme park finales go, this one pales in comparison with Disney's fireworks or Sea World's watery, holographic Neptune. There are a few noisy boats, some loud explosions, and much ado about nothing. If you're worried about getting stuck in parking-lot gridlock, skip it. Children may enjoy seeing the kind of chase scenes live they've seen on television. If you do decide to stay, amble back along the lagoon and pick your spot for the evening show. There are definitely bad and good views: The best are from the footbridge, at the opposite end of the lagoon on New York's South Street, as well as along Exposition Boulevard, the avenue along the lagoon adjoining Expo Center. Prime locations fill up at least 30 minutes before show time, so be warned. *Duration: 20 min. Crowds: Large, but there's plenty of room for all. Strategy: Bring a snack and claim your spot 30 min before show time. Audience: All ages. Rating:* ★

Expo Center

Taking up the southeastern section of the park, Expo Center contains another great group of Universal Studios attractions: Back to the Future . . . The Ride, Fievel's Playland, and E.T. Adventure.

⑰ If there's one ride that's on top of everyone's list it's **Back to the Future . . . The Ride.** This is the flight simulator to beat all others, even (probably) those yet to be built. Michael J. Fox, star of the 1985 movie, said that the ride actually delivered what the script imagined. When popstar Michael Jackson was visiting Walt Disney World, he made a special detour specifically to experience this ride—and rode it three times in a row. Even Disney-MGM's Star Tours, which easily outranks most other flight simulators, can't compare with this one. The cause of all the unbridled enthusiasm is a seven-story, one-of-a-kind Omnimax screen, which surrounds your De Lorean-shaped simulator vehicle so that you lose all sense of perspective as you rush backward and forward in the space-time continuum. It also helps that this simulator's motion is the most aggressive of all flight simulators—and there are no seat belts. Having your wallet slide out of your pocket is the least of your worries and a stiff neck is a distinct possibility. *Duration: 5 min. Crowds: Up to 2 hrs in busy seasons at peak times (between 11 and 3). Strategy: Arrive in the park at opening and dash on over—or be prepared to wait (and wait . . . and wait); lines drop off a hair about ½ hour after the mad mass rope-drop rush. Or go late. For view and motion, sit smack dab in the middle of the car. Audience: Older children and adults. No pregnant women, guests under 40" tall, or guests with motion sickness or heart, back, or neck problems. Rating:* ★★★

TIME OUT The **International Food Bazaar** is an efficient, multi-ethnic cafeteria serving Italian, American, German, Greek, and Chinese dishes at affordable prices (most of the entrées cost either $5.95 or $6.75). The Italian Caesar salad and Greek salads are especially welcome on a muggy day.

"I love you, you love me . . ." If you can't get enough of the big purple **⑱** dinosaur at home, here he is at Universal. **A Day in the Park with Barney** is filled with brilliantly colored trees and indoor clouds and stars. The big guy sings and does his TV schtick, and, although his star has dimmed a bit with the popularity of the Power Rangers, kids still go crazy. There are plenty of nifty things to play with once the show is over, too. *Crowds: Room for all. Strategy: Arrive 10–15 min early on crowded days for a good seat. Audience: Families with children. Rating:* ★★

⑲ For parents who are doing the baby swap on Back to the Future, or for younger children who need some time out, **Fievel's Playland,** just around the corner, is a true gift. Based on the adventures of Steven Spielberg's mighty, if miniature, mouse, this gigantic playground incorporates state-of-the-art amusements that are now de rigueur in entertainment parks: a four-story net climb equipped with tubes, ladders, and rope bridges; tunnel slides; water play areas; a harmonica slide that plays music when you slide along the openings; ball crawls; and a 200-foot water slide that you whiz down while sitting in Fievel's signature sardine can. *Duration: It's up to your preschooler. Crowds: Not significant, though waits do develop for the water slide. Strategy: On hot days, go after supper, or prepare to sweat. Audience: Toddlers, preschoolers, and their parents. Rating:* ★★

⑳ Spielberg's best-known creation receives his due at **E.T. Adventure,** located in a large structure adjoining Fievel's Playland. To the hoarsely murmured mantra of "Home, home," you board bicycles mounted on a movable platform and pedal through fantastic forests floating in mists of dry-ice fumes, magic gardens populated by such whimsical new Spielberg characters as the Tickli Moot Moot, and across the moon (remember to turn to catch your shadow) in an attempt to help the endearing extraterrestrial find his way back to his home planet. Though the ride begins like an outer-space version of Disney's It's a Small World, it picks up enough to have a thrill-ride bite. The music is as tear-jerking as ever, and so is the little surprise at the end when E.T. personally says goodbye. Another surprise, the waiting area—a pine-scented forest complete with E.T. beckoning you on—is one of the most pleasant at this park, although small children may find the darkness a little scary. *Duration: 5 min. Crowds: Sometimes not bad, but up to 2-hr wait during crowded periods. Strategy: Go early. Audience: All ages. No one suffering from motion sickness or heart, back, or neck problems; guests under 40" tall must ride in orbs. Rating:* ★★★

TIME OUT For all-American burgers and shakes in a full-service restaurant, one of the best choices is the guitar-shaped **Hard Rock Café.** The neck of the guitar extends out of the park into the parking lot, enabling area visitors to take their teenagers without buying an ☛ ticket. The rock music is classic but earsplitting, which makes conversation next to impossible—not always a bad thing when dining with teenagers. The walls are crammed with rock-and-roll memorabilia, a treat for hard-core fans who can recognize many of the items' obscure provenance. Allow some time for picking up that Hard Rock tee. So popular is the restaurant's store, you may well find yourself standing in line to get in a line inside the store. The music, however, is cool.

㉑ **AT&T at the Movies** doesn't seem to actually have much connection to the movies, but it is a nifty collection of interactive computer games. What's interactive mean, anyway? In this case, it means you can hear your words spoken by television characters. (Grandpa Munster running through Shakespeare is pretty funny.) It also means putting computer disguises on your face or hearing your voice as it would have sounded on a Victrola. *Strategy: Go near the end of the day while others are hustling to make the big rides. Crowds: It can be busy, but usually not a problem. Audience: All ages. Rating:* ★★

Dining

Most eateries are on Plaza of the Stars and Hollywood Boulevard. And their stellar locations are often matched by astronomical prices. Several restaurants accept reservations: Production Central's **Studio Stars** (☎ 407/363–8769), which has an all-you-can-eat buffet; San Francisco/Amity's **Lombard's Landing** (☎ 407/362–9955), designed to resemble a warehouse from 19th-century San Francisco; and the **Hard Rock Café** (☎ 407/351–7625; *see above*).

Shopping

Every ride and every attraction has its affiliated theme shop; in addition, Rodeo Drive and Hollywood Boulevard are pockmarked with money pits. Choice souvenirs include the Universal Studios' trademark movie clipboard; sepia prints of Richard Gere, Mel Gibson, and Marilyn Monroe; supercool sunglasses à la Blues Brothers; and, of course, all the gak you want to eat. Check out the "Do Not Disturb" signs from the Bates Motel at the **Bates Motel Gift Shop,** as well as Bates Motel stationery and bathrobes, and little plush King Konglets at Kongfrontation. Stop by Hollywood's **Brown Derby** for the perfect topper, from fedoras à la Indiana Jones to bush hats from *Jurassic Park*. Be advised that few of the attraction-specific souvenirs are sold outside of their own shop, so if you're struck by Fred Flintstone "yabba dabba doo" boxer shorts at the **Hanna-Barbera Shop,** seize the moment—and the shorts.

Access for Travelers with Disabilities

As in Walt Disney World's major parks, each attraction has an audio portion that will appeal to those with visual impairments and a visual portion to charm those with hearing impairments. But Universal Studios has also made an all-out effort not only to make the premises physically accessible for those with disabilities but also to lift attitudinal barriers. Power-assist buttons were added to heavy, hard-to-open doors, lap tables were provided for guests in shops, and bathroom facilities (already up to code) were modified with niceties such as insulating undersink pipes and companion rest rooms. In addition, all the employees now attend disability awareness workshops to remind them that people with disabilities are people first. And you can occasionally spot staffers using wheelchairs. Parts of the park with cobblestone streets now have paved paths, and photo spots have been modified for wheelchair accessibility. Various attractions have been retrofitted, so that most attractions can be boarded directly in a standard wheelchair; those using oversize vehicles or scooters must transfer to a standard model—these are available at the ride's entrance—or into the ride vehicle.

Services

Many employees have had basic sign-language training; even some of the animated characters speak sign, albeit—because many have only four fingers—an adapted version. Like Walt Disney World, Universal Studios Florida supplements the visuals with a special **guidebook** containing story lines and scripts in all of the attractions described below, unless otherwise noted. There is an **outgoing TTY** on the counter in Guest Relations, just inside the Main Entrance and to the right.

The park also publishes the **"Studio Guide for Guests with Disabilities,"** which pinpoints the special entrances available for those with disabilities (which often bypass the attraction's line). In addition, cassettes with narrative descriptions of the various attractions can be borrowed, along with portable tape players. You can get these and the various booklets at Guest Relations.

Attractions

Alfred Hitchcock's 3-D Theatre, "Murder, She Wrote" Mystery Theater, Ghostbusters, Animal Actors Stage Show, the **Gory, Gruesome & Grotesque Horror Make-Up Show, Beetlejuice's Graveyard Revue,** and the **Wild, Wild, Wild West Stunt Show** are all completely wheelchair-accessible, theater-style attractions. Guests with visual impairments will enjoy all of these shows, but sound and special effects make all but Alfred Hitchcock's 3-D Theater and "Murder, She Wrote" inappropriate for service animals.

HOLLYWOOD

Lucy: A Tribute is wheelchair accessible, but the TV show excerpts shown on overhead screens are not close-captioned.

PRODUCTION CENTRAL

Guests using an oversize wheelchair or scooter must transfer to a standard wheelchair to board the **Production Tram Tour.** The information in the narrative—interesting to those with visual impairments—is written down in the guidebook for the hearing-impaired. The **Nickelodeon Studios** tour is also completely accessible by guests using wheelchairs and enjoyable for guests with other disabilities. If you lip-read, ask to stay up front. The **Funtastic World of Hanna-Barbera** is completely accessible by guests using wheelchairs. However, your experience will be more intense if you can transfer to a ride seat and tolerate your vehicle's sudden sharp accelerations, climbs, stops, dives, and banked turns. If you can't, you can still experience the attraction, albeit from a stationary seat. Guests with other disabilities who enjoy other thrill rides will enjoy this one as well.

NEW YORK AND SAN FRANCISCO/AMITY

If you use a standard-size wheelchair or can transfer to one or to the ride vehicle directly, you can board **Kongfrontation, Earthquake—The Big One,** and **Jaws** directly. If their turbulence will be a problem for you, you shouldn't ride. Service animals should not ride. Note that guests with visual impairments as well as those using wheelchairs should cross San Francisco with care.

EXPO CENTER

To ride **E.T. Adventure,** you must transfer to the ride vehicle or to a standard-size wheelchair if you're not already using one. Service animals are not permitted. There is some sudden tilting and accelerating, but anyone with back, neck, or heart conditions can ride in E.T.'s orbs (the spaceships) instead of the flying bicycles.

Restaurants

All restaurants are wheelchair accessible. However, you can't take into the Hard Rock Café wheelchairs or scooters rented in the park.

Entertainment

There are special viewing areas at all of the outdoor shows, including **Dynamite Nights Stunt Spectacular.**

SEA WORLD

Many visitors are surprised to discover that there's a lot more to Sea World than Shamu, its mammoth killer-whale mascot. Aptly named, 135-acre Sea World is the world's largest zoological park and is devoted entirely to the mammals, birds, fish, and reptiles that live in the ocean and its tributaries. Sure, you can be splashed by Shamu and his other orca buddies, but you can also be spat at by a walrus, stroke a stingray, experience life as a manatee, and learn to love an eel (well, maybe).

What's even more astonishing is that the fun factor is closely tied to educational elements. Every attraction is designed to teach visitors about the beauty of the marine world and how that world is being threatened by human thoughtlessness. It's all very politically and environmentally correct. Yet the presentations are rarely dogmatic, never pedantic, and almost always memorable as well as enjoyable.

After a rough adolescence under previous owner Harcourt Brace Jovanovich (which included a threat of bankruptcy amid rumors that stressed-out killer whales had turned on their trainers), Sea World was purchased by Anheuser-Busch in 1989 and added to that company's stable of entertainment theme parks, whose Florida representatives now are Busch Gardens, Adventure Island, and Cypress Gardens. Sea World turns 23 in 1996 and, thanks to Anheuser-Busch's new management, is bigger and better than ever. Recent years have seen annual additions from polar bears to sea lions. Sea World seems to have at last found an identity that makes it shine.

The park rivals Disney properties for sparkling cleanliness, smiley staff, and attention to detail—the nautical flags flying over the entrance spell out "Sea World" in semaphore, and the strollers are shaped like upended dolphins (you push the tail).

It used to be you could whip through Sea World and still have time to play a few rounds of golf. No more. Count on spending an entire day—and wanting to return.

Essential Information

Tourist Information
Contact Sea World (7007 Sea World Dr., Orlando 32821, ☎ 407/351–3600; no TTY).

You're given a computer-generated map at the park entrance. An especially neat and considerate touch is the recommended show schedule, personalized according to your arrival time, that's printed out on it. In the park, a large board at the entrance lists all show times.

Inside the park, the main information center is **Guest Relations,** near the park entrance.

Getting There
Sea World is just off the intersection of I–4 and the Bee Line Expressway, 10 minutes south of downtown Orlando and 15 minutes from Orlando International Airport. Of all the central Florida theme parks, it's the easiest to find. Signs direct you to Exit 28 off I–4 and guide you the short distance to the parking lot.

PARKING
Parking costs $5 per car, $7 per RV or camper.

Admission
Regular one-day ☛ tickets cost $35.95 for adults, $30.95 for children 3–9, including tax. Two-day tickets, which must be used within one week, are $40.95 for adults, $35.95 for children. Discounted and multi-park single-day tickets to Cypress Gardens and Busch Gardens may be purchased at the ticket booth at the exit. AAA members who present their membership card receive a 10% discount.

Hours
Sea World is open daily 9–7; during the summer and on holidays, the park may stay open as late as 10 PM.

Services

BABY CARE

There are **diaper-changing tables** in or near most women's rest rooms, and in the men's rest room at the front entrance, near Shamu's Emporium. You can buy **diapers** at machines located in all changing areas and at Shamu's Emporium. A special area for **nursing** is alongside the women's rest room at Friends of the Wild gift shop, equidistant from Sea World Theater, Penguin Encounter, and Sea Lion and Otter Stadium. You will find **stroller rentals** at the Information Center ($5 for single, $10 for double; no deposit). However, no formula or baby food is sold on the premises; the nearest sources are a five-minute drive away at Gooding's Supermarket on International Drive, Publix supermarket and Eckerd's drugs on Central Florida Parkway, and Kmart on Turkey Lake Road.

CAMERAS AND FILM

Disposable Kodak Funsaver cameras are for sale on the premises, as are film and blank videotapes. There were neither camera nor camcorder rentals nor camera repairs on the premises at press time.

FIRST AID

First Aid Centers are behind Stingray Lagoon and near Shamu's Happy Harbor. Registered nurses are on duty.

GUIDED TOURS

Even if you already know the answer to the frequently asked question, "Do you paint Shamu?" it's worth spending the nominal extra fee to sign up for the 90-minute behind-the-scenes guided tours—**"Backstage Explorations"** or **"Animal Lover's Adventure"**—or the 45-minute **"Animal Training Discoveries,"** in which Sea World trainers discuss animal behavior and training techniques ($5.95 adults, $4.95 children 3–9). Tours leave every 30 minutes until 3 PM. Register at the guided tour center to the left of the Guest Relations/Information Center at the park entrance. Sign-language interpreters can be provided with advanced notice.

LOCKERS

They're inside the park entrance and to the right, next to Shamu's Emporium. The cost is $1.

LOST CHILDREN AND ADULTS

Lost parents and lost children should rendezvous at the Information Center just inside the park entrance. All employees who see lost-looking children have been trained to take them to the Information Center. A park-wide paging system helps reunite guests.

LOST AND FOUND

Go to the Information Center to reclaim your misplaced items or to drop off somebody else's.

MONEY

Foreign currency can be exchanged at the Special Services Window at the Main Gate (daily 10–3). An ATM linked to various bank and credit-card networks is at the exit gate.

PACKAGE PICKUP

When you make purchases anywhere in the park, your clerk can send them to Package Pickup, in Shamu's Emporium, on request. Allow an hour between making your purchase and your departure.

WHEELCHAIR RENTALS

Both standard and electric wheelchairs are available ($5 and $25 daily with driver's license).

Strategies for Your Visit

When to Go

Friday, Saturday, and Sunday are usually busier than the rest of the week, except during weeks that include Christmas, July 4, and Easter, when every day is equally busy.

Blitz Tour

The recommended itinerary and show schedule printed on the park map make a lot of sense. There's only one problem: Everyone else will be following them, too. Although there's room for all at the stadiums, the other attractions—especially Penguin Encounter and the Dolphin Community Pool—can get unpleasantly crowded, and there will be lines at Wild Arctic.

Instead, walk straight through the park to the **Sea World Theatre** to see "Window to the Sea," both to orient yourself and to get a sense of the larger vision of the park. Then whip into **Penguin Encounter** early, to visit one of the most spectacular attractions at its least crowded. While you are in the area, catch **Big Splash Bash,** the park's revamped, Broadway-style song-and-dance show. Proceed to **Terrors of the Deep,** to spend some quality time with a moray eel. Follow the crowds across the bridge to **Shamu Stadium**; while they're watching the first Shamu show, glimpse Orlando's only polar bears in a chilly tour of the park's newest and most elaborate attraction, **Wild Arctic.** Pick up a cuddly likeness of the northern version of a teddy bear from a nearby concession, then beat the crowds to lunch at Mango Joe's Café. Get a lakeside table and catch the early **Gold Rush Ski Show,** too.

While on this side of the lagoon, visit the sea lions at **Pacific Point Preserve,** plus **Manatees: The Last Generation?** and the **Shamu Breeding Pool and Nursery.** That should put you right in place for the afternoon Shamu show.

Wander back across the bridge and treat yourself to some interactive exhibits: There's the **Dolphin Community Pool, Stingray Lagoon,** and the **Caribbean Tide Pool,** where fondling the starfish is not to be missed; visit these exhibits during the day because the herring and smelt concessions close at dusk. Keep an eye on the time: You'll want to intersperse these with the shows at the **Whale & Dolphin Stadium** and the **Sea Lion & Otter Stadium.**

By now, you'll be feeling a little frayed. The soothing New Age music at the **Tropical Reef** strikes just the right note, especially once cranky children and their families have left for the day. The **"Water Fantasy"** is another good option. During high season, stick around for the closing laser and fireworks show, entitled Mermaids, Myths & Monsters, and watch King Neptune walk on water and dance across the central Florida sky.

On Rainy Days

Although Sea World gives the impression of open-air roominess, almost a third of the attractions are actually indoors and all the others are shielded from the elements by canopies, cantilevered roofs, or tautly stretched tarpaulins. Pick up a signature poncho—it's clear, with a black-and-white orca on the back—at one of the ubiquitous concession stands, and dive right in.

Other Tips

- Try to arrive early for Shamu shows, which generally fill to capacity on even the slowest days. They're not kidding about that splash zone, either. If you simply must experience an orcan belly flop, pack a set of dry clothes, especially in chilly weather.

- When the park hours are extended, wait until midafternoon to arrive. Then you can do most of your touring during the less steamy parts of the day and have dinner in the park.

- You may want to budget ahead for food for the animals (a major part of the close-up Sea World charm). A small carton of fish is usually $2.

- Set up a specific rendezvous time and location at the start of your visit in case you and your companions get separated.

Exploring Sea World

Sea World is organized around the nucleus of a 17-acre central lake. Rather than being divided into sections or "lands," as is the case at other Florida entertainment parks, Sea World's attractions flow into each other. As you enter, the lake is to your right. The right side of the park contains Shamu Stadium, Shamu Breeding Pool and Nursery, Shamu's Happy Harbor play area, Wild Arctic, Atlantis Water Ski Stadium, and Anheuser-Busch Hospitality Center, home of the hulking Clydesdale horses. The left side of the park is considerably denser, with all the other attractions stacked one on top of another. You can orient yourself by the Sky Tower (☛ $3), whose revolving viewing platform is generally visible even above the trees; it's directly opposite Shamu Stadium.

The computerized, color-coordinated map handed out at the entrance makes the park look much larger than it is. It's actually quite compact, but artful landscaping, curving paths, and concealing greenery make it very easy to get disoriented. When that happens, don't try to figure out the sometimes confusing signs; just find an aqua-shirted staff member and ask for directions. If you're panicked about missing a Shamu performance, just remember that the key is finding the lake; Shamu Stadium is no more than a 10-minute walk away.

This guide covers the attractions as you would encounter them if you were exploring the park in a clockwise direction.

Numbers in the margin correspond to points of interest on the Sea World map.

At the end of the entrance avenue is the first of many lagoons, this one
❶ embracing the **Tropical Reef,** an exhibit in which Sea World goes head to head with Epcot Center's older Living Seas pavilion and scores. An indoor (that is, air-conditioned) attraction, the centerpiece is a cylindrical mega-aquarium where more than 1,000 tropical fish swim around a 160,000-gallon man-made coral reef. Identification photos of Tinker's butterfly fish, black-and-white Moorish idols, bright blue-striped yellow sergeant majors, and their piscine pals are displayed just above eye level, but because the pesky things don't stay put under their portraits, matching fish to picture is like playing connect-the-dots with moving dots. Kids especially like to run circles around the tank in search of one particular species. There are also 17 miniaquariums set in pillars and around the perimeter, displaying king crabs, moray eels, and other single species as well as vignettes of undersea life. *Crowds: Not usually a problem. Strategy: Go toward the end of the day (because it's near the entrance, most people stop here on their way in). Audience: All ages. Rating:* ★★★

❷ Just opposite the Tropical Reef's exit is the **Caribbean Tide Pool,** whose lagoon is a touchy-feely version of the Tropical Reef. Under the watch-

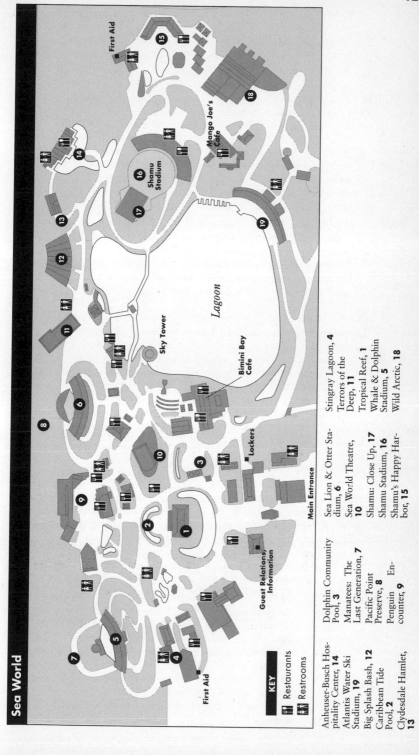

Sea World

KEY

🍴 Restaurants
🚻 Restrooms

First Aid

First Aid

Shamu Stadium

Mango Joe's Cafe

Sky Tower

Lagoon

Bimini Bay Cafe

Lockers

Guest Relations/Information

Main Entrance

Anheuser-Busch Hospitality Center, **14**
Atlantis Water Ski Stadium, **19**
Big Splash Bash, **12**
Caribbean Tide Pool, **2**
Clydesdale Hamlet, **13**

Dolphin Community Pool, **3**
Manatees: The Last Generation, **7**
Pacific Point Preserve, **8**
Penguin Encounter, **9**

Sea Lion & Otter Stadium, **6**
Sea World Theatre, **10**
Shamu: Close Up, **17**
Shamu Stadium, **16**
Shamu's Happy Harbor, **15**

Stingray Lagoon, **4**
Terrors of the Deep, **11**
Tropical Reef, **1**
Whale & Dolphin Stadium, **5**
Wild Arctic, **18**

ful eye of a Sea World guide, you can reach into the lukewarm water, pick up a starfish or a sea anemone, and ask such basic questions as "What do they do?" (Answer: "Not much.") *Crowds: Make it hard to get to the animals. Strategy: Go early or late. Audience: All ages. Rating:* ★★

③
④
Don't even bother to dry off your hands. Ringing the Caribbean Tide Pool and the Tropical Reef are the **Dolphin Community Pool** and **Stingray Lagoon,** two separate outdoor feeding and petting pools. Smelts are sold at concession stands next to each pool at three for $1 to feed the fish. Buy a batch and stroke the stingrays as they flap up (they feel like wet crushed velvet). This is one of the most rewarding experiences in the park for all ages, and the snack-happy animals are obligingly hungry all day. *Crowds: Can make it hard to get to the animals during busy seasons. Strategy: Go early—the smelt concession stand closes at dark. Audience: All ages. Rating:* ★★★

TIME OUT Adjoining the Dolphin Community Pool, full-service **Bimini Bay Café** dishes up light and tasty tropical cuisine in a pale pastel setting that would be refreshing even without the air-conditioning. The veranda tables have a great view of the action "backstage" at the water-ski show, the floats where the water-ski tow boats pick up their next load of daredevil stuntmen and stuntwomen.

⑤
⑥
Two of the most entertaining shows at Sea World are at **Whale & Dolphin Stadium** and **Sea Lion & Otter Stadium,** two gleaming white-and-navy-blue structures that dominate the left and top perimeter of this side of the park and are separated from each other by the overgrown refrigerator that houses Penguin Encounter. Whale & Dolphin Stadium, whose bright tropical colors and cheerful pink lighthouse evoke the Caribbean, is located just beyond Stingray Lagoon. Sea Lion & Otter Stadium, whose rather bland exterior conceals the wildly inventive, multilevel balconies (read: diving boards) and staircases (read: water slides) of the "Hotel Clyde and Seamore" set, is located at the top of the attractions on the left side of the park, just to the left of the spot where the central lake begins to curve.

The dolphin show spotlights one lucky child from the audience (to get yours picked, come early and ask one of the stadium attendants), six Atlantic bottlenose dolphins, and two false killer whales. The dolphins wave, leap, and do backflips; in one sequence, the trainer rides on their backs and then gets torpedoed into the air. The child from the audience stands on the side of the tank, commands the dolphins with hand gestures, and gets splashed. *Duration: 20 min. Crowds: You'll always get in. Strategy: Sit in the first four rows if you want to get splashed. Audience: All ages. Rating:* ★★★

"Hotel Clyde and Seamore," the current show in Sea Lion & Otter Stadium, is a comedy featuring break-dancing sea lions, an environmentally sensitive otter, and a heroic walrus that lumbers in and saves the day from blundering, littering humans. Show times are staggered so that there's time to explore the attractions between the two stadiums between shows. *Duration: 40 min, including the 15-min preshow. Crowds: No problem. Strategy: Sit toward the center for the best view, and don't miss the show's opening minutes. Audience: All ages. Rating:* ★★★

⑦
Sea World's commitment to the conservation of Florida's manatees, a gentle cross between a walrus and an oil barrel, is especially striking at **Manatees: The Last Generation?** just behind Whale & Dolphin Sta-

dium. Visitors tramp down a Plexiglas tunnel beneath the naturalistic, 3½-acre lagoon to **Manatee Theater,** where a film examines manatees' lifestyle and describes how human encroachment is threatening the species' survival. You can snoop at the lettuce-chomping giants and native fish, including tarpon, gar, and snook, in **Manatee Habitat,** a 300,000-gallon tank with a 126-foot seamless acrylic viewing panel; keep an eye out for mama manatees and their nursing calves. Other animals that share the manatee's world live in **Alligator Habitat,** a marsh display, and Bird Habitat. *Strategy: Go during a Shamu show, and not right after a dolphin show. Audience: All ages. Rating:* ★★★

8 The nonstop chorus of "aarrrps" and "yawps" leads the way to **Pacific Point Preserve,** a new 2½-acre home for California sea lions and harbor and fur seals, just behind Sea Lion & Otter Stadium. The naturalistic beaches, waves, and huge outcroppings of upturned coastal rock duplicate the rocky northern Pacific coast. (The weather, on the other hand, is distinctly Floridian.) Viewers stroll around the edge of the surf zone, a favorite hangout for fun-loving pinnipeds, and can peep at underwater activities through the Plexiglas wall at one side of the tank. Buy some smelt and watch the sea lions sing for their supper from close up. *Crowds: Not a problem. Strategy: Go anytime. Audience: All ages. Rating:* ★★★

There are 17 species of penguin, from the little crested fairy penguin to the large orange-striped king penguin, as well as puffins and murries, which scoot around a refrigerated re-creation of Antarctica at **Penguin Encounter,** a large white building between Whale & Dolphin Stadium and Sea Lion & Otter Stadium. The indoor viewing area is the chilliest spot in Sea World, but it's even colder inside the penguins' habitat; in fact, it snows daily. The birds love it, clustering under the icy precipitation, then waddling over to their frigid pool and taking the plunge. A Plexiglas wall on the viewers' side of the tank shows that the penguins are as graceful in the water as they are awkward on land. Sea World's penguin-breeding program has been so successful that it routinely supplies birds to other zoos. *Crowds: Frequently gridlocked, despite a moving walkway tactfully nudging visitors past the glassed-in habitat. Strategy: Go while the dolphin and sea lion shows are on. Audience: All ages. Rating:* ★★

10 The indoor **Sea World Theatre,** between Penguin Encounter and the central lagoon, screens "Window to the Sea," a brief overview of the park's research, conservation, and breeding efforts. (Sea World has emergency teams that routinely save beached whales, injured manatees, and other water animals.) The film starts out like a dreary PBS special but picks up enough to keep even children entertained. Footage of a killer-whale attack increases the gore factor that's so appreciated by some adolescents. If a behind-the-scenes tour seems more interesting now that you've had a look at the park's scientific side, skitter right back to the entrance—groups leave every half hour until 3 PM. *Duration: 20 min. Crowds: No problem. Audience: All but young children. Rating:* ★★

Later in the afternoon (usually starting at 5), the film presentation in Sea World Theatre is replaced with **Water Fantasy,** a delightfully kitschy demonstration of what you can do with a really state-of-the-art sprinkler system and some colored lights. The stage floor, a sort of giant wading pool, contains 36 revolving nozzles that spray water into fountains, waving plumes, and helices, all in time to a sound track of pop tunes. Still, this undemanding show and air-conditioned theater are a pleasant relief after all the intense animal interaction, and the youngsters will love it. *Duration: 20 min. Crowds: Not a problem.*

Strategy: Go when you want to sit down and cool off. Audience: All ages. Rating: ★

Continue around the central lagoon, ignoring the lure of the bridge short-cut to Shamu Stadium, to a large and innocuous white structure housing some thoroughly nasty critters. **Terrors of the Deep** is Sea World's attempt to make you love—or at least no longer be repulsed by—dangerous sea creatures such as eels, barracuda, venomous and poisonous fish, and sharks. Each animal is profiled via a video screen and educational posters ("There is little to love about the eel," one says, backing up its point by explaining how a slimy coat of mucus makes so-called blue eels appear green). Then you walk through a series of four Plexiglas tubes—surrounded by tanks—containing the world's largest collection of such animals. Sharks slide just feet overhead and eels slither out from their hiding places. Stop to absorb this neatly contained underwater nightmare in a large viewing theater with benches. Even at its most crowded—and this is another one of Sea World's most popular attractions—the walk-through tubes and overhead videos mean that even small children can get an eyeful. *Duration: Plan to spend 40 min. Crowds: Most significant when adjacent sea lion show gets out. Strategy: Go during the sea lion shows. Audience: All ages. Rating:* ★★★

Featuring 14 dancers, 2,400 seats, 45 set pieces, an 80-foot curtain of water, a school of ultraviolet fishes, and three 10-foot puppet-worms singing "Hey, Big Spender," the **Big Splash Bash** touts big numbers and delivers an earnest but ordinary show. *Duration: Kids get restless during the 30-min performance. Crowds: Not a problem. Strategy: Good when you need a rest. Rating:* ★★

Again following the lakeshore, you come to **Clydesdale Hamlet** and **Anheuser-Busch Hospitality Center.** A feature of all Anheuser-Busch parks, the walk-through hamlet houses hulking Clydesdale horses and provides a bucolic corral for their ponderous romping. A statue of a heroically endowed stallion, which youngsters are encouraged to scramble up on, makes a perfect generic theme-park photo opportunity. The Clydesdales are so incongruous in this marine-oriented setting that you have to agree with one teenager, who wisecracked, "Look, Dad, surf 'n' turf." The hospitality center, far from espousing the Teutonic overtones of its Busch Gardens cousin, is light and airy, combining cafeteria-style service with a bar serving Anheuser-Busch beverages. *Crowds: Never significant. Strategy: Go anytime. Audience: All ages. Rating:* ★

Little ones can't wait to scramble along the lakeshore path to **Shamu's Happy Harbor,** a 3-acre outdoor play area with crawlable, climbable, explorable, bounceable, and get-wetable activities, including a four-story net climb. Youngsters go wild for the "ball rooms"—two tents filled with thousands of Styrofoam balls that children can wade through (there are separate ones for toddlers and grade schoolers)—and the tent with the air-mattress floor, which is like a giant trampoline. There are pipes to crawl through and much more. With big sailing ships to explore and water to play in and around, it's different but just as dramatic as Disney-MGM's *Honey, I Blew Up the Kids* Movie Set Adventure Playground. Plus, Shamu's Happy Harbor is much more spacious and airy. *Crowds: Often a challenge. Strategy: Don't go first thing in the morning or you'll never drag your child away (but if you go in midafternoon, expect plenty of hubbub). Audience: Toddlers through grade schoolers. No height or age restrictions. Rating:* ★★

In fact, the only thing likely to distract your child from the net climb is directly opposite: **Shamu Stadium,** home to Sea World's orca mascot and hands-down the most popular feature in the park. Several shows daily showcase the whales' acrobatic, spectator-drenching antics. Fantastic flips and jumps are combined with video footage of orcas in the wild and gently educational factoids about the care and training of the giant mammals. After an unprecedented two births in late 1993—a baby boom by orca standards—Sea World revamped the show to focus on "Baby Shamu." Because killer whales do not reach their full size for four years, the kids are likely to be part of the show for a while. For a funkier version catch **Shamu's Night Magic.** Watching an orca bop to Madonna is not to be missed. Come early to get a seat. Sitting in the first tier will help you become part of the pre-show via a closed-circuit screen. Your head will be roughly the size of a Volkswagen. Snap a picture for a unique souvenir. *Duration: 25 min. Crowds: Sometimes a problem. Strategy: Go 45 min early for the early afternoon show. Close-up encounters through the Plexiglas walls are not to be missed, so trot on down. Audience: All ages. Rating:* ★★★

⑰ Adjoining the stadium, **Shamu: Close Up** allows unprecedented up-close-and-personal underwater viewing of the breeding and nursery area. Follow the signs around to the underground viewing stations for a unique glimpse of favorite whale pastimes, tummy-rubbing and back-scratching. The 1.7-million-gallon outdoor tanks are on the same level as the main pool in Shamu Stadium and have similar Plexiglas walls and viewing setups. Sea World can never predict when its whales will get pregnant, but its breeding program has been astonishingly successful. There's a good chance that you'll see a miniature Shamu looking remarkably like an inflatable pool toy, cavorting after its mother. *Crowds: Sometimes so large you'll have to edge your way to viewing areas. Strategy: Ideal time is during a Shamu show; otherwise, go early or late, or be patient. Audience: All ages. Rating:* ★★★

Walruses hoist themselves onto half-inch-thick ice with a groan as sea lions lazily lounge nearby, blinking their round, long-lashed eyes. A polar bear roars in the distance as a blast of cold air hits your face and salmon skim through clear, frigid water. A wide array of live animals, a simulated trek through the frozen Arctic, a chance to help with a little sub-**⑱** zero research, **Wild Arctic**—Sea World's most ambitious project to date—is part ride, part educational adventure, with 28 viewing stations and exhibits. Since opening in the spring of 1995, it's become a Sea World must-see. *Strategy: Go early, late, or during a Shamu show. Crowds: Expect a wait during peak season. Audience: All ages. Rating:* ★★★

TIME OUT **Mango Joe's Café,** a speedy, tropical-colored cafeteria between Shamu Stadium and Atlantis Water Ski Stadium, serves fresh fajitas, hefty salads, and delicious key lime pie, and the place has plenty of umbrella-shaded tables, many right on the lake. Some tables have a great view of the show.

⑲ The last attraction on the lagoon circuit, **Atlantis Water Ski Stadium** presents a themed water-skiing show on Sea World's central lagoon, complete with singing, dancing, and lots of stunts—a rip-roaring, gag-filled extravaganza that is to Cypress Gardens' performance what the Ice Capades is to Olympic figure-skating competitions. There's a sketchy theme, whose gossamer story is important only as an excuse for the usual suspects to present themselves: good guys (they do flips off ramps), bad guys (they specialize in skiing barefoot and on their faces to show how tough they are), gals (they get to show off skimpy costumes), and a clown or two. *Duration: 35 min. Crowds: Not a problem. Strategy: Be warned—the splash factor is significant in the first 10 rows; the terrace*

*at neighboring Mango Joe's Café and the deck at the Bimini Bay Café
are alternative viewing spots. Audience: All ages. Rating: ★★★*

Sea World has wisely decided not to compete directly with the can't-
be-beat bang of Disney's legendary closing fireworks. Instead, the new
Mermaids, Myths & Monsters caps off a nautically themed day using
lasers, fountains, and a few well-timed pyrotechnics. More a montage
than a miniseries, the show has a loose theme allowing you to witness
huge, seemingly 3-D versions of King Neptune, and a host of other characters walk, dance, and leap across the water. *Duration: 20 min. Crowds:
Room for all. Strategy: Follow the crowd after the last Shamu show,
sitting on the second tier to avoid getting wet from wind-borne spray.
Audience: All ages, although young children may be a little frightened
by the sheer size of the holograph-like images. Rating:* ★★★

Dining

In addition to the standard entertainment park fare of burgers, barbecue, and the usual burnt offerings sold at restaurants and concessions throughout the park, Sea World has two dandy places for lunch:
Mango Joe's Café and **Bimini Bay Café** (*see above*), from which you
have a close-up view of the frenetic activity on the floats where the water-
ski show stunts are set up.

Unfortunately, the pickings are slim for dinner. Mango Joe's closes down,
alas, leaving a meager choice of barbecued chicken and ribs at **Bucca-
neer Smokehouse** and sandwiches and salads at **Anheuser-Busch Hospitality Center.**

Luau

Alternatively, you can opt for entertainment in the form of the **"Aloha!"
Polynesian Luau Dinner and Show** at Bimini Bay Café. In an Anheuser-
Busch family version of *Blue Hawaii,* scantily clad dancers undulate
across the floor, bearing lei-draped platters of roast pig, mahimahi, piña
coladas, and hula pie. Reservations are required and may be made the
same day either at the luau reservations counter in the information center at the entrance or by telephone (☎ 407/363–2195 or 800/227–
8048). The cost is $27.95 adults, $18.95 children 8–12, $9.95 children
3–7, including one cocktail and all nonalcoholic drinks.

Shopping

There are some hard-hearted souls who can pass up a plush Shamu,
but they are few and far between. These are available all over the park.
Also extremely cuddly are the stuffed manatees sold at **Manatee Cove,**
near the manatee exhibit; proceeds from the toys go to benefit a manatee preservation organization. The **Friends of the Wild** shop near Penguin Encounter carries various items, including tropical fish earrings
and hair ornaments. If you've left the park before realizing that your
Aunt Betsy simply must have a Shamu slicker, visit the shop just outside the entrance.

Access for Travelers with Disabilities

Services

There are **TTYs for outgoing calls** at Bimini Bay Café, across from
Whale & Dolphin Stadium.

Attractions

Because many of the shows are in theaters and stadiums, guests using
wheelchairs will have an easy day at Sea World. With reserved seating

areas, the **Nautilus Showplace, Sea Lion & Otter Stadium, Sea World Theatre, Shamu Stadium,** and **Whale & Dolphin Stadium** are completely accessible, though entry usually requires an uphill climb along sloping ramps. The stadium shows usually fill to capacity, so plan to arrive 30–45 minutes before each show (45–60 minutes in peak seasons). At Shamu Stadium, the reserved seating area is inside the splash zone, so if you don't want to get soaking wet, get a host or hostess to recommend another place to sit. There is entertainment value in all of the theater and stadium shows for both hearing-impaired and visually impaired guests with a single exception: Performances in the Nautilus Showplace may be unrewarding for guests with visual impairments.

Penguin Encounter, Terrors of the Deep, and **Tropical Reef** are all wheelchair accessible. To ride the moving-sidewalk viewing areas in Penguin Encounter and Terrors of the Deep, guests must transfer to a standard wheelchair (available in the boarding area) if they do not already use one. Tropical Reef and Penguin Encounter have minimal entertainment value for guests with visual impairments. All will be enjoyable for guests with hearing impairments.

The **Anheuser-Busch Hospitality Center** is completely accessible. **Shamu's Happy Harbor** has some activities that are accessible to children using wheelchairs and anyone else who wants to climb, crawl, or slide.

The **"Aloha!" luau** is completely accessible.

Shops and Restaurants

Restaurants are accessible, but drinking straws are not provided here; this is out of concern for the safety of the animals. Bring your own. Shops are level, but many are so packed with merchandise that maneuvering in a wheelchair can be a challenge.

BUSCH GARDENS

When Anheuser-Busch opened a small hospitality center adjacent to its Tampa brewery in 1959, the company couldn't foresee the day that a couple of somnolent koalas and a ride called Kumba would be more of a draw than a draught would be. Busch Gardens, as the tropical biergarten was called, was seen as a useful place to stash the Busch family's collection of exotic animals and birds while tending to the real business: making and selling beer.

But 12 years later, the call of the wild proved so strong that Anheuser-Busch began to develop Busch Gardens into a multifaceted, Africa-themed park and zoo, with the brewery increasingly relegated to a sideshow. Rising profits demanded the creation of a separate corporate umbrella, and as a profit center spun off from the parent company, Busch Entertainment Corporation (BEC) was endowed with the mandate to expand and multiply in the field of leisure-time entertainment. Now owners of Busch Gardens; The Old Country in Williamsburg, Virginia; Adventure Island in Tampa; Sesame Place in Langhorne, Pennsylvania; the Sea World parks in Orlando, San Antonio, Aurora (Ohio) and San Diego; and Cypress Gardens in Winter Haven, BEC has become the second-largest theme park owner-operator in the world, right behind the Walt Disney Company.

There is little of the crowd and bustle of the Disney parks here. The animal displays and lush landscaping help to create a softer mood. The personnel are equally casual; they seem less stiff and programmed than some of the clean-shaven assembly-line workers at the home of the Mouse. Their relaxed attitude can seem disrespectful or charming, depending on your point of view. Another odd note is that some of the attractions, such as the Show Jumping Hall of Fame and the Questor flight simulator, have nothing to do with the African theme that led Busch Gardens to be dubbed "The Dark Continent" (a name later dropped in the interest of political correctness); in fact, they seem like a theme park version of monkey-see, monkey-do.

But that's merely a case of smudged icing on what's still a very satisfying cake. A member of the American Association of Zoological Parks and Aquariums, Busch Gardens ranks among the top four zoos in the United States. More than 3,200 birds, mammals, and reptiles are spread out on its 300 acres; the aviary houses some 600 rare and exotic birds, and about 500 African big-game animals roam uncaged on the 60-acre Serengeti Plain. Busch Gardens participates in the Species Survival Program, lending animals to other zoos for breeding as well as recording tremendous success with breeding endangered animals on the premises (top of the program's wish list is to host a pair of rare Chinese pandas).

The park itself is divided into nine areas linked to the common theme of turn-of-the-century Africa, plus the brewery. Animals are exhibited wherever possible—on islands, near concession stands, in spacious cages in the middle of a maze of lines, and in displays and shows in which they are the stars. But there's more than enough for the non–animal lover to do, what with numerous roller coasters and other gut-wrenching rides (beware the Kumba), water attractions, a Skyride, and shops galore. And there's always the brewery, whose self-guided tour is rarely crowded— a nice, if ironic, touch, considering it is the park's raison d'être.

Essential Information

Tourist Information
Contact Busch Gardens (Box 9158, Tampa 33674, ☎ 813/987–5283, no TTY).

On-site park information is available at **Guest Relations,** near the Main Entrance in Morocco.

A large signpost at the entrance lists performances scheduled for that day; show times for each performance are also posted in front of the individual stages and theaters.

Getting There
Busch Gardens is at the corner of Busch Boulevard and 40th Street, 8 miles northeast of downtown Tampa, 2 miles east of I–275, and 2 miles west of I–75. It will take you an hour and 15 minutes to drive the 81 miles from Orlando on I–4. Contrary to declarations in the brochures, Busch Gardens is *not* easy to find. The printed directions are fine until you get to Fowler Avenue, and then the signs indicating your route disappear and you are guaranteed to miss 40th Street, where you are supposed to turn. A better route is to follow the brochure directions to Fowler Avenue (Exit 54 off I–75 from Orlando; Exit 33 off I–275 from Tampa), then turn left onto 30th Street—a well-marked intersection with a bank of traffic lights. Then make another left onto Busch Avenue—another well-marked intersection with traffic lights. You will finally see Busch Gardens signs telling you to make another left onto 40th Street for the entrance to the parking lot.

PARKING
The cost for cars is $3.

Admission

Adults pay $34.60, children 3–9 $28.20. Senior citizens receive a 15% discount, and AAA members get 10% off. Tickets are also available for sister parks Sea World and Cypress Gardens.

Hours

The park is open daily 9–8 except during off-season and on holidays, when hours are shorter.

Services

BABY CARE

Facilities for **nursing** and **diaper-changing tables** are in Dwarf Village; only women's rest rooms have changing tables. You'll find **stroller rentals** at Stroller and Wheelchair Rental in Morocco ($4 for singles, $8 for doubles, including $1 deposit; doubles are safari trucks!). No formula, baby food, or disposable diapers are sold on the premises, but there are shopping centers all around the park, as well as a Kmart and Kash 'N' Karry about 1 mile east of the Main Entrance on Busch Boulevard.

CAMERAS AND FILM

Disposable **Kodak Funsaver cameras** are for sale at **Safari Foto**, near the Main Entrance, as well as at other stores throughout the park. You can rent **35mm cameras** ($6.95 per day with $50 deposit) at the **One-Hour Photo Shop**, also near the Main Entrance.

CAR SERVICE

If you have car trouble, raise your hood and the parking patrol will assist you.

FIRST AID

The infirmary is alongside the Festhaus in Timbuktu.

GUIDED TOURS

Numerous tours and programs here are designed to fan the animal conservation spark. One of the most popular is the three-hour **Behind-the-Scenes Tour,** daily at 8:30 AM, in which you ride the feeding truck and see just how many carrots those gorillas go through in one day. You can also reserve ahead to join periodic four-hour **Senior Safaris** as well as wonderful age-specific half-day, full-day, and multi-day programs for children ($18–$100; ☎ 813/987–5555).

LOCKERS

You'll find them in the Moroccan Village, near the Congo River Rapids; in Stanleyville, near the Tanganyika Tidal Wave; and in the Congo, at the Kumba and Congo River Rapids rides. The cost is 50¢.

LOST CHILDREN AND ADULTS

Go to Security at the Main Entrance or speak to any security officer (they wear white shirts, badges, and hats and look vaguely like sheriffs).

LOST AND FOUND

Report losses and finds of material goods at the Main Entrance's Security office.

MONEY

For currency exchange, go to the Guest Relations window near the Main Entrance in Morocco. There is an ATM just inside the Main Entrance, in Morocco; it's linked to the Plus, Honor, and Cirrus networks.

PACKAGE PICKUP

If you'd rather not lug around your purchases all day, have them sent from any store in the park to **Sahara Traders,** in the Moroccan village area near the entrance. You can pick them up on your way out. The service is free, but do allow an hour for delivery.

At Stroller and Wheelchair Rental in Morocco, you can rent standard chairs ($4, with $1 deposit) and motorized wheelchairs ($20, with $5 deposit). If yours disappears and needs replacing, ask in any gift shop.

Strategies for Your Visit

When to Go
Mondays are least crowded in summer, when local schools are out; weekdays are the most tranquil the rest of the year.

Blitz Tour
Figuring out the most efficient way of visiting Busch Gardens is only slightly less complicated than planning a safari. Pick up a list of shows at the entrance gate and loosely schedule your day around them; they are welcome sit-down breaks in a full day on your feet and some are even air-conditioned. Must-sees are the dolphin show, the bird show, the elephant wash, and the glitzy entertainment in the Moroccan Palace Theater. Also be sure to ride the Kumba, one of the best roller coasters around.

Make **Myombe Reserve** your first stop. Then hop on the **Trans-Veldt Railroad** at Nairobi Station and take it all around the park to Stanleyville. People on foot get to Stanleyville and the Congo in the afternoon; by visiting in the morning, you'll beat the lines on the rides—including the **Stanley Falls Log Flume,** the **Kumba,** and the **Tanganyika Tidal Wave**—and the animals will be more lively. Work your way north through the Congo to the **Congo River Rapids**—a refreshing splash at midday—and then catch the show at **Dolphin Theater.**

Busch Gardens is laid out so that the crowds tend to shuffle counterclockwise. Now go against the flow—through Timbuktu and back to Nairobi—to visit the **Elephant Wash,** et al. You're close enough to the **Moroccan Palace Theater** to make an afternoon show of **Hollywood on Ice** or to while away the time before the next one with a **Monorail** ride. If the line's not too long, try **Questor** (otherwise, save it until the end of the day).

Wander back through Morocco, past the brewery, and to the **Bird Gardens.** Time your visit for the last bird show; remember that the brewery tour is self-guided, so you can do that anytime.

Walk back up to Stanleyville and consider your late-afternoon options: You can go on the tidal wave again, see the rare white Bengal tigers get frisky at Congo's **Claw Island,** ride the **Skyride** back to Nairobi (it'll drop you off right opposite Questor), or take the train for a late-afternoon tour of the **Serengeti** (a worthwhile trip, although this often seems to be the time of day when the kudus get randy and ardently embrace other kudus). If you end up at Nairobi, have a restorative drink on the balcony of the **Colony Club** (Budweiser, Bud Light, and O'Doul's are on tap; red and white wine are also available) before hitting the Moroccan souk on your way out.

On Rainy Days
The Skyride may close temporarily because of lightning or high winds, but otherwise it's business-as-usual in the park.

Other Tips

- Keep in mind that the animals nap through most of the day, and you'll see the most action first thing in the morning and in the late afternoon.

- Unlike most central Florida parks, Busch offers national fast-food restaurants literally across the street. Readmission is allowed, so you can easily duck out for a burger.

- The water rides are designed to get you wet, very wet. If it's a cold or overcast day and you don't want to freeze, purchase a thin plastic poncho for about $3.50 or bring your own.

- If you want to snap loved ones in mid-ride (mid-scream?), look for photo staging spots at Congo River Rapids, Kumba, and the Tanganyika Tidal Wave.

- As soon as you arrive in the park, set up a specific rendezvous location and time in case you and your companions get separated.

Exploring Busch Gardens

Busch Gardens' nine different areas plus brewery are laid out in two concentric circles with an occasional appendage. The center is Timbuktu, an open-air carnival and bazaar. The main entrance is through Morocco; going counterclockwise along the winding paths, you'll encounter Myombe Reserve, Nairobi, the Serengeti Plain, the Congo, Stanleyville, Bird Gardens, and the Brewery, which abuts Morocco. A sharp elbow to the right from Myombe Reserve and Nairobi is the Crown Colony. Each of the areas is distinguished by its own distinctive architectural styles as well as regional music pumped through carefully camouflaged loudspeakers.

Morocco

The park's Main Entrance leads you through the gates of the tiled and turreted Moroccan fort, which houses the park administrative offices, and into a land of swirling colors and skirling music. Morocco itself contains two eateries—the Zagora Café and the Boujad Bakery—a resident snake charmer, the Moroccan Palace Theater, and numerous souvenir stands, arranged in a replica of an Arabic souk, or open-air marketplace.

It's hard not to fall into the shekel-flinging mode; Middle Eastern music wails through the speakers, brightly colored wool tassels droop overhead, brass urns glimmer, bangles shimmer, veils waft in the wind, and mouthwatering smells issue from the Boujad Bakery. Follow the main drag past the **Sultan's Tent,** a raised platform hung about with multicolored striped curtains, where a snake charmer snuggles up to a python and wraps it around her arms, waist, and neck. Show schedules are posted next to the Sultan's Tent. The snake charmer's main audience is a group of indifferent alligators, who loll about in a pond to the right of the Sultan's Tent. No hungry audience this: The alligators are so well fed and lazy that they ignore the plump koi fish that share their pond.

Numbers in the margin correspond to points of interest on the Busch Gardens map.

❶ Note that the blue-tiled, iron-fretted **Moroccan Palace Theater,** cater-corner to the alligators, asks you to travel at least a continent away when stepping into the cool comfort of its ice rink. An African-inspired park featuring an ice show: Go figure. Hollywood on Ice features 10 skaters and 2 singers, who all join together to create these frigid follies in a chorus line production backed by clips from Hollywood's golden age. You have to see it to understand the presence of the 17-foot inflatable dinosaur. Having made its debut in 1995, this show tries hard and, hey, at the very least it's air-conditioned—a good thing for those trekking through Timbuktu. *Duration: 30–40 min. Crowd: Sizable, but there's always enough room. Strategy: Shows four times daily; check schedules posted outside. Go when you want to sit down and cool off. Audience: All ages. Rating:* ★★

TIME OUT The **Zagora Café** in Morocco dishes out basic burgers, fajitas, and turkey sandwiches in an enormous open-air cafeteria. **Boujad Bakery** is the place for a cup of cappuccino and a *churro* (Mexican deep-fried sweet dough liberally dusted with confectioner's sugar). Breakfast is also available.

Crown Colony

Follow the path around the Moroccan Palace, under the Monorail overpass to a large cul-de-sac. This is the Crown Colony, a transportation and hospitality center with two distinctly non-African attractions they couldn't fit in elsewhere: the home of BEC's signature Clydesdale horses—a staple at every BEC park—and the requisite flight simulator.

The **Monorail** has only one station, and this is it. The lines snake past airy cages containing curious lemurs, which set the mood for the ride itself: a journey around the adjacent Serengeti Plain. The station is the Crown Colony terminus for a seven-minute **Skyride** above the Serengeti and through Timbuktu; except in bad weather, when it sometimes closes, ❷ it's a useful shortcut to the Congo, its other terminus. The **Clydesdale Hamlet** boasts the usual batch of oversize beasts galumphing around a corral and stables; a particularly patient one is periodically led out for photographs.

❸ Tucked away in a corner of the cul-de-sac is **Questor,** Busch Gardens' flight simulator. The gimmick here is that you are helping a mad scientist search for a magic crystal, a search that takes you to the center of the earth. As flight simulators go, the shake-up is pretty good but no competition for Disney-MGM's Star Tours or Universal's Back to the Future and certainly not worth what can be a long wait. But if the line is manageable, then give it a whirl. *Duration: 5 min. Crowds: Up to 1½ hr on crowded days. Strategy: In summer and holiday periods, go early or late. Audience: Older children and adults. Must be 42" to ride. Rating:* ★★

TIME OUT The **Colony Club,** done up to resemble a veddy British eatery from the good old *Out of Africa* days with portraits of top-hatted sahibs, used polo mallets, and nicely faded Oriental carpets, serves sandwiches, salad platters, and pizza in a downstairs counter-service restaurant. There's full service upstairs; *see* Dining, *below.*

Serengeti Plain

Looming just north of the Crown Colony and forming the eastern border of Nairobi and Timbuktu is the 80-acre Serengeti Plain, an open-air zoo where about 800 animals of 30 different species are allowed to run free in a re-creation of their natural habitats—all of which look remarkably similar to Florida pastureland. You'll see zebras, camels, impalas, giraffes, lions, gazelles, Cape buffalo, and kudus (a heftier impala), among other species. Don't be dismayed if it's raining; in fact, hasten right over to the Monorail to catch sight of all the animals instinctively turning their heads up into the rain. Though the Trans-Veldt Railroad skirts the eastern edge of the Serengeti, there are basically two ways to explore it: the **Skyride** and the **Monorail**. The Skyride takes you 49 feet above the Serengeti on a 1.1-mile one-way ride to the Congo; it gives you a great overview but not much detail. The Monorail is a classic Busch Gardens experience; unlike Disney's monorail, it's suspended from an overhead rail and trundles around the veldt at eye level to a zebra. A guide tells you a little about the animals as you edge along the track. If you believe the hype about seeing the animals in their natural environments, the omnipresent fence lines will be a shock. (At one point you can see the freeway from one side of the monorail car.) Busch Gardens could take some tips from sister-park Sea World about displaying animals. *Duration: Monorail 20 min, Skyride 7 min. Monorails leave every 5 min; Skyrides operate continuously. Crowds: You can always walk right on. Strategy: Go anytime. Audience: All ages. Rating:* ★★

Myombe Reserve: The Great Ape Domain

The **Myombe Reserve** is easily overlooked, thanks to superbly luxuriant rain-forest landscaping and a modest entrance opposite the Moroccan Palace Theater. Completed in 1992, it's one of the park's newer and much-heralded animal attractions. Some 3 acres have been lovingly landscaped into a home for an extended family of chimpanzees (formerly of Chimp Island in the Serengeti) and another family of Western lowland gorillas (whose scientific name is, according to an educational plaque, Gorilla gorilla gorilla). There's always a well-informed guide on hand to explain that gorillas rest 40% of the day and feed another 30%, or to point out the almost infinitesimal differences and complicated relationships between Sally, Smokey, and Samantha. Check out the Aldabra tortoises, which can weigh more than 500 pounds and live to be 100. *Crowds: Not significant. Strategy: Visit either first thing in the morning or late in the afternoon; both are close to feeding time, when both apes and chimps are more active. Audience: All ages. Rating:* ★★★

Nairobi

Myombe's rain-forested path leads you to Nairobi, a collection of buildings containing the animal nursery, the petting zoo, the Show Jumping Hall of Fame, the elephant display, and the Nairobi train station—a gingerbread clapboard structure straight out of *Out of Africa*.

❹ The **Animal Nursery** is a long, low building, with glass cages on the outside holding convalescing animals wrapped in nests of blankets; through the glass on the other side of the cages, you can see the laboratories and food preparation. Animals are fed at various times, so there's **❺** usually something going on. The **Petting Zoo** contains both Nubian and African pygmy goats, Barbados black-bellied sheep, ducks, rabbits, turtles, roosters, and hens. Visitors are allowed to feed only the goats and sheep (which are rotated throughout the day to keep them from being overfed); for the others, food is brought out on a tray for the twice-daily handout. *Crowds: Never significant. Strategy: Go anytime. Audience: All ages. Rating:* ★

❻ Although it has nothing to do with Africa, the **Show Jumping Hall of Fame** has everything to do with colonialism and family ties. Elizabeth Busch, a family member and a fanatic about horse jumping, needed a place to house her collection of antique riding saddles, horseshoes, ribbons, and portraits of famous horses, and this minuscule corner was found, right next to the reptiles. *Crowds: Not a problem. Strategy: Go anytime. Audience: Adults. Rating:* ★

138

SERENGETI PLAIN

MBUKTU

Kenya Kanteen
Elephant Wash
NAIROBI
Nairobi Train Station

MYOMBE RESERVE
The Great Ape Domain

CROWN COLONY
Colony Club
Skyride and Monorail Station

Sultan's Tent
Stroller/Wheelchair Rental
Automatic Teller
MOROCCO
Guest Relations
Marrakesh Theater
Main Entrance

KEY

Restaurants
Restrooms
Rail Line
Skyride
Monorail
Roller Coaster

❼ The big attraction in Nairobi is the **Elephant Display,** housing 22 Asian elephants; the most attractive part of the display is their swimming pool, in which elephant parents and children snort, swim, and clean off before getting dusty again. Every couple of hours, some of the elephants troop out to the Elephant Wash area next to the Kenya Kanteen, where a schedule is posted and where they take a garden hose and give each other showers while a keeper explains elephant habits. *Crowds: Can be significant for the Elephant Wash but you can usually see. Strategy: Go anytime. Audience: All ages. Rating:* ★★★

The Kenya Kanteen is a good place to watch out for the **Trans-Veldt Railroad,** an authentic reproduction of an East African steam locomotive (with, as the tour guide points out, an American cowcatcher for those pesky impala—none of which actually can come near the tracks) that chugs around the Serengeti and then circumnavigates the park in a 2½-mile journey, making stops near the Congo River Rapids and Stanleyville (about 10 minutes to the Congo Train Station and another 10 minutes to Stanleyville). It's a dandy way to see the Serengeti. *Duration: 30 min. Crowds: Steady, but you almost always find a seat. Strategy: It comes only every 30 min, so watch the mother elephants dunking the little ones in the elephant pool until you hear the whistle, then dash for the station. Audience: All ages. Rating:* ★★

Timbuktu

From Nairobi you can continue by foot through a blindingly white mud fort—rather austere compared with the fretwork-laced decorative tile of the Moroccan fort—into Timbuktu, a claustrophobic walled area housing at least three rides guaranteed to make you lose your lunch; a video arcade; the Festhaus, an incongruous little piece of Germany, with dirndled maidens and lederhosen-clad youth dancing around a beer-swilling, sausage-chomping crowd; numerous games of chance; the Crazy Camel carousel; kiddie rides; and the Dolphin Theater (if you can have lederhosen in Timbuktu, why not dolphins, too?).

❽ The first ride you'll see as you exit the mud fort is the **Sandstorm,** "the number-one ride for making guests throw up," as a Busch Gardens staffer eloquently put it. It doesn't look all that menacing, but the constant rotation of both your seat and the arm it's attached to should prove the point. *Duration: 2½ min. Crowds: Not a problem. Strategy: Go anytime. Audience: Older children, teens, adults. Rating:* ★★

❾ Screams issue equally from the **Phoenix,** a crescent that swings back and forth, higher and higher until it swoops sickeningly over the top, and **❿** the **Scorpion,** 1,805 feet of steel roller coaster twisted into a gigantic hoop with a 65-foot drop; it reaches a maximum speed of 50 mph. *Duration: Phoenix 2 min, Scorpion 2 min. Crowds: Lines can build at midday in busy periods. Strategy: Go early or late. Audience: Older children, teens, adults. No riders under 48" on Scorpion. Rating:* ★★

⓫ Tamer diversions include the **Crazy Camel,** a delightful carousel with brightly painted camels alongside the traditional horses; carnival-type games of chance ($1 or $2 usually buys three throws); and such children's rides as Busch Flyers and a pint-size version of the Phoenix (other diminutive attractions are housed in Dwarf Village, outside Stanleyville).

⓬ The show at the **Dolphin Theater** is modeled on the one at Sea World, and, in fact, the dolphins and trainers are borrowed from Busch Gardens' fishy cousin. The dolphin tank is smaller than Sea World's and lacks the Plexiglas sides that let you peer at the underwater activities during the show. But the two-dolphin show is delightful. Mick and Bud more than earn their 35 pounds of raw fish, jumping and waving their flippers and thoroughly enchanting everyone, including the one lucky child chosen to come up and play with them. (If your child is between 5 and 8, outgoing, and not scared by dolphins, arrive 15 minutes early and ask an usher if your child can be picked for the show. He or she will, however, be backstage learning the proper hand signals during a dandy section of the show when the trainer plays in the water with the dolphins.) *Duration: 20 min. Crowds: Never a problem. Strategy: Go in the middle of the day, when the other animals in the park are snoozing. Audience: All ages. Rating:* ★★★

Congo and Stanleyville

Another mud fort by the Dolphin Stadium marks the exit from Timbuktu and the entrance to the Congo and adjacent Stanleyville, which is practically indistinguishable from the Congo. Unlike the open, dusty plains of the Serengeti and Nairobi, the Congo and neighboring Stanleyville are delightfully shaded by lush plantings and lofty, leafy trees, under whose branches nestle African fetish statues and piles of expedition-supply boxes for that "Dr. Livingstone, I presume" touch. Hysterical shrieks from the area's several thrill rides remind you that the visitors, if not the natives, are perpetually restless.

⑬ Directly to your right after exiting Timbuktu are the aptly named **Ubanga-Banga Bumper Cars** and, across the bridge, two of Busch Gardens' star attractions: Kumba and the Congo River Rapids. *Bumper cars' duration: About 4 min. Crowds: Never significant enough to cause a wait except in midafternoons during busy periods. Strategy: Go anytime—and if there's a line, don't bother to wait. Audience: Older children, teens, adults. Rating:* ★★

⑭ **Kumba** contains nearly 4,000 feet of turquoise steel twisting at up to 60 mph through three first-of-a-kind coaster maneuvers: a "diving loop" (plunging you from 110 feet into a loop); a camelback, with a 360° spiral and three seconds of weightlessness; and the world's largest loop, with a height of 108 feet. That's in addition to spirals, cobra rolls, and a corkscrew ride in the dark. Kumba offers a surprisingly smooth ride without the neck-wrenching of most similar efforts. Catch a replay of your screaming face on three TV monitors near the exit. *Duration: 3 min. Crowds: Can mean long lines. Strategy: Go as soon as the park opens. Audience: Older children, teens, adults. No riders under 52 in. Rating:* ★★★

⑮ Stagger on to the popular **Congo River Rapids,** one of the all-time best water rides. Visitors sit in rafts that look like enlarged inner tubes, 12 to a raft, and experience a watery version of bumper cars. As you go bumping and bucketing through nearly ¼ mile of rapids and waterfalls (and through a dark cave), be sure to wrap your camera in a waterproof bag (you will be splashed)—and remember to smile for the spectators taking pictures from the bridge. *Duration: 5 min. Crowds: There's usually a line. Strategy: Go early to avoid waits and have the best time. Audience: Older children, teens, adults. Rating:* ★★★

⑯ ⑰ As you exit the Congo River Rapids, follow the screams to the right for the **Monstrous Mamba,** another revolving octopus ride. The **Python,** a steel roller coaster on 1,250 feet of track, hurls passengers through two hoops at 50 mph. *Duration: Monstrous Mamba 70 sec, Python 70 sec. Crowds: Significant only in busy seasons. Strategy: Go early or late in holiday periods. Audience: Older children, teens, adults. No riders under 47 in on Mamba, must be 39 in and accompanied by adult on the Python. Rating:* ★★

⑱ Somehow the hysteria doesn't seem to bother the somnolent Bengal tigers on nearby **Claw Island** (they are more active in the early morning and the late afternoon). Some particularly pleasant shady benches overlook the island and are a nice place to recuperate before hitting the next rides.

⑲ The **Stanley Falls Log Flume Ride,** which has a 40-foot drop, and the
⑳ **Tanganyika Tidal Wave,** with a 55-foot drop into a splash pool, are among the park's most popular rides, due as much to the certainty of getting wet as to their gut-turning drops. In fact, the tidal wave offers two possibilities for dunking: the ride itself and, for those who are chicken, the viewing bridge at the bottom of the drop, where a recording of Tchaikovsky's *1812 Overture* heralds the next wave. (A sign posted nearby politely reads, "This bridge is part of a water attraction. You will get soaked. Thank you.") Either huddle behind the Plexiglas shelter on the bridge or skitter off—fast. *Duration: Stanley Falls 3½ min, Tanganyika Tidal Wave 6 min. Crowds: Significant, with lines even on average days. Strategy: Ride early in the morning or in the evening. Audience: Older children, teens, adults. Rating:* ★★★

㉑ Just past the exit of the Tanganyika Tidal Wave is **Orchid Canyon,** a lovely 100-yard walk through 200-odd cascading orchids and bromeliads native to South Africa, the Philippines, and South America—it's a welcome respite from the sensory overload you'll get in the rest of the park. Meanwhile, placidly ignoring riders' screeches and distant pleas of "Aw, c'mon, Melissa, you *need* to go on this ride," lemurs, rhinoceroses, eland, and orangutans peacefully snooze away in spacious enclosures naturalized with rocks, trees, and, in the case of the orangutans, gymnastic equipment. A couple of thatched huts scattered throughout the Congo and Stanleyville contain snakes in wire boxes and inquisitive parrots perched in cages. Keepers are on hand to explain their behavior and hold them for you to stroke.

Stanleyville is also home to the **Stanleyville Theater,** where circus acrobats and ethnic dancers perform, and to the **Stanleyville Bazaar** and **Air Africa,** something like a Moroccan souk, with African craftspeople fashioning their wares outside. Some interesting handcrafted wares are available for sale.

TIME OUT The **Stanleyville Smokehouse** cafeteria serves slow-cooked chicken, beef, and ribs with corn on the cob and all the trimmings; the **Bazaar Café** offers hearty barbecue beef sandwiches. Between the two, the Stanleyville air is redolent of barbecue.

Move on by catching the train at the Stanleyville Train Station—a twin of Nairobi's station—located behind the Stanleyville Theater and near the orangutans' island. Or follow the path past the orangutans, onto the bridge over the train tracks, and down to Bird Gardens.

Bird Gardens

This area is home to Dwarf Village, the koala habitat, and 1,883 exotic birds representing 218 species, including one of the largest managed flocks of Caribbean flamingos (fed beta-carotene supplements to maintain their bright coral color).

㉒ Just over the ramp from Stanleyville is **Parrots of the Pacific,** where multicolored parrots, macaws, and cockatoos are arranged in a circle, in cages, beneath two sprawling live oaks. A staffer is usually on hand to answer questions.

㉓ The children's play area, shady **Dwarf Village,** is well equipped with rubber safety matting, although the rides are a tad old-fashioned; you won't find the high climbing nets and snazzy sliding tunnels of the newer parks. But there are ball crawls, bouncing rooms, a miniature carousel, toy trains, and—a nice touch—storytelling. Loudspeakers merrily belt out happy kiddie songs, giving a cheerful air to the area. Several times daily, conservation specialists tell animal stories, sometimes with live animals as props. The youngsters' seats: fake toadstools. *Crowds: Seldom a problem. Strategy: Wait until later in the day, or you may never get your youngsters away; or go at midday for a respite from the heat. Audience: Young children. Rating:* ★★

㉔ The path leads right to **Flamingo Island,** whose flock of Caribbean flamingos is worth well over $1 million. The flamingos are part of a national breeding program, so the number of birds in the flock is constantly changing. *Crowds: Not a problem. Strategy: Go early or late to see birds at their most active. Audience: All ages. Rating:* ★★

㉕ To the right of Flamingo Island is the entrance to the **Aviary,** a lushly landscaped walk-through cage in which 194 species flutter freely among the trees and stalk along the ground. *Crowds: Not a problem. Strategy: Go early or late to see birds at their most active. Audience: All ages. Rating:* ★★

㉖ The **Bird Show Theater,** an open amphitheater just behind Flamingo Island, displays macaws, condors, and eagles performing natural behaviors; bird enthusiasts rate it one of the best shows anywhere. You can have your photo taken with one of the squawking stars at the adjacent posing area just after each show. *Duration: 30 min. Crowds: Sometimes significant during holiday periods. Strategy: Arrive 15 min before show time in busy seasons. Audience: All ages. Rating:* ★★

㉗ A very elaborate display with Chinese motifs down the boardwalk past the aviary once housed a pair of pandas; now it's **Koala House,** home to a breeding group of four—one male and three females. You can usually spot some joeys (baby koalas), too, although a look at the impassive parents makes it hard to imagine that any two of them ever get worked up enough to procreate. For close-up viewing by visitors, the exhibit offers a people-mover and an elevated observation gallery. Also, pay a few quarters for pellets to feed the huge decorative fish in the adjoining pool. They beg. Really. *Crowds: Not a problem. Strategy: Go in late afternoon to see the animals at their most active. Audience: All ages. Rating:* ★

Brewery

㉘ The last major attraction is the **Brewery,** a self-guided walk through a working brewery that produces 2.7 million barrels of Budweiser annually. You'll occasionally spot the big tanker cars on the freight trains that rumble out of the park bearing beer for a thirsty nation. Using automatic video and audio displays, educational placards, and labels, the tour covers every step of the process, from choosing the hops to canning the product. You don't have to be a beer fanatic to enjoy yourself, but people with a special interest in the inception of Bud Light do tend to linger. Some people gallop along, peering from the glassed-in walkways at the aging vats and bottling lines. But the written and audio displays abundantly provide beer trivia, from George Washington's favorite recipe to the secret behind how the aluminum tabs get put on top of flip-top cans. *Duration: Allot around 20 min. Crowds: Never a problem. Audience: Older children and adults. Rating:* ★★

TIME OUT You won't be able to snap a cold one at the Brewery, but the **Hospitality House** right outside provides whistle-wetting wuffo on tap. After a full day at Busch Gardens, you'll need it. You can also order a delicious hero sandwich (called a Tampa Sandwich Platter). Even the outdoor setting is pleasant.

Dining

The majority of the gustatory offerings are of the red meat variety, smoked, wursted, or burgered. They are routinely washed down with Anheuser-Busch products, which are sold parkwide: Budweiser, Bud Light, Michelob, and nonalcoholic O'Doul's. Ice cream and popcorn stands are ubiquitous.

Steak, chicken, and pasta dishes are on the menu upstairs in the Crown Colony's **Colony Club,** a white-tableclothed full-service dining area whose huge windows give a great view of the Serengeti. The change in altitude affects the price only minimally, and the setting is one of the most relaxing in the park. It's also the fanciest place in the park. Unfortunately, the number of window tables is limited (so you have to eat very early or late to get one), and when the park closes early, seating may end around 4, though this varies.

Shopping

There are three must-have stuffed animals on the central Florida theme-park circuit, and two of them are here: white tiger puppets (sold at the **Stanleyville Bazaar**) and cuddly gorillas (sold at **J.R.'s Gorilla Hut,** just outside Myombe Reserve). The latter also stocks a delightfully long-limbed chimpanzee, whose Velcroed palms attach in an everlasting hug. In Stanleyville, the aforementioned Stanleyville Bazaar and **Air Africa** are chockful of pseudo-African schlock—along with some authentic, imported treasures—but you can find the perfect birthday trinket or Yuletide stocking-stuffer in the form of a set of carved wooden zoo animals, perhaps, or brilliantly colored, elephant-shaped napkin rings. The **Souk** is the stop for inexpensive bangles, moderately priced brass, and exorbitantly pricey Moroccan leather, not to mention a rainbow of gauze veils to swathe your own little Salome. If all you want to do is shop, 30-minute shopping passes are available for a deposit equaling the price of admission.

Access for Travelers with Disabilities

To many wheelchair users, the Busch Gardens experience will be represented less by the wild rides than by the animals, which are on display at almost every turn. Of the rides that make up a significant part of the experience for many other visitors, almost all are accessible by guests who can transfer from their own wheelchair into the ride vehicles.

Services

The park publishes a leaflet describing each attraction's accessibility. It's available at Guest Relations.

Attractions

All attractions are wheelchair accessible in **Morocco, Myombe Reserve,** and **Nairobi.**

CROWN COLONY, TIMBUKTU

For **Questor** in the Crown Colony and for **Crazy Camel, Phoenix, Sandstorm,** and **Scorpion** in Timbuktu, you must be able to transfer from your wheelchair into the ride vehicle, and you must also be able to continuously hold on to lap bars or railings, hold yourself upright, and absorb sudden and dramatic movements. Timbuktu's other rides also cannot be boarded in a wheelchair.

CONGO, STANLEYVILLE

Guests using wheelchairs must also transfer to ride vehicles at **Congo River Rapids, Ubanga Banga Bumper Cars, Monstrous Mamba,** and **Python** in Congo and at **Stanley Falls** and **Tanganyika Tidal Wave** in Stanleyville; as at Questor (*see above*), you must also be able to hold lap bars or railings for these, as well as sit upright and absorb sudden and dramatic movements. Transferring out of a wheelchair is also required for **Congo kiddie rides.**

BIRD GARDENS

To play in **Dwarf Village,** children must be able to leave their wheelchair. The **Brewery** is not wheelchair accessible; the tour involves walking limited distances and several flights of stairs.

Shops and Restaurants

All shops and restaurants in Busch Gardens are wheelchair accessible.

CYPRESS GARDENS

A botanical garden, amusement park, and waterskiing circus rolled into one, Cypress Gardens is a uniquely Floridian combination of natural beauty and utter kitsch. It was founded during the Depression by Dick and Julie Pope; she was a southern belle from Alabama with a green thumb, and he was a short, fast-talking real estate promoter and public relations whiz addicted to flashy jackets ("If I didn't wear the jackets," he once confided to *Life* magazine, "people would think I was a tall fire hydrant"). They created their dream in a snake- and alligator-infested cypress swamp on the shores of Lake Eloise in what are euphemistically referred to as the central Florida "highlands," and they opened for business on January 1, 1936. (Ticket receipts that day totaled $38, less than the price of a day's 🎟 for two adults today.) Cypress Gardens has been open ever since and is central Florida's oldest continuously running attraction.

Despite Dick's self-designated status as "Swami of the Swamps" and "The Man Who Invented Florida," Cypress Gardens owes its two best-known traditions to Julie. In charge of the park during World War II while Dick was in the Armed Forces, Julie promised free water-ski shows for the soldiers at a nearby military base. What started with some stunts by Dick Jr. and his friends quickly expanded into a fully choreographed program with a bevy of "aquamaids" and stunt skiers, who originated the flips, barefoot skiing, and pyramids now a part of all waterskiing shows—both at Cypress Gardens and at other entertainment parks. When a winter storm devastated the plantings at the entrance to the park, Julie dressed the women on the staff in antebellum-style hoopskirts and had them stand in strategic locations, waving and smiling to draw visitors' attention away from the blighted blooms. These "Flowers of the South" provide photo-ops to this day.

The park now encompasses more than 200 acres and contains more than 8,000 varieties of plants gathered from 75 countries. More than half of the grounds are devoted to flora, ranging from natural landscaping to cutesy-poo topiary to chrysanthemum cascades. A staff of more than 50 horticulturalists manages a 7-acre nursery complex, which turns out some 10,000 plants a week, and they produce annual chrysanthemum shows, poinsettia pageants, and a three-month spring flower extravaganza.

Essential Information

Tourist Information
Contact Cypress Gardens (Box 1, Cypress Gardens 33884, ☎ 813/324–2111; in FL, ☎ 800/282–2123; outside FL, ☎ 800/237–4826; no TTY).

Within the park, the principal **information booth** is just inside the main gate.

Getting There
To get here, take I–4 west to the U.S. 27S exit. From there, the route is well signed: Follow signs to Winter Haven; at Waverly, turn right (west) on Route 540, and go 5 miles. It's a 45-minute drive from Walt Disney World.

PARKING
The grassy parking area is divided into the North Lot and the South Lot; within these, rows are marked numerically. Parking is free.

Admission
☛ Costs $26.91 for adults, $16.45 for children 3–9, and 15% off for guests over 55, excluding tax. AAA members get 10% off. Discounted tickets for Sea World and Busch Gardens can also be purchased here.

Hours
The park is open daily 9:30–6; restaurants in the Suzhou Gardens area stay open until 9. Hours may be extended in peak seasons.

Services

BABY CARE
You'll find **stroller rentals** at the Bazaar Gift Shop ($4 per day, with no deposit). Baby needs such as **baby food, formula, diapers,** and **wipes** can be purchased at the Winn-Dixie supermarket, across the street from the park. There are no designated facilities for nursing.

FIRST AID
First aid is near the entrance to the Botanical Gardens.

GUIDED TOURS
Behind-the-scenes tours of the nursery, as well as botanical tours of the gardens, are available by special request. Call the main park information number (*see above*) to arrange such tours.

LOCKERS
They're near the main office, just inside the park entrance (50¢).

LOST THINGS OR PEOPLE
Report **lost children and adults** as well as **lost possessions** at the main park office.

MONEY
There are no ATMs or currency exchange facilities.

WHEELCHAIR RENTALS
You can rent **standard wheelchairs** ($4 a day, with no deposit) and **motorized wheelchairs** ($5 per hour, with a $10 minimum and a $25 maximum, plus a $25 deposit).

Strategies for Your Visit

There's no sense of amusement-park anxiety at Cypress Gardens. The slow pace is partly because few people dash to gape at a banyan tree and partly due to the clientele, most of whom are older. In any case, there's no need to rush; even at a sedate pace, you can see just about everything in six hours. In summer, when the park stays open past the usual 5:30 PM closing time, you can arrive at noon and not miss anything. Lines are seldom a consideration. However, lines do build up at the Electric Boat Rides in fine weather on weekends and during winter, a favorite traveling time of the older visitors that Cypress Gardens tends to attract. Therefore, start with the boat-rides and save a pedestrian perambulation of the gardens for later in the day.

Other Tips

- There are mailboxes near all exhibits, saying "Please Take One." Please do. The fliers inside contain interesting background on the attractions.

- If you have allergies, come prepared with antihistamines. The beautiful floral arrangements wreak havoc on susceptible sinuses.

Exploring Cypress Gardens

The souvenir-shop-ridden main entrance funnels visitors straight to the water-ski stadiums. To the right are the Botanical Gardens; to the left are the Exhibition Gardens and the amusement area.

Numbers in the margin correspond to points of interest on the Cypress Gardens map.

① The **Botanical Gardens Cruise** floats through the cypress-hung canals of the Botanical Gardens, passing waving belles, flowering shrubs, 27 different species of palm, and the occasional baby alligator. Doing this first gives you a sense of Cypress Gardens' slightly schizoid history.

With luck and the right timing, you should be able to lope from dis-
② embarkation right into the **Water Ski Stadiums** for a stunt-filled waterskiing revue. Unlike Sea World's splashy song-and-dance extravaganza, the show at Cypress Gardens is purely athletic, with a nominal Mardi Gras theme extending only to the costumes and music. Also unlike at Sea World, the front rows stay dry. But that doesn't mean it's naptime: Smiling aquamaids whiz along on one leg; the Rampmasters pivot, flip, and jump over each other at 35 mph; Corky the Clown skis backward; and the grand finale involves a four-tier pyramid with everyone waving American flags. It's corny, but lively enough to keep even children entertained. *Duration: 30 min (presented every 2 hrs). Crowds: Not usually a problem. Strategy: Arrive 5–10 min before show time and sit in either stadium; the view is equally good from both. Audience: All ages. Rating:* ★★★

The path from the ski stadiums to Southern Crossroads, the hub of
③ the amusement park area, meanders through the **Exhibition Gardens,** a prime belle-spotting site (the belles often sashay through here to freshen up at the Southern Mansion, a.k.a. Tara South). The landscaping philosophy is heroic in intent and hilariously vulgar in execution, especially for the special flower festivals: During the annual November Mum Festival, 2 million multicolored chrysanthemums cascade over the ledges of the 40-foot-high Mediterranean waterfall, decorate the walls of an Italian-style fountain, color four gargantuan floral hearts, and drape two topiary swans in an eye-spinning display of pink, purple, yellow, orange, and red. The yearly Poinsettia Festival runs from December through early January and features flying-reindeer topiaries and Christmas trees made of more than 40,000 red, pink, and white blooms. A new addition is the Garden of Lights, which gilds the park's natu-

Cypress Gardens

KEY

Restaurants

Restrooms

N

Lake Eloise

Florida Pool

Oriental Garden

Banyan Tree

French Garden

Gazebo

Overlook Vista

First Aid

Main Entrance

Main Office

Mediterranean Waterfall

Lakeview Terrace

Southern Crossroads

Crossroads Restaurant

Village Fare

Botanical Gardens Cruise, **1**

Botanical Gardens, **12**

Carousel Cove, **11**

Crossroads Arena, **4**

Cypress Junction, **7**

Cypress Roots, **5**

Cypress Theatre, **9**

Exhibition Gardens, **3**

Kodak's Island in the Sky, **8**

Water Ski Stadiums, **2**

When Radios Were Radios, **6**

Wings of Wonder: The Butterfly Conservatory, **10**

A new addition is the Garden of Lights, which gilds the park's natural beauty with thousands of twinkling strands.

④ The **Crossroads Arena,** at the far southern end of the park, is home to a rotating collection of circus-themed acts from acrobats to trained birds. If you get there before the show, you can often watch the performers rehearse. *Duration: 25 min, plus 15-min pre-show. Crowds: Not significant. Strategy: Try for the first or last show of the day, because the tent gets wickedly hot at midday. Audience: All ages. Rating:* ★★★

⑤ As you work your way back toward Southern Crossroads, it's easy to overlook **Cypress Roots,** an unprepossessing clapboard shack chock-ful of fascinating memorabilia about the "Maharaja of the Marshes" and his fair bride. Save a good 20 minutes for the video interview of the Popes and the same amount of time to read all the *Life* magazine clippings of Dick Sr.'s promotional exploits.

TIME OUT **Village Fare,** a conglomeration of fast-food outlets, serves pizza, salads, burgers, and roast beef on picnic tables covered with green-trellised tablecloths in an air-conditioned arena. The **Cypress Deli,** a hop and skip away, features submarine sandwiches and big salads.

⑥ Nostalgia gets a firm nudge at **When Radios Were Radios,** an antique radio museum, with its collection of hundreds of 1920s Philcos, West-⑦ inghouses, and their successors dating through the 1950s. **Cypress Junction,** one of the nation's most elaborate model railroad exhibits, bridges the generation gap with its whistling freights, sleek expresses, tunnels, weather hazards, and all sorts of other knick-knacks. At any given time, you'll see nearly two dozen trains operating on its 1,100 feet of track; nearly 5,000 miniature figures of people and animals add that extra bit of detail. Oddly enough, this menagerie of miniatures was originally created as a Christmas exhibit for the *National Enquirer* ⑧ in Lantana, Florida. **Kodak's Island in the Sky,** a 153-foot-high revolving platform, provides aerial views of the park's seasonal flower spectaculars and lush gardens as well as of nearby Winter Haven.

⑨ One of the most popular attractions is the bird show at the **Cypress Theatre,** not the least of the reasons being that it's air-conditioned. Bird tricks are now referred to as "behaviors," although the behaviors exhibited by the parrots and macaws lean more toward such tricks as riding a bicycle or singing "Oh, What a Beautiful Morning" than the natural responses demonstrated by the raptors at the Busch Gardens bird show. Still, there's rousing audience response to "sing along with Grackles."

Anheuser-Busch Corporation's purchase of Cypress Gardens has resulted in both the installation of its signature statue of a hulking Clydesdale and a significant investment of money. The latter has been ⑩ put to good use in the newest exhibit, **Wings of Wonder: The Butterfly Conservatory.** More than 1,000 butterflies representing more than 50 species flit about an enclosed Victorian-style greenhouse, whose 5,500 square feet contain three waterfalls, educational displays, and a couple of chrysalis chambers where you can watch new butterflies struggling out of their cocoon. Four new gardens surround the conservatory: a butterfly garden constructed in the shape of a butterfly wing (great for those aerial shots from Kodak's Island in the Sky); an herb and scent garden, complete with cooking demonstrations; a vegetable and fruit garden; and a rose garden.

⑪ **Carousel Cove** caters to fidgety kids who demand a reward for traipsing past antique radios and inanimate shrubbery. It's perfectly geared to grandparents and grandchildren, with none of Sea World's athletic net climbs. Most of the rides are closer to the old-fashioned, county-fair variety than to the high-tech wonders at most theme parks. There are the ball crawls and bouncing pads, where kids can work off excess energy while their weary relatives watch, as well as skee ball, ball tosses, swings, and classic kiddie rides such as the Red Baron (airplanes). Some carnival games ($1 a chance) are also available.

12 It's worth saving the **Botanical Gardens** for last for the same reason that you save room for dessert. Most of the plants are labeled, as part of the park's education program; the plantings are naturalized; and a saunter on winding paths beneath shady live oaks or the quiet in the chamber created by a giant banyan's hanging roots provides a delicious respite from the usual entertainment park rush. Photo-ops abound.

Dining

The food is fast and the service friendly, but don't expect much more than basic refueling choices on the menu. At the Southern Crossroads hub, **Crossroads Restaurant** is fairly upscale, with a sit-down restaurant and a similar salad-quiche-sandwich menu with touches of southern cooking. **Lakeview Terrace,** on the upper level of the more southerly of the pair of water-ski stadiums, has a terrific view of the waterskiing show, as well as food that won't diminish your attention. Cypress Gardens is located plunk in the middle of central Florida's citrus plantations, so you can always pick up some freshly squeezed orange juice at **Baker's Dozen, Village Fare,** and most other food locations in the park.

Shopping

Before entering the park, buy a straw fan at the **Bazaar Gift Shop** at the entrance—it's invaluable for hot afternoon performances at the Crossroads Arena and on steamy days. Once inside, pick up minitopiaries and tastefully flowered T-shirts and sweatshirts (which do not turn you into a billboard for Cypress Gardens) at **Gardening, Etc.,** in Southern Crossroads. On your way out, stop in the gift shop again for pastel parasols for the baby-belle in your life, a pair of flowered gardening gloves, or an all-too-apt copy of *Allergy Plants* to find out what just ambushed your sinuses.

The **Butterfly Shop,** near Wings of Wonder, has a unique collection of fluttery fancies for collectors and some nifty things for bug-loving children.

Access for Travelers with Disabilities

All of the garden attractions at Cypress Gardens are wheelchair accessible, as are all restaurants and shops. Children with disabilities may not be able to negotiate some of the rides in Carousel Cove without assistance.

SPLENDID CHINA

The Orlando area's newest attraction is more a superlative open-air museum than a theme park in the Mickey Mouse tradition. Instead of standing in long lines at thrill rides and glitzy shows, visitors here stroll among painstakingly re-created versions of China's greatest landmarks. Tinkling, meditative music plays in the background, and Chinese artisans demonstrate traditional woodworking, weaving, and other crafts. Think of a park featuring scaled-down versions of the Grand Canyon, the Alamo, and the White House, plus roping shows and high school marching bands, and you'll get an idea of what a "Splendid America" might be like.

It took $100 million and 120 Chinese craftspeople working for two years to craft the 60-plus replicas, which include both man-made structures, such as the Imperial Palace, and natural phenomena, such as the rock formations of the Stone Forest. Some of the monuments are life-size, while others have been greatly reduced in scale—each brick in the Great Wall, for example, is only 2 inches long. These detailed reproductions are even more impressive when you consider that the artisans used historically accurate building materials and techniques whenever possible. Whereas Universal Studios and WDW are working to out-automate each other, Splendid China is content to stress tradition over technology; the most advanced electronics you'll see here are the tiny lights that glow inside the buildings after dark.

Park developers had planned to let the park consist solely of the miniature monuments, thereby re-creating the successful formula that has brought millions of visitors to the prototype park, Shenzhen Splendid China, which opened near Hong Kong in 1989. U.S. advisers convinced them, however, that theme park-savvy Western visitors expected more bang for their buck, so a playground area for children and live entertainment were added. Despite the awareness that Florida's Splendid China needed to be tailored for different demographics, problems still arose that neither the Chinese creators nor their U.S. friends had foreseen.

Park officials certainly didn't figure on demonstrators, who showed up on opening day to protest China's occupation of Tibet. (The park includes a representation of Potala Palace, the official seat of the Dalai Lama, Tibet's exiled spiritual and secular leader.) And they never dreamed that early guests would trample through the displays, kick over hundreds of handmade clay figurines, or try to take home the delicately painted decorations that are cemented onto many structures. The park suffered more damage in its first few days than its cousin in Shenzhen did in six years of operation. The first stage shows were an equally uncomfortable meeting of Asian and Western sensibilities: Chinese announcers read from stilted text that seemed to describe every other performer as "breathtaking and elegant." Some park-goers simply walked out.

Things have evened out considerably since opening day, but the difficulties are a reminder that cultural differences can be extremely powerful. Maybe it is the unrelenting Florida rain and sunshine, but after only a year in operation, the park was looking a bit worn. Officials continue to try and find a way to make the root differences a foundation for Splendid China's appeal. Officials say the numbers have been less than what they expected but blame it on a slow tourism market. They also claim that many of the customers are repeat visitors. It may be true. Many guests come to the park out of curiosity and find themselves fascinated by the delicate craftsmanship that went into creating the displays, the thousands of years of history that the structures represent, and the religious mythology attached to many of the re-created shrines. Splendid China turns out to be just their cup of tea. Others are still just trying to figure it out.

Essential Information

Tourist Information

Contact Splendid China (3000 Splendid China Blvd., Kissimmee 34747; ☎ 407/397–8800 or 800/244–6226). Once you're at the park, **Guest Services** (☎ 407/397–8825) is located inside the main entrance to the right.

Getting There

Splendid China is about 12 miles from Orlando, or 2½ miles west of the I–4/U.S. 192 junction. From Orlando, take I–4 west toward WDW, and get off at Exit 25B—the signs will say "Disney," "Fort Wilderness," and so on. You are now on U.S. 192; continue west past all of the exits leading to Disney. Stay in the far-left lane and look for the dragon.

PARKING

There's no charge for parking at Splendid China.

AUTO NEEDS

Should you experience car trouble, head for **Central Reception,** just outside the gate, and an attendant will call an auto service for you.

Admission

Regular ☛ is $23.55 for adults, $13.90 for children 5–12. AAA members receive a 10% discount, as do senior citizens over 55.

Hours

The park is open daily 9:30–8; shops and restaurants in the Suzhou Gardens area stay open until 9:30. Hours may be extended in peak seasons.

Services

BABY CARE

There are **diaper-changing tables** available in women's rest rooms. No diapers are sold on the property, but they can be purchased at Eckerd's, just off U.S. 192 near the park's entrance. **Strollers** are for rent at Guest Services (single $4, double $7, no deposit).

CAMERAS

Film for most cameras is sold at Guest Services, as are **disposable 35mm cameras.** Guest Services also rents **video cameras** ($25 per day, $150 deposit).

FIRST AID

First-aid services are immediately inside the main entrance.

GUIDED TOURS

A four-hour walking tour of the park is $5 per person. Or, a VIP golf-cart tour will whip you, a guide, and up to four friends around the park in about 90 minutes; the tour is $45, regardless of the number of people.

LOCKERS

They're near Guest Services ($1).

LOST THINGS
OR PEOPLE

Go to Guest Services. There is a park-wide public-address system that can be used for contact in an emergency.

MONEY

You'll find an ATM at Guest Services, but no currency exchange facilities.

PACKAGE PICKUP

If you do your shopping before checking out the exhibits, ask the merchant about holding the item or having it sent to Guest Services; there's no official package pickup, but most vendors will be happy to oblige.

One thing Splendid China offers that's not found at any other park is a full-service travel agency. **China Travel Services** (☎ 407/397–8868), one of the largest travel agencies in China and a major investor in the park, has an office on-site. If the re-creations make you want to see the real thing, make reservations before you go home.

WHEELCHAIR RENTAL
You can rent **standard wheelchairs** ($5) and **electric scooters** ($25, with $50 deposit) from Guest Services.

Strategies for Your Visit

You can probably tour every exhibit in under four hours, but once you add some time for shopping, eating, and taking in a few shows, Splendid China makes for a good one-day trip. The park is really at its most magical at night. Try not to arrive until after noon; that way you'll be in plenty of time to catch the shows, eat some dinner, watch the final parade at 6:30ish, and then wander the exhibits until closing time.

When you get to the park, go to Harmony Hall and watch the 15-minute film *This Is Splendid China,* which explains the history behind the park. Also check with Guest Services for show times and any special events. Since lines are not an issue here, there's no pressing strategy needed for touring the attractions. One thing to note: The park map numbers the exhibits counterclockwise; if you tour in that direction, you'll end up at the underwhelming mausoleum of Dr. Sun Yat-sen in the middle of the park. If you head clockwise, you'll finish up your day with the most impressive sites—the Imperial Palace and the Great Wall.

One final caveat: The passive nature of the park makes it suitable mostly for older children and adults. Young kids and even restless teens may get bored because there's plenty to see but not much to do.

Rainy Days
Splendid China is very much an outdoor exhibit; once you're out among the displays there is little shelter from the elements. If rain is forecast, stay home or bring a poncho.

Exploring Splendid China

Besides the star attractions like the Great Wall and the Summer Palace, Splendid China also has reproductions of Chinese temples, pagodas, typical Chinese homes, and grottoes filled with religious statuary. Each display is accompanied by a short, written explanation or a recorded message or both, explaining its significance and history. The following text, which marks only the highlights, takes you on a clockwise tour of the park; we pause about two-thirds of the way through at the Temple of Light Amphitheater, where all of the live shows are presented; depending on what time the shows you're most interested in start, you may want to head for the theater first.

As you come through the turnstile, you enter Splendid China's version of Main Street: **Suzhou Gardens** is a re-creation of a 14th-century Chinese village. Inside the tile-roofed structures, you'll find most of the park's shops, several restaurants, and **Guest Services.**

Just adjacent to Guest Services is **Harmony Hall,** where the *This Is Splendid China* film is screened every 20 minutes. Although it contains some lovely footage of China and useful background information on the buildings and statues that the exhibits here are based on, the film does not explore the meticulous construction that went into building the park. *Duration: 15 min. Crowds: Not a problem. Strategy: See it first so you'll better understand the exhibits. Audience: All ages. Rating:* ★★

The **closing parade,** which kicks off each night at about 6:30, also starts near the main entrance and then winds through Suzhou Gardens. Featuring colorfully painted wooden floats, flotillas of traditional sedan chairs, and a slew of ornately adorned ladies, it's worth a watch. *Duration: 25 min. Crowds: Nothing significant. Audience: All ages. Rating:* ★★

Head left out of Suzhou Gardens' shopping plaza and into an area of replicated stone grottoes, the originals of which are used as temples. **Grotto 257** is a cave shrine; the interior features dark, rich colors and is authentic down to the smudges in the artwork and the missing digits on some of the statues. A number of the exhibits appear worse for wear because their prototypes were damaged during the Cultural Revolution or simply by the passage of time; the craftspeople chose to replicate these originals as authentically as possible, warts and all. Several grottoes down is the **Leshan Buddha,** a re-creation of the largest man-made statue in the world. The original, which took 90 years to build, stands 24 stories high. This version is about 35 feet high. Past the grottoes is a maze of odd obelisks, composing the **Stone Forest.** This unusual formation replicates a 200-acre park in southern Yunan Province, where pillars have been whittled out of the limestone by aeons of erosion.

At Nine Dragon Wall, head left to the **Summer Palace,** the traditional home of China's dowager empress. Aristocrats and other members of the court would come to stay during the summer to escape the heat in Beijing. As at the original, the many palace structures are reflected in a smooth pool. After the complex fell into ruins during the 19th century, the Empress Dowager Ci Xi had it rebuilt with money that was supposed to be used to expand the navy. The stone boat that you see moored at the water's edge—the prototype is made from marble—therefore takes on a certain ironic meaning. The **Temple of Heaven,** past Dr. Sun Yat-sen's Mausoleum, is a striking, blue-tiled structure. It was at this site in Beijing that the emperor, as high priest of his people, would spend time in fasting and prayer.

Now make a swing around the back of the park. Check out the Water Village—China's version of Venice—and the Lijiang River Scenery area (can you see the elephant in the rocks?). Behind the "river," in the far back corner of the park, is the controversial reproduction of **Potala Palace,** a dusty-rose-and-white structure. The original in Lhasa, Tibet's capital, is an amalgam of two palaces—the Red and the White—both commissioned by the fifth Dalai Lama (1617–82); it stands 13 stories high but seems even taller because the walls were constructed to lean inward, creating a false perspective.

TIME OUT When you're ready to take a break from the miniatures, head past Jingzhen Octagonal Pavilion, Dai Village, and Manfeilong Pagoda to the **Wind and Rain Court.** Cantonese and Shanghai cuisine, along with a limited Western selection, are served in this ersatz pagoda. One park staffer said this is the place to get good hamburgers if your taste buds aren't in the mood to mu shu.

Splendid China's live-action venue is the **Temple of Light Amphitheater.** A costume show and a demonstration of music and folk dances are each presented on alternating hours. Both are slow-moving affairs, a situation that is not improved by the mumbling Chinese announcer. Without narration, the **Costume Show** amounts to a bunch of attrac-

No matter where you go, travel is easier when you know the code.[SM]

dial 1 8 0 0 CALL ATT[®]

Dial 1 800 CALL ATT and you'll always get through from any phone with any card* and you'll always get AT&T's best deal.** It's the one number to remember when calling away from home.

*Other long distance company calling cards excluded.
**Additional discounts available.

AT&T
Your True Choice

tive young Asian women in high heels and silk who parade back and forth in time to music. The **National Art Ensemble Show** is a performance of traditional folk dances and music from across China and is considerably more interesting than the costume show. The dancers are skilled and the music intriguing, but once again, much of the symbolism of the movements is lost because the narration is hard to follow. *Duration of each: 40 min. Crowds: Not significant. Audience: All ages. Costume show rating: ★; Art Ensemble show rating: ★★*

Right next to the amphitheater is the **Panda Playground.** The ball crawls, slides, and maze are likely to entertain smaller children who are less than captivated by exhibits that don't move, make noise, or light up. Compared with other central Florida theme park playgrounds, however, this one is nothing to write home about. *Crowds: Not significant. Audience: Young children. Rating: ★*

An **Acrobatic Show** is held in an adjoining tent. Some cheesy magic tricks are followed by truly incredible feats of balance and flexibility. One woman stands on a bench about six feet off the ground and bends backward to pick up a coin with her mouth. This is easily the most entertaining show in the park. *Duration: 20 min. Crowds: Not significant. Audience: All ages. Rating: ★★★*

After getting your fill of Chinese entertainment, be sure to see the **1,000 Eyes and 1,000 Hands Guanyin Buddha Statue,** whose many hands are said to ease the troubles of the world. The nearby **Terra Cotta Warriors** are modeled on 7,000 life-size clay figurines unearthed by archaeologists in 1974. The original figures were realistic portraits of servants, soldiers, and cavalry in the employ of Emperor Ch'in Shih Huang Ti. When the emperor died, almost 2,000 years ago, the figures were buried with him as an honor guard. Splendid China's warriors—replicas of replicas, as it were—are housed in a cool cave.

Now take a walk along the **Great Wall,** keeping in mind that the 6.5 million tiny bricks used to make the wall were mortared into place by hand. This ½-mile-long expanse cannot begin to replicate the size of the original—the 1,500-mile-long behemoth that is the only man-made structure visible from space. As in China itself, Mongolia lies on the other side of this wall. Check to see if a wrestling demonstration is scheduled near the **Mongolian Yurt.** Mongolia's capital city, Ulan Bator, has a population of 500,000, more than half of whom live in yurts like these.

The **Imperial Palace** is the centerpiece of Beijing's famed **Forbidden City** and one of the most impressive sights at Splendid China. The compound in Beijing, built in the early 1400s as the home of the royal family, was constructed of materials brought from all over China and decorated with centuries' worth of loot; it housed so many people that as many as 6,000 cooks were needed to feed them. No commoner stepped inside the walls of its inner sanctum until the mid-20th century; some of China's emperors never stepped outside. Even the scale model here gives a sense of the immense size and the artistry that made such a lifestyle possible.

Dining

Splendid China has some splendid food. Even the cafeteria-style offerings at Suzhou Gardens' **Seven Flavors Court** are far better than normal park fare, and probably at least as good as your neighborhood take-out place. Try the nearby **Suzhou Pearl** if you're more in the mood for attentive service, elegant atmosphere, and gourmet versions of traditional Chinese dishes. (The empty room off the main area is the park owners' private dining room.) If you're out among the exhibits proper, try

Great Wall Terrace, near the 1,000 Hands Guanyin Buddha statue; it serves Mandarin and northern Chinese cuisine and has table service. Reservations are recommended at all the sit-down restaurants and can be made at Guest Services when you first arrive. If you want just a hot dog and a soda, carts are scattered throughout the park.

Shopping

As with the food, the merchandise available at Splendid China is a cut above typical theme-park tourist souvenirs. Of Suzhou Gardens' 11 shops, only **Nine Dragon Gifts** offers pedestrian goodies like T-shirts and key chains. For more exotic offerings, check out **Ancestral Artifacts'** handcrafted Chinese furniture, the nursery at **Pen Jing Gardens** (which sells bonsai trees), and **Loomed Creations'** lovely linens. Other unusual treasures such as teas, works of calligraphy, silk embroidery, hand-painted porcelain, and jade may make you wish you had more time and money to spend.

Access for Travelers with Disabilities

There are no special programs or guides available for guests with disabilities. Most of Splendid China's attractions are wheelchair accessible, but Sun Yat-sen's Mausoleum and the Guanyin Buddha Statue have stairs. Visitors must be able to transfer to a golf-cart-like tram for the VIP guided tour. Recorded messages in both English and Spanish discuss the various exhibits but probably do not provide enough information for visually impaired guests to have a full experience. All of the shops and dining areas are wheelchair accessible, although the stone streets in Suzhou Gardens may make for some rough riding.

4 Away from the Theme Parks

Updated by
Jennifer
Burgess

WHEN YOU'RE READY to put some distance between you and Mickey, you'll find that Orlando and the surrounding central Florida area have much more than theme parks. Nature buffs like to escape to the Ocala National Forest or the Florida Audubon Society Madlyn Baldwin Center for Birds of Prey. Art devotees head for Rollins College's Cornell Fine Arts Museum or the Charles Hosmer Morse Museum of American Art. New-Agers check out Casssadaga—more than half the residents of this town are psychics, mediums, and healers. And since this is central Florida, you'll also find such attractions as Wet 'n' Wild and Terror on Church Street. Indeed, you'll discover an abundance of sights—natural, unnatural, and supernatural—that are equally enjoyable and often less crowded and expensive than those at the theme parks.

OFF THE BEATEN TRACK

Lesser-known attractions like those that follow, when visited together, combine to make enjoyable day trips. Both of these suggested itineraries lie to the north. Not far from I-Drive, about a half hour's drive, is tony, suburban Winter Park; farther afield is grove-filled Lake County.

Tour 1: Winter Park

Once the winter refuge of wealthy northerners, Winter Park, though part of Orlando's metro area, maintains a proud, independent, and upscale identity. A pleasant day can be spent shopping, eating, and taking in the scenery along **Park Avenue** downtown, full of trendy boutiques and restaurants. Long and narrow **Central Park** stretches through the heart of the shopping district, and benches under the ancient trees offer a respite from the bustle. Away from downtown, the moss-covered trees form canopies over brick streets, and old estates surround canal-linked lakes.

Perhaps the best way to get a feel for Winter Park is from the deck of a pontoon boat on the **Scenic Boat Tour.** The relaxing, hour-long cruise sails past 12 miles of fine old homes and around the grounds of Rollins College, on one of Winter Park's three main lakes, which are connected by 100-year-old canals. Having celebrated its 56th anniversary not long ago, this tour is one of central Florida's oldest attractions. Turn right off I–4's Fairbanks Avenue Exit. At Park Avenue, turn left and head straight into downtown Winter Park. Turn right on East Morse Boulevard; the dock is at the end of the street. *312 E. Morse Blvd., Winter Park,* ☎ *407/644–4056.* ☛ *$5.50 adults, $2.75 children 2–12.* ☉ *Daily 10–4; boats leave every hr.*

Having seen it from the lake, you might want to stroll around the campus of historic **Rollins College,** a private liberal arts school at the south end of Park Avenue. It claims Mister (Fred) Rogers among its alumni—yes, this was once his neighborhood. Take time to look at the Spanish-style architecture, especially Knowles Memorial Chapel, home of the Bach Festival Society. Also on campus is the **Cornell Fine Arts Museum,** which has the largest collection of American and European art in central Florida. The permanent collection contains works ranging from the Renaissance to contemporary times. *1000 Holt Ave., Winter Park,* ☎ *407/646–2526.* ☛ *Free.* ☉ *Tues.–Fri. 10–5, weekends 1–5; closed major holidays.*

If you're interested in more art, there is a concentration of galleries on Park Avenue. Half a block east is the elegant **Charles Hosmer Morse**

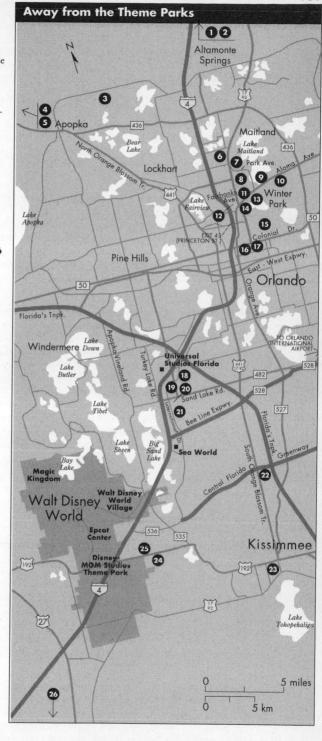

Away from the Theme Parks

Museum of American Art, which features an outstanding collection of stained-glass windows, blown glass, and lamps by Louis Tiffany. There's also a collection of paintings by 19th- and 20th-century American artists, as well as jewelry and pottery. *133 E. Welbourne Ave., Winter Park,* ☎ *407/645–5311.* ☛ *$2.50 adults, $1 students and children.* ☼ *Tues.–Sat. 9:30–4, Sun. 1–4.*

On Saturday, when the **Winter Park Farmer's Market** takes over a parking lot just west of Park Avenue, across the railroad tracks, you can see evidence of the real community that exists behind the upper-crust facade. The market is a long-standing tradition. Friends and neighbors gather to shop for fresh fruits and vegetables, breads and pastries, herbs, coffees, and plants. *W. Lyman and New York Aves., Winter Park,* ☎ *407/623–3275.* ☼ *Sat. 7–noon.*

Heading west out of town on Fairbanks Avenue, take the left fork onto Orange Avenue and, after ½ mile, turn left onto Denning Avenue for a visit to **Mead Gardens,** Winter Park's quite unusual park. Its 55 acres have intentionally been left to grow as a natural preserve. Walkers and runners are attracted to the trails that wind around the creek, and a recently constructed boardwalk provides a better view of the delicate wetlands. *S. Denning Ave., Winter Park,* ☎ *407/623–3334.* ☛ *Free.* ☼ *Daily 8–sundown.*

With entrances on both Rollins and Princeton streets (1 mile east off I–4 Exit 43), Orlando's **Loch Haven Park** is a grassy field with four of the city's cultural strongholds: Orlando Science Center, Orange County Historical Museum, Orlando Museum of Art, and Civic Theatre of Central Florida. All but the theater are open almost daily and have delightful gift shops chockablock with unusual items. The buildings, all air-conditioned, are delightfully cool on hot, humid days. The park itself doesn't offer much more than a pleasant walk from one building to another. However, off to the side are some old, shady oak trees—nice for a picnic—and a lovely lake is just across the street. The wide-open space hosts the Kite Festival in March and the Pet Fair in December, and it's frequently used by community groups for outdoor concerts and festivals.

Orlando Science Center is a place for action, and, best of all, touching is encouraged here. The Tunnel of Discovery has a variety of clever hands-on activities to teach the principles of physical science. Special traveling exhibits with themes ranging from dinosaurs to space travel all have interactive components. For preschoolers there's WaterWorks, where children, secured in plastic smocks, are turned loose to explore the properties of water. NatureWorks features an extensive collection of rocks and insects as well as live demonstrations with resident snakes, other reptiles, and amphibians. Films in the dome-shaped planetarium take viewers on a journey through the stars, and on weekend evenings Cosmic Concerts combines lasers and rock music in a psychedelic light show. There's a snack bar. *810 E. Rollins St., Orlando,* ☎ *407/896–7151.* ☛ *$6.50 adults, $5.50 children 3–11.* ☼ *Mon.–Thurs. and Sat. 9–5, Fri. 9–9, Sun. noon–5. Cosmic Concerts:* ☛ *$6.50; Fri. and Sat. 9* PM, *10* PM, *11* PM, *and midnight.*

Adjacent to the Science Center is more sedate **Orange County Historical Museum,** a storehouse of Orlando memorabilia, photographs, and antiques. Exhibits explore Native American and native Floridian culture, and they show off a country store, Victorian parlor, and print shop; call for an update on the always-changing traveling exhibits. Fire Station No. 3, an actual 1926 brick firehouse behind the museum, houses antique fire trucks, fire-fighting memorabilia, and collectibles. Though most items are for looking only, there are some firefighters' bunks, hats, and jackets for youngsters to investigate. *812 E. Rollins St., Orlando,* ☎ *407/897–6350.* ☛ *$2 adults, $1.50 senior citizens, $1 children 6– 11.* ☉ *Mon.–Sat. 9–5, Sun. noon–5.*

Across the park from the Science Center is the **Orlando Museum of Art.** The collection includes 19th- and 20th-century American art, displayed on a rotating basis year-round, and a permanent exhibit of pre-Columbian artifacts from a Mayan excavation. Young children will enjoy the first-class Art Encounter, created with the help of Walt Disney World. Hands-on activities, such as dressing up in colorful handwoven clothing from South America, stimulate imaginations and enhance children's understanding of the works in the galleries. Call for information on special exhibits. *2416 N. Mills Ave., Orlando,* ☎ *407/896–4231.* ☛ *$4 adults, $2 children 4–11.* ☉ *Tues.–Sat. 9–5, Sun. noon–5; tours Sept.–May, Wed. and Sun. 2 PM; Art Encounter Tues.–Fri. and Sun. noon–5, Sat. 10–5.*

The **Civic Theatre of Central Florida** stages productions throughout the year. The MainStage Series offers traditional Broadway musicals and dramas; the SecondStage Series has off-Broadway-style, cutting-edge works; and family classics are performed in the Theatre for Young People. *1001 E. Princeton St., Orlando,* ☎ *407/896–7365.*

A short distance from Loch Haven Park is **Leu Botanical Gardens,** Orlando's 56-acre horticultural extravaganza. Formerly the estate of the late industrialist and citrus industry entrepreneur Harry P. Leu, it has a collection of historical blooms, many varieties of which were established before 1900. You'll see ancient oaks, a 50-foot floral clock, an orchid conservatory, and one of the largest camellia collections in eastern North America (in bloom October through March). Mary Jane's Rose Garden, named after Leu's wife, is filled with more than 1,000 bushes; it is the largest formal rose garden south of Atlanta. The simple 19th-century Leu House Museum, once the Leu family home, preserves the furnishings and appointments of a well-to-do, turn-of-the-century Florida family. From Loch Haven Park, continue east on Princeton Street to the end. Turn right on Mills Avenue and left on Virginia Avenue; bear left at the fork and look for the garden entrance on the left, just after the traffic light. *1730 N. Forest Ave., Orlando,* ☎ *407/246–2620.* ☛ *$3 adults, $1 children 6–16. Garden open daily 9–5; museum Tues.–Sat. 10–3:30, Sun. and Mon. 1–3:30.*

Tour 2: Lake County

As you drive northwest out of Orlando on U.S. 441, you head into aptly named Lake County, an area renowned for its pristine water and excellent fishing. Watch the flat countryside, thick with scrub pines, take on a gentle roll through citrus groves and pastures with live oaks. The lean orchards still show signs of the devastation caused by an unusually harsh freeze several years ago.

About 45 minutes northwest of Orlando is the quaint valley community of **Mount Dora,** west off U.S. 441 on either Old U.S. 441 or Route 44B. Built around the unspoiled Lake Harris chain of lakes, the town has a slow and easy pace, a rich history, New England–style charm, and excellent antiques shopping (*see* Off the Beaten Track *in* Chapter 6, Shopping). Although the population of Mount Dora is less than 8,000, there is plenty of excitement here, especially in fall and winter. There is an art festival, a sailing regatta, a bicycle festival, a crafts fair, and many other events. Palm Island Park offers nature trails and fishing, and Gilbert Park has a public dock and boat-launching ramp, picnicking facilities, and a playground. Take in one of the prettiest views in central Florida from the city dock at the end of Fourth Avenue, next to the Mount Dora Yacht Club; on a misty day, the lakes seem to go on forever. Or just amble through the Main Street district. The Mount Dora Chamber of Commerce provides a self-guided tour map that tells you everything you need to know—from historic landmarks to restaurants. *Chamber of Commerce, 341 Alexander St., Mount Dora, ☎ 904/383–2165. Welcome center ⊙ Weekdays 9–5, Sat. 10–4, Sun. noon–4; after hrs, maps on display at the kiosk.*

A half-hour drive north of Mount Dora on Route 19 is **Ocala National Forest,** a 366,000-acre area between the Oklawaha and St. Johns rivers, known for its canoeing, hiking, swimming, camping, and invigorating springs. The visitor center, on Route 19, just north of Altoona, provides information on what to see and do. **Alexander Springs,** favored for its cold, fresh water, is just minutes away. From the center, continue north on Route 19 and turn right on Route 445; the entrance is on the left. After hiking down to the small beach, swim out, preferably with a snorkel and fins, to the steep drop-off at the head spring, where the water rushes out from rock formations below. It's not unusual to see friendly alligators sitting on the bank opposite the sandy beach, but you'll notice that natives leave the water before sundown—feeding time. Other choice springs in the national forest are Juniper and Salt springs. *Ocala National Forest visitor center, 45621 Rte. 19, Altoona, ☎ 904/669–7495. Center open daily 9–5. Alexander Springs: ☞ $2; open daily 8–8.*

SIGHTSEEING CHECKLIST

If you don't want to take a day trip, you might want to pick and choose individual attractions—peaceful, offbeat, enlightening, or just plain fun—to complement your time in the theme parks. You'll find there's more to culture here than Epcot Center, more to nature than Cypress Gardens, and more to animal life than Mickey and Shamu can offer.

The Natural World

Parks and Gardens

If your appetite for natural beauty has been whetted, take a one-hour drive south of Orlando to **Bok Tower Gardens,** a quirky yet appealing sanctuary of plants, flowers, trees, and wildlife native to subtropical Florida. Shady paths meander through pine forests in this peaceful world of silvery moats, mockingbirds and swans, blooming thickets, and hidden sundials. You'll be able to boast that you stood on the highest measured point in the state, a colossal 324 feet above sea level. The majestic 200-foot Bok Tower is constructed of coquina (from seashells) and pink, white, and gray marble. The tower houses a carillon with 57 bronze bells that ring every half hour after 10 AM. Each day at 3 PM there is a 45-minute recital, which may include Early American folk songs, Appalachian tunes, Irish ballads, or Latin hymns. There are also moonlight recitals.

The landscape was designed in 1928 by Frederick Law Olmsted Jr., son of the planner of New York's Central Park. On the grounds you'll find the 230-room, Mediterranean Revival–style Pinewood House, built in 1930. Take I–4 to U.S. 27 south. About 5 miles past the Cypress Gardens turnoff, turn right on Route 17A to Alternate U.S. 27. Past the orange groves, turn left on Burns Avenue and follow it about 1½ miles to the gardens. *Burns Ave. and Tower Blvd., Lake Wales, ☎ 813/676–*

1408. ☞ *$4 adults, $1 children 5–12.* ☉ *Daily 8–5. Pinewood House tours given Sept. 15–May 15, Tues. and Thurs. 12:30 and 2, Sun. 2; suggested donation $5 adults, $4 children under 12.*

In the heart of Orlando, on the eastern side of downtown, lies an inner-city victory, **Lake Eola Park.** Established in 1892, the family park experienced a series of ups and downs that left it run-down by the late '70s. With the support of determined citizens, the park gradually underwent a renovation, which restored the fountain and added a wide brick walkway around the lake. The security is such that families with young children use the well-lighted playground in the evening and downtown residents walk their dogs late at night in safety. The Walt Disney Amphitheater, perched on the lake, is a dramatic site for the annual Shakespeare Festival (March and April), as well as for weekend community concerts and *FunnyEola,* a free, family comedy show performed the second Tuesday of every month. However, the most fun to be had at the park is a ride in a swan-shaped pedal boat; the view at dusk, as the fountain lights up and the sun sets behind Orlando's growing skyline, is spectacular. Take the I–4 Robinson St. exit, turn right at the bottom of the ramp, and go ¼ mile. *Bordered by Robinson St. and Rosalind Ave., Orlando,* ☎ *407/246–2827.* ☉ *Daily 7 AM–midnight. Swan boats: rental fee $5.30 for ½ hr; open Sept.–May, daily noon–8; June–Aug., daily noon–10; max. 3 people per boat. Eola Park Café open weekdays 10–8, weekends 10–9.*

Leu Botanical Gardens, formerly the Leu estate, has gardens teeming with all kinds of flowers, including orchids, camellias, and roses (*see* Tour 1, *above*).

Mead Gardens is a 55-acre nature preserve in Winter Park (*see* Tour 1, *above*).

Recreation Areas

North of Orlando, **Ocala National Forest,** known for its springs, is good for canoeing, hiking, and swimming (*see* Tour 2, *above*).

Where the tannin-stained Wekiva River meets the crystal-clear Wekiva headspring, there is a curious and visible exchange—like strong tea infusing in water. (Wekiva is a Creek Indian word meaning "flowing water.") The **Wekiwa Springs State Park** sprawls around this area on 6,400 acres. The parkland is well suited for camping, hiking, and picnicking; the spring for swimming; and the river for canoeing and fishing. Canoe trips can range from a simple hour-long paddle around the lagoon to observe a colony of water turtles to a full-day excursion through less-congested parts of the river that haven't changed much since the area was inhabited by Timucuan Indians. Take I–4 Exit 49 (Longwood), and turn left on Route 434. Go 1¼ miles to Wekiwa Springs Road; turn right and go 4½ miles to the entrance, on the right. *1800 Wekiwa Circle, Apopka,* ☎ *407/884–2009.* ☞ *$3.25 per vehicle.* ☉ *Daily 8–sundown.*

Animals, Animals, Animals

A visit to 110-acre **Central Florida Zoological Park** will disappoint if you're expecting a grand metro zoo. However, this is a respectable display, of about 230 animals tucked under pine trees, and, like the city of Orlando, it continues to grow. The elephant exhibit is popular, as are the tortoises and the exotic and native snakes housed in the herpetarium. The zoo is becoming specialized in small and medium-size exotic cats, including servals, caracals, and jaguarundis, and there is an aviary that houses American bald eagles that have been grounded due to injury. Children love the Animal Adventure, which has domestic and farm animals to pet and feed; pony rides are offered from 10 to 4. Take I–4 Exit 52, and drive 1 mile east on U.S. 17–92 to the entrance, on the right. *3755 N. U.S. 17–92, Sanford,* ☎ *407/323–4450.* ☛ *$5 adults, $3 senior citizens ($1.50 on Tues.), $2 children 3–12.* ⊙ *Daily 9–5.*

More than 20 different species of hawks, eagles, owls, falcons, and vultures make their home at the **Florida Audubon Society Madlyn Baldwin Center for Birds of Prey.** There is an earnestness to this humble, working facility on Lake Sybelia in Maitland, which takes in 500–600 injured wild birds of prey each year. About 43% are able to return to the wild; permanently injured birds continue to live at the center and can be seen in the aviaries along the pathways and sitting on outdoor perches. The center also tracks eagles and occasionally sets up a closed-circuit monitor to observe a nest, so visitors can watch a genuine nature show. Take I–4 Exit 47A, then Maitland Boulevard East; turn right on Maitland Avenue, right on U.S. 17–92, right on Kennedy Boulevard, and right on Audubon Way. *921 S. Lake Sybelia Dr., Maitland,* ☎ *407/645–3826.* ☛ *$2 adults, $1 children 6–12.* ⊙ *Tues.–Sat. 10–4.*

Long before Walt Disney World, there was **Gatorland.** This campy attraction south of Orlando on U.S. 441 has endured since 1949 without much change, despite competition from major attractions. Through the monstrous aqua gator-jaw doorway (a definite photo op) lie thrills and chills in the form of thousands of alligators and crocodiles, swimming and basking in the Florida sun. In addition to the gators and crocs, there is a zoo that houses many other reptiles, mammals, and birds. A free train ride provides an overview of the park, and a three-story observation tower overlooks the breeding marsh, which is swamped with gator grunts, especially come sundown during mating season.

Don't miss the Gator Jumparoo show, in which gators leap out of the water for their food. The best Jumparoo is the first one in the morning, when the gators are hungriest. There's also a Gator Wrestling show, and though there's no doubt who's going to win the match, it's still fun to see the handlers take on those tough guys with the beady eyes. In the educational Snakes Alive show, high drama is provided by the 30–40 rattlesnakes that fill the pit around the speaker. Don't look for scrupulous Disney-style cleanliness here, and the personnel aren't polished with pixie dust either. This is a real Florida experience, and you'll walk out those aqua gator jaws knowing the difference between a gator and a croc. *14501 S. Orange Blossom Trail, between Orlando and Kissimmee,* ☎ *407/855–5496 or 800/393–5297.* ☛ *$10.95 adults, $7.95 children 3–11.* ⊙ *Daily 8–dusk.*

Friendly farmhands keep things moving on the two-hour guided tour of **Green Meadows Farm** in Kissimmee. There's little chance to get bored and no waiting in line because tours are always starting. Everyone who wants to gets to milk the fat mama cow, and chickens and geese are turned loose in their yard to run and squawk while city slickers try to catch them. Kids take a quick pony ride, and everyone gets jostled about on the old-fashioned hayride. Kids come away saying: "I milked a cow, caught a chicken, pet a pig, and fed a goat." Take I–4 Exit 25A (Kissimmee), go east on U.S. 192 for 3 miles to Poinciana Boulevard, turn right, and drive 5 miles. *1368 Poinciana Blvd., Kissimmee,* ☎ *407/846–0770.* ☛ *$12 age 2 and over.* ⊙ *Daily 9:30–5 (last tour at 4).*

Museums

Art/Science Museums

Glass, both stained and blown, is the main attraction at the

Charles Hosmer Morse Museum of American Art (*see* Tour 1, *above*).

Cornell Fine Arts Museum, at Rollins College, has a large collection of American and European art (*see* Tour 1, *above*).

Loch Haven Park contains Orlando's science, historical, and art museums and a community theater (*see* Tour 1, *above*).

It's local lore that the **Maitland Art Center,** a historic art museum near Lake Sybelia, is inhabited by the spirit of its artist-architect founder, Andre Smith. He began constructing his studio retreat in 1937, and the grounds and buildings themselves are works of art. The seemingly infinite reliefs and other details reflect Smith's fascination with Mayan and Aztec influences and further account for the mystical aura. An outdoor chapel is a favorite spot for weddings, and romantic gardens blend harmoniously with the natural surroundings. Inside, the galleries display an extensive collection of Smith's work as well as changing exhibits by local and national artists. Take I–4 Exit 47A and Maitland Boulevard East; turn right on Maitland Avenue and after ¾ mile, right again on Packwood Avenue. *231 W. Packwood Ave., Maitland,* ☎ *407/539–2181. Donations accepted.* ◎ *Weekdays 10–4:30, weekends noon–4:30.*

Offbeat Museums

The **Orlando Museum of Art** (*see* Tour 1, *above*) has a new look and is attracting national touring exhibits of artists like Andy Warhol and William Wegman (he of humorous Weimaraner-posing fame).

Old warbirds never die—they just become attractions at the **Flying Tigers Warbird Air Museum** in Kissimmee. The working aircraft restoration facility is nicknamed "Bombertown USA," because most of the planes here are bombers. Once they are operational, they are usually flown away by private collectors, but the museum also houses a permanent collection of about 30 vintage planes in its hangar, with a few big ones out on the tarmac. Tour guides are full of facts and personality and have an infectious passion for the planes. Go south on U.S. 441 to U.S. 192; turn right. After the Kissimmee Airport entrance, turn left on Hoagland Boulevard (Airport Road). *231 Hoagland Blvd., Kissimmee,* ☎ *407/933–1942.* ☛ *$6 adults, $5 senior citizens and children 5–12.* ◎ *Mon.–Sat. 9–5:30, Sun. 9–5 (extended for tour groups).*

A 10-foot-square section of the Berlin Wall. A pain and torture chamber. A Rolls-Royce constructed entirely of matchsticks. A 26-foot-by-20-foot portrait of Van Gogh made from 3,000 postcards. These and almost 200 other oddities speak for themselves in the **Ripley's Believe It or Not!** museum in the heart of tourist territory on International Drive. It is said that the fruits of Robert Ripley's explorations are to reality what Walt Disney World is to fantasy. The building itself is designed to appear as if it's sliding into one of Florida's notorious sinkholes. Give yourself an hour or two to soak up the weirdness here, but remember this is a looking, not touching, experience, which may drive antsy youngsters—and their parents—crazy. Take I–4 to Exit 29 (Sand Lake Rd.); turn left. Turn right on International Drive (second traffic light); museum is ¼ mile on left. *8201 International Dr., Orlando,* ☎ *407/363–4418.* ☛ *$8.95 adults, $5.95 children 4–11.* ◎ *Daily 10 AM–11 PM (extended for tour groups).*

Fun Houses and Miniature Golf

There are a variety of ways to attack the **Mystery Fun House.** You might just want to bring your quarters and visit the video arcade, for which there's no admission charge. Paying admission to the actual Fun House entitles you to a walk through the 18-chamber Mystery Maze, which comes with the warning that it is "90% dark" and full of gory and distorted images. Outside, there's an 18-hole Mystery Mini-Golf, a basic putt-putt course, laid out flat and simple, with some holes landing inside gator jaws, a gorilla, and so on. It isn't in the same league as Pirate's Cove (*see below*), a golfer's wonder. The real highlight is the Starbase Omega laser-tag game. Equipped with laser guns and wearing reflector belts, players are transported on a simulated spaceship ride to the arena, where they try to zap each other (to score points) and avoid being zapped by the UFO spaceship hovering overhead. Underfoot, the playing surface feels like an air mattress, adding a simulated low-gravity element to the game. Take I–4 to Exit 34B (Universal Studios). Turn right on Kirkman Road and right again on Major Boulevard. *5767 Major Blvd., Orlando,* ☎ *407/351–3355.* ☛ *Maze $7.95, minigolf $4.95, laser game $6.95, all 3 for $13.85.* ☉ *Daily 10 AM–11 PM (to midnight in peak seasons).*

You can play the crème de la crème of miniature golf at the two locations of **Pirate's Cove Adventure Golf.** Each site offers two 18-hole courses that wind around artificial mountains, through caves, over waterfalls, and into lush foliage. The beginner's course is called Captain Kidd's Adventure; a more difficult game can be played on Blackbeard's Challenge. The courses are opposite Mercado Mediterranean Village and in the Crossroads of Lake Buena Vista shopping plaza (*see* Shopping Villages *in* Chapter 6, Shopping). *8601 International Dr., Orlando,* ☎ *407/352–7378; Crossroads Center (I–4 Exit 27),* ☎ *407/827–1242.* ☛ *Captain Kidd's Adventure, $6.50 adults, $5.50 children 4–12; Blackbeard's Challenge, $7 adults, $6 children 4–12. Admission to both courses: $10 adults, $9 children 4–12. All-day (9–5) admission to either course: $12 adults, $9 children.* ☉ *Daily 9 AM–11:30 PM.*

Visit a haunted house year-round at **Terror on Church Street.** This showcase of horror in the heart of downtown, a few blocks east of Church Street Station, is a 25-minute walking tour through a high-tech labyrinth featuring 23 scenes from horror films with live actors and state-of-the-art sound effects. Lines are long on weekends, but they move along quickly because groups of eight leave every five minutes. The gift shop is stocked with gargoyles, eyeballs, and blood, as well as masks and makeup for re-creating your favorite slasher scenes. Terror targets the 12–22 age group but won't disappoint horror-film fans of any age. Follow signs off I–4 to the Church Street Historic District. *Church St. and Orange Ave., Orlando,* ☎ *407/649–3327.* ☛ *$12 adults, $10 students 17 and under; Florida residents, $10 adults, $8 students 17 and under.* ☉ *Sun.–Thurs. 7 PM–midnight, Fri. and Sat. 7 PM–1 AM.*

Water Parks

For aesthetics you can't beat Blizzard Beach and Typhoon Lagoon, with their landscaping and design in spectacular Disney style. But they don't have certain water slides that make the area's other water parks—Wet 'n' Wild and WaterMania—so popular. Both of these concrete and plastic attractions are packed in summer, and there are long lines at the popular rides. Both smell of chlorine and suntan lotion, and both are fashion shows of tacky swimwear. The basic difference is location.

Wet 'n' Wild is on International Drive, the cruise strip for restless teenagers. It attracts locals as well as out-of-towners, who constitute the greatest part of visitors to WaterMania, which is in Kissimmee.

WaterMania has all the requisite rides and slides without Walt Disney World aesthetics. However, it's the only water park around to have Wipe Out, a surfing simulator, where you grab a body board and ride a continuous wave form. The giant Pirate Ship in the Rain Forest, one of two children's play areas, is equipped with water slides and water cannons. The Abyss, similar to Wet 'n' Wild's Black Hole (*see below*), is an enclosed tube slide through which you twist and turn on a one- or two-person raft for 300 feet of deep-blue darkness. The park also offers a sandy beach, a picnic area, snack bars, gift shops, and periodic concerts, which can be enjoyed while floating in an inner tube. Its 18-hole miniature golf course won't win any local prizes, considering the competition, but does give you another way to pass the time while you're out of the water. It's in Kissimmee (½ mile east of I–4 and 1½ miles from Walt Disney World). *6073 W. Irlo Bronson Memorial Hwy., Kissimmee,* ☎ *407/239–8448 in Orlando, 407/396–2626 in Kissimmee, or 800/527–3092.* ☛ *$20.95 adults, $17.95 children 3–12.* ☼ *Sept. 5– Nov. 26, Dec. 26–June 2, daily 10–5; June 3–Aug. 20, weekdays 9:30– 7, weekends 9:30–8; Aug. 21–Sept. 4, weekdays 9:30–6, weekends 9:30–7. Closed Nov. 27–Dec. 25.*

Wet 'n' Wild, like WaterMania, is probably best known for its outrageous water slides, especially the Black Hole—a 30-second, 500-foot, twisting, turning ride on a two-person raft through total darkness propelled by a 1,000-gallon-a-minute blast of water. There's also an elaborate Kid's Park—for those 4 feet tall and under—full of miniature versions of the bigger rides. The latest addition is the Bubba Tub, a six-story, triple-dip slide with a tube big enough for the entire family. Take advantage of the half-price discount after 3 PM (5 in peak seasons), which not only saves money but also cuts down on exposure to the sun. Teens like the Top 40 concerts that take place frequently in summer. The park has snack stands, but visitors are allowed to bring their own food and picnic around the pool or on the lakeside beach. Take I–4 Exit 30A and make a left. *6200 International Dr., Orlando,* ☎ *407/351–3200.* ☛ *$20.95 adults, $17.95 children 3–9.* ☼ *Daily 10–5 (to about 9 in summer) except for Orlando's few really cold days.*

Explorable Towns

About 35 miles northeast of Orlando is **Cassadaga,** headquarters of the Southern Cassadaga Spiritualist Camp Meeting Association. More than half of the 300 residents are psychics, mediums, and healers, which makes it the nation's largest such community. The camp welcomes visitors either to sit in on one of the church services (10:30–11:45 AM Sunday or 7:30–8:15 PM Wednesday at the Colby Memorial Temple at the end of Stevens Street). Spiritualist services are nonsensational meditative gatherings, with the most unconventional aspect being the "message" portion, during which certified mediums deliver specific messages to attendees from spirits in the beyond. Visitors are also encouraged to get a reading from a camp member; it is suggested that the best way to find a medium who is right for you is by walking or driving through this rustic, five-block-by-five-block neighborhood and stopping at a house that is giving off the right energy. A community rich in spirit, it doesn't offer much to the material world, except the modest Southern Cassadaga Bookstore (1112 Stevens St.; ☼ Mon.–Sat. 9:30–5, Sun. noon–5). The people here are friendly and wholesome and accustomed to curiosity seekers, but they do request respect for their community. Take I–4 to Exit 54 (Cassadaga and Lake Helen). Turn right on Route 472 and right again on Route 4139 (first traffic light); continue 2 miles. *Cassadaga Spiritualist Camp, Box 319, Cassadaga,* ☎ *904/228–2880.*

Charming **Mount Dora** offers good antiques shopping and scenic lake views (*see* Tour 2, *above*).

5 Shopping

SHOPPING IS PART OF THE ENTERTAINMENT at Walt Disney World and throughout the Greater Orlando area. There's something in every price range in virtually every store, so even kids on allowances can get in on the act. You'll find everything from specialty stores, gift shops, and flea markets to factory outlets, department stores, and, of course, malls. Shop-till-you-droppers will be delighted to know that Orlando is packed with malls. It is virtually impossible to step outside your hotel room without seeing a mall or a sign advertising one. Whatever your shopping interests—Pongo and Perdita stuffed toys, Ralph Lauren blue jeans, flea-marketesque finds—the area provides a great opportunity to do a lifetime of shopping in a few days. Most stores accept traveler's checks and major credit cards.

Updated by
Marianne
Camas

WALT DISNEY WORLD

You'll be able to find Disney trinkets in every park, but there are a few shops throughout the property that carry unique items, like Magic Kingdom's Frontier Trading Post, where you can find western-style gifts. For top suggestions—such as the Emporium, the Magic Kingdom's largest gift shop—*see* the Shopping *sections in* Chapter 2. In addition, keep your eye out for wonderful finds tailored to special interests—tennis balls with Mickey Mouse logos, for instance, are available in the pro shops at the Contemporary and other hotels.

Magic Kingdom

Inside Cinderella Castle is the **King's Gallery,** where you can buy imported European clocks, chess sets, and tapestries while artisans perform intricate metalwork. Another nifty nook is **Harmony Barber Shop,** on the west side of Main Street, where old-time shaving items like mustache cups are sold. This will just whet your appetite for **Olde World Antiques** in Liberty Square, where you can find expensive antique jewelry, hutches, pewter, and brass. Fans of all things Pooh will find a charming array of items with the characters from the Hundred Year Woods at the **Briar Patch**, located just past the Splash Mountain exit in Frontierland. Serious collectors of Disney memorabilia will want to stop at **Disneyanea,** across the square from City Hall. Limited-edition sculptures, dolls, posters, and sometimes even park signs are available for purchase. To get monogrammed mouse ears, stop at the **Chapeau,** on the east side of Main Street (extremely crowded at the end of the day) or the **Mad Hatter,** in Fantasyland. The largest store for gifts is the **Emporium,** a Town Square landmark, where you can find everything from Mouseketeers' ear-gear to Madame Alexander dolls.

Epcot Center

The real shopping here is done in the special interest shops at the pavilions in World Showcase (*see* Epcot Center *in* Chapter 2, Exploring Walt Disney World). If your time in World Showcase is limited, check out **Disney Traders** and **Port of Entry,** the two shops at Showcase Plaza, located to the right of the Mexico pavilion. The best place for souvenirs, however, is on the way out: **Centorium** in Future World's Innoventions has the largest selection of goodies with Epcot Center logos.

Disney-MGM Studios Theme Park

Check out Sid Cahuenga's **One-of-a-Kind** shop, to the left as you enter the park. Alongside old movie posters, autographed pictures, and assorted, one-of-a-kind knickknacks are original costumes once worn by stars in feature movies. The **Animation Gallery,** at the end of the Animation Tour, sells original Disney animation cels, books, collectibles, and exclusive limited-edition reproductions. If you've been searching for Christmas decorations with a Disney theme, try **It's a Wonderful Shop,** near New York Street.

Disney Village Marketplace

Nestled along the shores of Buena Vista Lagoon, this complex of shops and boutiques is packed with art, fashions, crafts, and more. If you are looking for one-stop Disney shopping, this is the place. **Mickey's Character Shop** is the largest Disney merchandise store in the world. Children can buy trinkets for a dollar or two or choose among hundreds of stuffed animals—from Bambi and Thumper to Simba and Mufasa. Serious Disney fans can spend thousands for original cel paintings of animated movies or for porcelain sculptures of Cinderella or Alice in Wonderland. **Team Mickey's Athletic Club** offers sports clothing and equipment with the Mickey logo or Disney University items. **Toys Fantastic** has a phenomenal selection of Barbie dolls and accessories, along with the latest character collectibles. Artisans demonstrate their skills throughout the day at **Eurospain** and **Cristal Arts.** The **Christmas Chalet** sells holiday merchandise year-round. Both Disney-themed and traditional yule items are available. The prices here are no better or worse than anywhere else in the country. While parents shop, kids 12 and up can rent watercraft at the marina. There are plenty of places to grab a snack or to relax with a heartier meal. Relatively quiet in the morning, the complex gets busier as the day goes on, especially since Pleasure Island, which has clubs, eateries, theaters, and more shops, is nearby. *Lake Buena Vista,* ☎ *407/824–4321.* ☉ *Daily 9:30 AM–10 PM.*

Pleasure Island

Although best known as Disney's nightspot, Pleasure Island also has some nifty shops. (During the day, you can walk around Pleasure Island without paying an admission charge—it's just a short walk from Disney Village Marketplace, and not nearly as crowded.) **Reel Finds** is filled with movie and TV memorabilia (items are different from those sold at Disney-MGM). If you long to look like Indiana Jones, check out **Avigator's,** next door to the funky Adventurer's Club nightclub. **Suspended Animation** offers limited-edition cels and sculptures. **Changing Attitudes** will be a hit with the teen scene: It sells funky (and very un-Disneyesque) clothing and accessories. **Doodles** is the source for Pleasure Island memorabilia, hip T-shirts, and gag gifts.

GREATER ORLANDO AREA AND KISSIMMEE

Factory Outlet Malls

The International Drive area is filled with factory outlet stores, most on the northeast end. These outlets are clumped together in expansive malls or scattered along the drive, and much of the merchandise is dis-

172

Shopping

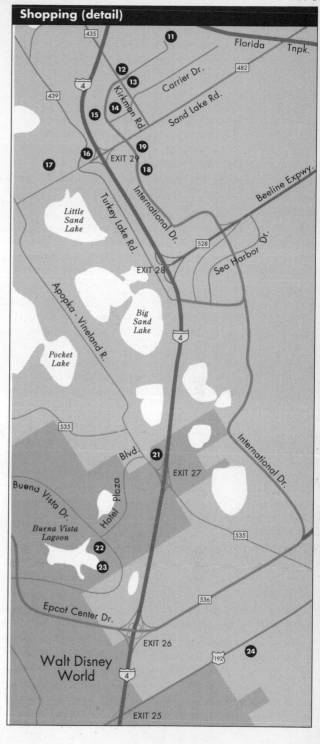

counted from 20% to 75%. You can find just about anything, some of it top quality, but be advised: These are not charming places to shop.

International Drive Area

Belz Factory Outlet World is the area's largest collection of outlet stores—nearly 170, in two malls and four nearby annexes. A good place to find discount name-brand clothes for the whole family, the complex includes such stores as Carole Hockman Lingerie, Maidenform, Danskin, Anne Klein, Jonathan Logan, Calvin Klein, Harvé Benard, Van Heusen, Burlington Brands, Just Kids, Bugle Boy, Oshkosh, Young Generations, Bally Shoes, Bass Shoes, Etienne Aigner, and Capezio. Especially popular are the outlets for athletic shoes: Converse, Reebok, and Sneakee Feet (which sells Reebok, Nike, and Adidas). There are also good buys in housewares and linens in such outlets as Fieldcrest/Cannon, Pfaltzgraff, Corning/Revere, Mikasa, and Fitz & Floyd. Don't worry about carting home breakable or cumbersome items; these stores will ship your purchases anywhere in the United States by UPS. Although the mall isn't fancy, it is clean and pleasant. Mall 2 offers a carousel for children and an adequate food court. The information booth sells discount tickets to all the non-Disney theme parks and offers a foreign currency exchange service. *5401 W. Oakridge Rd. (at the northern tip of International Dr.),* ☎ *407/352–9600.* ☯ *Mon.–Sat. 10–9, Sun. 10–6.*

All the dinnerware, flatware, glassware, and cookware you can imagine is at **Dansk Factory Outlet**—and all of it is at discount prices. Many of these items are seconds, limited editions, and discontinued styles. *7024 International Dr.,* ☎ *407/351–2425.* ☯ *Daily 9–7.*

A great place for jeans, **Denim World** carries Levi's, Lee, Bugle Boy, Jordache, and Wrangler and often offers two-for-one deals on shirts. Although the selection in children's sizes is limited, most women's and men's sizes can be found. There are plenty of salesclerks to help you dig through the stacks of jeans, and a seamstress will make alterations while you wait (10 minutes if you're first, much longer if there's a line). Parking is limited. *7623 International Dr.,* ☎ *407/351–5704.* ☯ *Daily 8 AM–midnight.*

Edwin Watts Golf Shop is a no-handicap shop for golfing equipment. *7297 Turkey Lake Rd.,* ☎ *407/345–8451.* ☯ *Weekdays 9:30–8, Sat. 9:30–6, Sun. noon–5.*

Quality Outlet Center and **Quality Center East** are two interconnected strip shopping centers containing more than 20 brand-name factory outlet stores, including American Tourister, Great Western Boots, Corning/Revere, Royal Doulton, Villeroy & Boch, Florsheim Shoes, Laura Ashley, Magnavox, and Mikasa. *5409 and 5529 International Dr. (1 block north of Kirkman Rd.),* ☎ *407/423–5885.* ☯ *Mon.–Sat. 9:30–9, Sun. 11–6.*

Special Tee Golf carries all brands of golf and tennis equipment and sportswear at discounted prices. *5400 International Dr.,* ☎ *407/352–3673.* ☯ *Mon.–Sat. 10–9, Sun. 11–5:30.*

U.S. 192 Area

Although **Kissimmee Manufacturers' Outlet Mall** doesn't look too appealing from the road, this strip shopping center contains a nice selection of shops. The approximately 20 stores include Bass Shoes, American Tourister, Van Heusen, Bon Worth, London Fog, Levi's, Fieldcrest/Cannon, Manhattan, Totes, Acme Boots, and Brandname Shoes (Reebok and L.A. Gear). *2511–2557 Old Vineland Rd., just off U.S. 192 (Irlo Bronson Memorial Hwy., 1 mi east of Rte. 535),* ☎ *407/396–8900.* ☯ *Mon.–Sat. 10–9, Sun. 11–5.*

Flea Markets

When you see signs for flea markets, remember that most are collections of shops run by small-time retailers, not gigantic garage sales with vendors set up at card tables. Most of the stock is usually new, not used.

With 400 booths, **192 Flea Market Outlet** is about one-quarter the size of Flea World (*see* Off the Beaten Track, *below*), but it's much more convenient to the major Orlando attractions and is open daily. The all-new merchandise includes toys, luggage, sunglasses, jewelry, clothes, beach towels, sneakers, and the obligatory T-shirts. *4301 W. Vine St. (also known as Irlo Bronson Memorial Hwy.), Kissimmee,* ☎ *407/396–4555.* ⊗ *Daily 9–6.*

Malls and Department Stores

While much of the rest of the country maintains a mall status quo, the Orlando area, with its burgeoning population and huge influx of tourists, continues to see mall construction. Several existing malls have been expanded, and a number of new ones are in the planning stages.

Central Orlando and Winter Park

Gayfers, JC Penney, Burdines, and Sears are the anchors of **Orlando Fashion Square.** The 130 specialty shops include such chain stores as Camelot Music, the Gap, Lerner, and Lechters. Bebe's has special children's wear, including mother-daughter outfits, christening gowns, and dresses for big occasions. The White House sells women's lingerie, sportswear, and formal dresses, but only in shades of white and ivory. And, just in case you missed something at the home of the Mouse, there's a large Disney store. Souvenir prices are the same as in the park; however, the store stocks some clothing items and memorabilia not found anywhere else. There's a large and popular food court. *3201 E. Colonial Dr. (3 mi east of I–4 Exit 41), Orlando,* ☎ *407/896–1131.* ⊗ *Mon.–Sat. 10–9, Sun. noon–5:30.*

International Drive Area

The **Florida Mall,** the largest in central Florida, includes Sears, JC Penney, Belk Lindsey, Gayfers, Dillard's, 200 specialty shops, seven theaters, and one of the better food courts around. The specialty stores are mostly those you've seen before: County Seat, the Limited, Radio Shack, Waldenbooks, Athlete's Foot, and Gordon's Jewelers. One recent addition is yet another Disney Store. At the Barefoot Mailman, however, you can purchase something special—authentic autographed pictures of Madonna, John Wayne, Michael Jackson, Elvis, and many others. Although the mall is supposedly divided into three distinct architectural areas (Victorian, Mediterranean, and Art Deco), you will probably not be aware of any striking differences. Because the mall attracts crowds of tourists, it offers many services, including car rental, airline reservations, check cashing, and currency exchange. Discount tickets to Universal Studios and other area attractions are also available here, as are brochures—many containing money-off coupons—describing local spots of interest. The **Florida Mall Terrace** is next door, with Byrons, Phar-Mor, Service Merchandise, Target, and more. *8001 S. Orange Blossom Trail (4½ mi east of I–4 and International Dr.), Orlando,* ☎ *407/851–6255.* ⊗ *Mon.–Sat. 10–9:30, Sun. 11–6.*

Shopping Villages

These quaint shopping areas are filled with gift shops, antiques shops, clothing stores, and restaurants. Some are primarily for tourists, with tourist prices, but all are much more pleasant and relaxed than the malls.

Central Orlando and Winter Park

Church Street Exchange is a decorative, brassy, Victorian-theme "festival marketplace" filled with more than 50 specialty shops; still others are across the street. At the Exchange's Pearl Factory, you can choose a pearl from an oyster to create your own pearl ring, pendant, or earrings and get an informative explanation of how oysters make pearls. At Kandelstix, craftspeople show how the unique, refillable, hand-carved candles are designed. Perhaps the best demonstration is at Augusta Jansson, where free candy samples are distributed during a lighthearted look at the process of making fudge. Units sells women's clothing and accessories created to mix and match on a three-sizes-fit-all basis. Udderly Country is a New England–style country store with a cow theme. You can also find many of the requisite upscale shops, such as Victoria's Secret and Benetton. Across the street from the complex is Bumby Emporium, a Church Street souvenir shop, and Buffalo Trading Company, where you can buy string ties, cowboy hats, and snakeskin boots; and across the railroad tracks is yet another collection of unusual shops and pushcarts, known as the Historic Railroad Depot. The Exchange has a small food court on the second floor (but remember there are some great restaurants on Church Street); children can spend some money on arcade and video games on the top floor at Commander Ragtime's Midway of Fun, Food and Games. *Church St. Station, 129 W. Church St., Orlando,* ☎ *407/422–2434.* ⊙ *Daily 11–11.*

The shops of **Ivanhoe Row,** in downtown Orlando, sell delightful but pricey antiques. The William Mosley Gallery carries a fine selection of 19th- and 20th-century paintings. Antiques to Cherish is known for its European and American silver, crystal, and porcelain, and Curator's Own has an unusual collection of African wood carvings and animal skins, American Indian and Eskimo crafts, and masks of all types. After antiquing, cross the street and take a stroll in the beautiful park surrounding Lake Ivanhoe. *1211–1231 N. Orange Ave. (I–4 Exit 43 to Princeton Ave. east to N. Orange Ave. and turn right), Orlando,* ☎ *407/896–9230 or 407/898–6050.* ⊙ *Mon.–Sat. 10–5.*

Longtime residents complain that **Park Avenue** is beginning to resemble a mall, as local one-of-a-kind stores are replaced by chains such as Banana Republic, Foot Locker, the Gap, Orvis, Laura Ashley, and Ann Taylor. Visitors, however, are usually charmed by this posh shopping district in Winter Park, with its tiny courtyards ringed by restaurants, galleries, bookstores, and other little shops. Perfumery on Park specializes in hard-to-find fragrances. The Center Street Gallery features original artwork, Russian lacquer boxes, and wonderful gifts. Antiques and other items for the home can be found at Far East Treasures, Table Dressing, and Gallery of Collectibles. (*see* Tour 1 *in* Chapter 4, Away from the Theme Parks). *Park Ave. between Fairbanks Ave. and Canton (east of I–4 Exit 45), Winter Park,* ☎ *407/644–8281. Most shops open Mon.–Sat. 10–5:30 (some also on Sun. noon–5).*

International Drive and WDW Area

The Crossroads of Lake Buena Vista, across the street from the entrance to the hotels at Lake Buena Vista, contains restaurants and nearly 20 shops that are convenient for tourists. Upscale and casual shops are geared toward sun and surf, electronics, and children, but the necessities, such as a 24-hour grocery and pharmacy, post office, bank, and cleaners, are also there. Though you'll find the usual franchised restaurants, there are also some local spots like the casual Pebbles (*see* The Orlando Area *in* Chapter 7, Dining). While you shop, your offspring can entertain themselves at Pirate's Cove Adventure Golf (*see* Fun

Houses and Miniature Golf *in* Chapter 4, Away from the Theme Parks). *12545–12551 Rte. 535 (off I–4 Exit 27), Orlando,* ☎ *407/827–7300. Hours vary.*

A neighborhood shopping center, the **Marketplace** provides all the basic necessities in one spot near International Drive. Stores include a pharmacy, post office, one-hour film processor, stationery and card store, bakery, dry cleaner, hair salon, optical shop, natural-food grocery, and 24-hour supermarket. Also in the Marketplace are three popular restaurants: Christini's, Enzo's, and the Phoenician (*see* The Orlando Area *in* Chapter 7, Dining). *7600 Dr. Phillips Blvd. (west of I–4 Sand Lake Exit), Orlando,* ☎ *407/345–8668. Hours vary.*

The Spanish-style **Mercado Mediterranean Village,** a relaxation stop for many bus tours, houses more than 60 specialty shops, such as Beach Club Orlando, which sells swimsuits and beach accessories; American Cola Company, which offers Coca-Cola and Anheuser-Busch memorabilia; and Once upon a Star, whose gifts and clothing have a movie motif. Earth Matters, a shop for environmentalists, sells items with a wildlife theme. A dinner theater and five restaurants (*see* Chapter 7, Dining) are found along the walkway that circles the festival courtyard, where live entertainment can be enjoyed at various times throughout the day. Near Mercado's front entrance is an office of the Orlando/Orange County Convention and Visitors Bureau. Here you'll find racks and racks of brochures on just about every conceivable area attraction. Discounted tickets to Universal Studios, dinner shows, and the water parks are sold here. The clean, quick, and large food court offers a selection of food from around the world. Although there is a variety show with animated birds for children every 20 minutes, this isn't a place you'll want to linger with your offspring. *8445 International Dr., Orlando,* ☎ *407/345–9337. Visitors bureau open daily 8–8, all others 10–10.*

Next door to Mercado is **Gooding's Plaza International,** a shopping plaza that caters to tourists. The 24-hour Gooding's Supermarket has a food court, one-hour photo developing, and an aisle devoted to Disney merchandise. Also here are an electronics store, Spec's music, and several restaurants, including a branch of the popular Jungle Jim's. *8255 International Dr., Orlando,* ☎ *407/352–4215. Hours vary.*

U.S. 192

The **Old Town** shopping-entertainment complex features a 1928 Ferris wheel, a 1909 carousel, and more than 70 specialty shops re-creating a turn-of-the-century Florida village. You can buy a nickel Coke at the General Store or gourmet popcorn at the Kissimmee Popcorn Company, watch the taffy maker at Coffelt's Taffy & Chocolates or the candlemaker at Candlelite, and, at Black Market Minerals, pan for gemstones and sharks' teeth or buy agate, onyx, quartz, or even dinosaur fossils. Every Saturday night there is a parade of classic automobiles. *5770 Irlo Bronson Memorial Hwy. (east of I–4), Kissimmee,* ☎ *800/843–4202; in FL, 800/331–5093.* ☉ *Daily 10 AM–11 PM.*

OFF THE BEATEN TRACK

Flea Markets and Antiques

Flea World claims to be America's largest flea market under one roof. More than 1,600 booths lend credence to the claim, but so much abundance sometimes means only that good bargains are hiding under unusually large piles of junk. Unlike flea markets in some areas, this one sells only new merchandise—everything from car tires, Ginsu knives, and pet tarantulas to gourmet coffee, leather lingerie, and beaded evening gowns. It's also a great place to buy cheap Florida and Mickey Mouse T-shirts. A free newspaper, distributed at the parking lot entrance, contains a map and directory. Kids love Fun World next door, which offers two unusual miniature golf courses, arcade games, go-carts, bumper cars, bumper boats, kiddie rides, and batting cages. *Located 3 mi east of I–4 Exit 50 on Lake Mary Blvd., then 1 mi south on U.S. 17–92, Sanford,* ☎ *407/321–1792.* ☉ *Fri.–Sun. 8–5.*

Advertised as Florida's biggest gathering of antiques and collectible dealers, **Renninger's Antique Center** is actually one large building with 150 "shops" arranged in rows of booths, similar to a flea market. Mother Daughter and the Victorian Rose sell fine 19th-century American and European furniture, Lyons Antiques specializes in American country furniture, and Lismore Antiques carries a large selection of steamer trunks. The aptly named Grandma's Attic, which is typical of many of the shops, offers china, quilts, toys, lamps, furniture, and collectibles from the 1890s through the 1950s. At bimonthly weekend Antique Fairs, as many as 500 antiques and collectibles dealers set up outdoor booths on the adjacent wooded, hilly acres; Renninger's triannual Extravaganzas draw 1,000 dealers. At the adjacent Renninger's Farmers' and Flea Market, 500 merchants sell fresh produce, meats, baked goods, crafts, and new and used household items. The best plan is to spend the morning at Renninger's and then move on to downtown Mount Dora in time for lunch. *U.S. 441, Mount Dora,* ☎ *904/383–8393 (Thurs.–Sun.). Admission charge ($10 Fri., $5 Sat., $2 Sun.) for Extravaganzas only.* ☉ *Weekends 9–5, with Antiques Fairs 7 weekends a year 8–5; Extravaganzas once each in Nov., Jan., and Feb., Fri. 10–5, weekends 7–5; Farmers' and Flea Market weekends 8–5.*

Historic Shopping Towns

History buffs will especially enjoy shopping in the dozen or so quaint little shops in **Longwood,** a typical late-19th-century Florida town of towering live oak trees and brick-paved streets. The heart of the town, the Longwood Hotel, now an office building, went up in 1886 as a winter resort for sun-seeking northerners. The turreted Bradley-McIntyre House (1885), open for tours on the second and fourth Wednesdays of each month from 11 to 4, was a winter "cottage" in Victorian days. The shops, many of which are housed in historic homes, are scattered throughout this quiet neighborhood. The Apple Basket specializes in folk art, hand-thrown pottery, braided rugs, country furnishings, and hand-blown glass ornaments at holiday time. The Enchanted Cottage stocks country and Victorian furniture. Legible Leftovers is Central Florida's biggest second-hand book store. The Culinary Cottage sells wonderful gourmet foods, decorative accessories, and rubber stamps. In the Browser's Barn you can find antiques and collectibles. Candles, Etc. features not only its namesakes but also cards, incense, potpourri, oils, and sealing wax. Have breakfast, lunch, or afternoon tea in Elmira's Pantry, a charming, old-fashioned tearoom. *2½ mi east of I–4 Exit 49 on Rte. 434, then north on Rte. 427 to first traffic light (Church Ave.), then left. Most shops open Mon.–Sat. 10–5.*

If you love antiques or if you're just tired of amusement parks, treat yourself to a day in **Mount Dora** (*see* also Tour 2 *in* Chapter 4, Away from the Theme Parks). Founded by homesteaders in 1874, this charming little town has 19th-century stores and houses tucked into rolling hills that overlook Lake Dora. There are dozens of crafts shops, boutiques, galleries, and antiques shops here. Schwab Antiques offers furniture, glass, china, silver, and clocks. Country Pine Newtiques has an extensive selection of Tom Clark gnomes, David Winter cottages, and other collectibles. The Art and Antique Union is a 16-dealer minimall. Arrive in time for lunch at Eduardo's Mexican & American Cantina or Windsor Rose Tea Room; stay for dinner at the Park Bench Restaurant, the Gables, or the Beauclaire Dining Room in historic Lakeside Inn, a famous turn-of-the-century resort that was later a favorite vacation spot of President and Mrs. Calvin Coolidge. *West off U.S. 441 on either Old U.S. 441 or Rte. 44B, Chamber of Commerce* ☎ *904/383–2165.*

Moviegoers may recognize **Sanford's** historic First Street, with buildings that date from the 1880s to the 1920s, as the place where Macaulay Culkin and Anna Chlumsky pedaled their bicycles in the movie *My Girl.* This sleepy town on the shores of Lake Monroe is sprinkled with crafts and antiques shops. I Remember That sells cut glass and Flow Blue china. The Country Courtyard offers quilting classes and supplies. Antiques and collectibles stock the Antique Station and Delightful Finds. The Cranberry House features handmade country and Victorian gifts. The First Street Gallery displays the work of some of Florida's best professional artists. The place to lunch is Soup to Nuts, a delightful little restaurant with a Vie de France bakery inside. Combine your shopping with a visit to the nearby Central Florida Zoological Park (*see* The Natural World *in* Chapter 4, Away from the Theme Parks) or a St. Johns River cruise (*see* Action! *in* Chapter 6, Sports and the Outdoors). *East on Rte. 46 off I–4 Exit 51. Most shops open Mon.–Sat. 10–5.*

Malls and Department Stores

With its renovation in 1989 and the addition of a food court in 1990, the **Altamonte Mall** has kept pace with and maybe even surpassed the others in the area. Sears, Gayfers, Burdines, and JC Penney department stores anchor the two-level property; its 165 specialty shops include branches of such chain stores as J. Riggings, Victoria's Secret, Foot Locker, Kay Bee Toys, B. Dalton, and Limited Express. To buy something unusual, try the San Francisco Music Box Company or, if you're really ready to splurge, the Wentworth Gallery, which has a fine selection of original art from around the world. Unlike the one-level malls in the area, this one has a light, airy, and spacious feeling. The many benches, central fountain, and towering palm trees invite you to relax. The neighboring **Renaissance Center** includes eight theaters, Byrons, Linens & Things, and Bookstop. *451 Altamonte Ave. (½ mi east of I–4 on Rte. 436), Altamonte Springs,* ☎ *407/830–4400.* ☉ *Mon.–Sat. 10–9, Sun. noon–5:30.*

6 Sports and the Outdoors

ACTION!

SPORTS: It's a word that's easy to associate with Orlando. When it comes to athletics, Orlando has more stature than many other cities its size. The Orlando Magic are big-time, and true baseball fans love the minor-league action. Local residents, who may visit the theme parks only when their great-aunt's in-laws are in town, fill the tennis courts and golf courses (there are some 60 in a 30-mile radius, staffed by nearly three dozen PGA pros). Anglers have their own place in the Orlando sun as well—on any of dozens of small lakes. And boating is big, both on these lakes and on backcountry rivers fed by clear, sweet springs.

Bicycling

At WDW

The most scenic bike riding in Orlando is on Walt Disney World property, along roads that take you past forests, lakes, golf courses, and Disney's wooded resort villas and campgrounds. Bikes are available for rent at **Caribbean Beach Resort** (☎ 407/934–2850) and **Fort Wilderness Bike Barn** (☎ 407/824–2742), and **Walt Disney World Village Resort** (☎ 407/827–6905) will rent you a bike for $3 an hour or $8 a day. Theoretically, bike rentals are only for those lodging on WDW property; in practice, rental outfits usually check IDs only in busy seasons. However, bikes must be used only in the area in which you rent them.

Elsewhere

Despite the presence of two large schools—the University of Central Florida and Rollins College—where you would expect to find large numbers of enthusiastic bicyclists, the Orlando area doesn't offer a lot in the way of biking opportunities. It's illegal to ride bikes on Orlando sidewalks (and the police discourage those who do), and bike trails are few and far between. Moreover, local motorists are often not particularly accommodating when it comes to sharing the road with two-wheeled traffic. There are some scenic routes, however.

The area near Rollins College, in Winter Park, offers views of lakes, tree-lined streets, and the homes of much of the area's old money. Most riders prefer to go west of town to the Clermont–Lake County area. Since it's out in the boonies, there isn't much traffic to worry about. There are lots of orange groves and some hills.

Florida Backroads, by Robert Howard ($14.95 in bookstores), contains detailed descriptions of biking areas, plus maps with mileage markers and routes for 40 excursions.

Fishing

Central Florida is covered with freshwater lakes and rivers teeming with all kinds of fish, especially largemouth black bass, but also perch, catfish, sunfish, and pike.

Licenses

To fish in most Florida waters (but not at Walt Disney World), anglers over 16 need a fishing license, available at bait-and-tackle shops, fishing camps, most sporting-goods stores, and Walmarts and Kmarts. Some of these locations may not sell saltwater licenses, or they may serve non-Florida residents only; call ahead to be on the safe side. The cost is $16.50

for seven days and $31.50 for one year (freshwater); $7 for three days, $17 for seven days, and $32 for one year (saltwater).

At WDW

Two-hour fishing trips on regularly stocked Bay Lake departing from **Fort Wilderness, Contemporary, Polynesian,** and **Grand Floridian Resort marinas** include boat, equipment, coffee and pastries, and guide for up to five anglers. These organized trips are the only way you're allowed to fish on the lake. Reservations are required. *Bay Lake Fishing Trips,* ☎ 407/824–2621. *Fee: $125. Trips daily at 8, 11:30, and 3.*

Bass specialists will head for the two-hour fishing expeditions (up to five anglers) that depart from the **Disney Village Marketplace marina.** *Captain Jack's Guided Bass Tours,* ☎ 407/828–2461. *Fee: $120. Trips daily at 7, 9:45, and noon.*

There's fishing off the dock at the **Ol' Man Island Fishing Hole.** Catch and release is encouraged, but you can have your fish packed in ice to take home. You'll have to clean them yourself, though. *Dixie Landings,* ☎ 407/934–5409. *Cane poles and bait: $3 per hr per person, $10 per hr for family of up to 6; no fee to use dock.* ☉ *Daily 7–4.*

A two-hour fishing trip down the Sasagoula River at **Dixie Landings** includes guide, rod, bait, and soft drinks. Reservations must be made in advance. *Dixie Landings,* ☎ 407/934–5409. *$35 per person. Trips daily 8 AM.*

Fishing without a guide is permitted in the canals in **Disney Village** (Dixie Landings, Port Orleans resorts) and at **Fort Wilderness** resort and campground. Poles and tackle can be rented from one of the "trading post" grocery stores located on the Fort Wilderness campground.

Elsewhere

Top central Florida waters include **Lake Kissimmee,** the **Butler** and **Conway chains of lakes,** and **Lake Tohopekaliga** (don't bother to pronounce it—it's "Lake Toho" to locals). Your best chance for trophy fish is between November and April on Toho or Kissimmee; for good creels, the best producer is usually the Butler area, whose additional advantage is its scenery—lots of live oaks and cypresses, plus the occasional osprey or bald eagle. Toho and Kissimmee are also good for largemouth bass and crappie. The Butler chain yields largemouth, some pickerel, and the occasional huge catfish. A variety of services are available, from equipment and boat rental to full-day trips with guides and guarantees.

FISHING CAMPS

There are a number of excellent fishing camps in the area in the form of lakeside campgrounds that draw a more outdoorsy crowd than you find elsewhere in the area.

East Lake Fish Camp, on East Lake Tohopekaliga, has a restaurant and country store, sells live bait and propane, and rents boats. You can also take a ride on an airboat. It has 283 RV sites, 40 tent sites, and 24 cabins. Try to make reservations for the cabins at least two weeks in advance during the winter and spring. *3705 Big Bass Rd., Kissimmee,* ☎ 407/348–2040. *RV sites $16 (2 people), tent sites $12, cabins $45 (2 people, $5 each additional).*

Red's Fish Camp, on West Lake Tohopekaliga, has 100 RV sites. Most of the full hookups are booked year-round, but electrical and water hookups are usually available, as are live bait, food, and drinks. *4715 Kissimmee Park Rd., St. Cloud,* ☎ 407/892–8795. *RV sites $12.*

Richardson's Fish Camp, also on West Lake Tohopekaliga, has 9 cabins with kitchenettes, 16 RV sites, 12 tent sites, boat slips, and a bait shop. *1550 Scotty's Rd., Kissimmee,* ☎ *407/846–6540. RV sites $19.50; tent sites $15; cabins $36 for 1 bedroom, $55 for 2 bedrooms, and $65 for 3 bedrooms.*

GUIDES

Guides fish out of each of the above fishing camps, and you can usually make arrangements to hire them through the camp office. Rates vary, but $125 for a half day and $175 (prices quoted are for two people) for a full day are good rules of thumb. Many area guides are part-timers who fish on weekends or take a day off from their full-time job to guide; the following are full-timers, who hit a variety of local lakes, including those listed above and private lakes.

Bass Bustin' Guide (BBG), in business 15 years, provides boat, tackle, transportation, and ice and soft drinks for bass fishing on local lakes—and guarantees fish! *5935 Swoffield Dr., Orlando,* ☎ *407/281–0845. ½ day from $125, full day from $175; extra person: $25 adult.*

Bass Challenger Guide (BCG) takes you out in boats equipped with tackle and drinks. Transportation can be arranged between fishing spots and local hotels. Bass is the only quarry, and they guarantee "No bass, no pay!" *Box 679155, Orlando,* ☎ *407/273–8045 or 800/241–5314. ½ day from $150, full day from $200.*

Cutting Loose Expeditions goes after bass, like the BBG and BCG (*see above*), but also arranges saltwater expeditions to the Indian River flats to light-tackle-cast for redfish, sea trout, tarpon, and snook. They'll arrange deep-sea charters out of Port Canaveral (*see* Chapter 10, The Cocoa Beach Area). All trips can include everything but food. They'll even pick you up at the hotel and take you to the fishing hole. *Box 447, Winter Park,* ☎ *407/629–4700 or 800/533–4746. ½ day from $175, full day $200–$300, $500–$600 offshore.*

Golf

With sunny weather practically year-round, Florida is a golfer's haven, offering more golf courses than any other state. Most of Florida is extremely flat, but many of the courses listed here have been sculpted by their designers to create rolling hills that make them more challenging. Many resort hotels let nonguests use their golf facilities. Some country clubs are affiliated with particular hotels, and their guests can play at preferred rates. If you're staying near a course you'd like to use, call and inquire.

Golfpac (Box 162366, Altamonte Springs 32701, ☎ 407/260–2288 or 800/327–0878) packages golf vacations and prearranges tee times at more than 40 courses around Orlando. Rates vary based on hotel and course, and 60–90 days' advance notice is recommended to set up a vacation.

What follows is a list of the best courses open to the public. All have dress codes, so call to find out the specifics at each, and be sure to reserve tee times in advance. The yardages listed are those from the blue tees. Since greens fees usually vary by season, the highest and lowest figures are provided, and all include mandatory cart rental.

At WDW

Where else would you find a sand trap shaped like the head of a well-known mouse? Walt Disney World has five championship courses—all on the PGA Tour route. Eagle Pines and Osprey Ridge are the newcomers, flanking the Bonnet Creek Golf Club just north of Fort

Wilderness. They join WDW's original courses, the Palm and the Magnolia, which flank the Shades of Green Resort, to the west, and the Lake Buena Vista course, near Disney Village Marketplace.

GREENS FEES

The three older Disney courses have the same fees and discount policies: Guests at WDW resorts pay $85; all others pay $95 regardless of season. Prices at Eagle Pines and Osprey Ridge go up to $100 and $115 from January through April. The twilight discount rate is $45 for everyone; this rate goes into effect at 2 PM during the winter and peak seasons and at 3 PM during the summer and off-seasons.

TEE TIMES AND RESERVATIONS

Tee times are available from 7:30 AM until dark on weekdays and from 7 until dark on weekends. You can book them up to 30 days in advance if you're staying at a WDW-owned hotel, 7 days ahead otherwise. For tee times and private lessons at any course, call 407/824–2270.

Eagle Pines, one of two new courses, was designed by golf-course architect Pete Dye. Greens are small and undulating, and fairways are lined with pines and punctuated by bunkers that broaden the challenge. *Golf View Dr., at Bonnet View Golf Club, north of Fort Wilderness. 6,722 yds. Par: 72. USGA: 72.3. 18 holes. Facilities: restaurant, private lessons, club and shoe rental, lockers, driving range, putting green.*

The **Lake Buena Vista** course winds among Disney Village Resort town houses and villas; greens are narrow—and hitting straight is important, since errant balls risk ending up in someone's bedroom. *Lake Buena Vista. 6,829 yds. Par: 72. USGA: 72.7. 18 holes. Facilities: restaurant, private lessons, club and shoe rental, lockers, driving range, putting green.*

The **Magnolia,** played by the pros in the Walt Disney World Golf Classic, is long but forgiving, with extra-wide fairways. *At Shades of Green. 7,190 yds. Par: 72. USGA: 73.9. 18 holes. Facilities: restaurant, private and small-group lessons, club and shoe rental, lockers, driving range, putting green.*

In designing **Osprey Ridge,** Tom Fazio leavened the challenge of the course with a relaxing tour into some of the still-forested, as yet undeveloped portions of the huge WDW acreage. Tees and greens as much as 20 feet above the fairways keep competitive players from getting too comfortable, however. Osprey Ridge opened in 1992 along with Eagle Pines. *Golf View Dr., Bonnet Creek Golf Club. 7,101 yds. Par: 72. USGA: 73.9. 18 holes. Facilities: restaurant, private lessons, club and shoe rental, lockers, driving range, putting green.*

The Palm, one of WDW's original courses, has been confounding the pros as part of the annual Walt Disney World Golf Classic for years. It's not as long as the Magnolia, or as wide, and there are more trees. And don't go near the water! *At Shades of Green Resort. 6,957 yds. Par: 72. USGA: 73. 18 holes. Facilities: restaurant, private and small-group lessons, club and shoe rental, lockers, driving range, putting green.*

Elsewhere

Greens fees at the following non-Disney courses fluctuate with the season. A twilight discount applies after 2 PM in busy seasons and after 3 PM during the rest of the year; the discount is usually half off the normal rate.

Cypress Creek Country Club is a demanding course with 16 water holes and lots of trees. *5353 Vineland Rd., Orlando, ☎ 407/351–2187. 6,955 yds. Par: 72. USGA: 73.6. 18 holes. Greens fees: $25–$38. Spe-*

cial policies: tee times 7 days in advance. Facilities: restaurant, private lessons, club rental.

Falcon's Fire Golf Club, designed by golf-architect Rees Jones, has one of Orlando's newest courses. Its strategically placed fairway bunkers demand accuracy off the tee. *3200 Seralago Blvd., Kissimmee, ☎ 407/ 397–2777. 6,473 yds. Par: 72. USGA: 72.5. 18 holes. Greens fees: $55– $72. Special policies: tee times 7 days in advance. Facilities: restaurant, lounge, private and group lessons, club rental, lockers, driving range, putting green.*

Located about 45 minutes from Orlando, **Grenelefe Golf and Tennis Resort** has three 18-hole courses amid gentle hills. Length is the key here. The West Course, designed by Robert Trent Jones Sr., plays to 7,325 yards from the championship tees. An absence of water hazards (there are just two ponds) softens the course somewhat. The East Course is very tight, with small greens and lots of changes in elevation. Designed by Ed Seay, it requires accuracy. The South, designed by Ron Garl and Andy Beane, has plenty of sand and water but wider fairways and larger greens. *3200 Rte. 546, Haines City, ☎ 813/422– 7511 or 800/237–9549. West Course 7,325 yds, par 72, USGA 75; East Course 6,802 yds, par 72, USGA 72.5; South Course 6,869 yds, par 71, USGA 72.6. 54 holes. Greens fees: $39–$110. Special policies: tee times 3 days in advance, but courses often closed to public at busiest time of year (Jan.–Apr.). Facilities: 3 restaurants, 2 lounges, snack bar, private lessons, club and shoe rental.*

The Lloyd Clifton–designed **Hunter's Creek Golf Course** has large greens and 14 water holes. *14401 Sports Club Way, Orlando, ☎ 407/ 240–4653. 7,438 yds. Par: 72. USGA: 72.8. 18 holes. Greens fees: $35– $55. Special policies: tee times 3 days in advance. Facilities: snack bar, private lessons, club rental.*

Marriott's Orlando World Center has a Joe Lee–designed course with 14 water holes and lots of sand. *1 World Center Dr., Orlando, ☎ 407/ 238–8660. 6,265 yds. Par: 71. USGA: 69.8. 18 holes. Greens fees: $60– $95. Special policies: tee times 7 days in advance for public, 90 days in advance for World Center guests. Facilities: 4 restaurants, sports bar, private and group lessons, club and shoe rental.*

MetroWest Country Club has a rolling Robert Trent Jones Sr. course, with few trees but lots of sand. *2100 S. Hiawassee Rd., Orlando, ☎ 407/299–1099. 6,500 yds. Par: 72. USGA: 70.3. 18 holes. Greens fees: $42–$65. Special policies: tee times 7 days in advance. Facilities: restaurant, private and group lessons, club rental.*

About five minutes from Walt Disney World's main entrance is **Orange Lake Country Club.** It has three 9-hole courses, all very similar. Distances aren't long, but fairways are very narrow, and there's a great deal of water, making the course very difficult. *8505 W. Irlo Bronson Memorial Hwy., Kissimmee, ☎ 407/239–0000 or 800/877–6522. Lake/Orange: 6,551 yds, par 72, USGA 72.2. Orange/Cypress: 6,680 yds, par 72, USGA 72.6. Cypress/Lake: 6,535 yds, par 72, USGA 72.3. Greens fees: $30–$65. Special policies: tee times 2 days in advance. Facilities: restaurant, cafeteria, pizzeria, driving range, putting green, private and group lessons, club rental.*

About 18 miles southeast of Disney World is the **Poinciana Golf & Racquet Resort**—69 bunkers and 17 water holes nestled in a cypress forest. *500 E. Cypress Pkwy., Poinciana (near Kissimmee), ☎ 407/933–5300 or 800/331–7743. 6,400 yds. Par: 72. USGA: 70.8. 18 holes. Greens* *fees: $30–$40. Special policies: tee times 7 days in advance, discount coupons accepted off season. Facilities: restaurant, lounge, driving range, putting green, private and group lessons, club rental.*

Timacuan Golf and Country Club has a two-part course designed by Ron Garl. Part I, the front nine, is open, with lots of sand; part II, the back nine, is heavily wooded. *550 Timacuan Blvd., Lake Mary,* ☎ *407/321–0010. 6,582 yds. Par: 72. USGA: 71.5. 18 holes. Greens fees: $40–$85. Special policies: tee times 3 days in advance. Facilities: restaurant, snack bar, club rental, driving range, putting green.*

Health Clubs

At WDW

Although most of the Walt Disney World health clubs accept only guests at Walt Disney World hotels (and some accept only guests of that particular hotel), some clubs have been known to stretch the rules—a fact worth noting if you're desperate for your workout.

Body by Jake, at the Dolphin, has step and regular aerobics classes, weights, personal trainers, treadmills, and stationary bikes. *The Dolphin,* ☎ *407/934–4264. Fee: $8 per day; $16 individual or $26 family for length of stay (hotel guests only).* ☉ *Daily 6 AM–9 PM. Guests at other hotels admitted only by the day; must pay cash. Sauna.*

The **Olympiad Health Club** has Nautilus and hand weights, stairclimbers, cross-country ski machines, and treadmills, plus a tanning bed and booth. Massages are offered at the club or in your room. *Contemporary Resort,* ☎ *407/824–3410. Fee: $8.48 per day; massage: $37 per ½ hr, $55 per hr, $70–$95 per hr in room.* ☉ *Daily 6:30 AM–8 PM. Open to all Disney guests. Sauna.*

The glittering **St. John's Health Spa** has Nautilus, cardiovascular equipment, treadmills, stairclimbers, rowing machines, and a sauna. Grand Floridian, ☎ *407/824–3000, ext. 2433. Fee: $5.30 per day; $10.60 per individual or $15 per family for length of stay; massage $37 per ½ hr, $55 per hr.* ☉ *Daily 6 AM–10 PM. Sauna.*

Exercise machines, a sauna, spa, and steam room are available at the **Ship Shape Health Club.** *Yacht and Beach Club,* ☎ *407/934–3256. Fee: $7 per day, $10 per individual or $20 per family for length of stay; massage $37 per ½ hr, $55 per hr, $70 per hr in room.* ☉ *Daily 6:30 AM–9:30 PM. Open only to Disney guests.*

Elsewhere

To find out what's hot when you visit, the best bet is to ask at your hotel, because clubs outside WDW come and go. And don't forget about the local YMCAs, longtime local favorites. To find the one nearest where you're staying, phone the Metropolitan YMCA office (☎ 407/896–9220). Most accept guests on a single-visit basis, for $5–$10 a day, and you don't have to be a Y member.

The **Downtown YMCA** has Nautilus, Cybex machines, free weights, racquetball, an Olympic-size pool, two gyms, and aerobics classes. It's an older property, but the weight room facilities were just revamped. *433 N. Mills Ave., Orlando,* ☎ *407/896–6901. Fee: $7 per day, $3.50 to YMCA members from outside Orlando.* ☉ *Weekdays 5 AM–9:30 PM, Sat. 8–6:30, Sun. 1–5.*

The **International Drive YMCA** is definitely more posh. It has Nautilus, free weights, racquetball, two swimming pools (one Olympic-size), and a diving well. Members can call ahead to reserve racquetball courts.

8422 International Dr., Orlando, ☎ 407/363–1911. Fee: $8 per day, $4 to YMCA members from outside Orlando, $20 per week. ☉ Weekdays 6 AM–9 PM, Wed. and Thurs. until 10, Sat. 8–4.

Horseback Riding

At WDW

Fort Wilderness Campground offers tame trail rides through backwoods. Children must be over nine, and adults must be under 250 pounds. *Fort Wilderness Campground Resort, ☎ 407/824–2832. Open to the public. Trail rides: $17 for 45 min. Rides daily at 9, 10:30, noon, and 2.*

Elsewhere

Private lessons in hunter, jumper, and dressage are given at **Grand Cypress Equestrian Center.** Supervised novice and advanced group trail rides are also available. Call at least a week ahead for reservations in winter and spring. *Grand Cypress Resort, 1 Equestrian Dr., ☎ 407/239–4608. Trail rides: $30 per hr for novice, $45 per hr for advanced; private lessons: $45 per ½ hr, $75 per hr. ☉ Daily 8–5.*

Poinciana Riding Stables offers basic and longer, more advanced nature trail tours along old logging trails near Kissimmee. Pony rides are also available, and the stable area has picnic tables, farm animals you can pet, and a pond to fish in. Reservations a day in advance are recommended for the popular advanced trails. *3705 Poinciana Blvd., Kissimmee, ☎ 407/847–4343. Trail rides: $29.95 for basic, $39.95 for advanced; pony rides: $4 for 10 min. ☉ Daily 9–5.*

Ice Skating

Orlando sees frost only about once every other year, so ice-skating fever is not taking the city by storm. There are a couple of options, however, if you feel the urge to chill out.

Orlando Ice Skating Palace is either grungy or a look into pre-Disney Orlando, depending on your point of view. But if you are homesick for a winter chill, this should do the trick. *3123 W. Colonial Dr., Parkwood Shopping Plaza, Orlando, ☎ 407/299–5440. ☛ Weekdays and Sun. $5.95 adults, $4.95 children under 12; skate rental $1.50. ☉ In summer Mon.–Sat. 12:30–3:30, 4–7, 7:30–10:30, also Sat. 11 PM–1 AM, Sun. 2–5, 7:30–10:30; in winter closed Mon.–Tues., reduced hours Wed.–Sun.*

Rock on Ice is definitely spiffier but seems touristy. *Dowdy Pavilion, 7500 Canada Ave., Orlando, ☎ 407/363–7465. Skate rental $1.50. Admission prices and open-skating times vary; call for more information.*

Jogging

At WDW

Walt Disney World has several scenic jogging trails. Pick up jogging maps at any Disney resort. **Fort Wilderness Campground** (☎ 407/824–2900) has a 2.3-mile jogging course with plenty of fresh air and woods as well as numerous exercise stations along the way. Early in the morning all the roads are fairly uncrowded, however, and make for good running. The roads that wiggle through **Disney's Village Resorts** are pleasant, as are the cart paths on the **golf courses.**

Elsewhere

Turkey Lake Park (3401 S. Hiawassee Rd., Orlando, ☎ 407/299–5581; park entry: $2 adults, $1 children under 12), not far from Disney, has a 3-mile biking trail that's also popular with joggers. Several wooded hiking trails also make for a good run. The park closes at 5.

In Winter Park, around **Rollins College,** you can jog along the shady streets and around the lakes, inhaling the aroma of old money. The **Orlando Runners Club** meets in the area every Sunday morning at 7 AM for 3-, 6-, and 12-mile jaunts; for details, call the Track Shack (1322 N. Mills Ave., Orlando, ☎ 407/898–1313; open weekdays 10–7, Sat. 10–5).

Tennis

At WDW

You can play tennis at any number of Disney hotels, and you'll find the courts a pleasant respite from the milling throngs in the parks. All have lights and are open from 7 AM to 10 PM, and most have lockers and rental racquets ($4–$5 an hour). There seems to be a long-term plan to move from hard courts to clay, and the Contemporary has already converted. All courts are open to all players, but court staff can opt to turn away nonguests when things get busy. (That doesn't often happen.)

The **Contemporary Resort** is the center of Disney's tennis program, with its sprawl of six clay courts. It has three backboards and an automatic ball machine. ☎ 407/824–3578. *Courts $12 per hr, $40 for length of stay. Court reservations available (up to 24 hrs in advance). Clinics with video replay ($35), private lessons ($37–$45 per hr, $20–$25 per ½ hr), video reviews $10 extra. Arrange-a-game services, ball machines, racquet rental $5.*

The **Dolphin** and **Swan** share eight asphalt courts. ☎ 407/934–4396. *Courts $12 per hr. Court reservations available to all (up to 24 hrs in advance). Clinics with video replay ($35), private lessons ($45 per hr, $25 per ½ hr), video reviews $10. Arrange-a-game services, ball machines, racquet rental $5.*

Fort Wilderness Campground has two courts out in the middle of a field; they're popular with youngsters. If you hate players who are too free about letting their balls stray across their neighbors' court, this is not the place for you. ☎ 407/824–2900. *No charge for courts. No court reservations. No instruction.*

At the **Grand Floridian,** the two clay courts attract a somewhat more tennis-minded crowd. ☎ 407/824–2438. *Courts $12 per hr. Court reservations (up to 24 hrs in advance). Private lessons $35 per hr.*

The **Yacht and Beach Club** has two blacktop courts. ☎ 407/934–3256. *No charge. Court reservations available (up to 24 hrs in advance). No instruction.*

Elsewhere

Lake Cane Tennis Center has 13 lighted hard courts. Four pros provide private and group lessons. *5108 Turkey Lake Rd., Orlando, ☎ 407/352–4913. Courts $2 per hr weekdays, $4 per hr weekends. Lessons $30 per hr, $15 per ½ hr.* ☉ *8 AM–10 PM.*

In addition to its golf courses, **Orange Lake Country Club** has 15 all-weather hard tennis courts, 9 of them lighted. It is five minutes from Walt Disney World's main entrance. *8505 W. Irlo Bronson Memorial Hwy., Kissimmee, ☎ 407/239–0000. Courts free for guests, $4 per hr for nonguests. Court reservations unnecessary. Private lessons $30 per hr. Clinics $10 per ½ hr. Racquet rentals $2.* ☉ *Daily dawn–11 PM for guests and 8–5 for nonguests.*

Orlando Tennis Center offers 16 lighted tennis courts (9 HarTru and 7 asphalt), 2 racquetball courts, and three tennis pros. *649 W. Livingston St., Orlando,* ☎ *407/246–2162. Courts $5.80 for 1½ hr on HarTru, $3.68 for 1½ hr on asphalt; raquetball $2.12 per hr, no ½-hr rates. Court reservations unnecessary. Private lessons: $30 per hr, group lessons $5.* ☼ *Weekdays 8 AM–10 PM, weekends and holidays 8–3.*

Red Bug Park has 16 lighted Plexipave courts and 8 outdoor four-wall racquetball courts. *3600 Red Bug Lake Rd., Casselberry,* ☎ *407/695–7113. Tennis courts $2 per hr before 5, $4 per hr after; racquetball $4 per hr. Court reservations available (up to 24 hrs in advance). Private lessons $34 per hr.* ☼ *Daily 8 AM–10 PM.*

Sanlando Park has 25 lighted Plexipave courts and 8 covered, fan-cooled racquetball courts. *401 W. Highland St., Altamonte Springs,* ☎ *407/869–5966. Tennis courts $2 per hr before 5, $4 per hr after on weekdays; racquetball $4 per hr. Court reservations available (up to 24 hrs in advance). Private lessons $32 per hr, $16 per ½ hr.* ☼ *Daily 8 AM–10 PM.*

Water Sports

At WDW

Boating is big at Disney, with the largest fleet of for-rent pleasure craft in the nation. There are marinas at the Caribbean Beach Resort, Contemporary Resort, Disney Village Marketplace, Fort Wilderness Campground, Grand Floridian, Polynesian Village, and Yacht and Beach Club, where you can rent Sunfish, toobies, catamarans, motor-powered pontoon boats, pedal boats, and tiny two-passenger Water Sprites—a hit with kids—for use on **Bay Lake** and the adjoining **Seven Seas Lagoon, Club Lake, Lake Buena Vista,** or **Buena Vista Lagoon.** Most rent Water Sprites; otherwise, each hotel has its own rental roster, and you're sure to find something of interest. The Polynesian Village marina rents outrigger canoes. Fort Wilderness rents canoes for paddling along the placid canals in the area. And you can sail and water-ski on Bay Lake and the Seven Seas Lagoon; stop at the Fort Wilderness, Contemporary, Polynesian, or Grand Floridian Resort marinas.

Elsewhere

Orange Lake, a private lake at the Orange Lake Country Club next to Walt Disney World, has all types of boating—in rowboats, paddleboats, canoes, wave runners, Jet Skis, and jet boats. You can even sign up for waterskiing school. *Rentals at Orange Lake Water Sports, 8505 W. Irlo Bronson Memorial Hwy., Kissimmee,* ☎ *407/239–4444. Fees: $5 per ½ hr for canoes, $35 per ½ hr for Waverunners, $60 per ½ hr for a power boat; Jet Skis $25 per ½ hr, $45 per hr, including instruction; waterskiing $35 per ½ hr, $60 per hr.* ☼ *Daily 10–6.*

There's a ski ramp and slalom course on 140-acre **Sand Lake,** a fairly quiet scenic expanse of water rimmed mainly by villas. Jet Skis keep swimmers firmly in the restricted swimming area. *Rentals available at Splash 'n' Ski, 10000 Turkey Lake Rd. (west off I-4 Exit 29, on Sand Lake Rd.), Orlando,* ☎ *407/352–1494. Jet Skis $35 per ½ hr, sailboards $25 per ½ day, waterskiing $45 per ½ hr.* ☼ *Mon.–Sat. 10–5:30.*

A boat ride on **Shingle Creek** provides views of giant cypress trees dripping with Spanish moss. You can get around by airboat or rent a quiet electric swampboat or a canoe. *Airboat Rentals, 4266 Irlo Bronson Memorial Hwy., Kissimmee,* ☎ *407/847–3672. Airboats $22 per hr, swampboats and electric boats $16 per hr, canoes $5 per hr.* ☼ *Daily 9:30–5.*

The **St. Johns River** winds through pine and cypress woods and past pastures where cows graze placidly, skirting the occasional housing development. There's good bird- and wildlife-watching; herons, ibis, storks, and sometimes bald eagles can be spotted, along with alligators and manatees. It's a favored local boating spot, for everything from a day of waterskiing to a weeklong trip in a houseboat. Rentals are available in DeLand (west of I–4 Exit 56 via U.S. 44). *Holly Bluff, 2280 Hontoon Rd., DeLand, ☎ 904/822–9992 or 800/237–5105: Pontoon boats $60 for 4 hrs, $100 per day ($125 on weekends); 44-ft houseboats $375 for 1 day, $700 for 2 days, $1,100 for a week; rates lower Dec.–Feb. Hontoon Landing Marina, 2317 River Ridge Rd., DeLand, ☎ 904/734–2474; in FL, 800/248–2474: Luxury houseboats $400–$1,395 for 1 day, $1,095–$2,495 for a week; Jet Skis $30 per hr, $150 per day; ski boats and pontoons $20 per hr, $100 per day; prices lower Dec.–Mar.*

Another great waterway for nature lovers is the **Wekiva River,** which runs through 6,397-acre Wekiva State Park into the St. Johns River. Bordered by cypress marshlands, its clear, spring-fed waters showcase a rich array of Florida wildlife, including otters, raccoons, alligators, bobcats, deer, turtles, and numerous birds. Canoes and battery-powered motorboats, whose quiet engines don't disturb the wildlife, are the best way to get around; they're available for rent. *Katie's Wekiva River Landing and Campground, 190 Katie's Cove, Sanford, ☎ 407/628–1482. Canoes $5 per hr (2-hr minimum), $1 each additional hr, $18 per day. Group trips, campsites, 4 cabins, picnic tables.*

Alexander Creek and **Juniper Creek,** in Ocala National Forest just north of the greater Orlando area, also offer wonderful wilderness canoeing, with abundant wildlife and moss-draped oaks and bald cypresses canopying the clean, clear waters. Some of these runs are quite rough—lots of ducking under brush and maneuvering around trees. *Alexander Springs Canoe Rental, County Rd. 445, ☎ 904/669–3522; canoes $10–$22 with $20 deposit and ID; open daily 8–dark. Juniper Springs Canoe Rental, State Rd. 40, ☎ 904/625–2808; canoes $20–$25 with $20 deposit and ID.*

FROM THE SIDELINES

Not everything in Orlando is wholesome, Disney-style family fun. Wagering a wad of cash at the fronton or the dog track is guaranteed to wipe the refrain from "It's a Small World" right out of your head. And even if you bet and lose steadily, you won't necessarily spend more than you would at most of the attractions. In addition, there are teams in various sports and leagues that play their regular seasons in and around Orlando, as well as major-league baseball clubs that make their spring-training homes in the area.

Baseball

Watching a minor-league or spring-training game in a small ballpark can take you back to a time when going to a game didn't mean bringing binoculars or watching the big screen to see what was happening. Minor-league teams play from April to September and spring training lasts only a few weeks in March and early April, but it can be a thrill to watch stars up close while you, and they, enjoy a spring break before getting back to work. Tickets to the minors usually run $3–$6; spring training seats cost $8–$10.

Minor Leagues

The **Orlando Cubs** are Chicago's Class AA Southern League affiliate. They play 69 home games at Tinker Field. *287 S. Tampa Ave. (west off I–4 Colonial Ave. Exit), Orlando,* ☎ *407/872–7593.*

The **Kissimmee Cobras** are Houston's Class A team in the Florida State League and play at Osceola County Stadium. Arrive early because tickets are sold only at the stadium on a same-day, first-come basis. *1000 Bill Beck Blvd. (west of I–4 Exit 65), Kissimmee,* ☎ *407/933– 5500, or 407/933–2520 for spring-training tickets.*

Spring Training

Major-league baseball teams hold spring training all over Florida: in **Baseball City** (Kansas City Royals), **Bradenton** (Pittsburgh Pirates), **Clearwater** (Philadelphia Phillies), **Dunedin** (Toronto Blue Jays), **Fort Lauderdale** (New York Yankees), **Fort Myers** (Boston Red Sox and Minnesota Twins), **Kissimmee** (Houston Astros), **Lakeland** (Detroit Tigers), **Melbourne** (Florida Marlins), **Plant City** (Cincinnati Reds), **Port Charlotte** (Texas Rangers), **Port St. Lucie** (New York Mets), **St. Petersburg** (Baltimore Orioles and St. Louis Cardinals), **Sarasota** (Chicago White Sox), **Vero Beach** (Los Angeles Dodgers), **West Palm Beach** (Atlanta Braves and Montréal Expos), and **Winter Haven** (Cleveland Indians). For dates and more information, get a copy of the free *Florida Spring Training Guide,* published each year in early February by the Florida Sports Foundation (107 W. Gaines St., Tallahassee 32399, ☎ 904/488– 8347).

Basketball

The **Orlando Magic** joined the National Basketball Association in the 1989–90 season and play in the 15,077-seat Orlando Arena. Seven-foot-one center Shaquille O'Neal and teammates have since driven the city to new heights of hoop fanaticism. Tickets to the '94 season sold out in one day, and the current waiting period for season tickets is 10 years. Your best bet for seeing a game is probably a sports bar (*see* Chapter 9, After Dark). *Box 76, 600 W. Amelia St. (2 blocks west of I–4 at Amelia St. Exit), Orlando; TicketMaster* ☎ *407/839–3900, box office* ☎ *407/649–2255, season tickets* ☎ *407/896–2442.* ☛ *$17–$30.*

Dog Racing

Sanford Orlando Kennel Club has dog-racing and betting as well as South Florida horse-racing simulcasts and betting. *301 Dog Track Rd., Longwood,* ☎ *407/831–1600.* ☛ *$1.* ☉ *Nov.–May, Mon.–Sat. at 7:30 PM; matinees Mon., Wed., Sat. at 12:30 PM.*

Seminole Greyhound Park, a newer, larger, and prettier track, is your other option for wagering on greyhounds and simulcast horse-racing. *2000 Seminola Blvd., Casselberry,* ☎ *407/699–4510.* ☛ *$1 general, $2 clubhouse (children half price).* ☉ *May–Oct., Mon.–Sat. at 7:30 PM; matinees most recently Mon., Wed., Sat. at 12:30 PM.*

Football

The **Orlando Predators** play in the indoor Arena Football League, which differs from the National Football League in that teams have only eight players, each of whom holds both offensive and defensive positions. Games are held May to August at the Orlando Arena. *600 W. Amelia St., Orlando,* ☎ *407/648–4444 or 407/872–7362.* ☛ *$10–$23.*

Jai Alai

Orlando-Seminole Jai-Alai, about 20 minutes north of Orlando off I–4, offers south Florida horse-racing simulcasts and betting in addition to jai alai at the fronton. *6405 S. U.S. 17–92, Fern Park,* ☎ *407/331–9191.* ☛ *$1 general, $2 reserved seating.* ⊘ *Wed.–Sat. at 7:30* PM*; matinees Thurs. and Sat. at noon, Sun. 1* PM.

7 Dining

Updated by
Rowland
Stiteler

IT DOESN'T TAKE LONG to figure out Orlando's culinary landscape—simply stated, Beauty-and-the-Feast decor is often at least as important as the cooking. But serious foodies can take heart, as fabulous cuisine—from designer pizzas to newer-than-now *nouvelle classique*—is available throughout Walt Disney World and the surrounding area; it just takes a little pleasant homework to find it. A short spin down International Drive or U.S. 192 near Walt Disney World gives a first impression that every franchise restaurant company in America is represented here. If they can batter it, fry it, microwave it, torture it, and serve it with a side of fries, you'll find it in central Florida. But not all the franchises are mere burger barns. Far from it. National chains put their best foot forward here because their Orlando outpost is seen by millions of international visitors. The McDonald's on International Drive is the largest in the nation; the new Planet Hollywood is the biggest and most elaborate in the chain.

Restaurateurs build monuments here, and most of them try to offer good food. The result is a fiercely competitive dining market, which also brings out the best from the home-town eateries that predate Disney. Keep in mind that the dining choices here, like the entertainment choices, are far more than you can sample on any one trip.

Local Specialties

Grouper—fried, blackened, or broiled—is the closest thing central Florida has to a local dish. Most natives don't eat much alligator tail, but almost every fish restaurant offers it for the tourists—and it's fun to give it a try. Also worthy are some of the treats imported from the Florida Keys and billed as local fare. Try the stone crabs (in season, October through March), the small, tasty Keys lobsters, and conch chowder. Fresh hearts of palm, served in the more upscale restaurants, are also a treat. One tip on key lime pie: If it's green, especially fluorescent green, you've been had. Authentic key lime pie is yellow, even if the fruit isn't.

Dinner Shows

Dinner shows are popular and quite numerous in Orlando, although as a rule the meal won't be as memorable as the entertainment. Walt Disney World has several tableside extravaganzas, like the extremely popular Hoop-Dee-Doo Musical Revue at the Fort Wilderness Campground area. If you can't score a reservation for the Disney hoop-along, there are Arabian nights–, Wild West–, king-and-queen-, and medieval-theme shows, to name just a few. For our assessment and all the details, *see* Chapter 9, After Dark.

Dress

Because tourism is king here, casual dress is the rule, and very few restaurants require jackets or other dress-up attire for men. Unless an eating establishment is in the higher end of the price range, you'll be safe wearing anything that wouldn't get you thrown out of a Burger King. And if your child is the only one wearing a hat with Goofy ears, you probably made a wrong turn and ended up in Georgia.

Reservations

Reservations are always a good idea in a market where the phrase "bus drivers eat free" is emblazoned on the city's coat of arms. Without reservations, the entire Ecuadorian soccer team or the senior class from Platt City High School may arrive moments before you and keep you waiting a long, long time. Save that experience for your visit to the attractions.

For restaurants within Walt Disney World, reservations are especially easy to make, thanks to its central reservations lines, 407/WDW–DINE and 407/560–7277. In addition, the WorldKey Information Center can be used for the very popular restaurants of Epcot Center (for information, see the Epcot Center section below). Remember that while Orlando is not a big town, getting to places is frequently complicated, so always call for directions.

Price

CATEGORY	COST*
$$$$	over $40
$$$	$30–$40
$$	$20–$30
$	under $20

per person, excluding drinks, service, and 6% sales tax

IN AND AROUND WALT DISNEY WORLD

Eateries abound in and near Walt Disney World. On the tourism warp drive called U.S. 192, between Walt Disney World and Kissimmee, most of the restaurants are either chains or large, overrated, and overpriced, with a few worthwhile exceptions. On the other hand, Lake Buena Vista (around Exit 27 on I–4) is full of good eating opportunities. International Drive is internationally known for its tackiness, but in recent years some good restaurants have popped up on the southern end of the boulevard, around the cavernous Orange County Convention Center.

American

$$$$ **Victoria and Albert's.** All the servers work in boy-girl pairs, calling them-
★ selves "Victoria" and "Albert," and they recite the day's specials in tandem, like some surrealistic recitation out of a Lewis Carroll fantasy—you almost expect them to start smashing pocket watches on the table. But don't let the strange theatrics scare you away. You are in for a real experience at this lavish, romantic dining room that many Disney executives consider to be the top restaurant they have to offer. The intimate room (seating about 60) fits the Victorian theme, with a domed ceiling, fabric-covered walls, marbleized columns, and lots of fresh-cut flowers. A harpist adds an ethereal touch. The seven-course, prix fixe menu ($65) changes substantially day to day. Chef Scott Hunnel loves creating exotic dishes but always offers something for more proletarian palates. Appetizers might include velvety veal sweetbreads and rare New Zealand venison, artichokes in a lusty *duxelles* (mushroom-based) sauce, or jumbo sea scallops served over seaweed salad with warm beet vinaigrette. Entrées range from sautéed breast of duck or tournedos of veal on braised onions to well-prepared sirloin or broiled Maine lobster. A deluxe version of the meal comes with four glasses of wine, each selected by the sommelier to complement a particular course. Two seatings (6 and 9 PM) are offered nightly. Expect to spend about $100 a person with drinks. Prix fixe for children 2–11 is $45. (Doesn't that baby-sitter sound better by the minute?) You leave with a menu with your name printed on it. ✕ *Grand Floridian Beach Resort, Walt Disney World Magic Kingdom Resort Area,* ☎ *407/WDW–DINE. Reservations required. Jackets requested. AE, MC, V. Kosher and vegetarian meals by advance order.*

$$$ **Artist Point.** New in 1994, but built to look a century older than that,
★ the Wilderness Lodge—a huge, jauntily brawny hunting-lodge-style hotel—is definitely worth a look, and this excellent restaurant offers

Dining

*All restaurants except those in Epcot Center

0   5 miles

0   5 km

SEE DETAIL MAP ON FACING PAGE

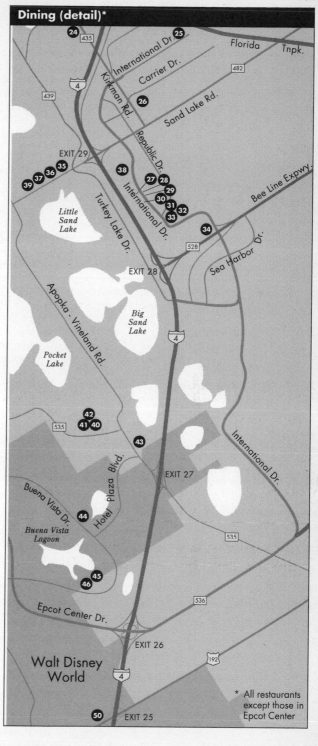

Dining (detail)*

* All restaurants except those in Epcot Center

those not booked at the Wilderness a good excuse to see the place. The northwestern salmon sampler is a good start, but you might also try the smoked duck breast, the maple-glazed steak, or the sautéed elk sausage. Most meats are hardwood grilled. The house specialty is the "trail dust shortcake," a buttermilk biscuit with strawberries, vanilla-bean ice cream, and whipped cream. Just to make sure you get that North-by-Northwest feeling, the sommelier can offer a suggestion from the selection of Washington State and Oregon vintage wines. Breakfast is an experience at the other restaurant in the hotel, Whispering Canyon Cafe, which features all-you-can-eat family meals with selections like smoked buffalo sausage and warm apple cakes. ✕ *Wilderness Lodge Resort, Walt Disney World Magic Kingdom Resort Area,* ☎ *407/WDW–DINE. Reservations accepted for Artist Point but not necessary for Whispering Canyon Cafe. AE, MC, V.*

$$ **Austin's.** That cameo on the front of the menu is Stephen F. Austin, kids, founder of the Republic of Texas and the inspiration for this ersatz Southwest eatery. Like many things in Orlando, Austin's is a fantasy, a Florida restaurant chain dedicated to Floridians' visions of what a Texas beef palace should be. But it's a good fantasy. The barbecued ribs and chicken are quite tasty, and the Galveston Bay—half a pound of ribs and a skewer of hickory-grilled shrimp—should satisfy those buckaroos who can't settle the age-old surf vs. turf quandary for themselves. The hickory-grilled fish is also good, especially when Norwegian salmon is available. If you've already been to Walt Disney World, the $6 price tag for the burgers won't faze you. This version comes with cheddar or Monterey Jack cheese, and your choice of the ubiquitous sesame seed bun or a healthy, whole-wheat edition. ✕ *8633 International Dr., Orlando,* ☎ *407/363–9575. AE, D, DC, MC, V.*

$$ **Cafe Tu Tu Tango.** This très-chic bistro doesn't have a dance floor, but
★ there's plenty of choreography here. Multiple kitchens bombard you with different courses, which arrive in waves if you follow the house custom and order a series of appetizers (which you seem to end up doing anyway, since the entrées are appetizer-size). The menu gives the address—on International Drive—a new meaning. Try the Cajun chicken egg rolls, for instance, with blackened chicken, Greek goat cheese, Creole mustard, and tomato salsa, if you want to get a compendium of the major cuisines of the world at one go. Trendy dishes like sun-dried tomato pizza and smoked chicken quesadillas give this place a certain hip spin that is in keeping with its origins in Miami's ultra-cool quarter, Coconut Grove. For added atmosphere (or perhaps just for the surrealism factor), artists work on paintings on easels while diners watch and sip drinks like the Matisse margarita and the Renoir rum runner. This place is part of the empire of Orlando-based restaurant magnate Robert Earl, who created Planet Hollywood and always wants to entertain customers as well as feed them. There's a limited selection of non-fancy food like burgers and pizza on the children's menu. Even though nothing on the entire menu is more than $8, it's not hard to spend $50 for lunch for two, especially if you follow your server's suggestion and order sangria early and often. ✕ *8625 International Dr., Orlando,* ☎ *407/248–2222. No reservations. AE, D, MC, V.*

$$ **Hard Rock Café Orlando.** The motto at this place is "Save the Planet," but that was before Hard Rock Orlando founder Robert Earl jumped ship and moved on to found Planet Hollywood with a galaxy of star partners. Both chains purvey a similar fantasy: a few hours of being cool just for standing in line and getting inside the restaurant. The Hard Rock Orlando, a huge, guitar-shaped building that is loaded down with memorabilia—including the collarless suits the Beatles wore on the *Ed Sullivan Show*—is adjacent to Universal Studios Florida and usually has a long line just from the Universal visitors. It's also a popular hang-out for members of the Orlando Magic NBA basketball team, and, yes, food is even served here. The menu and prices could be a lot worse, considering that the Rock is in a location where it would be popular no matter what it served. Best bets are the pig sandwich, made of pork shoulder hickory-smoked for 14 hours, and the reliable ⅓-pound char-broiled cheeseburger with all the trimmings. There is an extensive se-lection of beers. This place is a rock club and proud of it, so don't go if you can't tolerate the noise, which approaches the level of a 747 take-off. ✕ *Universal Studios Florida, 5800 Kirkman Rd., Orlando,* ☎ *407/ 351–7625. No reservations. AE, MC, V.*

\$\$ Pebbles. In the past few years this restaurant has become one of the most popular dining spots among Orlandoans—so popular that there are now three locations. They offer just the right blend of elegance and informality. Management says it targets the "casual gourmet" as its customer base. This is California cuisine, dude, with a Florida touch that brings grouper and other regional favorites into the picture. The Lake Buena Vista location will give you a chance to see how the lo-cals live. Good entrée choices include angel-hair pasta smothered with smoked duck, scallops, and Asian spices, and the Mediterranean salad, in which sun-dried tomatoes put in their obligatory appearance. The Caesar salad, tossed at tableside, is memorable. Good burgers, with your choice of several excellent cheeses, are also served here. This place is perennially voted best restaurant in the city by the readers of the daily *Orlando Sentinel* newspaper. Desserts here are worth the calories, and the wine list is intelligent without being a wallet-breaker. ✕ *In the Cross-roads Shopping Center near the Lake Buena Vista entrance to Walt Disney World, Orlando,* ☎ *407/827–1111; 17 W. Church St.,* ☎ *407/ 839–0892; 2516 Aloma Ave., Winter Park,* ☎ *407/678–7001; 2100 Rte. 434, Longwood,* ☎ *407/774–7111. No reservations. AE, D, DC, MC, V.*

\$\$ Planet Hollywood. On weekend nights, when the nearby Pleasure Is-land clubs are jumping, the line approaching this place is about as long as the chain of humanity that used to queue up at Lenin's Tomb in the pre-Yeltsin era. The rationale for standing in line here is similar: to see a piece of history. In this case, it's movie history, as assembled by club owners Demi Moore, Arnold Schwarzenegger, Sylvester Stallone, and Bruce Willis, and the biggest showman among the partners, restaura-teur Robert Earl. It was Earl who brought Hard Rock Café to Orlando, and it's easy to see a lot of Hard Rock at the Planet. Memorabilia, like the bus that was used in the movie *Speed* and the leather jacket worn by Schwarzenegger in *The Terminator,* rotate between the Orlando Planet Hollywood and its 17 sister restaurants around the country. There's also a souvenir shop just outside, where you can buy a few T-shirts while you wonder when you will actually get inside the restaurant. (Ac-tually, the wait is typically about two hours on most evenings. And if you want to minimize your wait, go in midafternoon: The menu does-n't change.) Food is secondary to the 20,000-square-foot building, com-plete with an indoor waterfall. The 110-foot-tall "planet" cost \$15 million, as much as Disney or Universal Studios Florida might spend to add a new attraction. The menu is built around fresh, healthful dishes like turkey burgers, smoked and grilled meats, unusual pastas and sal-ads, and a wide range of desserts. Among the better offerings are a Cre-ole pizza with shrimp, chicken, and Cajun sausage, and a tasty \$7.50 burger, a bargain in these parts. If someone else is driving, you should try a "Comet," the gargantuan souvenir-glass drink with vodka, rum, tequila, orange juice, and pineapple juice, for \$13. ✕ *Pleasure Island,*

Walt Disney World Village, ☎ *407/363–7827. No reservations. AE, DC, MC, V.*

$$ **White Horse Saloon.** Cattle ranchers would love this, the only hoe-down kind of place we know of in a four-star hotel. They would be mighty pleased at the way this western-theme saloon in the Hyatt Regency Grand Cypress sells their products: You can get a barbecued half-chicken for 20 bucks or pay a dollar more for prime rib. (If you want to go for the 28-ounce beef-worshiper's cut—that's 1½ pounds of corn-fed beef—it's $46.) All entrées come with sourdough bread, baked or mashed potatoes, and your choice of creamed spinach or corn on the cob. A hearty, hot apple pie with cinnamon-raisin sauce awaits those desperadoes who can still handle dessert. You also get music with your vittles. The Hand-Picked Trio, which has been here for years, plays in the evenings. ✕ *Hyatt Regency Grand Cypress, 1 Grand Cypress Blvd., Orlando,* ☎ *407/239–1234. Reservations advised. AE, DC, MC, V.*

Chinese

$$ **Ming Court.** In Orlando, restaurateurs know that if the chef doesn't get high marks, be sure the architect and interior designer do. Here, all parties concerned have done a fine job. Even though this place is on International Drive, a wall designed to look like a dragon's back gives an enclosed courtyard-like serenity to this Chinese palace of a restaurant. Diners look out through glass walls over a beautifully arranged series of floating gardens. Inside, little touches like rosewood chopsticks and linen tablecloths add to the classy feeling of the place. If you eat Chinese a lot, the menu probably doesn't have any dishes you haven't heard of, but the versions here are expertly prepared. The jumbo shrimp in lobster sauce, flavored with crushed black beans, costs more than you may be used to paying ($15), but it's very worthwhile. Another popular dish is the Hunan *kung pao* chicken, sautéed with red and green peppers and served with cashews and walnuts. Ming Court is within walking distance of the Orange County Convention Center and, incidentally, just across the street from several other good restaurants. ✕ *9188 International Dr., Orlando,* ☎ *407/351–9988. Reservations advised. AE, DC, MC, V.*

Continental

$$$$ **Arthur's 27.** The view from the 27th floor of the Buena Vista Palace Hotel, overlooking all of Walt Disney World and its environs, is breathtaking, but you may be even more lightheaded when you get a look at your check if you are not prepared to pay top dollar for a top-notch Continental meal. Handle the fiscal traumas up front with one of two prix-fixe dinner options: $60 (not including drinks and gratuities) for a six-course meal or $45 for a four-course special. Order à la carte and you will probably leave behind a couple of bills with Ben Franklin's picture on them. What you get for your money, however, is a well-prepared meal and a formal dining experience that will last two to three hours (even if you drum your fingers on the starched tablecloths). But if you love haute cuisine, and enjoy watching the sun go down behind the Epcot dome, you'll want to savor every minute at this place. All entrées come with some kind of heavenly sauce, like the rich, creamy cognac-based mixture that is spooned over the tenderloin of beef or the herb-rich garlic sauce that accompanies the roast loin of lamb. Desserts include a credible crème brûlée with raspberries and a chocolate cake to die for. Service can be pretentious, with waiters uttering clichés like "Excellent choice, sir" and making the changing of the plates seem like a Tomb of the Unknown Soldier ritual. Because there's only one seating a night, reservations as early as a month in advance are recommended. ✗ *Buena Vista Palace Hotel, Walt Disney World Village, Lake Buena Vista,* ☎ *407/827–3450. Reservations necessary. Jacket required. AE, D, DC, MC, V.*

Fast Food

$ **McDonald's.** The nation's largest McDonald's is no plain-Jane burger joint. Although the menu is standard, the frills are pure Orlando: a 7,500-square-foot playground full of slides, tunnels, and seesaws; a theater where musicians and magicians perform; even a gift shop, called Mickey D's, full of T-shirts. You can chow down in the tiki-bar-style Sunset Terrace area; the Maui Room, with a 600-gallon saltwater aquarium; or the Rock and Roll Room, featuring '50s memorabilia and a jukebox. ✗ *6875 Sand Lake Rd. and International Dr., Orlando,* ☎ *407/351–2185. No reservations. AE, MC, V.*

French

$$$ **La Coquina.** This gourmet restaurant bills itself as French with an Asian influence, and if you sample the pheasant and truffle wonton with foie gras and chives, you'll think this culture combo is quite worthwhile. The Hyatt Regency Grand Cypress culinary staff uses this restaurant as a showcase for its skills, and if you want a closer look, there's a special chef's table dining experience, in which your party eats in the kitchen (it can be arranged through the restaurant manager). If your children can't quite scarf down all their wasabi-seared tuna with soy or their glazed roast squab and foie gras, smaller portions at half the price are available for diners 12 and under. The high-point meal here is Sunday brunch, with a generous selection of goodies like waffles, omelets, tropical fruits, smoked fish, poached salmon, quartered duck, and pastries that make the $38 per person price seem like a real bargain. Brunch is truly a pleasant experience here, with nice touches like black swans swimming on the lake outside the window and a harpist calmly thrumming—excellent preparation for an assault on Space Mountain a little later in the morning. Lose the tank tops; men must wear shirts with collars and women must dress "appropriately," according to the printed dress code. Jackets are required for men at dinner. ✗ *Hyatt Regency Grand Cypress, 1 Grand Cypress Blvd., Orlando,* ☎ *407/239–1234. Reservations advised. AE, DC, MC, V.*

Italian

$$$ **Caruso's Palace.** From the interstate, this big, domed building looks like the Taj Mahal West (which would not seem overly odd in Orlando), but as you get closer to the baroque rotunda it's clearly a knockoff of an old Italian opera house. Nothing about this $5 million building is subtle; from the high, hand-painted ceiling to the imported Italian marble floors, the management wants this place to be as much an attraction as it is a restaurant. If you dine here, your appetite should be in scale with the mammoth building itself. All the entrées come with four other courses, including antipasto, soup or salad, a pasta course (even though some of the entrées themselves come with pasta), and rich Italian ice creams for dessert. If you really want to lay on the calories, however, there's a six-course sampler special that will make you feel Gleasonesque before you're finished. Some of the better entrées include steamed lobster with angel-hair pasta and beef selections like a thick, tender sirloin. ✗ *8986 International Dr., Orlando,* ☎ *407/363–7110. Reservations suggested. AE, D, DC, MC, V.*

$$–$$$ **Capriccio's.** Corporate executives and conventioneers, who make up a good part of this hotel's clientele, like the relaxed atmosphere of this place as a nice departure from the rubber-chicken circuit. The marble-topped tables are arranged on the tile floors so that everyone can view

the open kitchen and wood-burning pizza ovens, which turn out whole-wheat-flour pies ranging from *pizza margherita* (made with sun-dried tomatoes and smoked mozzarella, fontina, provolone, and Parmesan cheeses) to healthy *pizza bianca* (with mozzarella, goat cheese, and fresh thyme). If you're not in the mood for pizza, try one of the mesquite-grilled fish, beef, or chicken entrées, like the *pollo gonzo* (chicken in a lemon sage sauce). There's also a popular brunch offered on weekends. ✕ *Peabody Orlando Hotel, 9801 International Dr., Orlando,* ☎ *407/352–4000. AE, DC, MC, V. Closed Mon.*

$$ Ciao Italia. This is an odd place for a quiet, charming little Italian eatery, almost in the shadow of Sea World. But even though this quaint restaurant is in the middle of tourism's fast lane, nothing is hurried here. Every item on the menu is made to order, so you might want to bring along that dog-eared copy of *War and Peace* you never finished. Your patience will be rewarded, however: The Italian-speaking proprietors have managed to re-create a piece of Italy in central Florida. The proof is in the sweet New Zealand mussels, served with either white garlic or marinara sauce, and the light, colorful *pollo alla Tonino* (chicken breast with red and yellow peppers). For dessert, try the *tartufo* (chocolate-coated ice cream). ✕ *Across from Sheraton World Resort, 6149 Westwood Blvd., Orlando,* ☎ *407/354–0770. Reservations accepted. AE, D, DC, MC, V. Beer and wine only. No lunch.*

$$ Portobello Yacht Club. Operated by Chicago's venerable restaurateurs, the Levy brothers, this eatery has a much better lineage than the one the Disney brain trust made up. Supposedly (so the Disney Imagineers will tell you), the building was the home of Merriweather Adam Pleasure, the man for whom Pleasure Island was named. Of course, the man never existed, but that doesn't mean you won't find great pleasure dining here. Start with something simple—the chewy, tasty sourdough bread, served with roast garlic. Then move on to bigger and better things like the spaghettini alla portobello, a stick-to-your-ribs pasta dish with scallops, clams, shrimp, mussels, tomatoes, garlic, and herbs. There's always a fresh-catch special of the day. Since Pleasure Island is in Disney's own nightclub district, where party animals are a protected species, the people-watching can be quite interesting here, especially after a little sangria. This is a good spot for a late meal; it's open until midnight. ✕ *Pleasure Island, Walt Disney World,* ☎ *407/934–8888. Reservations accepted. AE, DC, MC, V.*

$–$$ Rosario's. This little place, in a New England–style clapboard house that looks refreshingly out of place in the unsightly jumble of motels known as Kissimmee, is understated and cheerful and serves Italian food that's above average. The *spaghetti aglio olio* is sauced with fresh garlic, basil, and diced tomatoes sautéed in olive oil. The hearty *pasta e fagioli* soup is filled with Italian white beans, prosciutto, escarole, and pasta and flavored with both brandy and a touch of marinara sauce. ✕ *4838 W. Irlo Bronson Hwy., Kissimmee,* ☎ *407/239–0118. Reservations advised. AE, D, DC, MC, V. Beer and wine only. No lunch.*

Japanese

$$ Ran-Getsu. The surroundings are definitely a Disney version of the Orient—but the food is fresh and carefully prepared. Sit at the curved, dragon-tail-shaped sushi bar and order the *matsu* platter—an assortment of *nigiri*- and *maki*-style sushi. Or, unless you're alone, you can have your meal Japanese style at the low tables overlooking a carp-filled pond and decorative gardens. Specialties include *sukiyaki* and *shabu-shabu* (thinly sliced beef prepared tableside in a simmering seasoned broth and served with vegetables). If you feel more adventurous, try the deep-fried alligator tail. ✗ *8400 International Dr., Orlando,* ☎ *407/345–0044. Reservations advised. AE, DC, MC, V. No lunch.*

Seafood

$$$ **Ariel's.** The centerpiece of this favorite of Disney executives, named for the Little Mermaid, is a 2,500-gallon saltwater tank. The finny fare comes from Florida, the Northeast, and the Northwest, and it's most often simply grilled over a hardwood fire. Want something more exotic? Start with the Tuckernut shellfish gumbo with andouille sausage and then have Ariel's strudel—chicken and ricotta wrapped in a flaky basil-perfumed pastry. ✗ *Disney's Beach Club Resort, Lake Buena Vista,* ☎ *407/ WDW–DINE. Reservations accepted. AE, MC, V. No smoking.*

$$–$$$ **Hemingway's.** There's usually a wait at this popular, elegant eatery that
★ overlooks the huge Hyatt Regency Grand Cypress pool, but when you begin to sample the wide variety of seafood specialties, you'll forget about the wait. Try the Old Man and the Sea special, which offers you a choice of grouper, swordfish, tuna, mahimahi, red snapper, pompano, or salmon, charbroiled or blackened, with Cajun, tartar, or béarnaise sauce. You can sample dishes that were inspired by all the phases of Hemingway's life, like the Spanish paella he might have eaten in Madrid before he wrote *For Whom the Bell Tolls.* The kitchen assumes you have a Papa-style appetite and includes mussels, clams, scallops, lobster, chicken, and sausage in this version. Beer-batter coconut shrimp with orange marmalade horseradish sauce is a house specialty. ✗ *Hyatt Regency Grand Cypress Resort, 1 Grand Cypress Blvd., Orlando,* ☎ *407/239–1234. Reservations highly recommended. AE, DC, MC, V.*

$–$$ **Atlantis.** It would be surprising if someone didn't choose this name for a seafood restaurant in a major hotel near Sea World of Florida, but rest assured, the food is more original than the moniker. The restaurant is elegant and moderately formal (but men won't need a jacket) and offers good fish selections, like various lobster dishes and grilled yellowfin tuna. ✗ *Stouffer Orlando Resort, 667 Sea Harbor Dr., Orlando,* ☎ *407/351–5555. Reservations available. AE, D, DC, MC, V. No lunch.*

$–$$ **Florida Bay.** The food in this seafood restaurant, which is within walking distance of the Orange County Convention Center, is tasty, well prepared, and fairly priced. As a starter, try the Oriental stir-fry white cheese pizza (actually on a pita); for entrées, you can't go wrong with the seafood dishes or the grilled-shrimp-and-mixed-greens special. Florida Bay gives the feeling of a Key West yacht club, with its turquoise-and-gray color scheme and cement floors. ✗ *8560 International Dr., Orlando,* ☎ *407/352–6655. No reservations. AE, D, DC, MC, V.*

Epcot Center

Epcot's World Showcase offers some of the finest dining to be found not only in Walt Disney World but in the entire Orlando area. The problems are that you have to pay Epcot admission to eat in these establishments; the top-of-the-line places, such as those in the French, Italian, and Japanese pavilions, can be expensive, and reservations hard to come by. On the other hand, most of them have a limited-selection children's menu with dramatically lower prices. Dress is informal—no one expects you to go all the way back to your hotel to tidy up. And if you have unruly youngsters in tow, you probably won't be alone. Kosher and vegetarian meals are available on request.

Reservations

All restaurants, unless otherwise noted, are open for both lunch and dinner daily. For both meals, reservations are a must. At Epcot, there are two ways of making reservations: either by calling the central reservations lines, 407/WDW–DINE or 407/560–7277 or, when actually on site at Epcot, by going to the WorldKey Information Centers—a system of interactive computer screens. To use the WorldKey system, here's the drill: As soon as you get to Epcot, head for Guest Services, at the base of Spaceship Earth, and line up in front of the World-Key Information Center. Or better still, go to the WorldKey kiosks located throughout the park, and avoid the logjam at the main location. Just ask any cast member (as all Disney employees are called) where to find the nearest kiosk. There's one near the Port of Entry shop, near the dock for the water taxi to Morocco, and another just before the bridge to World Showcase.

To make reservations using WorldKey, you should arrive early, because the most popular seating times in the busier restaurants are filled up within an hour of Epcot Center's official opening time (which may be as much as 30 minutes ahead of the published opening time). To avoid the battle of WorldKey, remember you can always book by phone (using numbers listed above). You can also opt to eschew the computer reservation bit and walk straight to the restaurant of your choice, where someone will be on hand to take reservations at 11 AM when they open for the day.

Alternatively, be flexible about your mealtimes. For the more popular establishments, it is much easier to get a reservation for lunch than for dinner, to get lunch reservations before noon, and to get dinner reservations for seatings before 6 PM and after 8 PM. And it's always worth stopping by the restaurant of your choice during the day in hopes of a cancellation.

No matter how you book, try to show up a bit early to be sure of getting your table. You can pay with cash; charge with American Express, MasterCard, or Visa; or, if you're a guest at an on-site hotel on Disney property, charge the tab to your room.

The following are your best bets for both good food and atmosphere.

British
$$ Rose and Crown. If you are an Anglophile and you love nothing more than a good thick beer, this friendly pub is the place to soak up both the suds and the British street culture. As with all World Showcase restaurants, the staff has been brought in from the appropriate country, so you can get a great foreign affairs lesson for the price of a meal. At day's end, visitors mingle with Disney employees while knocking down pints of Bass Ale and Guinness Stout with Stilton cheese. "Wenches" serve up simple pub fare, such as steak-and-kidney pie and fish-and-chips. Dark wood floors, sturdy pub chairs, and brass lamps create a warm, homey atmosphere. At 4, a traditional tea is served. The food is relatively inexpensive, especially at lunch, and the terrace has a splendid view of IllumiNations. All things considered, it's one of the best bets in Epcot.

French
$$$ Les Chefs de France. To create this sparkling French café-restaurant, three of France's most famous culinary artists came together: Paul Bocuse, who operates one restaurant north of Lyon and two in Tokyo; Gaston Lenôtre, noted for his pastries and ice creams; and Roger Vergé, proprietor of France's celebrated Mougins, near Cannes. The three developed the menu, trained the chefs, and look in (apparently not as frequently as they should, according to some reviewers) to make sure the food and service stay up to snuff. Start with a chicken-and-

duck pâté in a pastry crust, follow up with a classic *coq au vin* or broiled salmon with sorrel sauce, and end up with chocolate-doused ice-cream-filled pastry shells. Some people feel transported back to fin-de-siècle France, if only for an hour or two.

$$–$$$ **Bistro de Paris.** The great secret at the France pavilion—and, indeed,
★ in all of Epcot—is the Bistro de Paris, located around the back of the Chefs de Paris and upstairs. The sophisticated menu changes regularly and contains exciting offerings that reflect the cutting edge of French cooking. The dining salon is serene—and often filled with well-dressed French people, the mark of a successful transplant. Come late, ask for a window seat, and plan to linger to watch IllumiNations. The French wines are moderately priced and available by the glass.

German

$$ **Biergarten.** In this popular spot, Oktoberfest runs 365 days a year. The cheerful—some would say raucous—atmosphere is what you would expect in a place with an oompah band. Waitresses in typical Bavarian garb serve hot pretzels, hearty German fare such as sauerbraten and bratwurst, and stout pitchers of beer and wine, which patrons pound on their long communal tables—even when the yodelers, singers, and dancers aren't egging them on.

Italian

$$$ **L'Originale Alfredo di Roma Ristorante.** This is the most popular restaurant at Epcot, and its namesake dish, made with mountains of butter flown in from Italy, is one of the principal reasons. This restaurant was created, with the help of Disney, by the descendants of Alfredo de Lelio, who in 1914 founded Rome's Alfredo all'Augusteo restaurant and invented the now-classic dish—fettuccine sauced with cream, butter, and loads of freshly grated Parmesan cheese. But the true secret to the dish here is the butter. Insiders say the only Parmesan that goes into the mixture is what your waiter sprinkles on at the table. A very good variation of the trademark dish is the *fettuccine alla carbonara,* with lots of rich, crushed bacon that might make your cardiologist scream, but it's oh, so tasty. Stick with pasta, for the other menu items are undistinguished. Or try *lo chef consiglia* (the chef's selection)—a spaghetti or fettuccine appetizer, a mixed green salad, and a chicken or veal entrée. In addition, during dinner the Italian waiters skip around singing Italian songs and bellowing arias, a show in itself.

Japanese

$$–$$$ **Mitsukoshi.** This complex of dining areas overlooking tranquil gardens
★ is actually three restaurants. The **Yakitori,** a fast-food stand in a small pavilion modeled on a teahouse in Kyoto's Katsura Summer Palace, offers broiled skewers of chicken basted with teriyaki sauce, and *gyudon,* paper-thin beef simmered in a spicy sauce and served with noodles. At the **Tempura Kiku,** two dozen diners sit around a central counter and watch the chefs prepare sushi, sashimi, tempura, batter-dipped deep-fried shrimp, scallops, and vegetables. In the Mitsukoshi's third area—a series of five **Teppanyaki Rooms**—chefs skillfully chop vegetables, meat, and fish at lightning speed and then stir-fry them at grills set into communal dining tables. The **Matsunoma Lounge** to the right of this area pours Japanese sake, plum wine, and *saketinis*—martinis made with sake rather than vermouth. If you just want sushi, go to the lounge and you can usually avoid a wait.

Mexican

$$ **San Angel Inn.** The lush, tropical surroundings—cool, dark, and almost surreal—make this restaurant in the courtyard inside the Mexican pavilion perhaps the most exotic in Walt Disney World. It's popular among Disney execs as well as tourists, who treasure this place because it offers a great respite, especially when the humid weather outside makes central Florida feel like equatorial Africa. (But you probably won't see a Disney employee, even off duty, ordering one of the margaritas: They are so bad as to be legendary.) Candlelit tables are companionably close together, and the restaurant is open to a midnight-blue "sky" in the inside of the pavilion and filled with the music of folk singers, guitars, and marimbas. The best seats are along the restaurant's outer edge, away from the entrance and directly alongside the pavilion's "river," where boatloads of sightseers stream by; above looms an Aztec pyramid and volcano, whose soft, fiery light evokes a sense of the distant past. On the roster of authentic dishes, one specialty is *mole poblano*—chicken simmered until tender in a rich sauce of different kinds of chilies, green tomatoes, ground tortillas, cumin, and 11 other spices mixed with cocoa. Fresh tortillas are made every day and served with beef, chicken, and cheese fillings as well as fresh *salsa verde* (spicy green sauce).

Moroccan

$$–$$$ **Marrakesh.** This is the least popular of any of the World Showcase restaurants, possibly because the average American hasn't heard much about Moroccan food. Consequently, it's relatively easy to get seated, and once inside, you'll find belly dancers and a three-piece Moroccan band set a North African mood that feels almost like a set for a Disney Casablanca. The building itself, painstakingly constructed by artisans brought in from Morocco to handcraft the extensive carving, is impressive. The food is mildly spicy and relatively inexpensive. Try the couscous, the national dish of Morocco, served with vegetables; or *bastila,* an appetizer made of alternating layers of sweet-and-spicy pork and a thin pastry, redolent of almonds, saffron, and cinnamon.

Norwegian

$ **Restaurant Akershus.** Norway's tradition of seafood and cold-meat dishes is highlighted at the *koldtbord,* or Norwegian buffet, in this restaurant, comprising four dining rooms that occupy a copy of Oslo's Akershus Castle. Hosts and hostesses explain the dishes and suggest which ones go together, then send you off to the buffet table. There is no need to shovel everything you see onto your plate at one time—it is traditional to make several trips. First, take your appetizers (usually herring, which comes several ways here), then go for cold seafood such as gravlax. Pick up cold salads and meats on your next trip, and then, on your last foray, fill up on hot lamb, veal, or venison. The selection of desserts, offered à la carte, includes cloudberries—delicate fruits that grow on the tundra in season.

Other Options

Future World's two full-service restaurants are Living Seas' tiered **Coral Reef Room,** which serves a finny menu and has a view of the pavilion's jumbo aquarium through 8-foot-high windows, and the **Garden Grill,** where you can eat American fare with a twist as the restaurant revolves, giving you an ever-changing view of each of the biomes of the Living with the Land boat ride. In World Showcase, there's also China's **Nine Dragons,** which offers Chinese fare representing several regions—modified for American tastes—in a large, comfortable room decorated with Oriental motifs. If your hometown has a thriving Chinese community, you'll find the fare here uninspired, though the restaurant does seem to attract a large Asian following. Fast-food and cafeteria options are described as Time Outs in the Epcot Center section of Chapter 2, Exploring Walt Disney World.

Meals with Disney Characters

At these breakfasts, brunches, and dinners staged in hotel and theme park restaurants all over Walt Disney World, kids can snuggle up to all the best-loved Disney characters. Sometimes the food is served buffet style, sometimes it's sit-down. Prices and times vary, so call ahead. Reservations are often required; places where they are not are crowded, so show up on the early side if you hate to wait. Smoking is not permitted at any of these.

Breakfasts

No reservations are required for many of these events. You can drop in from 8 to 10:30 on Sundays at the *Buena Vista Palace* (☎ 407/827–2727; $10.95 adults, $5.95 children under 11); from 8 to 11 for a no-holds-barred buffet at the Contemporary Café in the **Contemporary Resort** (☎ 407/WDW–DINE; $12.95 adults, $7.95 children 3–11); from 7:30 to 11 in the Cape May Café at **Disney's Beach Club** ($12.95 adults, $7.95 children under 12); from 7:30 to 10:15 daily at the **Polynesian Resort**'s Papeete Bay Verandah (☎ 407/WDW–DINE; $12.95 adults, $7.95 children 3–11); Saturdays from 8 to 11 in the Garden Grove at the **Walt Disney World Swan** (☎ 407/934–1281; about $11 for adults, $7 for children, depending on whether you go for the buffet or order from the menu); and at the counter-service Stargate Restaurant in Future World's Innoventions East in **Epcot Center.** There, the characters are on hand from park opening until 10, with breakfast served for another hour; you don't have to buy food to enjoy the goings-on. Reservations are required for other breakfasts, including the one hosted by Mary Poppins, from 7:30 to noon in the 1900 Park Fare Restaurant in the **Grand Floridian** (☎ 407/824–2383; $14.95 adults, $9.75 children 3–11).

Sunday Brunch

The Disney characters show up for the lavish Sunday brunch from 8:30 to 12:30 at the Ristorante Carnivale at the **Walt Disney World Dolphin** (☎ 407/934–4025; $12.95 adults, $7.95 children 4–12). You can help yourself to everything from bacon and eggs and seafood crepes to pancakes and chocolate chip waffles in the distinctive circle-with-ears shape. Reservations are a good idea.

Dinner

Mickey's Tropical Revue, a luau character show, is presented daily at 4:30 PM at the **Polynesian Resort** (☎ 407/WDW–DINE; $29 adults, $22 young adults 12–20, $13 children 3–11). Mickey and Minnie are at the buffet served from 5 to 9 daily at the 1900 Park Fare Restaurant in the **Grand Floridian** (☎ 407/WDW–DINE; $18.50 adults, $9.95 children 3–11). Mickey also appears during dinner, served 5–10 PM daily, at **Chef Mickey's Village Restaurant** (☎ 407/WDW–DINE; entrées $9.75–$18.25, children's menu entrées from $8.75). You will need reservations for all of these. Every night at 8 (7 in winter months), near Fort Wilderness's Meadow Trading Post, there's also a **Character Campfire** and sing-along (free).

THE ORLANDO AREA

The following restaurants, in or near the city of Orlando, cater mostly to a local clientele.

American

$$ **Sam Snead's Tavern.** The prototype for a golf-theme grill, this lively restaurant is a tribute to the venerable pro champion Sam Snead. The wood-paneled walls are chockablock with pictures and memorabilia of his illustrious career. The kitchen does well with an eclectic variety of foods ranging from hamburgers and grilled chicken to veal chops and fish. The Caesar salad is excellent, as are the barbecued spareribs. The chocolate sack sounds weird but isn't: It's pound cake, ice cream, strawberries, and whipped cream packed into what looks like a paper bag made of chocolate, and it's much too much for one person. This is one of the few restaurants in town open as late as 1 AM. ✕ *2461 S. Hiawassee Rd., Orlando,* ☏ *407/295–9999. Reservations advised. AE, DC, MC, V.*

$ **Dexter's.** This hip college bar is so nondescript from the outside that the facade almost blends into the coin laundry next door. But inside you'll find a popular, trendy eatery and winery sophisticated enough to offer its own wine label and publish a monthly newsletter for those who appreciate a good vintage. Much of the clientele comes from Rollins College, a liberal arts school a block away, and the SoHo-like menu reflects that. If you are over 40, however, you won't feel out of place. One of the best entrées is chicken tortilla pie, a stack of cheese-laden tortillas that looks more like a spaceship than a pie; equally popular is the ratt pie, which is like the tortilla pie but filled with provolone and ratatouille. Jazz is featured frequently at night. ✕ *200 W. Fairbanks Ave., Winter Park,* ☏ *407/629–1150. AE, MC, V.*

American-International

$$$$ **Manuel's on the 28th.** How's this for one-upmanship? For a decade,
★   Arthur's 27 was Orlando's loftiest restaurant in terms of altitude, with a spot on the 27th floor of the Buena Vista Palace Hotel. In 1994, Manuel's on the 28th (as in 28th floor of the downtown Barnett Bank building) opened its doors and was almost immediately hailed by local dining critics as a culinary landmark. In many cases, restaurants with a view offer only that, but the cuisine here is excellent, with stellar offerings like seared loin of lamb in a cayenne-Scotch whiskey sauce, wood-roasted chicken and lobster in a coconut-lime sauce, and hickory-grilled muscovy duck breast with plum-ginger sauce. There is an extensive wine list and, an unusual offer, wines by the half glass. The restaurant offers several tasting packages. Though it's open only at dinner (and jackets are preferred), you may be allowed to come in during the day and just gawk at the view across the flat, green central Florida landscape. ✕ *390 N. Orange Ave., Orlando,* ☏ *407/246–6580. Reservations advised. AE, D, DC, MC, V. Closed Sun.–Mon. No lunch.*

$$–$$$ **Chatham's Place.** This is one of Orlando's best. The Chatham broth-
★   ers, Culinary Institute of America graduates, prepare everything to order here, and the staff is genuinely concerned that every patron has a perfect experience. The professional office building that the restaurant calls home, across the street from the Marketplace shopping mall, lends nothing in the way of atmosphere; nor is the decor anything to get excited about—hanging plants, glass-topped paisley tablecloths, and a view of the kitchen. But the meticulously prepared food rises above the setting. Try the black grouper with pecan butter, the rosemary-infused rack of lamb, or the duck breast, grilled to crispy perfection. ✕ *7575 Dr. Phillips Blvd., Orlando,* ☏ *407/345–2992. Reservations advised. MC, V. No lunch.*

$$ **Harvey's Bistro.** In the Barnett Bank building downtown, within walking distance of the arena and the Centroplex, this clubby newcomer, with paneled walls and white tablecloths, has quickly collected an enthusiastic business crowd at lunch and concert-, theater-, and arena-goers after dark. The menu offers a good selection of bistro and comfort foods. Soups are good (try the *petite marmite au gratin*), as

are the oven-roasted saffron scallops, the duck cassoulet with white and black beans, and the thin-crusted pizza with caramelized onions, fresh spinach, and goat cheese. Late hours are a plus. ✕ *390 N. Orlando Ave., Orlando,* ☎ *407/246–6560. Reservations advised. AE, D, DC, MC, V. Closed Sun. No lunch Sat.*

$$ **Moorefield's.** The trendy menu and fresh, sophisticated but homemade
★ dishes make you think Martha Stewart might be in the kitchen somewhere, but in this case it's owner-chef Elizabeth Moorefield. The menu changes constantly, but you can always find some variation of grilled salmon; roast pork; and perhaps the most popular dish on the menu, angel-hair pasta with artichoke hearts, hearts of palm, chevre, sun-dried tomatoes, and Parmesan. A popular appetizer is a minipizza topped with mushrooms and roasted garlic. About 20 carefully selected wines are offered by the glass. ✕ *123 S. Orange Ave., Orlando,* ☎ *407/872–6960. Reservations accepted. AE, MC, V.*

Chinese

$–$$ **Forbidden City.** The Hunan-style food at this restaurant in a reconstructed gas station is terrific. Start with the diced chicken with pine seeds in a package—icy lettuce cups wrapped around spicy chicken, which offer a delightful mix of cold and hot sensations. The sesame chicken—large chunks of sesame-coated poultry sautéed in a sweet sauce—goes perfectly with bright-green broccoli in a subtle garlic sauce. The traditional 10-ingredient lo mein is full of fresh shrimp, chicken, beef, and pork. You're in for a treat if you can get past the decor, or lack thereof; the former gas station's marquee is still there, and inside there are utilitarian tables and booths, with a few plastic plants to add that fresh, natural note. ✕ *948 N. Mills Ave., Orlando,* ☎ *407/894–5005. MC, V. Closed Sun. No lunch Sat.*

$–$$ **4-5-6.** With its mirrored walls and emerald green carpet, this restaurant is sleek and clean-looking, setting the stage for the food, which is made without MSG or preservatives. Dumplings sautéed in hot peanut butter sauce is a must for peanut butter fans. Specialties include chicken-three-ways (one platter that includes portions of General Tso's chicken, lemon chicken, and sliced chicken breast with snow peas), as well as Five Fresh Herbs Steamed Fresh Fish, made with sea bass. The friendly staff tries hard to accommodate, so be sure to speak up if you want your food spicy or served in a special casserole to keep it warm. ✕ *657 N. Primrose Dr., Orlando,* ☎ *407/898–1899. Reservations accepted. AE, MC, V. Beer and wine only.*

Cuban

$ **Numero Uno.** To the followers of this long-popular Latin restaurant,
★ the name is quite appropriate. Downtowners have been filling the place up at lunch for years. It bills itself as "the home of paella," and that's probably the best dish. If you have time and a good appetite, try the *paella Valenciana,* which takes an hour and 15 minutes on special order, with yellow rice, sausage, chicken, fish, Spanish spices, and a side order of plantains. If you don't have that long, go for traditional Cuban fare like shredded flank steak or the dish that half of Latin America eats daily, *arroz con pollo* (chicken and rice). Reservations are accepted only for parties of four or more. ✕ *2499 S. Orange Ave., Orlando,* ☎ *407/84–3840. AE, D, MC, V.*

Deli

$ **Ronnie's.** A former Orlando dining critic used to call this place Ronnie's "totalitessen," because of the silly and strictly enforced rules about such things as how many condiments you could have on the table at one time. But the owner's penchant for being a control freak can be forgiven because of the excellent, New York-deli-style food, including the cornerstone corned beef sandwich and Dr. Brown's soda. At lunchtime, city bigwigs fill up the back tables, and hours after other Orlando restaurants have turned out their lights for the night, Ronnie's is still serving coffee and Danish. The tuna fish salad is terrific. You can get takeout and baked goods next door. ✕ *Colonial Plaza, 2702 E. Colonial Dr. (between Bumby and Primrose Aves.), Orlando,* ☎ *407/894–4951. Cash or traveler's checks only.* ⊘ *Sun.–Thurs. until 11, Fri. and Sat. until 1* AM.

French

$$$ Le Cordon Bleu. Over the past two decades, Georges and Monique Vogelbacher have assembled a loyal clientele, who come back night after night for French cuisine with a Swiss touch. With its print wallpaper, lace curtains, and white tablecloths, the room is comfortable, and so is the menu, which offers the kitchen's well-prepared version of Caesar salad, superb roast rack of lamb (for two) with an array of seasonal vegetables, and poached Norwegian salmon. In keeping with the trend toward lighter cuisine, Le Cordon Bleu has placed a number of low-fat dishes and fresh fish specials on the menu as well. The bread is really good. ✕ *537 West Fairbanks Ave., Winter Park,* ☎ *407/647–7575. Reservations advised. AE, D, DC, MC, V. Closed Sun. No lunch Sat.*

$$ Le Coq au Vin. Louis Perrotte deserves a medal, not just for his culinary achievements in serving excellent French cuisine in Orlando for
★ about 15 years but for remaining modest. This French chef could run a stuffed-shirt kind of place with the best of 'em, because his food is as expertly prepared as any haute cuisine you'll find in the Orlando area. Instead, he chooses the self-effacing route, running a modest little kitchen in a small but charming house in south Orlando. Perrotte and his wife, Magdalena, who acts as hostess, make the place feel warm and homey, and it is usually filled with friendly Orlando residents. The traditional French fare is first-class and roused *Vogue*'s restaurant critic to raves: homemade chicken liver pâté, fresh rainbow trout with champagne sauce, and Long Island duck with green peppercorns. For dessert, try the crème brûlée, and pat yourself on the back for discovering a place that few tourists know about. The menu changes quarterly, as Perrotte celebrates the regional cuisines of his native France. Ask to be seated in the main dining room—it's the center of the action. ✕ *4800 S. Orange Ave., Orlando,* ☎ *407/851–6980. Reservations advised. AE, DC, MC, V.*

$$ Le Provence Bistro Français. This charming two-story restaurant in the heart of downtown Orlando does a fine imitation of an out-of-the-way bistro on the Left Bank in Paris. Reasonable prices and first-rate service add to the delightful surroundings and excellent food. For lunch try the *salade Niçoise,* made with fresh grilled tuna, French string beans, and hard-boiled eggs; or the *cassoulet toulousain,* a hearty mixture of white beans, lamb, pork, and sausage. At dinner you can choose between a six-course prix fixe menu, a less pricey four-course version, or à la carte options. ✕ *50 East Pine St., Orlando,* ☎ *407/843–1320. Reservations advised. AE, DC, MC, V. Closed Sun. No lunch Sat.*

Italian

$$$ Christini's. Orlando is short on the kind of upscale Italian restaurant you find so often in New York, so locals and tourists alike gladly pay the price at Christini's, one of Orlando's best for northern Italian cuisine. As a result, the place always feels as if there's a party going on, particularly in the center of the room. Owner Chris Christini is on hand nightly to make sure that everything is perfect. Try the pasta with lobster, shrimp, and clams or the huge veal chops, perfumed with fresh sage. ✕ *7600 Dr. Phillips Blvd., in the Marketplace, Orlando,* ☎ *407/ 345–8770. Reservations advised. AE, DC, MC, V.*

$$$ **Enzo's on the Lake.** Enzo's is one of Orlando's most popular restau-
★ rants, even though it's located on a tacky stretch of highway filled with used car lots. The Roman charmer who owns the place, Enzo Perlini, has turned a rather ordinary lakefront house in suburban Longwood, about 30 minutes' drive from I-Drive, into an Italian villa. It's worth the trip to sample the antipasto. The mussels, cooked in a heady broth of white wine and garlic, and the mild *bufalo mozzarella* cheese, flown in from Italy, make equally good starters. The *bucatini à la Enzo,* a combination of sautéed bacon, mushrooms, and peas served over long hollow noodles, is a very popular house specialty. The electricity in the air is such that even people with reservations don't mind waiting at the bar (as is often necessary); they simply get into the party. ✕ *1130 S. U.S. 17–92, Longwood,* ☎ *407/834–9872. Reservations neces-sary. AE, DC, MC, V. Closed Sun.*

$$–$$$ **Antonio's La Fiamma.** The wood-burning grill and oven, used expertly by the chef to turn out great grilled fish dishes, gourmet pizzas, and homemade bread are definitely the ticket to this restaurant's success. The main section of the restaurant is upstairs, where diners can watch the cooks at the back of the building working their magic. Try the fen-nel and radicchio salad topped with orange zest, cracked pepper, shav-ings of Gruyère, and extra-virgin olive oil. The *linguine alla cine di rapa,* linguini served with sautéed bitter greens, sausage, and slivered garlic, is a tantalizing marriage of tastes and textures. The *anitra con rosmarino all'agrodolce,* fully deboned and roasted duck with a sweet-sour sauce made of balsamic vinegar, rosemary, and honey, is heavenly. ✕ *611 S. Orlando Ave., Maitland,* ☎ *407/645–1035. Reservations advised. AE, MC, V. Closed Sun.*

$$–$$$ **La Scala.** Mirrored walls and gracious, sophisticated decor make this one of Orlando's most romantic restaurants. The fact that owner Joseph del Vento, a former opera singer, who once worked in New York's Tre Scalini, breaks into song every so often only adds to the charm. For pasta, order the dish called Chop, Chop, Chop—fresh seafood sautéed tableside, doused in marinara sauce, and served over fettuc-cine. ✕ *205 Loraine Dr., Altamonte Springs,* ☎ *407/862–3257. Reser-vations suggested. AE, DC, MC, V. Closed Sat. lunch and Sun.*

$$–$$$ **La Sila.** Although located in one of Orlando's ubiquitous strip shop-ping centers, La Sila offers consistently fresh, northern Italian cuisine in a gracious, sophisticated setting. Pasta lovers will appreciate the large and original selection of dishes, including a penne with arugula and fresh tomato sauce that's an ideal mixture of bitter and sweet. Because the restaurant's popularity continues to grow and because it's so con-venient to WDW and Universal Studios, reservations are a must. ✕ *4898 Kirkman Rd., Orlando,* ☎ *407/295–8333. Reservations ad-vised. AE, DC, MC, V. Closed Sun.*

$–$$ **Gargi's Italian Restaurant.** You can feel the building vibrate when Am-trak rolls by a few feet away, but that just adds charm to this delight-ful ma-and-pa pasta place. If you crave old-fashioned spaghetti and meatballs, lasagna, or manicotti made with sauces that you know have been simmering all day, this storefront hole-in-the-wall in Orlando's antiques district just a little north of downtown is the place. Well-heeled Orlandoans eat here before Orlando Magic games; it's also a favorite of waterskiers from Lake Ivanhoe across the street. Located off the beaten tourist track, but only a couple of hundred yards from I-4, it's a wel-come change from I-Drive. Get off I-4 at Ivanhoe (Exit 42); it's three minutes away. ✕ *1421 N. Orange Ave., Orlando,* ☎ *407/894–7907. Reservations accepted. Beer and wine only. MC, V. Closed Sun.*

Mexican

$ Amigo's. There are those who say the best Mexican food in central Florida is at Amigo's, two restaurants run by a family of transplanted Texans. Their strategy consists of building on good basics, like refried beans that would play well in San Antonio. Go for the Santa Fe dinner, so big it almost takes a burro to bring it to your table; you'll be able to sample tamales, enchiladas, chiles rellenos, and those heavenly frijoles and wash it down with a Mexican beer. ✗ *120 Westmoreland, Altamonte Springs,* ☏ *407/774–4334; 494 N. Semoran, Winter Park,* ☏ *407/657–8111. AE, MC, V.*

Middle Eastern

$ Phoenician. This is the latest addition to the rich culinary clique at the Marketplace. Hummus flavored with tahini, *baba ganoush* (roasted eggplant purée), and *lebneh* (soft, seasoned, yogurt-based cheese) top the menu. ✗ *7600 Dr. Phillips Blvd., in the Marketplace, Orlando,* ☏ *407/345–1001. No reservations. AE, MC, V.*

Pizza

$–$$ Donato's. This family-owned restaurant, the only one on the north end of International Drive, is just steps away from the Belz Factory Outlet Mall. There's a takeout deli and grocery store as you walk in. But taking the time to eat in one of the two large dining rooms is worthwhile. Although the decor is delicatessen, the food is abundant and well prepared. ✗ *5159 International Dr., Orlando,* ☏ *407/363–5959. AE, DC, MC, V.*

$–$$ Enzo's at the Marketplace. This pizzeria and deli combines the real Italian flavor of its Longwood sister with an atmosphere that's casual and a location that's more convenient for tourists. Owner Enzo Perlini, a food purist, imported the pizza ovens from Italy to ensure that his *pizza Napoli* would have the proper thin, crispy crust. It does. The toppings are Italian style—fresh tomatoes and mozzarella, seafood, or grilled vegetables. ✗ *7600 Dr. Phillips Blvd., in the Marketplace, Orlando,* ☏ *407/351–1187. AE, D, DC, MC, V.*

$–$$ Positano. One side of this cheerful restaurant is a bustling family-style
★ pizza parlor; the other is a more formal dining room. Although you can't order pizza in the dining room, you can get anything on the entire menu in the pizzeria, which serves some of the best New York–style pies in central Florida. Try the unusual and piquant *ziti aum, aum*— ziti with mozzarella, Parmesan, eggplant, and basil in a tomato sauce. ✗ *8995 W. Colonial Dr., in Good Homes Plaza, Orlando,* ☏ *407/291– 0602. Reservations in dining room only. AE, D, DC, MC, V.*

Seafood

$$ Straub's Fine Seafood. One school of economic thought in Orlando is that the farther you drive from Disney the less you pay for everything. Straub's holds up the culinary part of the equation with items like escargot to go (or to stay) for $6—less than you'd pay for a burger 30 miles away on U.S. 192 in Kissimmee. Straub's is one of those minimalist restaurants that put their emphasis on food, not atmosphere. Tablecloths are covered with Plexiglas, and when you walk into the place, you know there won't be a string quartet playing in the background. But owner Robert Straub, a fishmonger of many years, knows how to prepare a mean mesquite-grilled Atlantic salmon with a little béarnaise on the side. Straub fillets all his own fish and won't serve anything he can't get fresh. Blackened dolphin Cajun-style is quite good here, as is the angel-hair pasta with sautéed shrimp, pine nuts, capers, artichoke hearts, and fresh spinach. The menu states the calorie count and fat content of every fish item, but for the coconut-banana cream pie, made on premises, you just don't want to know. ✕ *5101 E. Colonial Dr., Orlando,* ☎ *407/273–9330; 512 E. Altamonte Dr., Altamonte Springs,* ☎ *407/831–2250. Reservations accepted. AE, D, DC, MC, V.*

Steak

$$$ Del Frisco's Prime Steak House. Orlando finally has a genuine New York–style steak house to call its own. The sound of Ol' Blue Eyes belting the standards swirls about a clubby dining room, where big, juicy sirloins and porterhouses are the entrées of choice. Scalloped potatoes and chopped spinach mixed with melted cheddar cheese and bacon bits come with the steaks and are sure to blow your low-fat diet. ✕ *729 Lee Rd., Orlando,* ☎ *407/645–4443. Reservations advised. AE, DC, MC, V. Closed Sun.*

$$$ Ruth's Chris Steak House. If you've never eaten in a country club but always wanted to, this sublime restaurant, with dark wood paneling, starched white tablecloths, and little lamps at each table, will give you the same feeling. This is a place for beef purists. The sirloins are pan-fried in butter and served à la carte only. Baked potatoes, spinach au gratin, and other accompaniments are all $3 to $5 extra. Even though the atmosphere makes you feel as if you should be wearing a blazer with a crest on it, jackets aren't required for men. ✕ *999 Douglas Ave., Altamonte Springs,* ☎ *407/682–6444. Reservations advised. AE, DC, MC, V.*

Thai

$$ Siam Orchid. One of Orlando's several elegant Asian restaurants, Siam Orchid occupies a gorgeous structure a bit off I-Drive. Waitresses, who wear costumes from their homeland, serve authentic fare such as Siam wings—a chicken wing stuffed to look like a drumstick—and *plalad prig,* a whole, deep-fried fish covered with a sauce flavored with red chili, bell peppers, and garlic. If you like your food spicy, say "Thai hot" and grab a fire extinguisher. ✕ *7575 Republic Dr., Orlando,* ☎ *407/351–0821. Reservations advised. AE, DC, MC, V.*

24-Hour

$$ Beeline Diner. This slick 1950s-style diner in the Peabody Hotel is not exactly cheap, but the salads, sandwiches, and griddle foods are tops. Though very busy at times, it can be fun for breakfast or a late-night snack. And for just a little silver, you get to play a lot of old tunes on the jukebox. ✕ *9801 International Dr., Orlando,* ☎ *407/352–4000. AE, DC, MC, V.*

Vietnamese

$ Little Saigon. As Orlando flourishes, so grow the ethnic restaurants, ★ including a variety of Vietnamese eateries and shops, about 1½ miles east of I–4's U.S. 50 exit. The folks at Little Saigon are friendly and love to introduce novices to their healthy and delicious national cuisine. Sample the spring rolls or the summer rolls (spring roll filling in a soft wrapper), then move on to the grilled pork and egg, served atop rice and noodles, or the traditional soup, filled with noodles, rice, vegetables, and your choice of either chicken or seafood; ask to have extra meat in the soup if you're hungry, and be sure they bring you the mint and bean sprouts to sprinkle in. Ask for an English-speaking waiter if you're unfamiliar with the cuisine. ✕ *1106 E. Colonial Dr., Orlando,* ☎ *407/423–8539. Reservations advised. MC, V. Beer and wine only.*

OFF THE BEATEN TRACK

Continental

$$$$ **Chalet Suzanne.** If you like to drive or are returning from a day at Cy-
★   press Gardens, consider making a dinner reservation at this family-
owned country inn and restaurant. Because of its charm and originality,
Chalet Suzanne has earned praise from restaurant critics. It might provide one of the most memorable dining experiences of your Orlando stay.
Expanded bit by quirky bit since it opened in the 1930s, this unlikely
country inn looks like a small Swiss village—right in the middle of the
orange groves. As an appetizer, try the broiled grapefruit, basted with a
butter, cinnamon, and sugar mixture and served with a grilled chicken
liver; then move on to shrimp curry, lobster Newburg, or filet mignon.
Crepes Suzanne are a good bet for dessert. All meals are prix fixe, with
seven courses; prices begin at $40 and are determined by the cost of your
entrée. ✕ *3800 Chalet Suzanne Dr., U.S. 27 north of Lake Wales, about
10 mi past Cypress Gardens turnoff,* ☎ *813/676–6011. Reservations
advised. Jacket required. AE, DC, MC, V. Closed Mon. in summer.*

8 Lodging

Updated by
Anto Howard

FORGET ABOUT BORA BORA—you're poolside under an azure sky at Disney's Polynesian Resort watching the Mickey-shaped ice cubes bob and dip in your tropical cooler. Is that Ariel swimming in the Popsicle-blue lagoon a hop, skip, and a snorkel dive away? After your first super-charged day discovering the wonders of central Florida, you're beginning to relearn those lounging and loafing skills so dear to every vacationer's heart. Booking yourself into the Polynesian was a wise choice and is turning out to be the perfect pick-me-up. On the other hand, if you haven't yet picked your fantasy accommodation in the Orlando area—which has more than 80,000 hotel rooms—the range of choices will dazzle.

The first big decision: to stay at a hostelry within WDW or one outside the property. There are advantages to each option. To help in finding your perfect room, we've reviewed hundreds of offerings throughout the main hotel hubs both in and surrounding WDW.

How to Choose

When examining your options, give careful thought to the kind of vacation you want. Consider what you want to see during your Orlando visit and how long you want to stay. Within a given price category, compare the facilities of the available establishments to make sure that you get exactly what you want; our charts (*see below*) will help you do this. Don't overlook the savings to be gained from cooking your own breakfast and maybe a few other meals as well, which you can do if you choose an establishment with cooking facilities. If you're traveling with children, remember to ask about the cut-off age, the age at which the management considers your offspring to be adults (and makes you pay accordingly, even when they share your room). Finally, don't overlook time spent in transit; if you're not staying at a property in or near WDW, you can waste a few hours a day sitting in traffic.

Staying in WDW

If you are coming to Orlando for only a few days and are interested solely in the Magic Kingdom, Epcot Center, and the other Disney attractions, the resorts on Disney property—whether or not they're owned by Disney—are the most convenient. Put aside your car keys, because Walt Disney World buses and monorails—free to guests at on-site resorts—are efficient enough to make it possible to visit one park in the morning and another after lunch (if you have a Park- or World-Hopper admission ticket). You have the freedom to return to your hotel for R&R when the crowds are thickest, and if it turns out that half the family wants to spend the afternoon in one of the parks and the other half wants to float around Typhoon Lagoon, it's not a problem.

On-site hotels were built with families in mind. Older children can travel on their own on the transportation system without inviting trouble. Younger children get a thrill from knowing that they're actually living in Walt Disney World. Rooms are usually large enough to accommodate up to five; villas sleep six or seven. All accommodations offer cable TV with the Disney Channel and a daily events channel.

If you're an on-site guest at a Disney hotel, a major perk is free transportation to the various Disney parks, either by monorail—which services three of the leading hostelries—or by motor launch, bus, or tram (the most frequent mode of transportation are buses, which depart every 15 minutes). Disney hotels offer other benefits to their guests. Each day on-site guests can get in to one of the three parks one hour before regular park opening—and even when the theme parks or water parks have reached capacity (as Blizzard Beach, Typhoon Lagoon, and Disney-MGM Studios sometimes do) on-site guests are guaranteed entry. Then there are the small conveniences: Guests at Disney-owned properties are able to charge to their room most meals and purchases throughout WDW. To golfers, it's important to know that Disney guests get first choice of tee times at the golf courses and can also reserve them up to 30 days in advance.

Staying Around Orlando

If you're planning to visit attractions other than WDW or if the Disney resorts seem too rich for your blood, then staying off-site holds a number of advantages. You'll enjoy more peace and quiet and may have easier access to Sea World and Universal Studios—as well as to Orlando's shopping, dining, and entertainment facilities. You're almost certain to save money.

The hotels closest to Walt Disney World are clustered in several principal areas: along **International Drive** within Orlando city limits; within the boundaries of **Kissimmee,** the town that is actually closest to Walt Disney World (where hotels tend to be small and cheap); and in the Disney **Maingate** area around WDW's northernmost entrance, just off I–4. Nearly every hotel in these areas provides frequent transportation to and from Walt Disney World. In addition, there are some noteworthy—if far-flung—options in the suburbs, the U.S. 192 area, and the Greater Orlando area. Since the city isn't so big, even apparently distant properties are seldom much more than a half hour's drive from Disney toll plazas (when traffic is running smoothly). If you're willing to make the commute, you're likely to save a bundle: Whereas accommodations at the Embassy Suites near Lake Buena Vista will cost you upwards of $120 a night, the sister property about 35 minutes away in Altamonte Springs charges around $80 for equally luxurious quarters. Some of the simpler motels with Kissimmee addresses will put you up for $40 a night or even less.

Reservations

All on-site accommodations may be booked through the **Walt Disney World Central Reservations Office** (Box 10100, Suite 300, Lake Buena Vista 32830, ☎ 407/W–DISNEY); persons with disabilities can call **WDW Special Request Reservations** (☎ 407/354–1853, TTY 407/939–7670) to get information or book rooms. Rooms at most non-Disney, chain hotels can be reserved by calling either the hotel itself or the toll-free number for the entire chain. Be sure to tell the reservationist exactly what you are looking for—Disney-owned property or not, price range, the number of people in your party, and the dates of your visit. If possible, stay flexible about dates; many hotels and attractions offer seasonal discounts of up to 40%.

Deposits

You must give a deposit for your first night's stay within three weeks of making your reservation. At many hotels you can get a refund if you cancel at least five days before your scheduled arrival. However, individual hotel policies vary, and some properties may require up to 15 days' notice for a full refund. Check before booking.

When to Book

Reserve several months in advance—as much as a year ahead if you want to snag the best rooms during high season.

Other Options

If neither the WDW Central Reservations Office nor the off-site hotels have space on your preferred dates, look into packages from American Express, Delta, or other operators, who have been allotted whole blocks of rooms. In addition, because there are always cancellations, it's worth trying even at the last minute; for same-day bookings, call the property directly.

Packages, including cruises, car rentals, and hotels both on and off Disney property, can be arranged through your travel agent or **Walt Disney Travel Co.** (1675 Buena Vista Dr., Lake Buena Vista 32830, ☎ 800/828–0228).

Ratings and Rates

Rates are lowest from early January to mid-February, from mid-April to mid-June, and from mid-August to the third week in December; low rates often remain in place longer at non-Disney properties. Always call several places—availability and special deals can often drive room rates at a **$$$$** hotel down into the **$$** range—and don't forget to ask if you're eligible for a discount. Many hotels offer special rates for members of, for example, the American Automobile Association or the American Association of Retired Persons.

CATEGORY	COST
$$$$	over $180
$$$	$120–$180
$$	$65–$120
$	under $65

All rates are for two adults traveling with up to two children during high season, plus 10% tax.

IN WDW: DISNEY HOTELS

Traditionally, guests have had to take a heavy hit in the wallet to stay in Disney-owned hotels. During the past several years, however, the number of moderately priced properties has boomed. With a wide selection of price ranges available, most lodging decisions come down to what area of WDW or what style of hotel strikes your fancy. Resort hotels predominate, but there are also campsites, trailers, and kitchen-equipped suites and villas. These accommodations are clustered together in four sections of Walt Disney World.

The **Magic Kingdom resort area** has ritzy hotels, all of which lie on the Magic Kingdom monorail route and are only minutes away from the park. Fort Wilderness Campground Resort, with trailers and RV and tent sites, is just southeast of this area. The **Epcot Center resort area,** south of the park, includes the luxurious Beach and Yacht Club Resorts as well as the popular Caribbean Beach Resort. Disney's newest high-end property, the Boardwalk Resort—which has a turn-of-the-century Atlantic City atmosphere—is opening near Epcot Center by summer '96. The **Disney Village resort area,** east of Epcot Center, is near Pleasure Island and the Disney Village Marketplace. Accommodations include two midprice resorts with an Old South theme as well as the Disney Village Resort, made up of town houses and villas equipped with kitchens. The newest complex, **All-Star Village,** lies near the intersection of World Drive and U.S. 192, south of Epcot Center and the Magic Kingdom.

Magic Kingdom Resort Area

Resort Hotels

$$$$ **Contemporary Resort.** If the Jetsons ever came to WDW, this 15-story
★ flat-topped pyramid is where they'd stay. Since the monorail runs right
through the heart of this awkwardly modern A-frame, it looks like some
intergalactic docking bay lifted straight out of a futuristic space age.
The Contemporary is a high-class, ideally situated resort complex that
seems to be bustling, in traditional Disney fashion, from the crack of
dawn until after midnight. Half the rooms are in the Tower, the main
building, and you'll have to pay extra for their spectacular views (those
in the front look out toward the Magic Kingdom's Cinderella Castle
and Space Mountain, a great backdrop for the flaming Florida sunsets and the regular nighttime fireworks show; those on the back side
have ringside views of the Electrical Water Pageant and the sun rising
through the mists of Bay Lake). Some guests report that Tower rooms
can be somewhat noisy at night—sounds rise through the busy atrium—
so if you're a light sleeper, you may prefer a room in the hotel's North
and South Gardens, where the other half of the rooms are located; the
best are on the shore of Bay Lake, but all cost less than Tower rooms.
(Try to avoid units described as having a view of the Magic Kingdom—
they have an even better view of the parking lot.) Regardless of location, all rooms have a small terrace and most have two queen-size beds
plus a small day bed. Main recreational facilities are right on the property; one of the swimming pools is WDW's largest, at 20 by 25 me-
ters. Kids happily disappear into the Fiesta Fun Center, one of the biggest
game rooms known to childkind. A short hop on the monorail—which
breezes right into the hotel every 10 to 15 minutes from 7 AM until two
hours after park closing—takes you to the Polynesian and Grand
Floridian hotels as well as to the Magic Kingdom and Epcot Center;
other destinations can be reached by motor launch and bus. 🏨 *WDW
Central Reservations, Box 10100, Lake Buena Vista 32830, ☎ 407/934–
7639; for same-day reservations, ☎ 407/824–1000; fax 407/824–3539.
961 rooms, 80 suites. 3 restaurants, 1 snack bar, 3 lounges, room service, 3 heated outdoor pools, lakeside beach, beauty salon,* health
club, 6 lighted tennis courts, supervised children's program, baby-sitting, volleyball, shuffleboard, marina, boat rentals, water skiing, game
room, guest laundry, concierge services. AE, MC, V.*

$$$$ **Grand Floridian.** At first you might think that a magical Disney time
★ machine transported this gilded-age masterpiece brick by brick from
some turn-of-the-century coastal hot spot to the shores of the Seven
Seas Lagoon. Actually, the gabled red roof, brick chimneys, rambling
verandas, and delicate gingerbread are grand-old yet brand-new, all built
from scratch on the site. Loving attention was paid to each detail, from
the crystal chandeliers and stained-glass domes to the ornate balconies
and aviary. Although equipped with every modern convenience, the moss-
green and salmon-pink rooms, with Victorian wallpaper, deep carpets,
and wall hangings, have real vintage charm, especially the attic nooks
up under the eaves. Deluxe suites are available in the smaller building
known as the Lodge. The Victorian theme extends to the resort's
charming monorail station as well. The monorail itself makes it easy
for guests to zip to the Magic Kingdom and Epcot Center from here;
bus and motor launch lines also connect to the parks. 🏨 *WDW Central Reservations, Box 10100, Lake Buena Vista 32830, ☎ 407/934–
7639 or 407/824–3000, FAX 407/824–3186. 769 rooms, 65 concierge
rooms, 71 suites. 5 restaurants, 4 lounges, room service, large outdoor
heated pool, beach, whirlpool, health club, 2 lighted tennis courts, ma-*

Walt Disney World Lodging

Name of Property	Number of Rooms/Suites	Number of Restaurants	Number of Lounges	Room Service	Complimentary Breakfast	
$$$$						
Buena Vista Palace and Palace Suite Resort	1,028	5	4	✓		
Disney's Village Resort	592	4	4	✓		
Grand Cypress Resort	676	5	4	✓		
Hilton at WDW Village	814	7	2	✓		
Marriott's Orlando World Center	1,504	7	2	✓		
Peabody Orlando	891	3	2	✓		
Stouffer Orlando Resort	780	5	2	✓		
Vistana Resort	722	2	1			
WDW Beach and Yacht Club Resorts	1,218	6	3	✓		
WDW Boardwalk Resort	392	4	4	✓		
WDW Contemporary Resort	1,041	4	3	✓		
WDW Dolphin	1,510	8	3	✓		
WDW Fort Wilderness Resort Homes	408	2	1			
WDW Grand Floridian	905	5	4	✓		
WDW Polynesian Resort	865	3	1	✓		
WDW Swan	758	4	3	✓		
$$$						
Courtyard by Marriott	323	1	1			
Embassy Suites Hotel at Plaza International	246		1		✓	
Embassy Suites International Drive South	245	1	1		✓	
Embassy Suites Orlando—North	210	1	1	✓	✓	
Embassy Suites Resort Lake Buena Vista	280	1	1		✓	
Grosvenor Resort	630	2	1	✓		

In-Room Kitchenettes	In-Room Microwaves	In-Room Coffeemaker	In-Room VCR	No. Swimming Pools	No. Tennis Courts (Lighted)	On-Site Golf	Arcade Game Room	Health Club	Boating	Supervised Children's Program	Baby-Sitting	Guest Laundry
✓	✓	✓	✓	3	3(L)		✓	✓		✓	✓	✓
✓	✓	✓		5			✓	✓	✓		✓	✓
✓	✓	✓		2	12(L)	✓	✓	✓	✓	✓	✓	✓
				2	2(L)		✓	✓		✓	✓	✓
				4	8(L)	✓	✓	✓		✓	✓	✓
				1	4(L)		✓	✓		✓	✓	✓
				1	5(L)		✓	✓		✓		✓
✓	✓	✓		5	13(L)		✓	✓		✓	✓	✓
				3	2(L)		✓	✓	✓	✓	✓	✓
✓				1	2		✓	✓	✓	✓	✓	✓
				3	6(L)		✓	✓	✓	✓	✓	✓
				4	8(L)		✓	✓		✓		✓
✓	✓	✓		3	1(L)		✓		✓	✓	✓	✓
				1	2(L)		✓	✓	✓	✓	✓	✓
				2			✓		✓	✓	✓	✓
				2	8(L)		✓	✓		✓	✓	✓
		✓		2			✓	✓			✓	✓
✓	✓	✓		1			✓	✓			✓	✓
				1							✓	✓
✓	✓	✓		1				✓			✓	✓
				1	1		✓	✓		✓	✓	
		✓	✓	2	2(L)		✓	✓			✓	✓

Walt Disney World Lodging

Name of Property	Number of Rooms/Suites	Number of Restaurants	Number of Lounges	Room Service	Complimentary Breakfast	
Guest Quarters Suite Resort	229	1	1		✓	
Parc Corniche Resort	210	1	1			
Sol Orlando Resort	150	1	1		✓	
Summerfield Suites Hotel	146		1		✓	
WDW Wilderness Lodge	726	3	1	✓		
Westgate Lakes	369	2	1			
$$						
All-Star Sports and All-Star Music Resorts	3,840	2*	2			
Best Western Kissimmee	282	1	1			
Caribbean Beach Resort	2,106	1*	1			
Clarion Plaza Hotel	810	2	1	✓		
Dixie Landings Resort	2,048	1/1*	1			
Enclave Suites at Orlando	321	1	1			
Holiday Inn Maingate East	670	6	2	✓		
Holiday Inn Sunspree Resort	507	1	1	✓		
Hyatt Orlando Hotel	922	4	1			
Orlando Heritage Inn	150	1	1	✓		
Orlando North Hilton	323	1	1	✓		
Park Plaza Hotel	27	1	1	✓	✓	
Perri House	6				✓	
Port Orleans Resort	1,008	1/1*				
Quality Suites Maingate East	225	1	1		✓	
Radisson Inn Maingate	580	1	1	✓		
Ramada Plaza Resort Maingate at the Parkway	718	1	2			

*Food Court

In-Room Kitchenettes	In-Room Microwaves	In-Room Coffeemaker	In-Room VCR	No. Swimming Pools	No. Tennis Courts (Lighted)	On-Site Golf	Arcade Game Room	Health Club	Boating	Supervised Children's Program	Baby-Sitting	Guest Laundry
		✓		1	2(L)		✓	✓			✓	✓
✓	✓	✓	✓	1		✓	✓				✓	✓
✓	✓	✓		1	1		✓	✓			✓	✓
✓	✓	✓	✓	1			✓	✓				✓
				1			✓		✓	✓	✓	✓
✓	✓	✓		1	1(L)		✓	✓	✓	✓	✓	✓
				4			✓				✓	✓
✓				2		✓						
		✓		7			✓		✓		✓	✓
			✓	1							✓	✓
				6			✓		✓			✓
✓	✓	✓		3	1(L)			✓			✓	✓
✓	✓	✓	✓	2	2(L)		✓			✓		✓
✓	✓	✓	✓	1				✓		✓		
				4	3(L)		✓	✓			✓	✓
				1							✓	✓
				1				✓			✓	✓
											✓	✓
				1								
				1			✓				✓	✓
✓	✓	✓		1			✓					✓
				1	2(L)			✓			✓	✓
				2	2(L)		✓	✓			✓	✓

Walt Disney World Lodging

Name of Property	Number of Rooms/Suites	Number of Restaurants	Number of Lounges	Room Service	Complimentary Breakfast
Residence Inn by Marriott on Lake Cecile	159				✓
Royal Plaza	396	2	2		
Sheraton Lakeside Inn	651	2	1	✓	
Travelodge Hotel	325	1	1		
Twin Towers Hotel and Convention Center	790	2	3	✓	
Wyndham Garden Hotel	167	1	1	✓	
$					
Comfort Inn Maingate	281	1	1		
Fairfield Inn by Marriott	135				
Fort Wilderness Resort Campsites	1,185	2	1		
Knights Inn—Maingate	120				
Park Inn International	197	1			
Quality Inn Lake Cecile	222				
Record Motel	57				
Red Roof Inn	102				
Sevilla Inn	46				
Shades of Green on WDW Resort	288	2	1	✓	
Wynfield Inn—Westwood	300				

In-Room Kitchenettes	In-Room Microwaves	In-Room Coffeemaker	In-Room VCR	No. Swimming Pools	No. Tennis Courts (Lighted)	On-Site Golf	Arcade Game Room	Health Club	Boating	Supervised Children's Program	Baby-Sitting	Guest Laundry
✓	✓	✓	✓	1					✓			✓
				1	4(L)		✓				✓	✓
				3	4(L)		✓		✓	✓	✓	✓
				1			✓				✓	✓
				1			✓	✓		✓	✓	✓
				1			✓	✓				
				1			✓					✓
				1			✓					
				3	2(L)		✓		✓			✓
✓				1			✓					✓
	✓			1			✓					
				1								✓
				1							✓	✓
				1								✓
				1								✓
				2	2(L)	✓	✓	✓				✓
				2			✓					✓

Best Western
Kissimmee, **48**

Buena Vista Palace, **23**

Clarion Plaza Hotel, **11**

Comfort Inn
Maingate, **34**

Courtyard by
Marriott, **26**

Embassy Suites International Drive South, **8**

Embassy Suites
Orlando North, **3**

Embassy Suites at
Plaza International, **6**

Embassy Suites Resort
Lake Buena Vista, **20**

Enclave Suites
at Orlando, **5**

Fairfield Inn
by Marriott, **9**

Grand Cypress
Resort, **19**

Grosvenor Resort, **30**

Guest Quarters Suite Resort, **21**

Hilton at WDW
Village, **27**

Holiday Inn
Maingate East, **40**

Holiday Inn
Sunspree Resort
Lake Buena
Vista, **25**

Hyatt Orlando Hotel, **38**

Knights Inn-
Maingate, **36**

Marriott's Orlando
World Center, **29**

Orlando Heritage
Inn, **12**

Orlando North
Hilton, **4**

Parc Corniche
Resort, **18**

Park Inn   International, **41**

Park Plaza Hotel, **2**

Peabody Orlando, **10**

Perri House, **17**

Quality Inn Lake
Cecile, **44**

Quality Suites
Maingate East, **39**

Radisson Inn
Maingate, **34**

Ramada Plaza Resort
Maingate at the Parkway, **37**

Residence Inn
by Marriott
on Lake Cecile, **45**

Record Motel, **46**

Red Roof Inn, **43**

Royal Plaza, **22**

rina, boat rentals, supervised children's program, baby-sitting, play-ground, guest laundry, concierge services. AE, MC, V.

$$$$ **Polynesian Resort.** When you arrive here you almost expect to be greeted with a conch-shell fanfare. The Great Ceremonial House, where visitors check in, sets the exotic mood at this resort, still the most popular of all owned by Disney. A three-story tropical garden (with more than 70 species of tropical plants) fills the lobby; orchids bloom alongside coconut palms and banana trees in the middle of the atrium, and volcanic rock fountains fill the arrival area with the harmonies of cascading water. If it weren't for the kids darting about in Mickey Mouse caps, you might think your travel agent sent you to Fiji by mistake. Rooms are in 11 two- and three-story "longhouses" arranged around this main building. All offer two queen-size beds and a twin bed in the living room to accommodate up to five, and except for some second-floor rooms, all have a balcony or patio. For the best view of the Magic Kingdom and the sandy, palm-trimmed Seven Seas Lagoon, stay in the Samoa and Maori sections, or the King Kamehameha rooms (where guests enjoy special check-in and check-out service, valet parking, complimentary Continental breakfast, afternoon snacks, and wine and cheese in the evening) of Tonga. Lagoon-view rooms are the most peaceful and the priciest. They also have a perfect view of the sparkling, once-nightly Electrical Water Pageant. If you're staying in Tonga, you can sit in the three-story glass conservatory and watch the nightly Magic Kingdom fireworks light the sky overhead. Rooms with garden and pool views are slightly less quiet and slightly less expensive; the least expensive rooms overlook the other buildings, the monorail, and the parking lot. One of the two pools is an extravagantly landscaped, free-form affair with rocks and caverns; both are great for (and beloved by) children, so if you want peace and quiet, head for the beach. Other recreational activities center on the hotel's marina, which rents boats. Exhausted parents never complain about the strict children-only policy at the Neverland Club, the hotel's child-care center, which even offers its young patrons their very own dinner show, Las Vegas style. No wonder more than half of the guests have been here before. Monorail, bus, and motor launch lines network the three parks from here. ◫ *WDW Central Reservations, Box 10100, Lake Buena Vista 32830, ☎ 407/934–7639; for same-day reservations, ☎ 407/824–2000; fax 407/824–3174. 751 rooms, including 102 concierge-serviced rooms, 12 suites. 3 restaurants, snack bar, lounge, room service, 2 outdoor heated pools, lakeside beach, boating, beauty salon, barbershop, game room, playground, volleyball, guest laundry, supervised children's program, baby-sitting, concierge services. AE, MC, V.*

$$$ **Walt Disney World Wilderness Lodge.** You'll almost feel like Lewis and
★   Clark as you follow a long, pine-sheltered, out-of-the-way road to get to this pricey, seven-story Disney hostelry modeled after the turn-of-the-century structures in national parks of the West. Of course, Disney does everything bigger and grander than history ever could, and the sheer size of this lodge—which sits on the southwest shore of Bay Lake—tells you this is no ordinary backwoods cabin. It's really a homage to the Great Indoors and recalls the days when tycoons with names like Vanderbilt were "roughing it" in rustic palaces in the great American woods. The towering five-story lobby is supported by pillars and beams that were once great tree trunks; the lobby's centerpiece is a huge, three-sided stone fireplace that Disney likes to say is 2 billion years old (it's constructed of rocks plucked from various strata of the Grand Canyon); and illumination is provided by enormous chandeliers shaped like tepees. A couple of authentic, 50-foot northwestern totem poles, real Indian headdresses, and other craft items add

to the splendor. The rooms are all decorated in western motifs, with hard-back leather chairs, patchwork quilts, and cowboy art on the walls. Each has either a balcony or a patio, and comes with two queen-size beds, or one queen and two bunk beds if requested. The hotel's show-stopper is its Fire Rock Geyser, a sort of faux Old Faithful, near the large swimming pool area, which itself begins as a hot spring in the main lobby, flows under a window wall to become "Silver Creek," and then widens into a rushing waterfall. You can satisfy a hankerin' for buffalo, elk, or other unusual western-style dishes, as well as some fine wines from the great Northwest, at Artist Point, a dining room inspired by the Craftsman era. Motor launches and buses connect you to all three parks. ✆ *WDW Central Reservations, Box 10100, Lake Buena Vista 32830,* ☎ *407/934–7639,* ｻX *407/824–3232. 697 rooms, 29 suites. 3 restaurants, lounge, room service, large heated swimming pool, children's pool, golf, game room, guest laundry, supervised children's program, baby-sitting. AE, MC, V.*

Camp and Trailer Sites

$–$$ If you're seeking a calm spot amid the theme-park storm, you need go no farther than the 700 acres of scrubby pine, tiny streams, and peaceful canals known as **Fort Wilderness Resort and Campground** on the shore of subtropical Bay Lake about a mile from the Wilderness Lodge Resort. This is about as relaxed as it gets in Walt Disney World. Sports facilities abound, bike trails are popular, and there's a marina where you can rent a sailboat to go out on Bay Lake. Nearby are WDW's River Country water playground and the Meadow Recreation Complex, which has lighted tennis courts and a fast-food snack bar. To experience this property, you can either bring your own tent or RV, or rent one of the fully equipped, air-conditioned Disney trailers (known as Wilderness Homes) parked on the property (*see below*). ✆ *WDW Central Reservations, Box 10100, Lake Buena Vista 32830,* ☎ *407/ W–DISNEY or 407/824–2900 for same-day reservations (and fax). Cafeteria, snack bar, grocery store, 3 outdoor heated pools, lakeside beach, bike paths, bike and canoe rental, fitness trail, petting farm, riding stable, guest laundry, game room, volleyball. AE, MC, V.*

$$$$ **Wilderness Homes.** In the old days people usually stayed in one of these when the rest of moderately priced Orlando was booked up. Then the word got out: cheap family accommodations available in a beautifully forested area. Now people are calling months in advance and requesting the same Wilderness Home they had last year. You won't find *House Beautiful* decor, but these perfectly comfortable accommodations put the relaxed friendliness of Fort Wilderness within reach of families who haven't brought their own RV and don't want to camp out. The larger trailers can accommodate four grown-ups and two youngsters; the bedroom has a double bed and a bunk bed, and the living room has a double sleeper sofa or Murphy bed. The smaller trailers, without the bunk beds, sleep four. Both types come with full kitchen, dishes, linens, a comfortable bathroom, air-conditioning, heat, daily housekeeping services, outdoor grill and picnic table, and even a color TV set with cable. ✆ *408 60- and 80-ft trailers.*

$ **RV and Tent Sites.** Bringing a tent or RV to Walt Disney World is one
★ of the cheapest ways to actually stay on WDW property, especially considering that sites accommodate up to 10. Tent sites with water and electricity are real bargains. RV sites cost more but come equipped with electric, water, and sewage hookups as well as outdoor charcoal grills and picnic tables; you can even get maid service for your trailer. Three hundred "preferred sites," those closest to the lake (numbering from 100 to 500, in the 700s, and in the 1400s), have higher prices but also

have cable TV hookups. Each group of sites has restrooms, showers, telephones, an ice machine, and a laundry room. ☎ *777 sites, including 300 preferred tent sites, 90 tent sites with water and electric hookups, and 387 trailer sites with water, electric, and sewage hookups.*

Epcot Center Resort Area

Resort Hotels

$$$$ **Walt Disney World Beach and Yacht Club Resorts.** Straight out of a Cape
★   Cod summer, these two properties—sited on a 25-acre lake—are coastal inns on a grand Disney scale. The five-story Yacht Club recalls turn-of-the-century New England seacoast resorts, with its hardwood floors, lobby full of gleaming brass and polished leather, oyster-gray clapboard facade, and evergreen landscaping; there's even a lighthouse on its pier. Rooms are similarly nautical, with white and blue naval flags on the bedspreads and a small ship's wheel on the headboard. Drawing on similar inspirations is the blue-and-white, three- to five-story Beach Club, where a croquet lawn, cabana-dotted white-sand beach, and staffers' 19th-century Jams and T-shirts set the scene. Guest rooms are summery, with wicker and pastel furnishings. Both establishments are refreshingly unstuffy, just right for families. Though each has its own restaurants and shops, the pair share certain facilities—including the Sand Castle Club for children and Stormalong Bay, a 3-acre water-recreation area, complete with a shipwreck to clamber over (its mast is an exciting water slide). The hotels are both accessible from Epcot Center via motor launch, and tram and bus lines also travel to the parks. ☎ *WDW Central Reservations, Box 10100, Lake Buena Vista 32830,* ☎ *407/934–7639 or 407/934–8000; fax 407/934–3850 (Beach);* ☎ *407/934–7000, FAX 407/934–3450 (Yacht). 1,158 rooms, including 30 concierge-serviced rooms and 30 suites. 6 restaurants, 3 lounges, room service, heated water recreation area and 2 pools, marina with boat rentals, health club, beauty salon, game room, guest laundry, golf, 2 lighted tennis courts, croquet court, volleyball court, concierge services, supervised program for children 3–12 (4:30–midnight), baby-sitting. AE, MC, V.*

$$$$ **Boardwalk Resort.** Disney's newest hotel brings back to life all the candy-
★   floss enchantment of America's great amusement piers. In the beginning, long before Disneyland ever existed, American holidaymakers unloosened their starched collars at amusement piers that dazzled with elaborately gingerbreaded structures, cotton-candy colors, and pavilions of extravagant design. The most famous was at Atlantic City, and now WDW's noted architectural master, Robert A.-M. Stern, pays homage to Disney's amusement park roots while celebrating vintage Americana at its most madcap. Complete with New England–style verandas, painted marquee signs, and saltwater-taffy touts, it comprises several buildings—ranging from Victorian to Deco—all side-by-side on a lakeside boardwalk. An inn-side view, however, reveals the Inn at the Boardwalk: WDW's smallest and most intimate deluxe hotel, it's accented with courtyards and family-size garden cottages. Thanks to the Muscles and Bustles health club, 10-piece bands, the dueling pianos of the Crazy Fingers Piano Bar, and Luna Park—a pool with a 200-foot water slide in the form of a classic wooden roller coaster—one will never be bored on this boardwalk. Bus, tram, and motor launch lines access the parks. *WDW Central Reservations, Box 10100, Lake Buena Vista 32830,* ☎ *407/W–DISNEY. 378 rooms, 14 cottages. Facilities: 4 restaurants, ESPN Sports Club, Dance Hall nightspot, room service, pool, tennis court, grass croquet court, 15 shops, New England town hall–style convention center. AE, MC, V.*

$$ Caribbean Beach Resort. Talk about tropical punch! Awash with the
★ bright, dizzying colors of the Caribbean, this hotel—the first of Dis-
ney's moderately priced accommodations—was a smash the moment
it opened. Just east of Epcot Center and Disney-MGM Studios, and
surrounding 42-acre Barefoot Bay, this property is composed of five
palm-studded island "villages." Each village is named for a different
Caribbean island—Aruba, Barbados, Jamaica, Martinique, and
Trinidad—and each has its own pool and guest laundry; all share a white-
sand beach. Bridges over the lake connect the mainland with the 1-
acre, path-crossed Parrot Cay, where there's a play area for children.
A mile-long promenade circles the lake and is favored by bikers, jog-
gers, and old-fashioned romantic strollers. The hub of the resort is a
complex called Old Port Royale, which is decorated with pirate's can-
nons and tropical birds and has stores, a food court, and a tropical
lounge. Each village has a different style of decor, but in general the
rooms are attractive and pastel-hued and come equipped with mini-
bars and coffeemakers. They are smaller than rooms in more expen-
sive Disney resorts, but roomy enough for smaller families. You don't
have the dining options that you do at other hotels in the same price
range. Otherwise, the only thing missing is a supervised children's
program. Bus lines network to all parks. ☎ *WDW Central Reserva-*
tions, Box 10100, Lake Buena Vista 32830, ☎ *407/W–DISNEY,* FAX
407/934–3288. 2,106 rooms. Food court, lounge, whirlpool, large heated
outdoor pool with pirate fort and adjacent wading pool, 6 smaller pools,
beach, playground, game room, bike rentals, marina with boat rentals,
guest laundry, jogging track, baby-sitting. AE, MC, V.

Disney Village Resort Area

Resort Hotels

$$ Dixie Landings Resort. Disney's Imagineers drew inspiration from the
antebellum splendor of the Old South's architecture for this sprawl-
ing, moderately priced resort northwest of Disney Village Marketplace and Lake Buena Vista, not far from Fort Wilderness. Rooms are
in three-story plantation-style mansions (any of which a Scarlett or a
Rhett would be proud to call home) and two-story rustic bayou
dwellings. All rooms are the same size and accommodate up to four
in two double beds; they are elegantly decorated with wooden armoires,
and the faucets on the sinks are of gleaming brass. The guest registration area looks like the interior of an old steamboat. The quaintly designed food court offers burgers, sandwiches, breakfast items, and
pizza. The pool, a 3½-acre, old-fashioned swimming-hole complex
called Ol' Man Island, looks like an oversize version of something out
of a Mark Twain novel; it has slides, rope swings, and an adjacent play
area. A marina rents out Water Sprites and other craft. Alas, there's
no children's program. Transportation is provided by bus and motor
launch lines. ☎ *WDW Central Reservations, Box 10100, Lake Buena*
Vista 32830, ☎ *407/W–DISNEY,* FAX *407/934–5777. 2,048 rooms. Food*
court, full-service restaurant, pizza delivery, whirlpool, large heated out-
door pools with adjacent wading pools, play area, game room, boat-
ing, guest laundry. AE, MC, V.

$$ Port Orleans Resort. Disney's version of New Orleans's French Quarter
deftly emulates the charm and romance of the original. Ornate row-house
buildings whose wrought-iron balconies are overgrown with climbing
vines are clustered around squares lushly planted with magnolia trees.
If you choose to go for an evening walk on the lamplit sidewalks that
edge the complex's alleyways, don't be surprised to find yourself on Bour-
bon Street, for all the routes are named after French Quarter thorough-

fares. Crescent City specialties such as red beans and rice, jambalaya, Cajun chicken, beignets, and croissants are on the menu (along with the usual burgers, deli sandwiches, and pizza) at the Sassagoula Floatworks Factory, the hotel's food court. Bonfamille's Café, the hotel's full-service dining room, offers Creole and other Louisiana-style fare. Kids love the large, free-form "Doubloon Lagoon," which is one of the most exotic of all Disney hotel pools: The serpentine body of Neptune twists through the water and becomes a water slide; you zoom out through his mouth. The marina rents the usual assortment of boats. Note that most rooms here have two double beds to accommodate four; for quarters with one king-size bed, book early. Try to get one with a view out over the garden, though these are a little more costly. The hotel doesn't have a child-care program. Bus and motor launch lines access all parks. ☎ *WDW Central Reservations, Box 10100, Lake Buena Vista 32830, ☎ 407/ W–DISNEY or 407/934–5502, FAX 407/934–5777. 1,008 rooms. Food court, full-service restaurant, pizza delivery, whirlpool, large pool area, children's pool, game room, baby-sitting, concierge services, guest laundry, bike rentals. AE, MC, V.*

Villas with Kitchens

$$$$ The secret's out: You don't have to stay at a hotel if you come to WDW. If you're holidaying with your family or a group of friends you might favor the good-value, self-catering option presented by the five clusters of villas at **Disney's Village Resort.** These share a single check-in point, the Village Resort Reception Center. To get around within the village, a car or rented bike or golf cart is necessary, while buses offer transport to the parks. The accommodations are not quite as plush as those in the resort hotels, but they are more personal and homey. You certainly get more space than in a hotel room, not to mention proximity to great golf, WDW's most extensive shopping, and the lively after-dark action of Pleasure Island. ☎ *WDW Central Reservations, Box 10100, Lake Buena Vista 32830, ☎ 407/934–7639 or 407/827–1100, FAX 407/934–2741. 4 restaurants, 4 lounges, room service, 5 outdoor pools (3 heated), 84 whirlpools, full kitchens, game room, playground, health club, fitness trail, baby-sitting, guest laundry, boat rentals. AE, MC, V.*

$$$$ **Fairways Villas.** The name hints at this complex's proximity to the links: These officially titled Two-Bedroom Deluxe Villas sit beside the Lake Buena Vista Golf Course, one of WDW's best. Built of cedar like the One-Bedroom Suites, these guest quarters are more tastefully decorated than those of some of the other villas and are very spacious. Done in muted mauves and blues, each sleeps eight in two bedrooms with two double beds each, a loft with a queen-size bed, and a living room with a Murphy bed. ☎ *64 units.*

$$$$ **Grand Vista Suites.** These attractively furnished accommodations, originally designed as two-story, 2,000-square-foot condominiums for a housing development, are now available to rent. All the comforts of a luxury hotel are offered, including nightly turndown service and stocked refrigerators. ☎ *4 units.*

$$$$ **One-Bedroom Suites.** The smallest and least expensive of the villas, these were designed to meet the needs of business people attending meetings at the nearby WDW Conference Center. The accommodations are built of cedar and have one bedroom with two queen-size beds, a day bed in an adjacent parlor, microwave, coffee/tea maker, and a wet bar but no kitchen—they're the only villas without one. A few deluxe units with whirlpools sleep six, but most of the suites accommodate five. ☎ *316 units.*

$$$$ One- and Two-Bedroom Villas. These facilities have fully equipped kitchens and either one or two bedrooms. The one-bedroom units have a king-size bed in one room and a double Murphy bed in the living room and sleep up to four. The two-bedroom units, which sleep six, have a sofa bed in the living room, a king-size bed in one bedroom, and a queen-size or two doubles in the other. ⊞ *39 one-bedroom units, 89 two-bedroom units.*

$$$$ Treehouse Villas. Take your vacation experience to a whole new level
★ with these out-of-the-way forest retreats on stilts, officially known as the Two-Bedroom Resort Villas with Study. Isolated within a serene, heavily wooded area ribboned with canals, these won't exactly make you feel like Tarzan or Jane, but the woods do occasionally reverberate with a howl or two late at night. Each villa accommodates six and has a kitchen and breakfast bar, two bathrooms, and two bedrooms with queen-size beds on the main level, plus a double-bedded study. There is a utility room with washer and dryer on a lower level. ⊞ *60 units.*

All-Star Village

Resort Hotels

$$ All-Star Sports and All-Star Music Resorts. What could America possibly love more than Mickey Mouse? Sports and music, perhaps. The buildings at each resort carry out one of five sports themes (baseball, football, tennis, surfing, and basketball) or five music themes (Broadway, country, jazz, rock, and calypso). Don't worry about being able to tell one from the other; gargantuan exterior ornamentations define each themed area. Stairwells in the shape of giant bongos stand on each side of Calypso, a three-story silhouette of a sax player adorns Jazz, and so it continues in Sports with 30-foot tennis rackets striking balls the size of small cars, baseball bats as big as oak trees, and football helmets you could climb into. Each resort has two pools: In Sports, the Grand Slam pool is shaped like a baseball diamond, while Music's Calypso pool is in the form of a giant guitar. The Sports and Music resorts mark Disney's entry into the economy-priced hotel market, and so, under the elaborate packaging, the buildings are basically well-maintained motels. Each room has two double beds, a closet rod, an armoire, and a desk. The End Zone and Intermission food courts offer a predictable selection of fast foods, from pizza to barbecue. The complex is in the northwest quadrant of the World Drive/U.S. 192 interchange, southwest of Disney-MGM Studios and Epcot Center; transportation to other WDW sites is by bus. ⊞ *WDW Central Reservations, Box 10100, Lake Buena Vista 32830,* ☎ *407/W–DISNEY,* ☎ *407/939–7333 (Sports), 407/939–7222 (Music). 1,920 rooms at each resort. 2 food courts, 2 poolside bars, 4 pools, 2 merchandise centers, guest laundry, game room, baby-sitting. AE, MC, V.*

OTHER HOTELS IN WDW

Though not operated by the Disney organization, the Swan and the Dolphin just outside Epcot Center, the military's Shades of Green Resort near the Magic Kingdom, and the seven hotels along Hotel Plaza Boulevard (near the Disney Village resort area) call themselves "official" Walt Disney World hotels. While the Swan, Dolphin, and Shades of Green hostelries offer the special privileges of on-site Disney hotels, such as free transportation to and from the parks, the Hotel Plaza resorts do not (although these hotels do offer their own transport systems).

Hotel Plaza

$$$$ **Buena Vista Palace and Palace Suite Resort at Walt Disney World Vil-**
★ **lage.** This bold, sand-colored tower, the largest hotel at Lake Buena
Vista, seems small and quiet when you enter its lobby. Don't be fooled.
Better indications of its enormity are its sprawl of parking lots, the height
of its taller tower, and its huge roster of facilities, right down to a business center with translation and secretarial service. Restaurants and
lounges include the Australian-themed Outback and the Laughing
Kookaburra Good Time Bar next door, and the Top of the Palace Lounge
and the formal Arthur's 27 (*see* Chapter 7, Dining), which offer a ringside seat for the local sunsets and Epcot Center's nightly laser-and-fire-
works show. Upper-floor rooms in the main hotel are more expensive;
the best ones look out toward Epcot Center's Spaceship Earth. Ask for
a room in the main tower, where the original rooms are, to avoid the
late-night noise that reverberates through the atrium from the Kookaburra. All bedrooms come with one king- or two queen-size beds. Suites
in the adjacent Island Resort accommodate up to eight people—a nice
alternative for larger families or people who just want extra space. All
rooms have private balconies or patios; in the Island Resort section,
rooms come with queen-size sleeper sofas and dining areas with coffeemaker and microwave. The hotel sits right on Lake Buena Vista,
where a private marina provides Water Sprites, jet boats, sea cycles,
and other craft. 🖹 *1900 Lake Buena Vista Dr., Lake Buena Vista 32830,*
☎ *407/827–2727 or 800/327–2990,* ℻ *407/827–6034. 1,028 rooms.*
5 restaurants, 4 lounges, snack bar, room service, 1 indoor-outdoor
heated pool, 1 lap pool, 1 wading pool, health club, whirlpool, sauna,
playground, 3 lighted tennis courts, beauty salon, game room, sand
volleyball court, business center, supervised children's program in sum-
mer, baby-sitting, guest laundry. AE, DC, MC, V.

$$$$ **Hilton at Walt Disney World Village.** One of the leading establish-
★ ments along Hotel Plaza Boulevard, the Hilton is also among the most
expensive. An ingeniously designed waterfall tumbles down off the covered entrance to the hotel and into a stone fountain surrounded by palm
trees so hefty you'd think they were on steroids. Another fountain adorns
the lobby, which is enlivened by floral carpeting, shell-shaped cornices,
and two large tanks of tropical fish. Guest rooms positively sparkle in
bright yellow and mauve and, although not huge, are cozy and contemporary. Each has a king-size bed or two double beds, and amenities include a minibar, cable TV, and in-room movies. Prices vary
dramatically from one location, floor, and season to another. Keep in
mind that if you must book a room at the lowest rate—on a lower floor
with a mediocre view—the check-in clerk can assign you to a better
room if one is available, at an extra charge of $30 to $40. The Vacation Station, a hotel-within-a-hotel, is aimed at the kids, with a video
arcade, Sunday morning breakfast with Mickey and Minnie, and a supervised playroom with large-screen television and six-bed dormitory
that operates every evening; meals are served on schedule, and the cost
is $4 an hour. 🖹 *1751 Hotel Plaza Blvd., Lake Buena Vista 32830,*
☎ *407/827–4000; for reservations, 800/782–4414; fax 407/827–*
3890. 787 rooms, 27 suites. 7 restaurants, 2 lounges, room service, 2
outdoor heated pools, outdoor whirlpool, 2 lighted tennis courts, su-
pervised program for children 4–12 (4:30 PM–midnight daily), baby-
sitting, health club, business center, lobby shops, guest laundry, valet
parking. AE, DC, MC, V.

$$$ **Courtyard by Marriott.** Once under the Howard Johnson name, this
hotel has undergone a recent multimillion-dollar renovation by the Court-
yard arm of Marriott (which offers the chain's more moderately priced

accommodations). The 14-story atrium is now accented with gazebos, white-tile trim, and tropical gardens, all creating a tranquilizing place where guests can enjoy a gourmet breakfast under white umbrellas. By evening, you'll find the energy center has shifted to the Tipsy Parrot, the hotel's welcoming bar. Guest rooms are Marriott-modern and feature handy coffeemakers. ☎ *1805 Hotel Plaza Blvd., Lake Buena Vista 32830,* ☎ *407/828–8888 or 800/223–9930,* FAX *407/827–4623. 323 rooms. Restaurant, lounge, 2 heated pools, children's pool, whirlpool, game room, playground, exercise room, baby-sitting, guest laundry. AE, DC, MC, V.*

$$$ **Grosvenor Resort.** Offering a wealth of facilities and comfortable rooms for a fair price, this attractive member of the Best Western chain is the best deal in the neighborhood. Rooms are average in size but colorfully decorated and have many amenities, including minirefrigerator, coffeemaker, and VCR (rent movies in the lobby). Public areas are spacious, with a Colonial-Caribbean decor. Baskerville's, decorated with Sherlock Holmes memorabilia, serves traditional fare and hosts a weekly Saturday night murder mystery dinner show, with the Baker Street sleuth himself turning up to grill the witnesses (including you perhaps) and sort out the clues. ☎ *1850 Hotel Plaza Blvd., Lake Buena Vista 32830,* ☎ *407/828–4444 or 800/624–4109,* FAX *407/828–8192. 624 rooms, 6 suites. 2 restaurants, lounge, room service, 2 heated outdoor pools, children's pool, whirlpool, game room, 2 lighted tennis courts, playground, shuffleboard, basketball court, volleyball court, rental movies and videocameras, baby-sitting, guest laundry. AE, DC, MC, V.*

$$$ **Guest Quarters Suite Resort.** Lodgings in this modern, L-shaped, con-
★   crete-and-tinted-glass structure are all in one- or two-bedroom suites. That extra room can make all the difference when the kids—or the alleged grownups—decide they want to spend all night retelling (and embellishing) the adventures of the day gone by. Convenient for small families or groups who want to avoid the hassle of cots and the expense of two separate hotel rooms, each bedroom has a king-size or two double beds, and the separate living area is equipped with a sofa bed, so the suites can sleep up to 6 or 10 respectively (if not particularly comfortably). There's a television in each room plus another in the bathroom, as well as a refrigerator, wet bar, and coffeemaker; microwave ovens are available on request. ☎ *2305 Hotel Plaza Blvd., Lake Buena Vista 32830,* ☎ *407/934–1000 or 800/424–2900,* FAX *407/934–1011. 229 units. Restaurant, lounge, ice cream parlor, pool bar, heated pool, children's pool, 2 lighted tennis courts, whirlpool, exercise room, jogging trail, baby-sitting, guest laundry. AE, DC, MC, V.*

$$–$$$ **Royal Plaza.** Would you like to sleep in the same place Burt Reynolds and Barbara Mandrell do? When in Orlando, the two celebrities stay here, in suites named after them. The rest of the time you can book these rooms—complete with photos, gold records, and other memorabilia donated by the stars themselves. For the most part, this casual, lively establishment is popular among families. Each of the generously proportioned rooms has a terrace or balcony, and the best ones overlook the pool. Be sure your quarters aren't too close to the ground floor if you have any interest in sleeping late or napping in the afternoon. The Giraffe, the hotel's Top-40 nightclub, hops until the wee, wee hours. ☎ *1905 Hotel Plaza Blvd., Lake Buena Vista 32830,* ☎ *407/828–2828 or 800/248–7890,* FAX *407/827–3977. 386 rooms, 10 suites. 2 restaurants, 2 lounges, heated outdoor pool, whirlpool, sauna, 4 lighted tennis courts, guest laundry, baby-sitting. AE, DC, MC, V.*

$$–$$$ **Travelodge Hotel.** An old, black London taxi is parked outside the front entrance and the lobby is very British, with polished chandeliers, deep green carpet, a two-story winding staircase, and big, broad wicker chairs. Though otherwise unexceptional, this is a quality property and a good choice for families, especially now that its guest rooms have been refurbished with attractive furniture, touches of brass, and hues of baby blue, peach, and soft green. Each room comes with one king-size or two double beds and private balcony. For nightly entertainment—and great vistas of Epcot Center—head for Topper's, on the 18th floor. ☏ *2000 Hotel Plaza Blvd., Lake Buena Vista 32830, ☎ 407/828–2424 or in FL, 800/423–1022; outside FL, 800/348–3765; fax 407/828–8933. 325 rooms. Restaurant, lounge, 2 snack bars, heated pool, playground, game room, guest laundry, baby-sitting. AE, DC, MC, V.*

Epcot Center Resort Area

$$$$ **Walt Disney World Dolphin.** Not everyone takes to this Sheraton-op-
★ erated bit of whimsy, but no one denies that its wild, imaginative ambience is fast making it a leading Disney landmark. Two mythical 56-foot sea creatures—labeled dolphins by the hotel's noted architect, Michael Graves—perch atop each end of the building; between them soars a 27-story pyramid, one of the highest structures in Walt Disney World. A waterfall cascades down the facade from seashell to seashell and then into a 54-foot-wide clamshell supported by other giant dolphin sculptures; in true Florida spirit, the building's coral-and-turquoise facade displays a mural of giant banana leaves. Inside, chandeliers are shaped like monkeys, and room decor is equally jocular with palm tree-shaped lamps and wildly colorful bedspreads. The best rooms overlook Epcot Center and have a stunning view of its nightly fireworks show. Special registration and concierge services are available to those staying in the Tower (12th through 20th floors). The Grotto Pool features a high-speed water slide. With its emphasis on the convention trade, this hotel, despite its zany decor, is more urban and adult than many other on-site properties. Kids, however, will feel right at home at Camp Dolphin, the hotel's supervised program for children. Bus, tram, and motor launch lines access the parks. ☏ *1500 Epcot Resorts Blvd., Lake Buena Vista 32830, ☎ 407/934–4000 or 800/227–1500, FAX 407/934–4884. 1,185 rooms, 140 suites, 185 Tower rooms. 8 restaurants, minibars, in-room safes, 3 lounges, room service, 4 outdoor heated pools, lakeside beach, 8 lighted tennis courts, beauty salon, game room, boat rentals, exercise room, supervised program for children 3–11 (4 PM–midnight), baby-sitting, multilingual concierge services. AE, DC, MC, V.*

$$$$ **Walt Disney World Swan.** Facing its twin property, the Dolphin, across Crescent Lake, the Swan is another example of the postmodern "Learning from Las Vegas" school of entertainment architecture characteristic of design genius Michael Graves, the hotel's architect. Two 45-foot swans grace the rooftop of this coral-and-aquamarine hotel, which is connected to the Dolphin by a covered causeway. Inside, Graves canopied the ceiling with tall, gathered papyrus reeds and lined up a regiment of columns with palm-frond capitals. Guest rooms, located in the 12-story main building and in two seven-story wings, are decorated in floral and geometric patterns; the quirky theme continues with pineapples painted on the furniture and exotic bird-shaped lamps. As at the Dolphin, the atmosphere is more grown-up and less family oriented than that at many other on-site properties, though there are certainly plenty of facilities that families will appreciate, including Camp Swan, a supervised children's program. Bus, tram, and motor launch

lines connect this Westin-managed hotel with the parks. ☎ *1200 Epcot Resorts Blvd., Lake Buena Vista 32830,* ☎ *407/934–3000, 800/248–7926, or 800/228–3000; fax 407/934–4499. 758 rooms (45 concierge rooms on 11th and 12th floors). 4 restaurants, in-room safes, refrigerators, 3 lounges, room service, 2 heated outdoor pools, beach, health club, 8 lighted tennis courts, beauty salon, game room, boat rentals, supervised program for children 3–11 (4 PM–midnight), baby-sitting. AE, DC, MC, V.*

Magic Kingdom Resort Area

$–$$ Shades of Green on Walt Disney World Resort. Formerly the Disney Inn, this quiet resort, only two minutes by car from the Magic Kingdom, is now operated by the U.S. Armed Forces Recreation Center. Vacationing active-duty and retired personnel from all branches of the armed forces as well as those in the reserves, National Guard, and Department of Defense are eligible to stay here, and rates vary with your rank. Flanked by three world-class golf courses, the hotel offers spacious, country-style rooms that accommodate up to five in two queen-size beds and a comfortable sleeper sofa. Choose among views of the fairways, lush gardens, or pools. ☎ *WDW Central Reservations, Box 10100, Lake Buena Vista 32830,* ☎ *407/824–3600. 288 rooms. 2 restaurants, lounge, room service, 2 pools, children's pool, 2 lighted tennis courts, golf, game room, health club, guest laundry. AE, MC, V.*

INTERNATIONAL DRIVE

If you plan to visit other attractions besides Walt Disney World, the sprawl of newish hotels, restaurants, and shopping malls known as International Drive—"I-Drive" to locals and "Florida Center" in formal parlance—makes a convenient base. Parallel to I-4 (and accessible from Exits 28, 29, and 30), it's just a few minutes south of downtown Orlando. It's also near Sea World, Universal Studios, Wet 'n' Wild, and several popular dinner theaters.

Each part of the Drive has its own personality. The southern end is classier; the concentration of cheaper restaurants, fast-food joints, and inexpensive malls increases as you go north.

$$$$ Peabody Orlando. At 11 AM every morning, the celebrated Peabody
★ Ducks exit a private elevator into the enormous marble-floored lobby and waddle their way across a special red carpet to the little marble fountain in which they pass the day, basking in the glory of high-class fame: Eat your heart out, Donald. At 5 PM, to the delight of gathered crowds, the royal marching mallards repeat the ritual in reverse. Built by the owners of the landmark Memphis, Tennessee, Peabody Hotel, this 27-story structure looks like three high-rise office blocks from afar. But don't be put off by its austere exterior. Inside, the place is very impressive and handsomely designed. The most panoramic of the oversize beige-and-cream rooms have views of Walt Disney World, and every one comes with minibar and hair dryer; those in the Peabody Club on the top three floors enjoy special concierge service. There are three noteworthy restaurants: Capriccio's, serving Italian fare; Dux, with new American cuisine ranked by some gourmands among the best in Orlando; and the Beeline, a 24-hour 1950s-style diner (*see* Chapter 7, Dining). Located across the street from the Orange County Convention Center, the hotel attracts rock stars and other performers as well as conventioneers and duck lovers. ☎ *9801 International Dr., Orlando 32819,* ☎ *407/352–4000 or 800/732–2639,* ℻ *407/351–9177. 891*

rooms. 3 restaurants, 2 lounges, room service, pool, children's pool, 4 lighted tennis courts, tennis lessons, whirlpool, health club and spa, supervised children's program, baby-sitting, golf privileges, concierge services. AE, D, DC, MC, V.

$$$$ **Stouffer Orlando Resort.** This bulky building directly across the street from Sea World looks more like a Federal Reserve Bank than a comfortable hotel. Longer than a football field, its atrium lobby is billed as the world's largest (at 65,000 square feet). Occupying the entire core of the building, it is full of waterfalls, goldfish ponds, and palm trees; as guests shoot skyward in sleek glass elevators, exotic birds twitter in a large, hand-carved, gilded Victorian aviary. It's nice to be greeted with a glass of champagne when you register, but the spaciousness of the guest rooms, which are central Florida's largest, and the luxury of their marble bathrooms are even more pleasant. The most expensive rooms face the atrium, but if you're a light sleeper, ask for an outside room to avoid the music and party sounds that come from gatherings there. ☎ *6677 Sea Harbor Dr., Orlando 32821, ☎ 407/351–5555 or 800/468–3571, FAX 407/351–9991. 780 rooms. 5 restaurants, 2 lounges, room service, heated pool, children's pool, whirlpool, 5 lighted tennis courts, health club, sauna, game room, volleyball court, supervised children's program, baby-sitting, beauty salon, concierge services, guest laundry, golf privileges. AE, D, DC, MC, V.*

$$$–$$$$ **Westgate Lakes.** Formerly the Sonesta Villa Resort, this complex of
★ multi-unit town houses not far from International Drive is like a huge luxury apartment complex on a lake. Each unit is small but homey and comfortable, with a kitchenette, dining area, living room, small patio, bedroom, one or two bathrooms, and private ground-floor entrance; some units are bilevel. Guests can sail and waterski on the lake, sun themselves on the sandy beach, or golf at nearby clubs. If you want to cook at "home" but are too busy to shop, the hotel will pick up groceries for you and deliver them while you're out. ☎ *10000 Turkey Lake Rd., Orlando 32819, ☎ 407/352–8051 or 800/766–3782, FAX 407/345–5384. 369 units. 2 restaurants, lounge, pool bar and grill, ice cream parlor, heated outdoor pool, children's pool, 11 whirlpools, water sports (water-ski, Jet Ski, and paddleboat rental), health club, 2 lighted tennis courts, supervised children's program, baby-sitting, volleyball, shuffleboard, jogging path, game room, grocery delivery service, guest laundry. AE, D, DC, MC, V.*

$$$ **Embassy Suites Hotel at Plaza International.** The concept of an all-suites hotel that serves a free buffet breakfast and complimentary cocktails, pioneered by the Embassy Suites chain, has proved very popular in Orlando (there are currently four Embassy Suites hotels in the area). There are several reasons for this: The arrangement is comfortable—each unit has both a bedroom and a full living room equipped with wet bar, refrigerator, pull-out sofa and two TVs—and, more to the point, the cost is modest (less than that of a single room in the top hotels). This member of the chain has a central atrium that contains a lounge where a player piano sets the mood. The two-room suites can sleep up to six, and their kitchenettes, equipped with microwave, refrigerator, and coffeemaker, make it possible to eat in. ☎ *8250 Jamaican Ct., Orlando 32819, ☎ 407/345–8250 or 800/327–9797, FAX 407/352–1463. 246 rooms. Lounge, indoor-outdoor pool, exercise room, whirlpool, sauna, steam room, complimentary breakfast and cocktails, baby-sitting, game room. AE, D, DC, MC, V.*

$$$ **Embassy Suites International Drive South.** Another of the all-suite chain of hotels, this member has a expansive lobby with marble floors, pillars, hanging lamps, and old-fashioned ceiling fans. Tropical gardens with mossy rock fountains and palm trees add to the atrium's distinctive southern ambience. Elsewhere, ceramic tile walkways and brick arches complement the tropical mood. ☎ *8978 International Dr., Orlando 32819,* ☎ *407/352–1400 or 800/432–7272,* ℻ *407/363– 1120. 245 suites. Restaurant, lounge, complimentary breakfast and cocktails, indoor pool, whirlpool, steam room, sauna, supervised children's program, baby-sitting. AE, D, DC, MC, V.*

$$$ **Parc Corniche Resort.** This resort is a good bet for golf enthusiasts: It's framed by an 18-hole Joe Lee–designed golf course. Each of the one- and two-bedroom suites is decked out in pastels and tropical patterns and has a patio or balcony with a golf course view as well as a kitchen. The largest accommodations, with two bedrooms and two baths, can sleep up to six. The resort serves a complimentary Continental breakfast daily, and Sea World is only a few blocks away. ☎ *6300 Parc Corniche Dr., Orlando 32821,* ☎ *407/239–7100 or 800/446–2721,* ℻ *407/239–8501. 210 suites. Restaurant, lounge, heated pool, wading pool, whirlpool, golf, playground, game room, baby-sitting, guest laundry. AE, D, MC, V.*

$$$ **Summerfield Suites Hotel.** "Time to go to bed, kids—yes!—in your own room." How many times have you wanted to say that on your vacation? Sleeping from four to eight people, the one- and two-bedroom units at the all-suites Summerfield are a great option for big families. Parents relish the chance for a little peace, and the youngsters enjoy the feeling of grown-up privacy and, more importantly, the chance to control their own TV fate (there is a box in each room). Two-bedroom units, the most popular, have fully equipped kitchens, plus a living room with TV and VCR. Plush landscaping manages to give the place a secluded feel even though it's on International Drive. The courtyard shelters a small but pretty pool, with a poolside bar where you can get hot dogs and burgers. If you don't want the hassle of whipping up eggs in the morning, you can sample the hotel's free Continental buffet— or stop in at one of the restaurants in the Mercado Mediterranean Village across the street. ☎ *8480 International Dr., Orlando 32819,* ☎ *407/352–2400 or 800/833–4353,* ℻ *407/352–4631. 146 suites (42 with 1 bedroom, 104 with 2). Lounge, in-suite kitchen, heated outdoor pool, children's pool, whirlpool, convenience store, game room, exercise room, guest laundry, rental movies. AE, D, DC, MC, V.*

$$–$$$ **Enclave Suites at Orlando.** With three 10-story buildings surrounding an office, restaurant, and recreation area, this all-suite lodging is less a hotel than a condominium complex. Here, what you would spend for a room in a fancy hotel gets you a complete apartment, with significantly more space than you'll find in other all-suite hotels. Accommodating up to six, the units have full kitchens, living rooms, two bedrooms, and small terraces. This is a great deal for families or small groups of friends (good friends) who don't mind skipping the hotel hustle, and the studio suites are wonderful for couples. The Enclave Beach Cafe is popular with local yuppies. ☎ *6165 Carrier Dr., Orlando 32819,* ☎ *407/351–1155 or 800/457–0077,* ℻ *407/351–2001. 321 suites. Restaurant, lounge, in-suite kitchens, 2 heated outdoor pools, indoor pool, whirlpool, sauna, exercise room, lighted tennis court, playground, baby-sitting, guest laundry. AE, D, DC, MC, V.*

$$–$$$ **Twin Towers Hotel and Convention Center.** When it opened in the mid-1970s, this was the largest convention hotel between Miami and Atlanta. It's still a hotbed of business-trippers, but a $30 million renovation has targeted the huge theme-park tourist market. The we-try-harder attitude and the great location right at the entrance to Universal Studios Florida give it a head start. And don't worry about noisy conventioneers—the meeting and convention facilities are completely isolated from the guest towers. The comfortable, if nondescript, rooms

are oversize and have wicker furnishings, one king- or two queen-size beds, cable TV, and in-room movies. Among the dining-and-drinking options are a deli open around-the-clock, the Palm Court Restaurant (which serves three meals daily), and the Everglades Lounge (with live entertainment and a large-screen TV). ⌕ *5780 Major Blvd., Orlando 32819, ☎ 407/351–1000 or 800/327–2110, ꜰᴀx 407/363–0106. 760 rooms, 30 suites. 2 restaurants, 3 lounges, deli, room service, pool, children's pool, whirlpool, exercise room, sauna, game room, playground, supervised children's program, baby-sitting, guest laundry. AE, D, DC, MC, V.*

$$ Clarion Plaza Hotel. You'll see no shortage of wide-eyed convention-eers sporting name tags at this 12-story hotel alongside the Orange County Convention Center. Yet leisure travelers are gradually discovering both the hotel's prime location, minutes from attractions, and its long list of amenities generally found only at more expensive properties. The guest rooms are simple but large and elegant, with two queen-size beds and a nice little extra: a video-game unit hooked up to the TV. The dining line-up is exceptional for a hotel in this price range: There's the 24-hour Lite Bite; the upbeat Café Matisse, a coffee shop that serves elaborate buffets; and the richly paneled Jack's Place, which serves steaks, seafood, and huge desserts on tables dressed in crisp white linens amid autographed caricatures of famous movie stars. ⌕ *9700 International Dr., Orlando 32819, ☎ 407/352–9700 or 800/627–8258, ꜰᴀx 407/352–9710. 810 rooms. 2 restaurants, lounge, coffee shop, lobby bar, in-room safes, in-room VCRs, room service, heated outdoor pool, whirlpool, game room, baby-sitting, guest laundry. AE, D, DC, MC, V.*

$$ Orlando Heritage Inn. Standing out like a curiosity among the very mod-
★ ern car parks, gas stations, and high-rises of International Drive, the exterior of this two-story, pale-pink structure was inspired by the owner's love for *Gone with the Wind*. It has white railings on all balconies, a first-floor veranda with big wooden rocking chairs and four brass ceiling fans, and, on top, a polished weather vane. Inside the lobby atrium, the decor moves to imitate a later, Victorian-era Florida. In the guest rooms, folk art hangs on walls, lace curtains adorn the double French doors, and quilted spreads cover the beds. Dinner shows are presented in the rotunda several nights weekly. ⌕ *9861 International Dr., Orlando 32819, ☎ 407/352–0008 or 800/447–1890, ꜰᴀx 407/352–5449. 150 rooms. Restaurant, lounge, dinner theater, in-room safes, room service, heated outdoor pool, baby-sitting, guest laundry. AE, D, DC, MC, V.*

$–$$ Wynfield Inn–Westwood. If you don't want a room with just the bare essentials yet don't have the budget for luxury, this two-story motel is a find. Its cheerful, contemporary rooms are smartly appointed with colorful, floral-print bedspreads, peach walls, and understated wall hangings. Complimentary coffee and tea are served in the lobby every day. The staff is friendly and helpful and acts more like the staff of a "do-anything-to-please" independent motel. Children 17 and under stay free in their parents' room (with a maximum of four guests per room). ⌕ *6263 Westwood Blvd., Orlando 32821, ☎ 407/345–8000 or 800/346–1551, ꜰᴀx 407/345–1508. 300 rooms. 2 outdoor pools (1 heated), pool bar, game room, guest laundry. AE, D, DC, MC, V.*

$ Fairfield Inn by Marriott. This understated, few-frills, three-story hotel—the Marriott Corporation's answer to the Motel 6 and Econolodge chains—is a natural for single travelers or small families on a tight budget. It's squeezed between International Drive and the highway and doesn't have the amenities of top-of-the-line Marriott properties, but nice perks such as complimentary coffee and tea, free local phone calls, and cable TV give a sense of being at a much fancier property. ☎ *8342 Jamaican Ct., Orlando 32819,* ☎ *407/363–1944 or 800/228–2800,* FAX *407/363–1944. 135 rooms. Heated outdoor pool, game room. AE, D, DC, MC, V.*

MAINGATE

Outside the northernmost entrance to WDW, just off I–4, the Maingate area is full of large hotels unaffiliated with Walt Disney World, mostly sprawling, high-quality resorts catering to Walt Disney World vacationers. Although they share a certain sameness with resorts the world over, they vary in size and price. As a rule, the bigger the resort and the more extensive the facilities, the more you can expect to pay. If you're looking for a clean, modern room, you cannot go wrong with any of them. All are equally convenient to Walt Disney World. One may emphasize one recreational activity more than another, so your ultimate decision may depend on how much time you plan to spend at your hotel and which of your strokes—your drive or your backhand—requires the most attention.

$$$$ **Grand Cypress Resort.** If you polled those familiar with Orlando to
★ name its most spectacular resort, few would hesitate to name the Grand Cypress. With more than 1,500 acres, it is huge and offers virtually every resort facility, and then some—even a 45-acre nature preserve. Golf facilities are first-class, with 45 Jack Nicklaus–designed holes (four courses and a high-tech golf school). The huge, 800,000-gallon swimming pool resembles an enormous grotto, has a 45-foot water slide, and is fed by 12 cascading waterfalls. And as you'd expect of a first-class Hyatt resort, the hotel has a striking 18-story atrium filled with tropical plants. Accommodations are divided between the 750-room Hyatt Regency Grand Cypress and the 146-unit Villas of Grand Cypress. The one-, two-, three-, and four-bedroom villas, near the fairways, are luxuriously furnished and include cathedral ceilings and tile floors; the larger ones have a full kitchen. The restaurants are excellent (*see* Chapter 7, Dining). There's just one drawback: the king-size conventions that the Grand Cypress commonly attracts. ☎ *Hyatt Regency Grand Cypress, 1 Grand Cypress Blvd., Orlando 32836,* ☎ *407/239–1234 or 800/233–1234,* FAX *407/239–3800. 676 rooms. Villas of Grand Cypress, 1 North Jacaranda, Orlando 32836,* ☎ *407/239–4700 or 800/835–7377. 146 villas. 5 restaurants, 4 lounges, room service, 2 outdoor pools (1 heated), 3 whirlpools, health club, 45-hole golf complex with clubhouse and golf school, 12 tennis courts (6 lighted), 2 jogging trails, fitness course, bicycle rental, equestrian center, croquet court, water sports on lake (paddleboat, sailboat, and canoe rentals), game room, health club, supervised children's program, babysitting, guest laundry. AE, D, DC, MC, V.*

$$$$ **Marriott's Orlando World Center.** To call this Marriott massive would be an understatement. The lineup of amenities seems endless. One of the four swimming pools is the largest in Florida, and every other amenity you could imagine seems to be on-site, including a golf course. The lobby is a huge, opulent atrium, adorned with 16th-century Asian artifacts. Luxurious villas—the Royal Palms and Sabal Palms—are available for daily and weekly rentals. If you like your hostelries cozy, you'll consider the size of this place a definite negative; otherwise, its single unappealing aspect is the hordes of conventioneers it attracts. ☎ *8701 World Center Dr., Orlando 32821,* ☎ *407/239–4200 or 800/228–9290,* FAX *407/238–8777. 1419 rooms, 85 suites. 7 restaurants, 2 lounges, room service, 3 heated outdoor pools, 1 heated in-*

door pool, children's pool, 4 whirlpools, health club, 18-hole golf course, 8 lighted tennis courts, miniature golf course, 2 volleyball courts, game room, beauty salon, supervised children's program, baby-sitting, guest laundry. AE, D, DC, MC, V.

$$$$ Vistana Resort. Consider this peaceful resort if you're interested in tennis: Its clay and all-weather tennis courts can be used without charge; private or semiprivate lessons are available for a fee. It's also a good bet if your family is large or you're traveling with a group of friends. The spacious, tastefully decorated villas and town houses spread over 95 landscaped acres and have two bedrooms each plus a living room and all the comforts of home, including a full kitchen and a washer and dryer. The price may seem high, but considering that each unit can sleep six or eight, the place is a positive bargain. ⌨ 13500 State Rd. 535, Orlando 32821, ☎ 407/239–3100 or 800/877–8787, ℻ 407/239–3111. 722 units. 2 restaurants, 1 lounge, 5 heated outdoor pools, 5 children's pools, 6 whirlpools, health club, 3 basketball courts, shuffleboard, miniature golf course, game room, convenience store, supervised children's program, baby-sitting, guest laundry. AE, D, DC, MC, V.

$$$–$$$$ Embassy Suites Resort Lake Buena Vista. This is a typical example of the popular all-suite chain (see International Drive, above), although some local folks have been shocked by this hotel's wild turquoise, pink, and yellow facade. Clearly visible from I–4, it has become something of a local landmark. But it's an attractive option for other reasons. It's just 1 mile from Walt Disney World, 3 miles from Sea World, and 7 miles from Universal Studios Florida. The central atrium lobby, loaded with tropical vegetation and soothed by the sounds of a rushing fountain, is a great place to enjoy the complimentary breakfast and complimentary evening cocktails. ⌨ 8100 Lake Ave., Lake Buena Vista 32830, ☎ 407/239–1144 or 800/362–2779, ℻ 407/238–0230. 280 suites. Restaurant, lounge, deli, indoor-outdoor heated pool, children's pool, whirlpool, fitness room, lighted tennis court, shuffleboard, basketball, volleyball, fitness course, supervised children's program, baby-sitting, game room, playground. AE, D, DC, MC, V.

$$–$$$ Holiday Inn Sunspree Resort Lake Buena Vista. You might be impressed by the sweeping, covered entrance to its striking, terra-cotta-colored facade, but what really earns the kudos at this place is the way it seems to be built around the idea of family fun. All employees (including managers) have to graduate from Clown College (an eight-week intensive course in balloonology, magic tricks, costume design, clown ethics, and the seven clown commandments). This ensures that Camp Holiday—a free children's program of magic shows, arts and crafts, movies, cartoons, and other supervised activities day and night—is the finest program around. Children even have their own restaurant, the Kid's Kottage, where they eat for free if a parent is dining in the main restaurant, and the hotel rents beepers so that parents can have some time to themselves without worrying about the kids. It's also an excellent value. Furnished with two queen-size beds or one king-size bed and a sleeper sofa, all rooms have a TV and VCR plus a kitchenette. The showpiece of the hotel courtyard is a wonderfully huge pool. ⌨ 13351 State Rd. 535, Lake Buena Vista 32830, ☎ 407/239–4500, 800/366–6299, or 800/465–4329; fax 407/239–8463. 507 rooms. Restaurant, lounge, deli, snack bar, room service, kitchenettes, heated outdoor pool, wading pool, 2 whirlpools, health club, billiards, playground, free supervised program for children 2–12 (8 AM–midnight; must be potty-trained). AE, D, DC, MC, V.

$$–$$$ **Ramada Plaza Resort Maingate at the Parkway.** The only Ramada Re-
★ sort to earn the title Plaza, this bright, spacious Ramada may offer the
best deal in the neighborhood: attractive setting, good facilities, and
competitive prices. Its delicatessen comes in handy when you want to
assemble a picnic. Generously proportioned rooms are decked out in
tropical patterns, with pastel colors and pineapple shapes carved in white
wooden furniture; those with the best view and light face the pool. ☎
*2900 Parkway Blvd., Kissimmee 34746, ☎ 407/396–7000 or, in FL,
800/225–3939; outside FL, 800/634–4774; fax 407/396–6792. 712
rooms, 6 suites. Restaurant, 2 lounges, deli, snack bar, 2 outdoor
pools (one heated), children's pool, 2 whirlpools, fitness center, sauna,
2 lighted tennis courts, volleyball, game room, baby-sitting, guest laundry. AE, D, DC, MC, V.*

$$ **Hyatt Orlando Hotel.** Instead of a single tower, this very large hotel con-
sists of 10 two-story buildings in four clusters. Each cluster is a com-
munity with its own heated pool, whirlpool, park, and playground at
its center. The rooms are spacious but otherwise unmemorable. The
lobby is vast and mall-like, with numerous shops and restaurants; the
Foi-Foi is upscale Italian, and there is also a very good deli. If you'll
be spending most of your time attacking Orlando attractions, the rea-
sonable rates and convenience (it's the closest independent property
to WDW) will more than make up for the unremarkable nature of the
place. ☎ *6375 W. Irlo Bronson Memorial Hwy., Kissimmee 34746,
☎ 407/396–1234 or 800/228–3336, FAX 407/396–5090. 888 rooms,
34 suites. 4 restaurants, deli, lounge, 4 heated outdoor pools, 4
whirlpools, 3 lighted tennis courts, 4 playgrounds, health club, jogging
trail, game room, baby-sitting, guest laundry. AE, D, DC, MC, V.*

$$ **Perri House.** Exactly 1 mile from the Magic Kingdom as the crow flies,
★ this six-room bed-and-breakfast on a serene side road is a unique lodg-
ing in build-it-bigger-and-they-will-come Orlando: Part-hostelry, part-
bird preserve, Perri House will be, by 1996, an Audubon Society–
recognized Bird Sanctuary, complete with observation paths, a pond,
feeding station, and a small birdhouse museum. About 200 trees and
more than 1,500 bushes have been planted—many awaiting the addition of birdhouses. Already you can awaken to the cries of bobwhites,
downy woodpeckers, red-tail hawks, and an occasional bald eagle.
Nick and Angi Perretti planned and built the circular house so that each
room has an outside entrance. Guests dally at will in the "swan-and-
roses" living-room area and have free run of the kitchen, where a Continental breakfast is served gratis. The bird- and blossom-themed
bedrooms come with either two queen- or one king-size four-poster bed,
private bathroom, and TV. The furnishings are childproof and kids are
welcome. ☎ *10417 State Rd. 535, Lake Buena Vista 32830, ☎ 407/876–
4830 or 800/780–4830, FAX 407/876–0241. 6 rooms. Outdoor pool,
complimentary Continental breakfast, bird sanctuary. AE, D, MC, V.*

$$ **Wyndham Garden Hotel.** After traipsing through Orlando's theme
★ parks and malls, what many visitors want most is to lounge around
their living room just the way they do at home. Formerly the Double-
tree Club Hotel, this six-story complex lets you do just that: It pro-
vides a 5,000-square-foot living room full of big couches, with a
better-than-at-home big-screen TV fitted with a Nintendo unit. Homey
touches abound and the service and amenities more than make up for
the less-than-inspiring facade. ☎ *8688 Palm Pkwy., Lake Buena Vista
32830, ☎ 407/239–8500 or 800/996–3426, FAX 407/239–8591. 167
rooms. Restaurant, lounge, room service, heated outdoor pool, whirlpool,
health club, game room. AE, D, DC, MC, V.*

U.S. 192 AREA

If you're looking for anything remotely quaint, charming, or sophisticated, move on. The U.S. 192 strip—a.k.a. the Irlo Bronson Memorial Highway, the Spacecoast Parkway, and Kissimmee—is a neon-and-plastic theme park crammed with mom-and-pop motels, bargain-basement hotels, cheap restaurants, fast-food spots, nickel-and-dime attractions, gas stations, and minimarts in mind-numbing profusion. But if all you want is a decent room with perhaps a few extras for a manageable price, this is Wonderland. Room rates start at $20 a night—lower at the right time of year, if you can cut the right deal—with most costing $30 to $70 a night, depending on facilities and proximity to Walt Disney World. Among the chain hotels—Best Western, Comfort Inn, Econolodge, Holiday Inn, Radisson, Sheraton, Travelodge, and so on—are a pride of family-owned properties, many of which are run by recent immigrants.

Whatever your choice, you will find basic rooms, grounds, and public spaces that vary little from one establishment to the next. Keep in mind that the newer the property, the more comfortable your surroundings. Of course, the greater the distance from Walt Disney World, the lower the room rates. A few additional minutes' drive may save you a significant amount of money, so shop around. And if you wait until arrival to find a place, don't be bashful about asking to see the rooms. It's a buyer's market.

$$$ **Sol Orlando Resort.** The brochure on this resort-hotel complex stretches a point when it says it has the charm of a small village in the Spanish region of Andalusia. The red-tile-and-stucco villas and palm-studded grounds are indeed attractive, but it's the spacious accommodations that are truly noteworthy. Each of the one-, two-, and three-bedroom units has a living and dining area, a kitchen, and two TVs; the three-bedroom villa has 1,200 square feet of living space and sleeps up to eight comfortably. Complimentary breakfast is also included. ⛇ 4787 *W. Irlo Bronson Memorial Hwy., Kissimmee 34746,* ☎ *407/397–0555,* FAX *407/397–0553. 150 villas. Restaurant, lounge, heated outdoor pool, wading pool, whirlpool, health club, lighted tennis court, air-conditioned squash and racquetball court, game room, convenience store, guest laundry, minigolf complex next door. AE, D, DC, MC, V.*

$$–$$$ **Quality Suites Maingate East.** This hotel, built in 1989, is an excellent option for a large family or group of friends. The spacious green-and-mauve rooms, designed to sleep six or ten, come equipped with a microwave, refrigerator, and dishwasher. Suites have two bedrooms with two double beds each and a living room with a double pull-out couch. A complimentary Continental breakfast is offered, and free beer and wine are served afternoons at the pool-side bar. Kids will enjoy the motel's restaurant: A toy train chugs along overhead. No-smoking suites are available. ⛇ *5876 W. Irlo Bronson Memorial Hwy., Kissimmee 34746,* ☎ *407/396–8040 or 800/848–4148,* FAX *407/393–6766. 225 units. Restaurant, lounge, poolside bar, heated outdoor pool, whirlpool, kitchenettes, playground, game room, convenience store, guest laundry. AE, D, DC, MC, V.*

$$–$$$ **Residence Inn by Marriott on Lake Cecile.** Of the all-suite hotels on U.S. 192, this complex of four-unit town houses is probably the best. One side of the complex faces the highway; the other overlooks an attractive lake, where you can sail, waterski, Jet Ski, and fish. Forty units are penthouses accommodating four, with complete kitchens, small living rooms, loft bedrooms, and fireplaces. All others accommodate two and are laid out like studio apartments but still have full kitchens

and fireplaces. Each suite has a private entrance. While the price may seem high considering the location, there is no charge for additional guests, so you can squeeze in the whole family at no extra charge, and both the Continental breakfast and a grocery shopping service are complimentary. ☎ *4786 W. Irlo Bronson Memorial Hwy., Kissimmee 34746,* ☎ *407/396–2056 or 800/468–3027,* FAX *407/396–2296. 159 units. Heated outdoor pool, whirlpool, basketball court, playground, guest laundry. AE, D, DC, MC, V.*

$$ **Best Western Kissimmee.** Overlooking a nine-hole, par-three executive golf course, this independently owned and operated three-story hotel is a hit with golf-loving senior citizens as well as families. The two swimming pools in the garden courtyard are amply shaded to protect tender skin from the sizzling sun. The spacious rooms are done in soft pastels, with light wood furniture and attractive wall hangings. Units with king-size beds and kitchenettes are available. The hotel's restaurant, Casual Cuisine, serves breakfast and dinner buffet-style as well as from a varied, full-service menu. ☎ *2261 E. Irlo Bronson Memorial Hwy., Kissimmee 34744,* ☎ *407/846–2221 or 800/944–0662,* FAX *407/846–1095. 282 rooms. Restaurant, lounge, pool bar, 2 outdoor pools (1 heated), playground, picnic area, adjacent 9-hole golf course. AE, D, DC, MC, V.*

$$ **Holiday Inn Maingate East.** Everything seems to be the biggest something in Orlando, and Maingate East is the world's largest two-story Holiday Inn. The service is good, despite the size, but that's not the only reason to stay here. The whole interior recently got a multimillion-dollar makeover; all rooms now have a TV and VCR, and kitchenettes are fully equipped. You can rent videotapes and buy snacks and groceries in the lobby, and some of the restaurants serve buffet-style—an added convenience. Camp Holiday's kids' program operates much as it does at the Holiday Inn Sunspree Resort (*see* Maingate, *above*). ☎ *5678 W. Irlo Bronson Memorial Hwy., Kissimmee 34746,* ☎ *407/ 396–4488, 800/366–5437, or 800/465–4329; fax 407/396–1296. 670 rooms. 6 restaurants, café, 2 lounges, room service, 2 Olympic-size pools (1 heated), wading pool, 2 whirlpools, 2 lighted tennis courts, 2 game rooms, supervised program for children 3–12 (8 AM–midnight; must be potty-trained), in-room kitchenettes, 2 playgrounds, small convenience store, VCRs and rental movies, guest laundry. AE, D, DC, MC, V.*

$$ **Radisson Inn Maingate.** This sleek, twin-towered, seven-story modern
★ hotel, just a few minutes from WDW's front door, has cheerful guest rooms, large bathrooms, and plenty of extras for the price. It's not fancy, but it is perfectly adequate. The best rooms are those with a view of the pool. Two floors in each tower are reserved for nonsmokers. ☎ *7501 W. Irlo Bronson Memorial Hwy., Kissimmee 34746,* ☎ *407/396– 1400 or 800/333–3333,* FAX *407/396–0660. 575 rooms, 5 suites. Restaurant, lounge, deli, poolside bar, room service, heated outdoor pool, whirlpool, exercise room, 2 lighted tennis courts, jogging trail, baby-sitting, guest laundry. AE, D, DC, MC, V.*

$$ **Sheraton Lakeside Inn.** This comfortable, if undistinguished, resort, a complex of 15 two-story balconied buildings spread over 27 acres by a small man-made lake, offers quite a few recreational facilities for the money. The nondescript beige rooms are available in the standard two double or one king-size bed configurations, and each has a refrigerator and safe. The children's program has arts and crafts, movies, and miniature golf in a comfortable play area. ☎ *7769 W. Irlo Bronson Memorial Hwy., Kissimmee 34746,* ☎ *407/239–2650 or 800/848– 0801,* FAX *407/396–2222. 651 rooms. 2 restaurants, lounge, deli, room service, 3 outdoor pools (2 heated), wading pool, 4 lighted tennis* *courts, supervised program for children 5–12 (Tues.–Fri. 2–9 PM, Sat. 11–5 PM), baby-sitting, miniature golf, 2 game rooms, paddleboat and fishing equipment rental, guest laundry. AE, D, DC, MC, V.*

$ **Comfort Inn Maingate.** This hotel is close to Walt Disney World—just a mile away—so you can save a bundle without unduly inconveniencing yourself. Standard rooms are light and airy with a mauve-and-soft-blue color scheme; deluxe rooms, overlooking a landscaped garden, have refrigerators, coffeemakers, and hair dryers. Children 17 and under stay free, and those under 12 eat free. ☎ *7571 W. Irlo Bronson Memorial Hwy., Kissimmee 34746,* ☎ *407/396–7500 or 800/228–5150,* FAX *407/396–7497. 281 rooms. Restaurant, lounge, outdoor pool, game room, gift shop, guest laundry. AE, D, DC, MC, V.*

$ **Knights Inn–Maingate.** Part of a national chain, this one-story motel, with a prefab Old World facade, is not exactly an English charmer, but it does offer spacious, clean rooms at budget prices; some have kitchenettes and sofas. ☎ *7475 W. Irlo Bronson Memorial Hwy., Kissimmee 34746,* ☎ *407/396–4200 or 800/843–5644,* FAX *407/396–8838. 120 rooms. Heated outdoor pool, kitchenettes in some rooms, game room, guest laundry. AE, D, MC, V.*

$ **Park Inn International.** The Mediterranean-style architecture of this property on Cedar Lake is not likely to charm you off your feet, but the friendly staff might. Ask for a room as close to the water as possible. There is a restaurant, but for an extra $10 you can get a room with a kitchenette. ☎ *4960 W. Irlo Bronson Memorial Hwy., Kissimmee 34741,* ☎ *407/396–1376 or 800/327–0072,* FAX *407/396–0716. 197 rooms. Restaurant, outdoor pool, whirlpool, game room, guest laundry. AE, D, DC, MC, V.*

$ **Quality Inn Lake Cecile.** Rooms at this plain-Jane inn are adequate, not fancy—but those close to the lake are prettier as well as quieter. ☎ *4944 W. Irlo Bronson Memorial Hwy., Kissimmee 34746,* ☎ *407/396–4455 or 800/846–4855,* FAX *407/396–4182. 222 rooms. Outdoor pool, lakeside beach, guest laundry. AE, D, DC, MC, V.*

$ **Record Motel.** This simple property is the kind of mom-and-pop operation with few frills and rock-bottom rates that made U.S. 192 famous. Clean rooms with free HBO, complimentary morning coffee, and a solar-heated pool are the basic attractions here. What the place lacks in luxuries and ambience it more than makes up for with the friendliness of its staff, who'll gladly direct you to equally inexpensive restaurants. ☎ *4651 W. Irlo Bronson Memorial Hwy., Kissimmee 34746,* ☎ *407/396–8400,* FAX *407/396–8415. 57 rooms. Heated outdoor pool, baby-sitting, guest laundry. AE, D, MC, V.*

$ **Red Roof Inn.** If you want a clean, quiet room but don't want to gamble on an independent, this three-story chain motel delivers consistently. The small, comfortable rooms are decorated in blues and grays. A big plus are the many fast-food and budget-priced eateries within walking distance. The complimentary daily newspaper and coffee each morning are pleasant surprises. ☎ *4970 Kyng's Heath Rd., Kissimmee 34746,* ☎ *407/396–0065 or 800/843–7663,* FAX *407/396–0245. 102 rooms. Outdoor pool, heated whirlpool, guest laundry. AE, D, DC, MC, V.*

$ **Sevilla Inn.** This classy, family-operated motel built in 1985 and ex-
★   panded in 1990 is one of the best buys in the Orlando area. Stucco and wood on the outside, the three-story building has up-to-date rooms with colorful bedspreads, tasteful wall hangings, a fresh paint job, and cable TV. If you need a place to just drop your bags and get some rest between theme parks, this is a good bet. The pool area, encircled by palm trees and tropical shrubs, looks like something you'd find in a much fancier resort. Free coffee is available every morning. ☎ *4640*

W. Irlo Bronson Memorial Hwy., Kissimmee 34746, ☎ 407/396–
4135 or 800/367–1363, FAX 407/396–4992. 46 rooms. Heated outdoor
pool, guest laundry. AE, D, MC, V.

ORLANDO SUBURBS

Travel farther afield and you can get more comforts and facilities for
the money, and maybe even some genuine Orlando charm—of the warm,
cozy, one-of-a-kind country inn variety.

Altamonte Springs

Staying among the suburban developments, office parks, and shopping
malls of Altamonte Springs may not be as glamorous as dwelling with
the Disney characters. But accommodations in this suburb 30 to 40
minutes' drive from the theme parks cost on average one-third less than
comparable lodgings elsewhere in the Orlando area. The suburban atmosphere offers relief from the frantic tourist scene farther south. In
addition, the area is convenient to Enzo's on the Lake, one of Orlando's
best restaurants, as well as to the jumbo Altamonte Mall (see Chapters 5, Shopping, and 7, Dining).

$$$ Embassy Suites Orlando—North. What makes this member of the all-
suite chain (see International Drive, above) different is its location right
on the edge of Crane's Rost Lake. Otherwise, all the suites are up to
the high Embassy Suites standard and look out onto a lush, tropical
atrium. Although the sound of the waterfalls can be soothing, the
same can't be said for that of the conventioneers at the tables around
them. So for guaranteed peace and quiet, choose a suite on one of the
upper floors. The accommodations are spacious and flawlessly kept,
the staff friendly and helpful, and the complimentary cooked-to-order
breakfast makes a great send-off for your day in the theme parks. There's
fishing on the lake, and a scenic 1-mile jogging trail surrounds it. Cen-
tral Florida's biggest shopping mall is a short walk from the front en-
trance. 🏨 225 E. Altamonte Dr., Altamonte Springs 32701, ☎ 407/
834–2400 or 800/362–2779, FAX 407/834–2117. 210 suites. Restau-
rant, lounge, room service, in-suite kitchenettes, indoor heated pool,
exercise room, fishing, gift shop, baby-sitting, guest laundry. AE, D,
DC, MC, V.

$$ Orlando North Hilton. Though the emphasis at this eight-story concrete-
and-glass tower is on the business traveler, tourists will also appreci-
ate the hotel's quiet elegance. The comfortable rooms are decorated
with peach and dark-green florals and brass accents. Renovated in fall
1992, this hotel also has two floors of more pricey one- and two-bedroom Executive Suites and individual rooms with concierge service. The
pool is sunny and surrounded by palm trees, and the bar beckons at
cocktail time. 🏨 350 S. Lake Blvd., Altamonte Springs 32715, ☎ 407/
830–1985, FAX 407/331–2911. 318 rooms, 5 suites. Restaurant, lounge,
room service, heated outdoor pool, whirlpool, health club, baby-sitting, guest laundry. AE, D, DC, MC, V.

Winter Park

Winter Park, a small college town and Orlando's poshest and best-es-
tablished neighborhood, is full of chichi shops and restaurants. If its
heart is the main thoroughfare of Park Avenue, then its soul must be
Central Park, an inviting greensward dotted with huge trees hung with
Spanish moss. It feels a million miles away from Orlando's tourist track,
but it's just a short drive from the major attractions.

$$–$$$ **Park Plaza Hotel.** Small and intimate, this 1922-vintage establishment—complete with wrought-iron balcony—feels almost like a private home, with nice touches including a newspaper slid under your door each morning and complimentary breakfast brought to your room. The key to a special stay here is a front garden suite, with a living room. These open onto a long balcony usually abloom with impatiens and bougainvillea and punctuated by wicker tables and chairs to enhance people-watching on chic Park Avenue or Central Park. All rooms have either a double, queen-, or king-size bed, but those in the back can be small and cramped. On the first floor is one of Orlando's most popular restaurants, the Park Plaza Gardens. This old-fashioned spot is definitely not for people who want recreational facilities or other special amenities—nor is it suitable for young children. ▣ *307 Park Ave. S, Winter Park 32789,* ☎ *407/647–1072 or 800/228–7220,* ℻ *407/647–4081. 27 rooms. Restaurant, lounge, room service, jogging path, baby-sitting, guest laundry. AE, DC, MC, V.*

9 After Dark

Updated by
Mary Meehan

I F YOU KNOW that adults traveling without children make up half of the more than 13 million travelers who visit Walt Disney World, it won't surprise you if the sidewalks don't roll up when the sun goes down. A recent surge in the number of nightspots in the Orlando area shows no sign of letting up. Nightclubs in Orlando proper have significantly more character than those in the areas around Walt Disney World. Orlando even has those all-night dance parties called raves, and those velvet ropes you have to stand behind to be blessed with access to the hottest clubs. It's gone practically cosmopolitan. There was even a mini-riot a few years back involving a downtown nightclub crowd. But for very-late-night action, head for WDW. By virtue of Disney's independent legal status, clubs on Disney property are allowed to stay open later than bars elsewhere; you can get a drink there as late as 2:45 AM.

WALT DISNEY WORLD

Inside Walt Disney World, every hotel has its quota of bars and lounges pushing specialty drinks in all colors of the rainbow. At the hotels and at Pleasure Island—Disney's dedicated after-dark destination—jazz trios and bluegrass bands, DJs and rockers tune up and turn on their amps after dinner's done. Plus, there are two long-run dinner shows that give you and your family an evening of song, dance, and dining, all for a single price.

In the following text, "informal" means wear anything you want, while "casual" is a little dressier. Unless otherwise noted, men never need a jacket or jacket and tie.

Dinner Shows

The **Hoop-Dee-Doo Revue,** staged at Fort Wilderness's rustic Pioneer Hall, may be corny, but it is also the liveliest show in Walt Disney World. A troupe of jokers called the Pioneer Hall Players stomp their feet, wisecrack, and otherwise make merry while the audience chows down on barbecued ribs, fried chicken, corn on the cob, strawberry shortcake, and all the fixin's. There are three shows nightly, and the prime times sell out months in advance in busy seasons. But you're better off eating dinner too early or too late rather than missing the fun altogether— so take what you can get. And if you arrive in Orlando with no reservations, try for a cancellation. *Fort Wilderness Resort,* ☎ *407/934– 7639 in advance (☎ 407/824–2748 on the day of the show).* ☛ *$35 adults, $25 ages 12–20, $17 children 3–11. Reservations required. Seatings at 5, 7:15, and 9:30 PM. No smoking.*

The **Polynesian Luau** is an outdoor barbecue with entertainment appropriate to its colorful South Pacific setting at the Polynesian Resort. Its fire jugglers and hula-drum dancers are entertaining for the whole family, if never quite as endearing as the napkin-twirlers at the Hoop-Dee-Doo Revue. There are two shows nightly, plus an earlier wingding for children, called Mickey's Tropical Luau, wherein Disney characters do a few numbers, decked out in South Seas garb. *Polynesian Village Resort,* ☎ *407/934–7639. Admission to Polynesian Luau: $33 adults, $25 ages 12–20, $17 children 3–11. Admission to Mickey's Tropical Luau: $29 adults, $22 ages 12–20, $13 children 3–11. Reservations normally necessary at least a month in advance. Polynesian Luau* *seatings at 6:45 and 9:30 PM. Mickey's Tropical Luau seating at 4:30 PM. AE, MC, V. No smoking.*

IllumiNations

You won't want to miss Epcot Center's grand finale, a laser show that takes place every night, just before the park closes, along the shores of the World Showcase lagoon. Orchestral music, including Tchaikovsky's *1812 Overture,* fills the air. The show starts with laser images moving on screens mounted on barges in the middle of the lagoon. Later, multicolored neon lasers streak across the sky in time to the music while fireworks explode high overhead and low to the water. More laser designs flicker on the clouds of smoke left behind. At the end, lasers trace the outline of the continents on Spaceship Earth, so that it looks like a slowly turning globe. It's a stellar performance.

Some places around the lagoon offer much better vantage points than others. The best locations are the Matsu No Ma Lounge in the Japan pavilion, the patios of the Rose and Crown in the United Kingdom pavilion, and Cantina de San Angel in Mexico. Another good spot is the World Showcase Plaza between the boat docks at the Showcase entrance, but this is often crowded with visitors who want to make a quick exit after the show. If you want to join them here, claim your seat at least an hour in advance. Because the fireworks create a good deal of smoke, use the old lick-the-finger test to see which way the wind is blowing, and position yourself accordingly.

Pleasure Island

Locals as well as tourists patronize this 6-acre after-dark entertainment complex, which, like many other Disney creations, has a fictitious history to go along with its craftily constructed facades. Ostensibly, the island's derelict factories and warehouses are left over from the sail-making business of 19th-century entrepreneur Merriweather Adam Pleasure. The complex is connected to Disney Village Marketplace and the mainland by three footbridges. In addition to seven clubs, the island has a few restaurants, shops, and a 10-screen AMC cinema that starts showing movies at 1:30 PM.

Things are always changing on Pleasure Island. New attractions include a '70s dance haven, a jazz club, and, adjoining the Pleasure Island complex, one of the glitziest of all Planet Hollywood restaurants; the nightly New Year's Eve party—complete with fireworks—that started a couple of years ago is still going strong. One thing hasn't changed, and that's the pay-one-price admission that gets you into all the clubs and shows except the movie house. There may be an opportunity to glimpse some stars or stars of the future. Star Search, based at Disney-MGM, films its band competitions at Pleasure Island. National acts also occasionally perform and film videos at the park. *Pleasure Island,* ☎ *407/934–7781. The complex is located off of Buena Vista Drive. Cover: $19.61 (includes admittance to all clubs). No cover for shops and restaurants. Reservations not necessary. Clubs open 7 PM–2 AM year-round, shops 10 AM–1 AM, restaurants usually 11:30 AM–midnight. Children accompanied by parent or adult admitted to all clubs except Mannequins (same cover as adults).*

The **Adventurers Club** features the Audio-Animatronics showcased in many Disney rides and is supposed to re-create a private club of the 1930s. Apparently quiescent mounted trophies may start talking, your bar stool may begin sinking, and it's sometimes questionable if the person at the next table is a guest or part of the live entertainment. *Guests under 18 must be accompanied by an adult.*

The **Comedy Warehouse** has evolved from a predictable troupe of comedians to an improvisational setup in which even Mickey and Walt are fair game. Nationally known acts perform in the club's Comics of the Month series, and Entertainment Television tapes its "Stand-Up/Sit-Down Comedy Show" here. There are five shows nightly. *Guests under 18 must be accompanied by an adult.*

In case the lava lamps and disco balls don't tip you off, the '70s are back at **8trax,** one of Pleasure Island's newest clubs. Slip on your love beads, strap on your platform shoes, and groove to the recorded tunes of Iron Butterfly, the Village People, or Donna Summer. *Guests under 18 must be accompanied by an adult.*

Most of the locals who come to Pleasure Island can be found dancing to Top-40 hits at **Mannequins Dance Palace,** a high-tech nightclub with a revolving dance floor, elaborate lighting, and such special effects as bubbles and snow. *Guests must be 21 or older.*

Live country-and-western music is the focus of the southwestern-style **Neon Armadillo Music Saloon,** where you can also crack unshelled peanuts, drink a cold beer, or find a partner for the Texas two-step. *Guests under 18 must be accompanied by an adult.*

One of the better places for jazz in central Florida, the **Pleasure Island Jazz Company** presents nightly performances by accomplished soloists through six- or seven-piece bands. The decor recalls a '30s speakeasy, and the well-stocked tapas bar and assorted wines-by-the-glass add a smooth '90s touch. *Guests under 18 must be accompanied by an adult.*

The three-tier **Rock & Roll Beach Club** is always crowded and throbbing with the rock music of the 1950s and 1960s. The live band and disc jockeys never let the action die down. *Guests under 18 must be accompanied by an adult.*

They'll be back—that's what the stars promised as they left the December 1994 opening of **Planet Hollywood.** Although we'd like to believe it, we doubt this latest satellite in the Stallone-Schwarzenegger-Willis universe will be a star magnet. There will, however, be an array of movie memorabilia, much of it with a central Florida connection (for example: the motorcycle from Wesley Snipes's *Passenger 57,* which was filmed north of Orlando in Sanford). Try a slab of Ebony and Ivory Brownie or some Cap'N Crunch Chicken. *1506 E. Buena Vista Drive, next to Pleasure Island at Walt Disney World Resort,* ☎ *407/827–7828. No cover charge.* ◷ *11 AM–1 AM; bar, 11 AM–2 AM. AE, MC, V.*

Other After-Dark Doings

Electrical Water Pageant
This is one of Disney's small wonders, a 10-minute floating parade of sea creatures outlined in tiny lights, with a terrific blipping, bleeping, toe-tapping electronic score. You can see it from key beaches on Bay Lake and the Seven Seas Lagoon beaches at the Polynesian (at 9), the Grand Floridian (9:15), Fort Wilderness (9:45), the Contemporary (10:05), and, in busy seasons, the Magic Kingdom (10:20). Times occasionally vary so check with Guest Services.

Fireworks
WDW is one of the earth's largest single consumers of fireworks. Traditionally, there have been spectacular short shows at the Magic King-

dom and Disney-MGM Studios at 10. Times vary during the year, so check with Guest Services just to be certain. You can also find them at Pleasure Island as part of the every-night-is-New-Year's-Eve celebrations.

Movies

With all the only-in-WDW activities, it seems a shame to do what you can always do at home. But there are nights when your feet won't walk even one more step. Try the tenplex theater at Pleasure Island (☎ 407/827–1309). It's state-of-the-art and plays all the latest.

Nightcaps

Even the busiest hotels have quiet corners. At the Contemporary Resort, try the **Top of the World Lounge,** with its view of the Magic Kingdom, the tiny white lights lining the Main Street rooflines, and, in busy seasons, nightly fireworks. This is one of the few Disney locales that require a jacket. At the Polynesian, Disney bartenders ring all the variations on rum punch and piña coladas at the **Tambu Lounge.** At the Grand Floridian, **Narcoossee's** serves jumbo beers. At the Caribbean Beach, **Captain's Hideaway** is the spot, with its tropical potables. At the Dolphin, try the **Copa Banana,** where the tabletops look like pieces of fruit. At the Beach Club, **Martha's Vineyard Lounge** pours a good selection of wines. At Disney Village Marketplace, drop in at **Cap'n Jack's** for huge, beautiful strawberry margaritas, which incorporate not only strawberries but also special strawberry tequila. The **Village Lounge,** at the Village Marketplace, is another friendly corner; here you can party till the wee hours.

Clubs and Bars

The **Giraffe Lounge,** a flashy disco in the Hotel Royal Plaza at Lake Buena Vista, is full of spinning colored lights. It's small, and classy it ain't, but there's a lot going on, including live bands five nights a week, happy hour daily, and themed buffets (Mexican, Cajun, etc.); the place is usually densely packed on weekends. *Hotel Royal Plaza, Lake Buena Vista,* ☎ *407/828–2828. No cover charge.* ☉ *4 PM–2 AM; happy hour 4–9:30, buffets 4–8:30. AE, MC, V.*

Baja Beach Club is the two-story, inland answer to a beach party. Playing hits from the '60s to the '90s, there is an open deck serving sandwiches and just-grilled burgers and a sand volleyball court out back. Every 15 minutes a spunky, spandexed dance troupe performs. *8510 Palm Pkwy., Lake Buena Vista,* ☎ *407/239–9629. No cover charge.* ☉ *Tues.–Sat. 8 PM–3 AM. AE, DC, MC, V.*

SpectroMagic

The Disney Imagineers have outdone themselves once again with this Magic Kingdom parade incorporating the latest gee-whiz technology in sound and lighting. If you thought the Main Street Electrical Parade couldn't be topped, you just have to see this one: It proceeds down Main Street and through the park nightly at 9—and again at 11 during peak seasons, when the park stays open until midnight. Check with Guest Services. The early showing is for parents with children, while the later running gets night owls and others with the stamina and the know-how to hang around in order to enjoy the Magic Kingdom's most pleasant, least crowded time of day.

THE ORLANDO AREA

Disneyesque street signs with bright colors and engaging graphics are not the only new things in downtown Orlando. Nightspots have sprung up and are thriving in areas that used to be deserted after the office workers went home. Orlando's club owners figured out that there's big money to be made by luring tourists into the city center. The result is a diverse collection of clubs and nighttime activities offering everything from cutting-edge dance palaces and quiet coffeehouses to jousting tournaments and murder-mystery buffets. Even locals who haven't ventured out in a few years are surprised.

The Arts

If the fantasy wears thin, check out the Orlando fine arts scene in *The Weekly,* a local entertainment magazine, or the "Calendar" in Friday's *Orlando Sentinel.* They are available at newsstands. The average ticket price for locally produced shows rarely exceeds $12 and is often half that.

Orlando has an active agenda of dance, classical music, opera, and theater, much of which takes place at the **Carr Performing Arts Centre** (401 W. Livingston St., Orlando, ☎ 407/849–2020). The **Civic Theater of Central Florida** (1001 E. Princeton St., ☎ 407/896–7365) presents a variety of shows, with evening performances Wednesday through Saturday, and Sunday matinees.

During the school year, Winter Park's **Rollins College** (☎ 407/646–2233) has a choral concert series that is open to the public and is usually free. During the last week in February there is a Bach Music Festival (☎ 407/646–2182), which has been a Winter Park tradition for nearly 60 years. Also at the college is the Annie Russell Theater (☎ 407/646–2145).

The **Orange County Convention and Civic Center** (☎ 407/345–9800), at the south end of International Drive, and the **Orlando Arena** (☎ 407/849–2020), downtown on West Amelia Street, play host to many big-name performing artists.

Church Street Station

Church Street Station is a complete entertainment complex, made up of old-fashioned saloons, dance halls, dining rooms, and shopping arcades (*see below*) that nearly match Disney in their attention to detail. It all started in the 1970s, when Church Street was distinguished by nothing more than a dilapidated hotel, a few run-down buildings, and a tired old train station. Developer Bob Snow started with just one bar, Rosie O'Grady's, then acquired neighboring properties as his business grew (and boomed). Now both sides of the block are restored. The newest addition to the complex is the **Church Street Exchange,** a razzle-dazzle marketplace with more than 50 specialty shops and restaurants on the first two floors and a jumbo games parlor on another (*see* Chapter 5, Shopping).

Unlike much of what you see in Walt Disney World, this place doesn't just look authentic—it actually is. The train on the tracks is an actual 19th-century steam engine; the calliope was especially rebuilt to whistle its original tunes. Just about everything down to the cobblestones that clatter under the horse-drawn carriages is the real McCoy.

You can either spend an entire evening in one part of the complex or wander from area to area, soaking up the peculiar atmosphere of each. Either way, you pay a single admission price. Food and drink cost extra and are not cheap. Parts of the complex are open during the day, but the area is usually quiet then; the pace picks up at night, especially on weekends, with crowds thickest from 10 to 11, when the streets can get insanely busy. Be forewarned that fall weekends, when a big football game is at the Citrus Bowl, will be very crowded. Also, there are special themed parties—crowded, alcohol-drenched, frat-type festivals—throughout the year on holidays such as St. Patrick's Day. Call ahead around holidays to check, especially if you're thinking of taking the children. The street scene alone is entertaining—saxophone players, singers, and balloon-bending clowns are among the street performers you're likely to spot. *129 W. Church St., Orlando, ☎ 407/422–2434. ☛ $15.95 adults, $9.95 children 4–12 (includes admission to all of the following clubs; no admission required to enter Church Street Exchange, to wander through Church Street Station, or to eat in Lili Marlene's). AE, MC, V.*

Rosie O'Grady's Good Time Emporium, the original bar on Church Street, is a turn-of-the-century saloon with dark wood, brass trim, a full Dixieland band blaring out from a gazebo stage, banjo shows, tap dancers, and vaudeville singers. Is this a set for *The Music Man* or an evening at the Moulin Rouge? It's difficult to say. Multi-decker sandwiches and hot dogs are available from 11 AM to 2 AM, along with sodas and such drinks as Flaming Hurricane Punch (served in a souvenir glass). ☉ *11 AM–2 AM. Shows at 7:30, 9, 10:30, and midnight.*

Quiet **Apple Annie's Courtyard** offers recorded easy-listening music from Jimmy Buffett to James Taylor for your enjoyment either before or after dinner. It's also a good place to rest your feet after you've finished walking through the Church Street Exchange, to have a drink, and to do some people-watching. ☉ *11 AM–2 AM.*

Lili Marlene's Aviator's Pub and Restaurant has the relaxed atmosphere of an English pub and the finest dining on Church Street. Food is hearty, upscale, and very American—mostly steaks, ribs, and seafood. Walls are wood paneled and decked with biplane-era memorabilia; from the ceiling hangs a large-scale model aircraft. There's no music. ☉ *For lunch 11–4, dinner 5:30–midnight.*

Phineas Phogg's Balloon Works, a Top-40 dance club, plays tunes on a sound system that will blow your argyle socks off. It draws a good-looking yuppie tourist crowd and a few locals, mostly young singles over 21 but with a sprinkling of old-timers showing off their moves on the dance floor. Much of the young crowd feels it is worth the price of admission into the Station just to come here. The place is jammed by midnight. ☉ *7 PM–2 AM. Must be at least 21 to enter.*

In the **Orchid Garden Ballroom,** decorative lamps, iron latticework, arched ceilings, and stained-glass windows create a striking Victorian setting rather like an arcade where visitors sit, drink, and listen to a first-rate band pounding out popular tunes from the 1950s to the present. ☉ *7:30 PM–2 AM. Shows at 8:30, 9:30, 10:45, midnight, and (Fri. and Sat. only) 1 AM.*

Cracker's Oyster Bar, behind the Orchid Garden, is a good place to get a meal of fresh Florida seafood and pasta or slam down a few oysters with a beer chaser. ☉ *11 AM–midnight; lunch 11–4, dinner 4–midnight.*

The **Cheyenne Saloon and Opera House** is the biggest, fanciest, rootin'-tootin' saloon you may ever see. Occupying a tri-level former opera house, the place is full of moose racks, steer horns, buffalo heads, and Remington rifles; the seven-piece country-and-western band that plays there darn near brings the house down. With all the pickin', strummin', fiddlin', hollerin', and do-si-do-in', it's a fun place to people-watch. It's also one of the few places at Church Street to draw a big crowd every night. Make sure you wear your best stompin' shoes and cowboy hat, and practice up on your catcalls. The upstairs restaurant serves chicken-and-ribs fare. ⊗ *8:30 PM–2 AM; lunch 11–4, dinner 5– midnight. Shows at 8:30, 10, 11:30, and (Fri.–Sat. only) 1 AM.*

Clubs and Bars

If you were to judge only by the bars and nightclubs around Kissimmee, Lake Buena Vista, and International Drive, you would think that no one from Orlando ever went out. Not so. It's just that locals go elsewhere—and they have no shortage of options. Early in the week, many of the clubs are mostly deserted much of the night. Depending on your tastes, the absence of wall-to-wall crowds might make a visit worth the trip.

Downtown Orlando

Zuma Beach, a sun-and-surf-themed dance club (formerly Dekko's) where it's not unusual to see a guy in a flatteringly snug wetsuit checking your ID, has a massive light show and an ear-splitting sound system. Check out the Lifeguard Station, the upstairs bar, for drink specials and games. A new look hasn't changed this dress-to-impress crowd—lots of minidresses and too-hip-to-touch ties. There are occasional progressive nights for the 20ish. *46 N. Orange Ave.,* ☎ *407/648– 8727. Cover: $6.* ⊗ *Mon. 8 PM–2 AM, Tues. and Wed. 9 PM–2 AM, Thurs. 9 PM–4 AM, Fri. and Sat. 5 PM–4 AM. AE, MC, V.*

The Edge, *the* current hot dance spot and concert venue in downtown Orlando, is a multilevel converted warehouse with light shows and smoke; the pounding dance music is played just below the pain threshold. The musical offerings are schizophrenic: They vary from night to night and will probably change by the time you get here. Big-name alternative and rock acts also perform frequently in an adjoining concert field. *100 W. Livingston,* ☎ *407/426–9166. Cover: $4–$5.* ⊗ *Wed.–Sat. 9 PM–wee hours. AE, MC, V.*

Howl at the Moon has found the perfect solution to the rowdy bar patron who insists on crooning loudly with the band. Orlando's first singalong bar encourages its patrons to warble the pop classics of yesteryear or favorites like the "Time Warp" and "Hokey Pokey" (turn yourself around). This isn't karaoke: Everybody sings at once, so the noise level is just below a sonic boom, but toss back a couple of long-neck beers or one of the house specialty drinks—served in souvenir glasses—and you won't care any more. Piano players keep the music rolling in the evening, and the World's Most Dangerous Wait Staff adds to the entertainment. No food is served, but the management encourages you to bring your own or order out; several nearby restaurants deliver. *55 W. Church St., 2nd floor of Church St. Marketplace,* ☎ *407/841–4695. Cover: $2–$4 Wed.–Sat., free Sun.–Tues.* ⊗ *Daily noon–2 AM; piano players Sun.–Thurs. 8 PM–2 AM, Fri. and Sat. 6 PM–2 AM. AE, D, MC, V.*

Pinkie Lee's, a jazz club with leather booths, a gourmet menu, and brass accents, is among the most grown-up of Orlando's downtown nightspots. The entertainment is usually top-notch, and the weekend cover charge reflects that. Quiet and not as crowded as some of the clubs catering to a younger crowd, it's a good place to get away alone, together. (See if the hotel has a baby-sitting service.) *380 W. Amelia St.,* ☎ *407/872– 7393. Cover: $7.50 Tues.–Thurs., $10–$18 Fri.–Sat.* ⊗ *Tues.–Thurs. 11 AM–midnight, Fri. 11 AM–2 AM, Sat. 6 PM–2 AM. AE, DC, MC, V.*

Elsewhere

Bennigan's, another young-singles spot, is a favorite of people who work in the area. Orlando Magic basketball star–rapper and national television persona extraordinaire Shaquille O'Neal supposedly eats here often. It draws crowds in the early evening and during happy hours from 2 to 7 PM and from 11 PM to midnight, with food served almost until closing. *6324 International Dr., Orlando, ☎ 407/351–4436. ☉ 11 AM–2 AM (food until 1:30 AM). AE, D, MC, V.*

As you can tell from the name of this tiny bar-and-restaurant, **Dad's Road Kill Café** strives to be different. The bar area is littered with things to keep you busy as you drink your beer and wine: games, puzzles, a computer, plus the obligatory pool table and dart boards. On Friday and Saturday nights, there's low-key live entertainment. The menu is eclectic, a little pricey, and better than most. To get there from I–4 take the Lee Road exit, head east to Orlando Avenue, turn left and go almost 1 mile, and look for the strip mall on the corner of Lake and Orlando. *106 Lake Ave., Maitland, ☎ 407/647–5288. No cover charge. ☉ Tues.–Sat. 11 AM–2 AM (food until 1 AM). AE, MC, V.*

The Mill is a microbrewery and home to some of the best just-baked muffins you'll find in Orlando. Plus, it is a good venue to view some local rock bands in a casual, not horribly crowded atmosphere. The food is good, too. After the supper crowd, this place picks up some of the more laid-back students from Rollins College, which is just down the street. The bands usually start about 9:30 PM. *330 W. Fairbanks Ave., Winter Park, ☎ 407/644–1544. Cover: $4–$5. ☉ Tues.–Sat. until 2 AM, Sun. until midnight. Entertainment about 4 nights a week, never on Mon.; call to check. Kitchen closes at 10 PM Tues.–Thurs., 11 PM on weekends. AE, MC, V.*

Sullivan's Entertainment Complex is a newly renovated country-and-western dance hall with much right-friendly charm, where people of all ages and many families come to strut their stuff. Even Yankees are welcome. Big-name performers entertain on occasion; a house band plays from Tuesday through Saturday. Free country-dance lessons are offered on Sunday, Monday, Tuesday, and Thursday. *1108 S. Orange Blossom Trail (U.S. 441), ☎ 407/843–2934. Cover: $2 and up depending on the show. ☉ Mon.–Sat. 2 PM–2 AM, Sun. 6 PM–2 AM, with bands 8–2 (food until 2). AE, MC, V.*

Yab Yum is a bohemian refuge from the hustle and bustle of downtown Orlando. Local bands with names like Angel of the Odd or Gunga Din play on most Fridays and Saturdays. The crowd is heavy on aspiring-poet types, who hunch over espressos while giving form to their latest angst; luckily, you don't have to be tormented to enjoy a sandwich, the specialty coffees, or a tasty slab of fresh carrot cake or espresso flan. Beer, wine, and other drinks are also served. *25 Wall St. Plaza, Orlando, ☎ 407/422–3322. Cover on band nights: $4. ☉ Mon.–Thurs. 8:30 AM–1 AM, Fri. 8:30 AM–2:30 AM, Sat. 11:30 AM–2:30 AM. No credit cards.*

Dinner Shows

Dinner shows are an immensely popular form of nighttime entertainment around Orlando. For a single price, these hybrid eatery-entertainment complexes deliver a theatrical production and a multiple-course dinner. Performances run the gamut from jousting to jamboree tunes and tend to be better than the usually forgettable meal; unlimited beer, wine, and soda are usually included, but mixed drinks will cost you extra. What the shows lack in substance and depth they make up for in color and the enthusiasm of the performers. The result is an evening of light entertainment, which youngsters in particular will enjoy. Shows have seatings between 7 and 9:30 (usually one performance a night, but an extra show can be added during peak tourist periods), and at all but Mark Two, you sit with strangers at tables for 10 or more; that's part of the fun. Always call to make reservations in advance, especially for weekends. If you're in Orlando in an off-season, try to take in these dinner shows on a busy night—a show playing to a small audience can be pathetic and embarrassing. Also be on the lookout for discount coupons: You'll find them in brochure racks in malls, in hotels, and at the Orange County Convention and Visitor's Bureau in the Mercado Shopping Village on International Drive.

U.S. 192 Area

The **Arabian Nights** looks like an elaborate palace outside; inside it's more like an arena, with seating for more than 1,200 at long tables and a glass-enclosed skybox for private functions. The show features some 25 acts with more than 80 performing horses, music, special effects, and a chariot race; keep your eyes open for a unicorn. The three-course dinners are of prime rib or vegetarian lasagna. *6225 W. Irlo Bronson Memorial Hwy., Kissimmee,* ☎ *407/396–7400; in Orlando, 407/239–9223 or 800/553–6116; in Canada, 800/533–3615.* ☛ *$34.95 adults, $19.95 children 3–11. Reservations advised. AE, D, DC, MC, V.*

Capone's Dinner and Show returns to the gangland Chicago of 1931, when mobsters and their dames represented the height of underworld society. The evening begins in an old-fashioned ice cream parlor, but say the secret password and you'll be ushered inside Al Capone's private Underworld Cabaret and Speakeasy. Dinner is an unlimited Italian buffet that's heavy on pasta. Beer and sangria are included. *4740 W. Irlo Bronson Memorial Hwy., Kissimmee,* ☎ *407/397–2378.* ☛ *$35.99 adults, $18 children under 12. Reservations advised. AE, D, MC, V.*

Medieval Times, in a huge, ersatz-medieval manor house, portrays a tournament of sword fights, jousting matches, and other games on a good-versus-evil theme, featuring no fewer than 30 charging horses and a cast of 75 knights, nobles, and maidens. Sound silly? It is. Yet if you view it through the eyes of your children, this two-hour extravaganza is fabulous. That the show takes precedence over the hearty meat-and-potatoes fare is obvious from the dining setup: Everyone sits facing forward at long, narrow banquet tables stepped auditorium-style above the tournament area. Additional diversions, in the $2 million Medieval Life area, include a dungeon and torture chamber to tour, and demonstrations of antique blacksmithery, woodworking, and pottery-making. *4510 W. Irlo Bronson Memorial Hwy., Kissimmee,* ☎ *407/239–0214 or 800/229–8300. Medieval Times* ☛ *$32 adults, $21.95 children 3–12. Performances: daily 8 PM, 6 PM show occasionally added in high season. Medieval Life* ☛ *$8 adults, $6 children. Reservations required. Medieval Life open daily 4 PM–8 PM. AE, D, MC, V.*

Wild Bill's Wild West Dinner Show, in the 22-acre Fort Liberty complex, has the kind of slapstick theatrics and country-western shindigging that children really enjoy, including cancan girls, an authentic Texas lariat master, and Native American dancers. The chow, served by a rowdy chorus of cavalry recruits, is beef soup, fried chicken, corn on the cob, pork and beans, and pie and ice cream. Also part of the complex is an 1870s Main Street with shops, a stockade filled with western gifts and souvenirs, and a Brave Warrior Wax Museum. Between 11 AM and 2 PM, many of the acts in the dinner show perform in impromptu fashion in the courtyard. *5260 W. Irlo Bronson Memorial Hwy., Kissimmee,* ☎ *407/351–5151 or 800/883–8181.* ☛ *$31.95 adults, $19.95 children 3–11. Performances: daily 7 PM. Museum: $4 adults, $2 chil-*

dren 4–11. *Reservations advised. AE, DC, MC, V. No smoking in the showroom.*

International Drive Area

King Henry's Feast. In a faux castle near the Orange County Convention Center, Orlando's own King Henry VIII holds court as a group of jesters, jugglers, dancers, magicians, and singers entertain; ostensibly, he is celebrating his birthday and commencing his quest for a seventh bride. Meanwhile, saucy wenches serve forth potato-leek soup, salad, chicken, and ribs. *8984 International Dr., Orlando,* ☎ *407/351– 5151 or 800/883–8181.* ☛ *$31.95 adults, $19.95 children 3–11. Performances: daily 7 PM, 9:30 PM show occasionally added in high season. Reservations advised. AE, D, DC, MC, V.*

Mark Two, Orlando's first true dinner theater, stages complete Broadway musicals such as *Whose Life Is It, Anyway?*, *West Side Story*, and *George M.* throughout the year and musical revues chockablock with Broadway tunes during the Christmas holidays. For about two hours before curtain, you can order from the bar and help yourself at buffet tables laden with institutional-grade food; dessert arrives during intermission. Sets, costumes, music, and choreography are all done in-house; direction is by the theater's owner; and actors are mostly local. Under the circumstances, you wouldn't expect the world's best *Oklahoma!* and you don't get it. But it can be a pleasure to revisit these old favorites while sitting comfortably with a drink in hand. Each show runs for six to eight weeks, with eight shows a week, including matinees. Note that unlike other dinner theaters, the Mark Two offers only tables for two and four. Young children usually find it impossible to sit through the shows, and the steep charge provides ample reason to leave them with a babysitter. *Edgewater Center, 3376 Edgewater Dr., Orlando (west from I–4 Exit 44),* ☎ *407/843–6275 or 800/726– 6275.* ☛ *$29–$33 adults, $24–$28 children under 12. Reservations advised. Performances Wed.–Sat. 8 PM; Wed., Thurs., Sat. 1:15; Sun. 6:30. Closed Mon. and Tues. AE, D, MC, V.*

If Sherlock Holmes has always intrigued you, head for **Sleuths Mystery Dinner Show,** where your four-course meal and unlimited soft drinks are served up with a healthy dose of conspiracy. The whodunit performance stops short of revealing the perpetrator; you get to question the characters and attempt to solve the mystery. Maybe it was the butler? Seven mysteries are rotated throughout the year. *7508 Republic Dr., Orlando,* ☎ *407/363–1985 or 800/393–1985.* ☛ *$31.95 adults, $21.95 children. Reservations required. Performances Mon.–Sat. 6 and 9, Sun. 7:30. AE, D, MC, V.*

Sports Bars

So you're stuck in Orlando and the hotel bar isn't showing State U's biggest game of the year? No problem. Among about a dozen sports bars around town, the following pair offer dozens of games every week and are usually willing to tune their satellites in to pick up your requests.

With two big-screen televisions and a couple of satellite dishes, **Bloopers** is your regular high-testosterone sporting establishment. There is cold beer on tap and grunting, sweating men battling it out in vivid color. If it's not too crowded they sometimes oblige to flip through to find your favorite team. Don't ask, however, when Florida State or the University of Florida are playing. *Delta Orlando Resort, 5715 Major Blvd.,* ☎ *407/351–3340.* ☺ *Mon.–Thurs. 4 PM–1 AM, Fri. and Sat. noon–1 AM. AE, MC, V.*

Coaches Locker Room, a two-level sports palace, boasts 7 satellite dishes, 20 satellite receivers, 6 big-screen TVs, and 12 smaller monitors. Coaches shows every pro-football contest, plus every other kind of sport imaginable. The buffalo wings are worth trying. It's in the strip mall behind T.G.I. Friday's at the intersection of I–4 and Route 436. *249 W. Rte. 436, Altamonte Springs,* ☎ *407/869–4446.* ◷ *11* AM*–2* AM *(food until 2* AM*). AE, D, DC, MC, V.*

10 The Cocoa Beach Area

Including the Space Coast

Updated by
Dee Rivers

THE MOST DIRECT ROUTE from Greater Orlando to the coast, the Beeline Expressway, is arrow straight, cut through forests of long-needle pine and laid across the yawning savannas of the south-to-north St. Johns River, which begins life as a tiny stream in a place called Hell and Blazes, Florida. In this countryside of cedars, red maples, and palmettos, American egrets, blue herons, and shy limpkin wade and fish for dinner; ibis tend their chicks; and anhinga perch where they can, spreading their wings to dry. High above watery prairies yellow with wild mustard and butterflies, hawks hunt and osprey soar over their nests that crown stately sabal palms, Florida's official tree. It feels a million miles from the artificial worlds of the theme parks, and it's one good reason to make the trip from Orlando to Brevard County, on the east coast, only an hour away. The laid-back beach communities are another. Although the winter season alone counts about 460,000 vacationers, the area's white sands are much less densely developed than Daytona area beaches. Sun worshipers don't have to worry about being run over as they frolic or stroll—no cars are allowed on the sands. Moreover, the area is home to Kennedy Space Center and Spaceport USA and offers water sports, fishing, golf, nature, nightlife, and some distinctive shopping.

Accommodations, restaurants, and shopping are relatively close to each other and to all of the region's points of interest. And if you're lucky enough to be in town during a space shot, you'll be treated to a spectacular sight.

If you have the time, the best plan is to set aside two or three days to enjoy the area.

EXPLORING THE COCOA BEACH AREA

Jump-start the day with a brisk walk or jog along the beach to witness a spectacular sunrise. Then head for Spaceport USA at the Kennedy Space Center, which is free—perhaps the best entertainment bargain in Florida. To get here from the beach go north on A1A and watch for signs. From Orlando, take the Beeline Expressway east to Kennedy Space Center's Spaceport.

Kennedy Space Center

To get an overview of the area and some historical background, take the two narrated **bus tours:** One passes by some of NASA's office and assembly buildings, including current launch facilities and the space shuttle launching and landing sites. The other goes to Cape Canaveral Air Force Station, where early launch pads and unmanned rockets illuminate the beginnings of the space program. Security concerns mandate that many sights be viewed through a tour bus window. However, live and recorded narrations are provided during both tours, and there are historical exhibits at camera stops.

Even more dramatic are three IMAX films shown in the only back-to-back twin IMAX theater complex in the world. Projected onto a 5½-story screen, **The Dream Is Alive**, an awesome 40-minute film shot mostly by the astronauts, takes you from astronaut training and a thundering shuttle launch to an astronaut's-eye view of life aboard the shuttle while in space. **Destiny in Space** presents first-time views of the shuttle orbiting the Earth and thrilling flyovers of Mars and Venus. These two films are shown every 45 minutes in the IMAX I Theater. **The Blue**

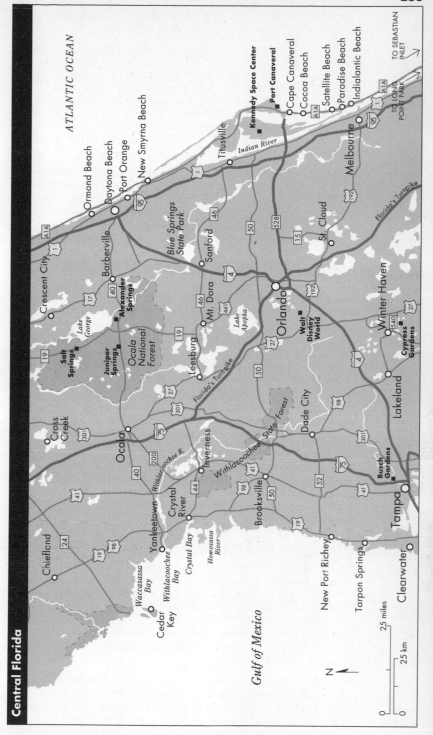

Central Florida

ATLANTIC OCEAN

Gulf of Mexico

TO SEBASTIAN INLET

TO LONG POINT PARK

Cape Canaveral
Port Canaveral
Kennedy Space Center
Cocoa Beach
Satellite Beach
Paradise Beach
Indialantic Beach
Melbourne

Ormond Beach
Daytona Beach
Port Orange
New Smyrna Beach
Titusville
Indian River

Crescent City
Barberville
Blue Springs State Park
Sanford
St. Cloud
Winter Haven

Lake George
Alexander Springs
Mt. Dora
Lake Apopka
Orlando
Walt Disney World
Cypress Gardens

Salt Springs
Juniper Springs
Ocala National Forest
Leesburg
Lakeland

Cross Creek
Ocala
Dade City
Busch Gardens

Inverness
Withlacoochee State Forest
Crystal River
Brooksville

Chiefland
Yankeetown
Withlacoochee R.
Tampa

Waccasassa Bay
Withlacoochee Bay
Crystal Bay
Homosassa River
New Port Richey
Tarpon Springs
Clearwater

Cedar Key

Florida's Turnpike

N

25 miles
25 km

Planet—an environmental look at the Earth seen from 200 miles high—
is shown three times a day in the IMAX II Theater.

In addition, you can stroll through the Spaceport's outdoor **rocket garden,** its lawns bristling with rockets, and tour a museum filled with
spacecraft that have explored the last frontier. For a close-up of how
space-related products have affected our daily lives, see *Satellites and
You,* a free multimedia presentation at **Spaceport Central.** *Kennedy Space
Center,* ☎ *407/452–2121. Bus tours: $7 adults, $4 children 3–11. IMAX
film: $4 adults, $2 children 3–11. Complex open daily 9 AM–dark; last
tour 2 hrs before dark; IMAX films shown daily 10–5:40. Closed on
certain launch dates (call ahead).*

At the **United States Astronaut Hall of Fame** museum, one block east
of U.S. 1, at the entrance to Spaceport USA, you can enter the world
of virtual reality, thanks to a new interactive display where you can
lose your breath because of the 3-G pull of a mock G-force trainer. For
a quiet interlude, view videotapes of historic moments in the space program. This is also home to U.S. Space Camp, which offers young people a hands-on learning environment that budding astronauts will
love. ☎ *407/269–6100.* ☛ *$7.95 adults, $4.95 children 3–11.* ☉
Daily 9–5, longer in summer.

Port Canaveral

After you leave the Space Center, going southbound on U.S. A1A, the
first traffic light you reach marks the entrance to Port Canaveral, a once-
bustling commercial fishing area still home to a small shrimping fleet,
several cruise ships, and charter and party fishing boats. Quaint in its
own way, the port offers a glimpse into the Florida off the tourist path,
particularly **Jetty Park,** where friendly conversations are unavoidable;
many locals like after-dark fishing from the jetties. Shops offer area
souvenirs and several restaurants with great waterway views specialize in fresh-catch family fare.

Cocoa Beach

If you continue westbound on Route 520 and turn left onto Brevard
Avenue after you cross over the Intercoastal Waterway bridge, you'll
end up in downtown Cocoa. A welcome respite from plastic and neon,
Victorian-style **Cocoa Village** is a cluster of restored turn-of-the-century
buildings and cobblestone walkways, where visitors can enjoy some 50
restaurants and specialty stores, including Flashbacks's antique collectibles
and the Monster ("the world's smallest surf shop"—open in April
only). *South of Rte. 520 at Brevard Ave. in Cocoa,* ☎ *407/631–9075.*

At 300 Delannoy Avenue, one street east of Brevard Avenue, is antique,
high-ceilinged **Travis' Hardware** (☎ 407/636–1441), a real vintage hardware store where, if you go there for thumbtacks or tape, you may not
come out for four hours. **Ron Jon Surf Shop** (4151 N. Atlantic Ave.,
Cocoa Beach, ☎ 407/799–8840) is marketing madness, a castle that's
as purple, pink, and glittery as any amusement park monolith, except
that it's plunked down in the middle of the beach community. It's a
local attraction in its own right.

To see what the land was like in other eras, visit the **Brevard Museum
of History and Natural Science.** Not to be missed is the museum's newest
acquisition, the Windover Archeological Exhibit of 7,000-year-old artifacts indigenous to the region. Don't overlook the hands-on discovery rooms and the Collection of Victoriana. The museum's nature
center has 22 acres of trails encompassing three distinct ecosystems—
sand pine hills, lakelands, and marshlands. To get here from Cocoa
Beach, take Route 520 to U.S. 1 and Michigan Avenue, then turn west

and follow the signs. *2201 Michigan Ave., Cocoa Beach,* ☎ *407/632–1830.* ☛ *$3 adults, $1.50 students.* ⊙ *Tues.–Sat. 10–4, Sun. 1–4.*

BEACHES

On Florida's mid-Atlantic coast from Ormond Beach south to Sebastian Inlet, there are about 100 miles of white-sand beaches. Generally, those below Satellite Beach—south of Cocoa Beach—tend to be rocky, with an uneven bottom.

The 57,000-acre **Canaveral National Seashore** (☎ 904/428–3384) in Titusville—30 miles north of Cocoa Beach on U.S. A1A—is home to more than 250 species of birds and animals. The area is unspoiled and hilly with dunes, and the strand itself is sprinkled with seashells. Surf and lagoon fishing is available, and a hiking trail leads to the top of an Indian shell midden at Turtle Mound. There's a visitor center on U.S. A1A. Weekends are busy and parts of the park are closed before launches, sometimes as much as two weeks in advance, so call ahead.

Playalinda Beach (☎ 407/267–1110), part of the national seashore, is the longest stretch of undeveloped coast on Florida's Atlantic Seaboard. It is remote, with pristine sands; hundreds of giant sea turtles come ashore here from May to August to lay their eggs, and the extreme northern area is favored by nude sun worshipers. Eight parking lots anchor the beach at mile intervals. There are no lifeguards, but park rangers patrol. Take Avon's Skin So Soft in case of horseflies. To get here, follow U.S. 1 north into Titusville to Route 406 (I–95 Exit 80), follow Route 406 east across the Indian River, then Route 402 east for 12 more miles. Do visit the **Merritt Island Wildlife Refuge** (☎ 407/861–0667; open weekdays 8–4:30, Saturday 9–5), which you'll pass on this stretch, to see up close, along nature trails, the same kind of scenery you whizzed past on the Beeline.

U.S. A1A and Route 520 will take you to **Cocoa Beach,** where amenities include dressing rooms, showers, playgrounds, picnic areas with grills, snack shops, and surfside parking lots. Beach vendors offer necessities, and guards are on duty in summer.

Satellite Beach is a sleepy little community just south of Patrick Air Force Base. Although no great shakes in the surfing world, it is the best place on the coast to surf right now. The only amenities are several picnic areas.

Small, scenic, 1,600-foot **Paradise Beach** (☎ 407/779–4008) is part of a 10-acre park north of Indianlantic on U.S. A1A. It has showers, rest rooms, a refreshment stand, and lifeguards in summer. Picnic tables must be reserved.

The 576-acre **Sebastian Inlet State Recreation Area** (☎ 407/984–4852), 12 miles south of Melbourne on U.S. A1A, offers 3 miles of interesting beach good for swimming, surfing, and snorkeling. The beach is rocky and the sand coarser than elsewhere along the coast, and the underwater drop-off is often sharp. It's fun for treasure hunters, because storms occasionally wash up pieces of eight from the area's ancient Spanish shipwrecks. Sebastian is also a favorite destination for Florida anglers. Warning: Come seriously prepared for what Floridians call their state bird—the ubiquitous mosquito! The park has a bathhouse, a concession, a fishing jetty, a boat ramp, campsites (☎ 407/589–9659), and the McLarty Treasure Museum (☎ 407/589–2147), built to commemorate the loss of the Spanish Treasure Fleet of 1715.

SPORTS

The **Recreation Complex of Cocoa Beach** (5000 Tom Warriner Blvd., ☎ 407/868–3333) offers a variety of sports facilities. Its 27-hole championship golf course meanders for 4 miles along the Banana River. Touching the shores of 17 lakes, the course is also home to much wildlife. The extensive complex offers an Olympic-size swimming pool, gymnasium, 10 lighted tennis courts, a restaurant, and a riverside pavilion with picnic tables.

Biking

Although there are no bike trails as such in the area, biking is allowed on the beaches and the Cocoa Beach Causeway. Bikes can be rented hourly, daily, or weekly at Ron Jon Surf Shop (*see* Exploring the Cocoa Beach Area, *above*).

Fishing

Check *Florida Today*, the local newspaper, or bait-and-tackle shops to find out what's biting where. There's **surf casting** for bluefish, pompano, sea bass, and flounder; success is mixed and depends on the season. Anglers **fishing from piers** sometimes pull in mackerel, trout, sheepshead, and tarpon; the Titusville pier has good shrimping. All major beach towns have lighted piers (admission usually $1–$4). You can also fish from some bridges. And there are several **deep-sea charters** around Port Canaveral; contact Cape Marina (800 Scallop Dr., ☎ 407/783–8410), Miss Cape Canaveral (630 Glen Cheek Dr., ☎ 407/783–5274), or Pelican Princess (655 Glen Cheek Dr., ☎ 407/784–3473).

Watersports

Boat America (1891 E. Merritt Island Causeway, ☎ 407/678–2860) offers a variety of boat rentals and enough nautical knowledge to help you set your own course. Pack a lunch and explore Banana River's lovely unspoiled islands, seek out wildlife in Intercoastal Waterway canals, or fish the deep waters off Port Canaveral's harbor. Pontoons, runabouts, Jet Skis, and wave runners are available for half- or full-day rental.

DINING

Moderate prices and fresh seafood are the rule, but some restaurants have unusual themes. The Cocoa Beach Pier is home to several eating establishments: In addition to the Pier Restaurant (*see below*), there's **Oh Shucks** (☎ 407/783–4050), where you can get oysters on the half shell and burgers; **Marlin's** (☎ 407/783–7549), which serves light meals indoors; and the **Boardwalk** (☎ 407/868–0420), an open-air bar where finger food reigns and live music livens up weekends.

$$$ **Bernard's Surf.** Astronauts don't come to Bernard's for the view; there are no windows in its dining rooms. They come for steaks and local fish, particularly the snapper à la surf, which is topped with a creamy seafood sauce of crab, shrimp, and scallops. Rusty's Raw Bar, the more casual part of the restaurant, offers 20 different seafood dishes as well as burgers and fries. ✕ *2 S. Atlantic Ave., Cocoa Beach,* ☎ *407/783–2401. Reservations advised. AE, D, DC, MC, V.*

$$$ **Mango Tree Restaurant.** Candles, fresh flowers, white linen tablecloths, rattan basket chairs with fluffy cushions, and eggshell-color walls hung with tropical watercolors by local artists set a romantic mood here. The intimate dining room overlooks a garden aviary that is home to doves and pheasants. Try the broiled grouper topped with scallops, shrimp, and hollandaise sauce. ✕ *118 N. Atlantic Ave., Cocoa Beach,* ☎ *407/799–0513. Reservations advised. AE, MC, V. Closed Mon.*

$$ **Ashley's.** The friendly servers in this snug wood-and-stucco restaurant will loan you the "U.S. Ghost Register" to read about the history of the place while you decide whether you want steak, seafood, or any of a wide range of other American favorites. Ladies may sense a presence in the powder room, purportedly the restless ghost of an ill-fated town girl; another spirit haunts the staircase, occasionally rudely pushing guests. NBC recently featured this spooky venue in *The Other Side,* its prime-time program about the paranormal. Although Ashley's has a Rockledge address, it's only about 20 minutes from Cocoa Beach. ✕ *1609 S. U.S. 1, Rockledge,* ☎ *407/636–6430. Reservations advised on weekends. MC, V.*

$$ **Black Tulip Restaurant.** At this romantic bistro, a tree provides the dining room's centerpiece; fresh flowers and candlelight reflected in mirrored walls enhance the Floridian cuisine, including mahimahi with scallops and herbs, as well as such Continental dishes as roast duckling with apples and cashews. The restaurant is in restored Cocoa. ✕ *207 Brevard Ave., Cocoa,* ☎ *407/631–1133. Reservations recommended. AE, DC, MC, V.*

$$ **Dockside.** Physically adjacent to Gatsby's Food and Spirits, Dockside is even more casual. You can eat outdoors on the deck and drink at the outside bar. House specialties are Black Angus beef and fresh swordfish. Sundays at Dockside are a local tradition, for both the champagne brunch and the entertainment—usually a local band—that follows in the afternoon. ✕ *480 W. Cocoa Beach Causeway, Cocoa Beach,* ☎ *407/ 783–2380. Reservations advised for brunch. AE, DC, MC, V.*

$$ **Flamingos.** Located in the Radisson Resort at the Port hotel—and close to the cruise-ship piers—this new spot has earned high kudos from foodies for its Floridian-inspired spin on Continental specialties. The decor is haute Caribbean: beige walls, paintings of flamingos, wicker trim, bouquets of red jasmine flowers, and finger bowls. Florida-gulf red snapper topped with crabmeat and orange hollandaise and the shrimp with caper-seafood stuffing are two favored entrées. Try, if you dare, the Ultimate Chocolate Sensation—a chocolate mocha-meringue debauch, complete with white chocolate, chocolate mousse, warm fruit, and crème de cacao. ✕ *8701 Astronaut Blvd., Cape Canaveral,* ☎ *407/ 784–0000. Limited seating. Reservations advised. AE, D, MC, V.*

$$ **Gatsby's Food and Spirits.** This friendly eatery on the banks of the Banana River offers prime rib, steaks, and seafood amid portraits of old-time movie stars, potted palms, brass railings, and other Roaring '20s touches. The bartender is famous for his penni wieni wo wos (sometimes known as shooters)—shots of peach schnapps, vodka, and cranberry juice. ✕ *480 Cocoa Beach Causeway, Cocoa Beach,* ☎ *407/ 783–2380. Reservations advised. AE, DC, MC, V.*

$$ **Heidelberg.** Roast duck and fillet Madagascar are the specialties at this elegant establishment, with its crisp linens, fresh flowers, and dark-red color scheme. All the soups and desserts are homemade; try the apple strudel and the rum-zapped almond-cream tortes. ✕ *7 N. Orlando Ave., opposite City Hall, Cocoa Beach,* ☎ *407/783–6806. Reservations advised. AE, MC, V.*

$$ **Lloyd's.** This latest addition to Port Canaveral's family-oriented dining spots snugs alongside the port's working docks, a venue that provides diners a spectacular view of coming-and-going cruise ships, net-draped shrimp boats, fishing pelicans, and—the topper—a drop-dead perfect vista for shuttle launches. The extensive menu brags that diners can not only see their catch come off the boat, they can order

"the fish-of-the-hour." A large, airy upstairs bar with darts and a pool table offers elevator access, and a rooftop deck is home to live music on weekends. ✕ *610 Glen Cheek Dr., Port Canaveral,* ☎ *407/784–8899. Reservations accepted for large parties only. AE, D, MC, V.*

$$ Pier Restaurant. In this elegant restaurant in a shopping, dining, and entertainment complex on Cocoa Beach Pier, you can enjoy fresh fish in a room with floor-to-ceiling windows that overlook the ocean. Try the mahimahi, or the grouper, which you can order broiled, blackened, grilled, or fried. ✕ *401 Meade Ave., Cocoa Beach,* ☎ *407/783–7549. Reservations advised. AE, DC, MC, V.*

$ Alma's Italian Restaurant. Five crowded, noisy dining rooms keep the waitresses here busy. The specialties of the house are fresh-caught grouper Italian style and veal Parmesan. The cellar stocks more than 200 imported and domestic wines. The restaurant has a warm, casual atmosphere with red-checked tablecloths, stone floors, and a large stained-glass window. ✕ *306 N. Orlando Ave., Cocoa Beach,* ☎ *407/783–1981. Reservations advised. AE, DC, MC, V.*

$ Herbie K's. This 1950s rock-and-roll diner has become a landmark since its 1987 opening. Servers dress, walk, and talk the '50s—you'll see saddle shoes and revisit such expressions as "Daddy-o" and "doll-face." Famous for its burgers, Herbie K's also serves home-style blue plate specials and old-fashioned ice-cream desserts. It's great for families. ✕ *2080 N. Atlantic Ave., Cocoa Beach,* ☎ *407/783–6740. AE, D, DC, MC, V.*

$ Lone Cabbage Fish Camp. The natural habitat of wildlife and local characters—Arnold Palmer loves the place—Lone Cabbage sits on the St. Johns River 9 miles north of Cocoa city limits on Route 520 and 4 miles west of I–95. The catfish, frogs' legs, turtle, country ham, and alligator on the menu make the drive well worthwhile. A fun family outing, this one-of-a-kind spot also has a dock where you can fish, buy your bait, or rent a canoe for a trip on the St. Johns. On the first and third Sunday of every month, there's a fish fry and spirited country-and-western hoedown—definitely not for the shy. ✕ *8199 Rte. 520, Cocoa Beach,* ☎ *407/632–4199. No credit cards.*

LODGING

Most lodging in Cocoa Beach is on U.S. A1A around its intersection with Route 520.

$$$ Holiday Inn Cocoa Beach Resort. When two adjacent beach hotels were redesigned and a promenade park landscaped between them, the Holiday Inn Cocoa Beach Resort was born. Public rooms are plush and modern, and there are many facilities. Options include standard, king, or oceanfront suites (which include a living room with sleeper sofa), or you can opt for a villa or bilevel loft. All come with cable TV, including free Showtime. ▦ *1300 N. Atlantic Ave., Cocoa Beach 32931,* ☎ *407/783–2271,* ⅎ𝔸𝕏 *407/784–8878. 500 rooms. Olympic-size outdoor heated pool, 2 lighted tennis courts, children's program, babysitting. AE, DC, MC, V.*

$$$ Radisson Resort at the Port. This elegant resort directly across the street from Port Canaveral is the closest beach-area resort to Walt Disney World, and though it's not on the ocean, the hotel provides complimentary transportation to Ron Jon's Surf Shop and the cruise ship terminals at Port Canaveral. Rooms have a Caribbean motif, with wicker appointments, hand-painted wallpaper, coffee machines, hair dryers, and ceiling fans; they come with one king-size or two double beds and have TVs with cable and HBO. The pool is lavish, in the best central Florida fashion, tropically landscaped and complete with a cascading 95-foot mountain waterfall. Facilities are equally abundant, as you'd expect of a resort of this caliber. ☎ *8701 Astronaut Blvd., Cape Canaveral 32920,* ☎ *407/784–0000 or 800/333–3333, FAX 407/784–3737. 200 rooms. Flamingos Restaurant, pool, children's pool, whirlpool, 2 lighted tennis courts, fitness center, convention center (with fax, photocopying, and secretarial support), playground, game room, guest laundry, complimentary local transportation, daily shuttle to Orlando International Airport. AE, D, DC, MC, V.*

$$ **Wakulla Motel.** This motel has the best occupancy rate on the beach. Its completely furnished five-room suites, designed to sleep six, are ideal for families; they include two bedrooms, a living room, dining room, and fully equipped kitchen and have cable TV with HBO. The grounds are landscaped with tropical vegetation. ☎ *3550 N. Atlantic Ave., Cocoa Beach 32931,* ☎ *407/783–2230, FAX 407/783–0980. 116 suites. 2 heated outdoor pools, shuffleboard court, outdoor grills, guest laundry.*

$ **Comfort Inn and Suite Resort.** This hostelry is across the street from the ocean and within walking distance of more than a dozen restaurants. You can choose from standard double rooms, minisuites, one-bedroom ocean-view suites, and fully equipped efficiencies. All are clean, comfortable, and decorated in light, tropical colors. The poolside bar has a waterfall, and there's a pond full of tropical fish, in addition to the many facilities. ☎ *3901 N. Atlantic Ave., Cocoa Beach 32931,* ☎ *407/ 783–2221, FAX 407/783–0461. 40 rooms, 40 minisuites, 40 ocean-view suites, 40 efficiencies. Lounge, pool, whirlpool, lighted volleyball court, shuffleboard, table tennis, playground, BBQ grills. AE, D, DC, MC, V.*

$ **Pelican Landing Resort on the Ocean.** This two-story beachfront motel is friendly and warm, so many guests call it a home away from home. Rooms have ocean views, microwaves, and TVs with cable and HBO; one even has a screened porch. Boardwalks to the beach, picnic tables, and a grill round out the amenities. ☎ *1201 S. Atlantic Ave., Cocoa Beach 32931,* ☎ *407/783–7197. 11 units. Beach, efficiencies with fully equipped kitchens. D, MC, V.*

NIGHTLIFE

In the Olde Cocoa area, the **Cocoa Village Playhouse** (300 Brevard Ave., Cocoa Beach, ☎ 407/636–5050)—the area's community theater—mounts plays and musicals featuring local talent from September through March. The rest of the year the stage hosts touring professional productions, concerts, and, in summer, shows aimed at children on vacation.

Bumpers is a cozy '50s-style lounge where they spin oldies for happy dancers amid memorabilia of the Eisenhower era; a 1957 Chevy serves as the DJ's booth, for example. Food is available from Herbie K's, the diner that shares the premises. *2080 N. Atlantic Ave., Cocoa Beach,* ☎ *407/783–9222.* ◔ *Mon.–Thurs. 4 PM–midnight, Fri. and Sat. 4 PM–2 AM. AE, D, DC, MC, V.*

Dino's, an intimate piano bar with mood lighting and great music all week, is a place to jam, sing, or just listen. A jazz combo plays on Friday and Saturday. There's a small dance floor. *315 Cocoa Beach Causeway, Cocoa Beach,* ☎ *407/784–5470.* ◔ *Noon–2 AM. AE, D, DC, MC, V.*

COCOA BEACH AREA ESSENTIALS

Getting Around

The Beeline Expressway (Rte. 528) is accessible from either I–4 or the Florida Turnpike. Tolls for the trip, up to $2.45 for a car, are a bargain-basement fare for the scenery. The coast is about 90 minutes from WDW, 60 minutes from Orlando.

If you're heading to Cocoa Beach, don't get off the Beeline at any of the Cocoa exits. The expressway eventually turns into U.S. A1A, the beach area's main artery, which is also called Atlantic Avenue. U.S. A1A's junction with Route 520, a few miles south of the Beeline changeover, marks the heart of Cocoa Beach.

Important Addresses and Numbers

Medical Emergency

Cape Canaveral Hospital (701 W. Cocoa Beach Causeway, or Rte. 520, Cocoa Beach, ☎ 407/799–7111).

Tourist Information

Contact the **Brevard County Tourist Development Council** (2725 St. Johns St., Melbourne 32940, ☎ 407/633–2110 or 800/936–2326) and the **Cocoa Beach Area Chamber of Commerce** (400 Fortenberry Rd., Merritt Island 32952, ☎ 407/459–2200 or 800/572–4636). Both can provide general information as well as dates for rocket launches.

11 Portrait of Walt Disney World®

THE MOUSE AND THE DYNAMO

By Andrew Holleran

I COULDN'T SLEEP the night before I went to Walt Disney World. A Floridian for more than 20 years, living two hours away by car, I had always patriotically avoided even going near the place. My family went. My neighbors went. (One of them, a 75-year-old man, has gone every year for 15 years to see what's new.) For my part, however, it depressed me that the Egyptians gave us the Pyramids, the Greeks the Parthenon, the French the cathedral of Chartres, and our cultural contribution was . . . a celluloid mouse.

Indeed, the morning I drove to Orlando I felt I was making the sort of pilgrimage people used to make to Mont-Saint-Michel or Jerusalem. "You know, he almost put it in St. Louis," I said to my sister as we drove south on Route 19 through Ocala National Forest. "But Adolph Busch, the beer baron, stood up at a dinner they gave for Disney and said anyone who built a theme park and did not sell beer inside was crazy. So, on the plane back to California, Disney said, 'Forget about St. Louis.'" Why? "Because, he had no intention of selling beer. He disliked the odor of beer on hot days in amusement parks—like the parks in southern California he used to take his daughter to in the '30s and '40s."

I could have told her more. After reading Richard Schickel's *Disney Version,* John Taylor's *Storming the Magic Kingdom,* and an article by John McAleenan in the Orlando *Sentinel* about the actual building of Disney World, I was bursting with tidbits like that. The fact that Disney went ahead in 1954 with the building of Disneyland was chiefly because he could promote it on his weekly television show. That amusement parks were dying in the '50s, and the manufacturers of rides refused to build Disney the new ones he had in mind. That on the day Disney World opened, the people who built it actually wondered if anyone would come. That Disney himself had come up against obstacles throughout his career, and ended up one of the most tenacious, determined, and resilient men in the history of American business. In fact, I was more fascinated by Disney's career (with these low points that people seem to have forgotten) than by his amusement parks. But I didn't mention any of this. I dropped my sister off in Apopka, a small town 10 miles from Orlando, and continued on alone to Orlando.

Walt Disney World is not in Orlando exactly but sits 20 miles southwest of downtown. It lies on both sides of a busy highway called I–4, on 28,000 acres of what used to be pinewoods, cattle pastures, and swampland, between two cities in two counties: Orlando, in Orange County, and Kissimmee, in Osceola County. Actually, Disney World exists in a world of its own—a separate entity, both physically and legally. Bill Donegan, an Orange County commissioner, likes to compare it to the Vatican.

The reason there's a lot of space between Disney World and the two cities it lies between is that Walt Disney wanted it that way. When Disney decided to put his second theme park in Florida, he wanted enough land around it to form a buffer against the sort of commercial crud that had marched up Harbor Boulevard in Anaheim to the very edge of Disneyland, and to enable him to build his own hotels to house the guests who were staying outside Disneyland. So, where Disneyland sits on 180 acres, Disney World occupies 28,000—roughly the area of Boston. ("If he had it his way," says Joe Fowler, an ex-admiral who helped construct Disney World, "we would have bought 50,000 acres.")

In the mid-'60s, big parcels were easy to find in central Florida; it was still mostly rural. In his first flight over the unbroken pinewoods in 1965, Disney saw an island

---

This essay has been excerpted and adapted from an article that originally appeared in the August 1990 issue of *Wigwag* magazine.

in the middle of a lake down below and, imagining the fun he could have with it, said, "This is great. Buy it." (It later became Discovery Island, a bird sanctuary and zoological park.) He bought the land—for about $180 an acre—without letting the real estate agent and lawyer who handled the transaction know his identity. The publisher of the Orlando *Sentinel* learned the truth only by agreeing to keep it a secret; if the news got out, the deal was off. He kept the secret. In those days, everybody wanted growth. Forty-eight hours after the news that 28,000 acres had been acquired by Disney, land adjacent to his went up to $80,000 an acre. Anyone who studies Walt Disney's remarkable career will discover this: He was a sharp businessman.

But he was not—and this is what's so strange, driving down I–4 in the middle of this boom—always the success we see today. His pedigree was one of failure. His father, one of 11 children born in Ontario and raised in Kansas, went south to Florida as a young man to grow citrus. (He met Walt's mother, a schoolteacher on vacation, there.) A freeze wiped out his grove, and he went north to Chicago, where he got work as a carpenter on the Columbian Exposition of 1893. For the next 10 years he worked as a small contractor. "My mother used to go out on a construction job and hammer and saw planks with the men," said Walt, who was born in Chicago in 1901, the youngest of four sons. His first name was that of the Congregational minister who christened him; his second, Elias, that of his father. When he was five, his father moved again, acquiring a farm near Marceline, Missouri. Four years later, the failure of the farm forced Walt's father to auction off the livestock and move once more, to Kansas City. There Walt worked a predawn newspaper route, in blizzards so bitter they gave him nightmares as an adult. He also took art classes. Right after the armistice in 1918, he went to France, where he sold fake German helmets as souvenirs to American G.I.s and painted the Croix de Guerre on their jackets for 10 francs apiece (his first paying art job). Back home, a job waited for him in a Chicago jelly factory his father had bought. But he returned instead to Kansas City to get newspaper work, and ended up starting an animation business. It was not a success at first. Business was so poor, in fact,

he had to tell his one big customer (a dentist who wanted an educational film for kids) that he couldn't meet him to discuss the project because he had no shoes: His only pair was being fixed. In 1923, at the age of 21, he gave up, like his father—but this time Disney went west, to Hollywood.

Each venture he pursued came, after some small success, to a dead end. When the banks lent him money—after the success of *Snow White and the Seven Dwarfs*—to build a studio, they insisted it be constructed so that if it failed it could be converted into a hospital (which is why the hallways are wide enough for a bed to be rolled down the middle). In 1939, *Snow White* won an Academy Award (a big statue for Snow White, seven tiny ones for the dwarfs). In 1940, *Pinocchio* was such a bomb that bankers cut off credit to his company. But each time he reached a dead end, he came up with something. Mickey Mouse was invented near bankruptcy, on a train to Los Angeles from New York, where Disney had just learned that his Eastern distributor had lured his best people away. He started making nature movies only because his feature-length animation-film career petered out in 1959 with *Sleeping Beauty* (another flop). He survived because he plowed whatever profits he did make into his own company (Walt Disney Productions), lived modestly in a town where other studio heads aped the English aristocracy, always drove a hard bargain (on actors, the saying went: "Disney gets you on the way up or the way down"), and never surrendered the rights to a single one of his films or to the merchandising connected with them. This strategy made him one of the few moguls to survive into the '60s with his studio intact.

Intact and insular: The Disney organization was always a family enterprise. All four brothers ended up living in Los Angeles—they played croquet together at Roy's house on summer Sundays—but the company consisted of only Walt and Roy. Roy handled the finances. Walt was the creative half, though Richard Schickel says he could barely draw the images for which his studio became famous; another man, Ub Iwerks, was responsible for much of the animation that has burned itself into the national consciousness.

In 1953, Disney alienated Roy by forming a private company called Retlaw (Walter spelled backward) to control the merchandising rights to the name Walt Disney. Because the name Walt Disney was on just about everything connected to the studio, and Retlaw's income went to Walt and his two daughters, Roy was furious. The feud went on for nearly a decade, during most of which they refused to speak to each other. The feud ended up dividing the company into "Walt men" (marketing, studio, theme parks) and "Roy men" (finance, legal, administrative), and the schism lasted long after the brothers' deaths—Walt's in 1966 and Roy's in 1971.

While the brothers were living, however, even their feud couldn't alter the united front the Disney company presented to outsiders. Not only did Walt retain the rights to every film he made (something other studios surrendered, especially when TV came along) and control the merchandise associated with his characters, but he also formed a company to distribute the movies. Yet even this was not enough. When the banks cut off his line of credit in 1940, Disney was forced to issue stock to raise enough money to complete *Fantasia,* and issuing stock meant the Disney company was no longer his. Eventually, the stock would be bought by pension funds, institutional investors, and tycoons like Sid Bass, Irwin Jacobs, and Ivan Boesky. Disney did not live to see the struggle that ended with raiders almost dismembering the company. He did live, however, to see his studio finally hit it big with *Mary Poppins* (for a time, the sixth biggest-grossing movie ever) and, before that, to realize another of the many ideas everyone told him was crazy: Disneyland.

By the time Disney came to Orlando, looking for a place to build a second theme park, he had become a shrewd and canny businessman, and he had also been burned. He had learned the importance of controlling his product. Disney World was his second child, and he meant to avoid all the mistakes he'd made with the first. Those mistakes—the reason Disney World is 20 miles from downtown Orlando on its own tract of 28,000 acres—all involved the same thing: letting others have control. When he was building Disneyland, for instance, a local utility group appealed to his belief in private enterprise and persuaded him to let the company supply him with electricity. (Disney was such a staunch Republican that when L.B.J. decorated him with a medal in 1964, he wore a Goldwater button on his lapel.) Then one day he went down to the park and was horrified to see high-tension wires converging on his domain. The company refused to bury them unless he paid for it. (He did.) When security guards from another outside firm failed to show the right attitude toward his guests (never "customers"), Disney fired them, hired his own, and sent every Disney employee (actually, people who work at Disney World and Disneyland are never called employees but, rather, "cast members") to the University of Disneyland, in Anaheim, to make sure they remained friendly, no matter how tired they were. What Disney wanted was to do things his way.

Florida let him. After he'd obtained everything he could through private means, he got the rest of what he wanted through the Florida legislature: control over the land. The bill Florida passed in 1967 to welcome Disney is called the Reedy Creek Improvement District Act. What the act did was set up a special taxing region called the Reedy Creek Improvement District (after a small stream on the property), which was authorized to provide its own pest and flood control, waste-removal systems, fire protection, and building codes. The last provision was especially important to Disney. The Disney company says it asked for the Reedy legislation to remove from Orange and Osceola counties the burden of supplying an infrastructure, and allow Disney to build its own state-of-the-art structures. But according to an Orange County official, Disney really wanted Reedy Creek so it could avoid the lengthy process of obtaining building permits from the county. This is how Disney continues to beat its competitors to the punch. Its Disney-MGM Studios, for instance, opened months before Universal's theme park, 15 miles to the north, even though Universal broke ground a year before Disney did. Disney has always been faster than people thought possible. When the construction firm originally hired to build Disney World said it would not be able to finish on time, Disney fired them and hired its own team, headed by a former general who'd overseen the Normandy invasion and a former admiral—both graduates of M.I.T.—and met the deadline by working 24-hour shifts.

Indeed, Reedy Creek is not only immune to local building codes and permits, it is also free of having to pay impact fees; the impact fee on the average house built in Orange County today is $4,400. The fee for a Disney hotel with 7,000 rooms, Bill Donegan figures, would come to more than $18 million.

On the other hand, Reedy Creek contributes a lot of money to the local county governments. Besides levying taxes within its boundaries (Disney paying for Disney), it pays property taxes to Orange and Osceola counties as well. To date, Disney has paid $181 million in taxes to Orange County alone, half of which has been allocated to its schools. So, despite comparisons to the Vatican, Reedy Creek is not quite independent. And while there may be other special taxing districts, none of them are as famous, rich, or spectacularly successful as Reedy Creek.

In fact, the very success of Disney World has become its particular problem. Disney likes to point out that the phenomenal growth that has quadrupled the population of Orlando since 1960 would have occurred with or without Disney. One of the reasons Walt Disney chose the Orlando area was that growth was forecast. Disney is proud of the fact that it's the area's largest employer (more than 31,500 jobs). It also points out that the average visitor to central Florida spends only 4 of 13 days at Disney World. And yet—because of Disney World's hotel-building boom (Orlando already has more hotel rooms than Manhattan, but the area's occupancy rate is 81%, which is very high); its addition of a third theme park (the Disney-MGM Studios); its water parks (Typhoon Lagoon, River Country), campgrounds, and nightclubs; and its avowed intention to make Disney World the center of convention business in the Southeast—it appears to folks beneath the castle that Disney wants to create a resort so all-inclusive that a guest never needs to leave it for anything but the plane home. This makes perfect sense for Disney, but it makes everyone around Disney World, particularly the hotels and attractions that live on Disney's spillover, nervous.

All this growth raises the question of who should pay for Disney World's astonishing success. The obvious problem is Orange County traffic. Because Disney does not have to pay impact fees, Orange County persuaded it in 1988 to chip in $1.3 million to improve the roads that feed into the highway leading to the Magic Kingdom (the infamous I-4); in exchange, Orange County made a matching grant and promised not to sue Reedy Creek for the next seven years. This was called the Interlocal Agreement. Bill Donegan, who says he'd have signed the original Reedy Creek Improvement District Act, voted no on the Interlocal Agreement. "It's a matter of balance. Quality of life," he says. "Disney-bashing is now a way of life."

That noted, most visitors still feel a thrill when they realize that they are finally coming to, yes, Walt Disney World! The first signs of Disney World are two huge hotels, looming above the highway, from whose pediments two gigantic swans, two gigantic dolphins, and several gigantic seashells look down like Ozymandias on the passing scene. Even before learning that they are the work of Michael Graves (Disney has hired some very fancy architects for its hotels), I thought, Now, this is fun.

It's even more fun to get off I-4 and turn up a winding road into Disney's green domain (containing not only theme parks, hotels, campgrounds, lakes, and 7,200 acres of wilderness preserve but also a tiny village where Disney employees live). The road curves through dense woods to a sort of turnpike toll station (where you get a $4 parking ticket), ending in one of three immense parking lots (one for each park), where a cheerful Disney employee—I mean, cast member—directs you to a parking space. Then you get into a long train of what look like linked golf carts and are taken to the entrance of whichever park you're visiting: Epcot, the Magic Kingdom, or the Disney-MGM Studios.

Of the three theme parks in Disney World—the Magic Kingdom, opened in 1971, Epcot Center in 1982, and the Disney-MGM Studios in 1989—the newest is the smallest. Its parking lot holds 4,500 cars, while Epcot Center and the Magic Kingdom each have parking spaces for

12,000. (This is why the Disney-MGM Studios parking lot closed as early as 8:30 AM recently—when it fills up, the doors close.) The moment you enter Disney World you have the sensation that you're in the hands of invisible engineers. The experience is always fluid. The long lines do keep moving, and every line has a sign beside it saying how long the wait is.

What you wait in line for varies from park to park. The Studios are a re-creation of a Hollywood back lot, including directors who ask you if you want to be in their movie. Epcot consists of corporate showcases clustered near the entrance and a chain of 11 national pavilions ringing a lagoon. The pavilions are clever pastiches of indigenous landmarks (the Eiffel Tower, a Japanese teahouse, a Moroccan Casbah), most of which contain shops, restaurants, and theaters where films about each country are shown. The films are free; the shops and restaurants are not, and the feeling that you are in the hands of expert people-movers is surpassed only by the feeling that an awful lot of money is changing hands rapidly.

A cynical friend had warned me that Epcot Center is basically a big shopping mall, but it's really more than that. For one thing, it's full of performers, and the performers at all three parks are as important an element of the experience as the physical plant itself; acrobats, singers, comedians, and storytellers are constantly assembling, dispersing, and reappearing as you walk from one attraction to the next. The Magic Kingdom, in fact, has a famous subterranean system of corridors so that the cowboys, for instance, don't have to walk through the audience to stage their gunfights. Nor, for that matter, do the people who supply the restaurants; Disney didn't want his guests seeing Coke being delivered. The Magic Kingdom is, after all, supposed to be an illusion.

It's also curiously small, and smallness is part of the strategy—to make it toylike. Frontierland blends imperceptibly into Fantasyland, which is just around the corner from Tomorrowland, which leads you to Main Street, U.S.A., at the end of which is Cinderella Castle, where Cruella de Vil is singing a torch song on the castle steps while cowboys are having a shootout in Frontierland, a Mississippi steamboat is

coming round the bend of a tiny river, and a brass band is playing near the Liberty Oak. The Magic Kingdom is the most intimate, shopworn, and emotionally charged of the three theme parks. Though they share the same cleanliness and the same extraordinary cleverness—Disney World, like God, is in the details—the Magic Kingdom is the most Disney of the parks. Only twice was the illusion shattered, when I noticed very small things: a broken door handle on the monorail, an attendant telling a man that his daughters weren't allowed to stand on the railing to watch Cruella de Vil—odd moments when reality intruded for just a second.

Mostly, though, the illusion holds as you walk around. And you walk around a lot. Indeed, the paradox of Disney World is that once you arrive, the chief cause of Orlando's troubles with Disney—the traffic that has filled county roads to the brim—completely vanishes. In Disney World you go by foot, monorail, or boat. (There are lots of lakes here; water was an important part of Disney's dream. Ironically, the big lake he admired from the air proved, on close inspection, to have brown water, which, the Disney people feared, visitors would think was dirty. So they drained the lake, dug up the muck, replaced it with sand, and filled it back up again.) You walk in and continue to walk—all day, into the night. "Do people faint?" I asked someone the second day of my visit. "No," she said, "but they do get sunburnt."

The sun here is so strong that just before opening, the Magic Kingdom had to be repainted because the colors that created the desired mood in Anaheim were all wrong in Orlando's clear glare. In Disney's original plan Epcot lay beneath a glass dome to keep out excess heat and humidity, but the dome never materialized. So, entering Epcot, I was out under the big blue Florida sky in a large park of broad lawns, impeccable flower beds, architectural fantasies, and fountains—a sort of permanent World's Fair. Epcot, actually, is an acronym that stands for Experimental Prototype Community of Tomorrow. Disney, who thought of his parks as always changing, always improving—who got pleasure from knowing that the trees he planted would get bigger and more beautiful—wrote: "Epcot . . . will never cease to be a living blueprint of the future, where people actually live a life they can't find anywhere else in the world today." Besides a dome, it was to have had schools, churches, offices, apartments, stores, parks, golf courses, marinas, a monorail, a vacuum-tube trash-disposal system, a central computer controlling everything from streetlights to hotel reservations, and petless residents who behaved—as visitors to Disneyland were expected to— "properly." But Epcot has turned out to be what Star Wars was for Reagan: only a dream.

In a small theater off the town square of the Magic Kingdom, you used to be able to see a film about Disney, narrated by Walt himself. In it was a sketch of his proposal for Epcot. Set in a flat plain surrounded by the glowing circles of what might be monorails, its skyscrapers rise into the sky exactly as we thought they would, back in the '50s, in cities of the future. The reality could hardly be more ironic. Epcot has pinewoods, manicured flower beds, and perfectly circulating lakes and streams; Orlando provides the skyscrapers—off in the distance, on a broad flat plain. It's a prototype of the problems that plague all Florida cities in the last decade of the century: where to put the cars, how to provide housing for the poor, how to control sprawl. (Bill Donegan says that after he voiced his complaints about all this at an urban affairs conference at Harvard, an official from Cleveland told him he envied Orlando's problems.) These are the problems of every place that is not an amusement park.

For that, to my astonishment when I finally got there, is all Disney World really is: an amusement park. A very nice amusement park. *Very* well done, but still, for all the brouhaha—the symbolism that politicians, intellectuals, and commentators find irresistible; the staggering financial success; the brilliant engineering and problem solving—just an amusement park. (In fact, there were so many English accents the day I went that I felt I was at Brighton. England surpassed Canada in 1989 as the country that sent the most visitors, followed by Germany, Brazil, and Mexico.) It's a place to spend the day walking from one exhibit to another, buying postcards and souvenirs, eating ice cream, watching movies about France or China in circular theaters surrounded by

giant screens, looking at masses of other people (strangely self-edited, as if Disney had chosen them, too), strolling past small children (and adults) being photographed with Pluto. ("How does he breathe?" I asked the attendant. "The way a dog breathes," he answered. "I mean the person inside," I said. "That's not a person," he explained. "That's Pluto.")

It's a place where litter is picked up immediately if anyone is so disreputable as to drop something on the ground, and where, standing on a Venetian bridge watching a crowd watch a juggler in the street by the Doge's Palace, I tapped on the balustrade and wondered, What is all this made of? (Fiberglass.) It's a place where you see kids in crazy hats (my favorite: the Donald Duck baseball cap, with a brim that quacks when squeezed) and where you'll overhear a boy standing next to you in line suddenly gasp, "Quick! Run! There's my parents!" It's—this came as a shock—a very big amusement park.

And yet it's not *really* just an amusement park—we all know that. The phrase Walt Disney concocted is "themed entertainment experience," which is actually a much more accurate description. There are no bumper cars here. This is a three-dimensional representation of the art world Disney created, and its appeal is subconscious and finally irresistible. (Emperor Hirohito of Japan used to wear, on informal occasions, a Mickey Mouse watch.) Schickel says that Disney removed the "secrets and silences" from childhood— subjected us all to the same sentimental kitsch. And it's true that Disney has a hold on childhood; one mother I know complained that a trip to Disney World seems to have become an American child's *right*. The Disney company knows this. The reason that Disney releases its classic animation features every seven years is that seven years is time enough for a new crop of children to grow up. And one of the factors in Disney's revival after the doldrums and confusion following Walt's death was the simple desire of a new generation of parents to take their kids to the Disney productions *they* had seen as children. Some product! Disney deals in family, childhood, nature, fairy tales, and the sort of timeless America that a lot of people feel vanished with *Son of Flubber*. (Until the mid-'70s, women were discouraged from wearing halter tops in Disneyland, and alcoholic drinks have been served here only recently, after dark, at large corporate parties.) The cleanliness, the sexlessness of Disney's world, is part of its appeal. The joke around the company—when Disney was alive, in fact—was that Walt himself could never have worked at Disneyland. He had a mustache, liked a stiff drink at the end of the day, and swore. To this day, cast members are forbidden to have facial hair.

During the uncertain years following Disney's death, when company executives still felt him looking over their shoulders, everyone was aware that while the country itself had changed, Disney had to remain true to itself or lose its identity altogether. Faced with the fact that a hit movie for kids was now *Porky's,* Walt's son-in-law, Ron Miller, launched a new company in 1983—Touchstone Pictures—to enable Disney to keep up with the changing times without surrendering its special place in the American mind. (Even so, its first picture was *Splash.* Today there are some far less Disneyesque films on the market.) Everyone realized that Disney stood, ineluctably, for certain things. Things that give you goose bumps. The Disney company is so closely identified with a certain American gentility that when Saul Steinberg, the Wall Street investor, held a meeting of his staff in 1984 to consider a buyout of the company (with the backing of Michael Milken, the one-time junk-bond king), he was warned that news of a Jewish raider acquiring Disney and selling off the pieces might produce an anti-Semitic backlash. The raid proceeded anyway, and fending it off caused a shakeup in the Disney organization that not only reunited the two sides of the feuding family but also resulted in the hiring of Michael Eisner and the late Frank Wells as chairman and president. The rest, as they say, is history. On January 29, 1987, Snow White and the Seven Dwarfs paraded onto the floor of the New York Stock Exchange to dramatize Disney's highest-ever first-quarter earnings.

Each year, the current president of Walt Disney Attractions gives Orange and Osceola counties a "State of Our World" address, outlining what Disney is considering over the next 5 or 10 years. There is still a lot of the 28,000 acres to be developed.

Some of it is bog, but even so, what remains can't be covered with theme parks alone. Disney is thinking about a major new shopping mall, an office development, and in 10 years, perhaps, another park. ("No one really knows what Disney is thinking," one local official says.) In the meantime, its neighbors try to deal with their own future.

The feeling in the surrounding area seems often to be one of paranoia—that Disney is smarter, faster, and bigger than anyone else, and it is trying to duplicate in Reedy Creek anything a tourist might leave the Disney grounds to find. Reedy Creek comptroller Ray Maxwell scoffs at this idea. "There is plenty for everyone," he says. Indeed, he points out, Orlando makes so much money selling to Disney World itself that even if tourists *were* shuttled directly from the airport to Disney World and back, it would mean just as much business for Orange County, with none of the wear and tear. As far as the roads go, he says that most of the highways around Disney World are funded by the federal and state governments, not by the county. When Orange County refused to improve Route 535, a road Disney employees use to get to work, the state repaved it, believing that the public would benefit from improving the access of Disney's employees to their workplace. The geographical boundaries of Reedy Creek are easy to ascertain—they're fixed with a surveyor's exactitude—but the political boundaries are not.

To a commissioner like Donegan, Disney World is an arrogant city-state escaping its fair share of the costs of growth around Orlando. To Ray Maxwell, this is sheer jealousy: Disney is the reason for the incredible prosperity. (The assessed value of Osceola County was $500 million in 1974 and $5 *billion* in 1990.) The growth of Orlando, he says, is no greater than the growth in other parts of the state. The infrastructure Disney built when it arrived in Reedy Creek was infrastructure Orange and Osceola counties could not have provided themselves.

But the squabbles between Disney and central Florida are over something less tangible than money: culture. Disney executives were amazed when they came here to buy land in 1965 and one of the largest property owners sold them 7,500 acres on a handshake (a handshake he did not renege on when he learned the identity of his buyer). That was the way things were done in Florida in those days; the property owner only wanted permission to graze his cattle on the land till Disney opened. Florida—central Florida, certainly—was then a culture of ranchers, farmers, sleepy county courthouses, and timber companies. Now Disney sells an estimated 30 million tickets a year (the company no longer gives out attendance figures, because they affect the price of its stock), and people come here from all over America, and the world, to spend vacation time. (Summer, Christmas, and spring break are the busiest times; Monday is the busiest day, when people begin their vacations with fresh energy.) These people have caused change. Change would have come to Orlando anyway, no doubt, but Disney World has become its embodiment. A friend who has lived in Orlando since 1946 explains it this way: "Disney put us on the map. But I'm not sure I want to be on the map."

I know just what he means. At the same time, having finally come here, I'm impressed. Disney World is so well run and so well thought out—so technologically and environmentally sophisticated—that after I'd been here awhile I began to think the problem was with Orange County, not Reedy Creek: that maybe Disney should run Orlando, too. (A thought that also occurred to Ray Bradbury, who was so dazzled by Disneyland, he asked Walt Disney to run for mayor of Los Angeles. Disney thought it over, then replied, "Why should I run for mayor when I'm already king?") But as smart and innovative as the Disney operation is, it's not going to run Orlando or Kissimmee. It's a corporation run for the benefit of its stockholders—a testament to the ability of private enterprise. Here is everything technology, expertise, and energy can bring to bear on a large piece of property surrounded by the chaos of millions of people in pursuit of money, retirement, power, and golf.

That is why I lingered in the Magic Kingdom longer than I thought I would—mesmerized in particular by the town square—and finally went upstairs in City Hall to ask a Disney publicist, Pam Parks, about Disney's relationship with the real world.

"Disney-bashing waxes and wanes," she said, smiling. "I would be astonished if the local politicians supported Disney without reservation." Feeling that I was not going to get any more out of her about the political nuances of the situation, I inquired about a story I'd heard outside the gates: that Walt Disney, lover of technology and the future, believed in cryogenics (freezing the dead so that if a cure for what killed them is developed years from now they can be thawed out and brought back to life). "I must ask you a crazy question," I said. "Is Disney frozen?"

"His nephew Roy was here with his daughter a while ago," Parks replied, "and that's one of the things *he* said: 'Can you believe people actually think he's freeze-dried and lying in the castle?' "

"In the castle!" I said. The idea was immediately appealing: Disney up in one of the turrets with Cinderella, frozen in a futuristic fridge. This park, as Richard Schickel points out, is so much the ultimate expression of one man's ideas and taste that a frozen Disney would not be entirely out of place. I went downstairs and sat on a bench beneath the portico of City Hall to examine my Mickey Mouse hat (a yarmulke with two ears sticking out; you can have your name embroidered on the back, for free), write postcards (Snow White and Dopey), and watch the Whitmanesque spectacle of all these healthy, well-built families walking by in tasteful all-cotton sports clothes. (Shirts and shoes must be worn at all times, but there are no fat people in too-tight shorts.) I sat there for a long time, strangely happy. It was spellbinding: a sort of *Volkfest*, a huge swarm of European and American families—the people who came here to escape Europe, settled Australia, and would like to go next to the moon, no doubt, or Mars.

To be honest, I'd expected something different. Fear, loathing, a clammy dread—all combined to produce what I call red-alert insomnia: the sensation that someone is pouring battery acid through your brain. I'd even reread *The Education of Henry Adams* before coming, to prepare myself for a cultural epiphany, if not apocalypse. I reread *The Education* because, after seeing the Chicago Exposition of 1893—the one Walt's father helped put up—and the Paris Exposition of 1900,

Adams titled a chapter in his autobiography "The Dynamo and the Virgin." The Dynamo was the symbol of the new, modern, industrial state—the one we've been living in since 1900. The Virgin was the symbol of Eve, the feminine principle, the presiding spirit of his beloved Middle Ages. Had Adams been alive to see Disney World, he would have had to rename his chapter "The Mouse and the Virgin." But Disney World wasn't exactly apocalyptic, now that I was here to see for myself. It was just a very nice amusement park that families can come to together. (So important to family life, the family vacation.) It was also more old-fashioned than new. The future wasn't what impressed me here. The space rides and deep-sea laboratory seemed sort of corny, what might excite a 10-year-old. It was what I was looking at now that cast a spell: the past. Specifically, this charming replica of a square in some midwestern town at the beginning of the century—not far from Marceline, Missouri, perhaps. (Every brick, shingle, and gas lamp on Main Street, U.S.A., Disney had explained, is only five-eighths of its true size. "This cost more," he said, "but made the street a toy, and the imagination can play more freely with a toy. Besides, people like to think their world is somehow more grown-up than Papa's was." Shrewd man!)

The lights came on and twinkled in the trees. The stores were jammed. The recorded waltzes played, while poor Pluto—whoever was inside it—continued to stand in the garden to one side of City Hall, hugging small children, who sometimes beamed and sometimes panicked at his embrace. It was a set for *The Music Man*. It was the whole sentimental dream of Victorian life, of the American Midwest, that deepened and deepened its spell, there in the central Florida dusk. And its final irony is that this place, this wholly artificial town square, provided before my eyes the street life—the human interaction, the mingling—that our car-cities of the present have completely erased from contemporary existence. One gets in a car or flies in a plane many miles to come here to find the gemütlichkeit that cars and planes have obliterated. Disney World, which specializes in the past (Main Street, steamboats, cowboys, castle) and the future (Voyage to Mars, George Lucas, lasers, Tomorrowland), leaves the present to Orange County. Which is why I sat there, wondering how I was going to get back to the parking lot, get in the car, and drive home.

DISNEY: FURTHER READING

STILL THE MOST PERCEPTIVE book on Disney is *The Disney Version,* by Richard Schickel (Simon & Schuster, 1985). Disney's art is featured in *Disneyland: The Inside Story,* by Randy Bright (Harry N. Abrams), and a comprehensive history of the great Disney animation tradition is provided in *Disney Animation: The Illusion of Life,* by Frank Thomas and Ollie Johnston (Abbeville, 1981). For a good read about Disney and other animators, look for *Of Mice and Magic* (NAL Dutton, 1987), by Leonard Maltin. *Walt Disney: An American Original* (Pocket Books, 1980), by Bob Thomas, is full of anecdotes about the development of WDW, and Marc Elliot's *Walt Disney: Hollywood's Dark Prince* (Birch Lane Press, 1993) is a controversial look at the life of WDW's creator.

Index

INDEX

NOTES

NOTES

NOTES

NOTES

NOTES

NOTES

NOTES

NOTES

"Grown-up Mouseketeers can now have their own Disney guidebook."
— *Gourmet Magazine*

For the 20 million adults who visit
Walt Disney World each year without kids!

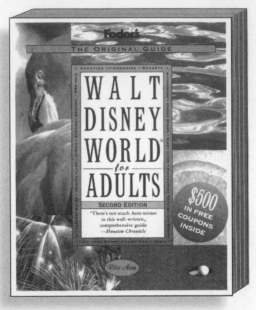

This completely updated new edition includes
all the latest changes at the world's #1 tourist
—and honeymoon—destination.

Walt Disney World for Adults provides up-
to-date information on hotels, restaurants,
sports facilities, as well as essential adult-only
information, including pocket pagers, in-park
computer networks, nightlife strategies, and
where to buy an evening dress, that makes
this the best guidebook of its kind.

**Five hundred dollars worth of
money-saving coupons in each book!**

At bookstores everywhere, or call
1-800-533-6478.

Your guide to a picture-perfect vacation

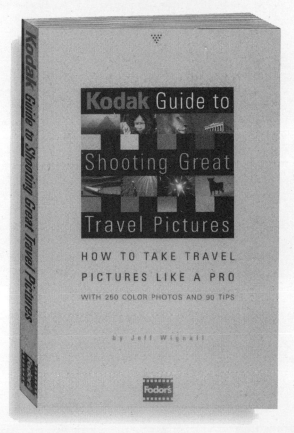

Kodak and Fodor's join together to create the guide that travelers everywhere have been asking for—one that covers the terms and techniques, the equipment and etiquette for taking first-rate travel photographs.

The most authoritative and up-to-date book of its kind, **The Kodak Guide to Shooting Great Travel Pictures** includes over 200 color photographs and spreads on 100 points of photography important to travelers, such as landscape basics, under sea shots, wildlife, city street, close-ups, photographing in museums and more.

$16.50   ($22.95 Canada)

At bookstores everywhere, or call 1-800-533-6478.

Fodor's Travel Publications

Available at bookstores everywhere, or call 1–800–533–6478, 24 hours a day.

Gold Guides

U.S.

Alaska

Arizona

Boston

California

Cape Cod, Martha's
Vineyard, Nantucket

The Carolinas & the
Georgia Coast

Chicago

Colorado

Florida

Hawaii

Las Vegas, Reno,
Tahoe

Los Angeles

Maine, Vermont,
New Hampshire

Maui

Miami & the Keys

New England

New Orleans

New York City

Pacific North Coast

Philadelphia & the
Pennsylvania Dutch
Country

The Rockies

San Diego

San Francisco

Santa Fe, Taos,
Albuquerque

Seattle & Vancouver

The South

U.S. & British Virgin
Islands

USA

Virginia & Maryland

Waikiki

Washington, D.C.

Foreign

Australia &
New Zealand

Austria

The Bahamas

Barbados

Bermuda

Brazil

Budapest

Canada

Cancún, Cozumel,
Yucatán Peninsula

Caribbean

China

Costa Rica, Belize,
Guatemala

The Czech Republic
& Slovakia

Eastern Europe

Egypt

Europe

Florence, Tuscany
& Umbria

France

Germany

Great Britain

Greece

Hong Kong

India

Ireland

Israel

Italy

Japan

Kenya & Tanzania

Korea

London

Madrid & Barcelona

Mexico

Montréal &
Québec City

Morocco

Moscow, St.
Petersburg, Kiev

The Netherlands,
Belgium &
Luxembourg

New Zealand

Norway

Nova Scotia, New
Brunswick, Prince
Edward Island

Paris

Portugal

Provence &
the Riviera

Scandinavia

Scotland

Singapore

South America

South Pacific

Southeast Asia

Spain

Sweden

Switzerland

Thailand

Tokyo

Toronto

Turkey

Vienna & the Danube

Fodor's Special-Interest Guides

Branson

Caribbean Ports
of Call

The Complete Guide
to America's
National Parks

Condé Nast Traveler
Caribbean Resort and
Cruise Ship Finder

Cruises and Ports
of Call

Fodor's London
Companion

France by Train

Halliday's New
England Food
Explorer

Healthy Escapes

Italy by Train

Kodak Guide to
Shooting Great
Travel Pictures

Shadow Traffic's
New York Shortcuts
and Traffic Tips

Sunday in New York

Sunday in
San Francisco

Walt Disney World,
Universal Studios
and Orlando

Walt Disney World
for Adults

Where Should We
Take the Kids?
California

Where Should We
Take the Kids?
Northeast

Special Series

Affordables
Caribbean
Europe
Florida
France
Germany
Great Britain
Italy
London
Paris

Fodor's Bed & Breakfasts and Country Inns
America's Best B&Bs
California's Best B&Bs
Canada's Great Country Inns
Cottages, B&Bs and Country Inns of England and Wales
The Mid-Atlantic's Best B&Bs
New England's Best B&Bs
The Pacific Northwest's Best B&Bs
The South's Best B&Bs
The Southwest's Best B&Bs
The Upper Great Lakes' Best B&Bs

The Berkeley Guides
California
Central America
Eastern Europe
Europe
France
Germany & Austria
Great Britain & Ireland
Italy
London
Mexico

Pacific Northwest & Alaska
Paris
San Francisco

Compass American Guides
Arizona
Canada
Chicago
Colorado
Hawaii
Hollywood
Las Vegas
Maine
Manhattan
Montana
New Mexico
New Orleans
Oregon
San Francisco
South Carolina
South Dakota
Texas
Utah
Virginia
Washington
Wine Country
Wisconsin
Wyoming

Fodor's Español
California
Caribe Occidental
Caribe Oriental
Gran Bretaña
Londres
Mexico
Nueva York
Paris

Fodor's Exploring Guides
Australia
Boston & New England

Britain
California
Caribbean
China
Florence & Tuscany
Florida
France
Germany
Ireland
Italy
London
Mexico
Moscow & St. Petersburg
New York City
Paris
Prague
Provence
Rome
San Francisco
Scotland
Singapore & Malaysia
Spain
Thailand
Turkey
Venice

Fodor's Flashmaps
Boston
New York
San Francisco
Washington, D.C.

Fodor's Pocket Guides
Acapulco
Atlanta
Barbados
Jamaica
London
New York City
Paris
Prague
Puerto Rico

Rome
San Francisco
Washington, D.C.

Rivages Guides
Bed and Breakfasts of Character and Charm in France
Hotels and Country Inns of Character and Charm in France
Hotels and Country Inns of Character and Charm in Italy

Short Escapes
Country Getaways in Britain
Country Getaways in France
Country Getaways Near New York City

Fodor's Sports
Golf Digest's Best Places to Play
Skiing USA
USA Today The Complete Four Sport Stadium Guide

Fodor's Vacation Planners
Great American Learning Vacations
Great American Sports & Adventure Vacations
Great American Vacations
National Parks and Seashores of the East
National Parks of the West

Before Catching Your Flight, Catch Up With Your World.

Fueled by the global resources of CNN and
available in major airports across America,
CNN Airport Network provides a live source

of current domestic and
international news,

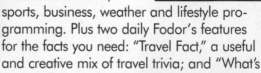

sports, business, weather and lifestyle programming. Plus two daily Fodor's features
for the facts you need: "Travel Fact," a useful
and creative mix of travel trivia; and "What's

Happening," a comprehensive round-up
of upcoming events in major cities
around the world.

With CNN Airport Network, you'll never
be out of the loop.

Wet'n Wild®

$3 OFF

™

$3⁰⁰ OFF

All-Day Studio Pass

Regular admission price $37⁰⁰ (plus tax)

RIDE THE MOVIES!

At Universal Studios Florida® you'll find yourself "in the movies" at every turn! So get ready to ride the blockbusters like E.T.®, Back to the Future®...The Ride℠, Earthquake® and more as you see how movie magic is recreated at THE #1 MOVIE STUDIO AND THEME PARK IN THE WORLD!

20% OFF

Food and beverages purchased for your party (up to six) at Studio Stars Restaurant or Finnegan's Pub.

$3⁰⁰ OFF
All-Day Studio Pass

$3.00 discount valid through 12/31/96. Coupon valid for up to 6 people and must be presented at the time of purchase. This offer has no cash value and is not valid with any other special discounts. Subject to change without notice. Parking fee not included.

6183920001990

DINE HOLLYWOOD-STYLE

Be a part of the scene at the Studio Stars Restaurant (across from Ghostbusters®) or drop into Finnegan's Pub for Irish spirits, ales and entertainment. Your 20% discount is good for a party of six! Remember to present this coupon when ordering.

HERE'S YOUR OWN PERSONAL VIEW OF THE WORLD.

Here's the easiest way to get up-to-the-minute, objective, personalized information about what's going on in the city you'll be visiting—before you leave on your trip! Unique information you could get only if you knew someone personally in each of 160 destinations around the world. Everything from special places to dine to local events only a local would know about.

It's all yours—in your Travel Update from Worldview, the leading provider of time-sensitive destination information.

Review the following order form and fill it out by indicating your destination(s)

and travel dates and by checking off up to eight interest categories. Then mail or fax your order form to us, or call your order in. (We're here to help you 24 hours a day.)

Within 48 hours of receiving your order, we'll mail your convenient, pocket-sized custom guide to you, packed with information to make your travel more fun and interesting. And if you're in a hurry, we can even fax it.

Have a great trip with your Fodor's Worldview Travel Update!

Fodor's WORLDVIEW TRAVEL UPDATE

Insider perspective

Time-sensitive

Customized to your interests and dates of travel

DESTINATIONS

Worldview covers more than 160 destinations worldwide. Choose the
destination(s) that match your itinerary from the list below:

Europe
Amsterdam
Athens
Barcelona
Berlin
Brussels
Budapest
Copenhagen
Dublin
Edinburgh
Florence
Frankfurt
French Riviera
Geneva
Glasgow
Lausanne
Lisbon
London
Madrid
Milan
Moscow
Munich
Oslo
Paris
Prague
Provence
Rome
Salzburg
Seville
St. Petersburg
Stockholm
Venice
Vienna
Zurich

United States
(Mainland)
Albuquerque
Atlanta
Atlantic City
Baltimore
Boston
Branson, MO
Charleston, SC
Chicago
Cincinnati
Cleveland
Dallas/Ft. Worth
Denver
Detroit
Houston
Indianapolis
Kansas City
Las Vegas
Los Angeles
Memphis
Miami
Milwaukee
Minneapolis/St. Paul
Nashville
New Orleans
New York City
Orlando
Palm Springs
Philadelphia
Phoenix
Pittsburgh

Portland
Reno/Lake Tahoe
St. Louis
Salt Lake City
San Antonio
San Diego
San Francisco
Santa Fe
Seattle
Tampa
Washington, DC

Alaska
Alaskan Destinations

Hawaii
Honolulu
Island of Hawaii
Kauai
Maui

Canada
Quebec City
Montreal
Ottawa
Toronto
Vancouver

Bahamas
Abaco
Eleuthera/
  Harbour Island
Exuma
Freeport
Nassau &
  Paradise Island

Bermuda
Bermuda Countryside
Hamilton

**British Leeward
Islands**
Anguilla
Antigua & Barbuda
St. Kitts & Nevis

British Virgin Islands
Tortola & Virgin
  Gorda

**British Windward
Islands**
Barbados
Dominica
Grenada
St. Lucia
St. Vincent
Trinidad & Tobago

Cayman Islands
The Caymans

Dominican Republic
Santo Domingo

Dutch Leeward Islands
Aruba
Bonaire
Curacao

**Dutch Windward
Island**
St. Maarten/St. Martin

French West Indies
Guadeloupe
Martinique
St. Barthelemy

Jamaica
Kingston
Montego Bay
Negril
Ocho Rios

Puerto Rico
Ponce
San Juan

Turks & Caicos
Grand Turk/
  Providenciales

U.S. Virgin Islands
St. Croix
St. John
St. Thomas

Mexico
Acapulco
Cancun & Isla Mujeres
Cozumel
Guadalajara
Ixtapa & Zihuatanejo
Los Cabos
Mazatlan
Mexico City
Monterrey
Oaxaca
Puerto Vallarta

South/Central America
Buenos Aires
Caracas
Rio de Janeiro
San Jose, Costa Rica
Sao Paulo

Middle East
Istanbul
Jerusalem

**Australia & New
Zealand**
Auckland
Melbourne
South Island
Sydney

China
Beijing
Guangzhou
Shanghai

Japan
Kyoto
Nagoya
Osaka
Tokyo
Yokohama

Pacific Rim/Other
Bali
Bangkok
Hong Kong & Macau
Manila
Seoul
Singapore
Taipei

INTERESTS

For your personalized Travel Update, choose the eight (8) categories you're most interested in from the following list:

1.	Business Services	Fax & Overnight Mail, Computer Rentals, Protocol, Secretarial, Messenger, Translation Services
	Dining	
2.	All-Day Dining	Breakfast & Brunch, Cafes & Tea Rooms, Late-Night Dining
3.	Local Cuisine	Every Price Range—from Budget Restaurants to the Special Splurge
4.	European Cuisine	Continental, French, Italian
5.	Asian Cuisine	Chinese, Far Eastern, Japanese, Other
6.	Americas Cuisine	American, Mexican & Latin
7.	Nightlife	Bars, Dance Clubs, Casinos, Comedy Clubs, Ethnic, Pubs & Beer Halls
8.	Entertainment	Theater – Comedy, Drama, Musicals, Dance, Ticket Agencies
9.	Music	Classical, Opera, Traditional & Ethnic, Jazz & Blues, Pop, Rock
10.	Children's Activites	Events, Attractions
11.	Tours	Local Tours, Day Trips, Overnight Excursions
12.	Exhibitions, Festivals & Shows	Antiques & Flower, History & Cultural, Art Exhibitions, Fairs & Craft Shows, Music & Art Festivals
13.	Shopping	Districts & Malls, Markets, Regional Specialties
14.	Fitness	Bicycling, Health Clubs, Hiking, Jogging
15.	Recreational Sports	Boating/Sailing, Fishing, Golf, Skiing, Snorkeling/Scuba, Tennis/Racket
16.	Spectator Sports	Auto Racing, Baseball, Basketball, Golf, Football, Horse Racing, Ice Hockey, Soccer
17.	Event Highlights	The best of what's happening during the dates of your trip.
18.	Sightseeing	Sights, Buildings, Monuments
19.	Museums	Art, Cultural
20.	Transportation	Taxis, Car Rentals, Airports, Public Transportation
21.	General Info	Overview, Holidays, Currency, Tourist Info

Please note that content will vary by season, destination, and length of stay.

Name _____

Address _____

City _____ State _____ Country _____ ZIP _____

Tel # ( ) - Fax # ( ) -

Title of this Fodor's guide: _____

Store and location where guide was purchased: _____

INDICATE YOUR DESTINATIONS/DATES: You can order up to three (3) destinations from the previous page. Fill in your arrival and departure dates for each destination. **Your Travel Update itinerary (all destinations selected) cannot exceed 30 days from beginning to end.**

		Month	Day	Month	Day
(Sample) **LONDON**	From:	6 /	21	To: 6 /	30
1	From:	/		To:	/
2	From:	/		To:	/
3	From:	/		To:	/

CHOOSE YOUR INTERESTS: Select up to eight (8) categories from the list of interest categories shown on the previous page and circle the numbers below:

1 2 3 4 5 6 7 8 9 10 11 12 13 14 15 16 17 18 19 20 21

CHOOSE WHEN YOU WANT YOUR TRAVEL UPDATE DELIVERED (Check one):
❏ Please send my Travel Update immediately.
❏ Please hold my order until a few weeks before my trip to include the most up-to-date information.
Completed orders will be sent within 48 hours. Allow 7–10 days for U.S. mail delivery.

ADD UP YOUR ORDER HERE. SPECIAL OFFER FOR FODOR'S PURCHASERS ONLY!

	Suggested Retail Price	Your Price	This Order
First destination ordered	$ 9.95	$ 7.95	$ 7.95
Second destination (if applicable)	$ 6.95	$ 4.95	+
Third destination (if applicable)	$ 6.95	$ 4.95	+

DELIVERY CHARGE (Check one and enter amount below)

	Within U.S. & Canada	Outside U.S. & Canada
First Class Mail	❏ $2.50	❏ $5.00
FAX	❏ $5.00	❏ $10.00
Priority Delivery	❏ $15.00	❏ $27.00

ENTER DELIVERY CHARGE FROM ABOVE: + [ ]

TOTAL: $ [ ]

METHOD OF PAYMENT IN U.S. FUNDS ONLY (Check one):
❏ AmEx ❏ MC ❏ Visa ❏ Discover ❏ Personal Check (U. S. & Canada only)
❏ Money Order/International Money Order

Make check or money order payable to: Fodor's Worldview Travel Update

Credit Card __/__/__/__/__/__/__/__/__/__/__/__/__/__/__/__/ Expiration Date:__/__

Authorized Signature _____

SEND THIS COMPLETED FORM WITH PAYMENT TO:
Fodor's Worldview Travel Update, 114 Sansome Street, Suite 700, San Francisco, CA 94104

OR CALL OR FAX US 24-HOURS A DAY
Telephone **1-800-799-9609** • Fax **1-800-799-9619** (From within the U.S. & Canada)
(Outside the U.S. & Canada: Telephone 415-616-9988 • Fax 415-616-9989)

(Please have this guide in front of you when you call so we can verify purchase.)
Code: FTG   Offer valid until 12/31/97